DO THEY WALK ON WATER?

Do They Walk on Water?

Federal Reserve Chairmen and the Fed

Leonard J. Santow

Foreword by Henry Kaufman

Westport, Connecticut
London

Library of Congress Cataloging-in-Publication Data

Santow, Leonard Jay.
    Do they walk on water? : Federal Reserve chairmen and the Fed / Leonard J. Santow ; foreword by
Henry Kaufman.
        p. cm.
    Includes bibliographical references and index.
    ISBN 978-0-313-36033-6 (alk. paper)
    1. Board of Governors of the Federal Reserve System (U.S.)—Evaluation. 2. Board of Governors
of the Federal Reserve System (U.S.)—Officials and employees. 3. Monetary policy—United States.
I. Title.
HG2563.S26   2009
332.1'10973—dc22   2008029268

British Library Cataloguing in Publication Data is available.

Library of Congress Catalog Card Number: 2008029268
ISBN: 978–0–313–36033–6

First published in 2009

Praeger Publishers, 88 Post Road West, Westport, CT 06881
An imprint of Greenwood Publishing Group, Inc.
www.praeger.com

Printed in the United States of America

The paper used in this book complies with the
Permanent Paper Standard issued by the National
Information Standards Organization (Z39.48-1984).

10 9 8 7 6 5 4 3 2 1

A VOICE FROM THE PAST

"The Research department [at the New York Fed] was full of intellectual stimulation. From the ranks of my colleagues came some of the top economists in the U.S. such as Albert Wojnilower and Henry Kaufman, both of whom had escaped from (Nazi) Germany. I think that the trying experiences they had honed their personalities and ways of working.

"Wojnilower was a sort of genius who was able to look at things in ways that were different from what was usually accepted, and had superior intuition. Kaufman became famous for his interest rate forecasts.

"In the 1960s, Wojnilower, Kaufman, Leonard Santow from the Dallas Fed in Texas, and I began to have regular exchanges of opinion, calling our group the 'Foursome.'"*

---

*My Personal History by Paul Volcker, a series of personal interviews published by Nihon Keizai Shimbun, October 1–31, 2004 (translated from Japanese).

CONTENTS

FOREWORD

I did not read this book with detachment. Early in my career, I was charged with the task of tracking and attempting to predict the actions of the U.S. Federal Reserve. I have also been a close friend of Leonard Santow for decades. Although my career took a turn into other research and investment banking activities, Leonard continued to hone his Fed watching skills, building a reputation over nearly half a century that is virtually without peer.

In this stimulating and informative book, the author brings together decades of knowledge and wisdom about monetary policy—not as an exercise in hindsight, but from his rare vantage point as a top-ranked analyst immersed in the real-time flow of data on which the Fed bases its decisions. He also makes over thirty recommendations for improving monetary tactics and policy approaches. If only half of these were adopted, financial markets and the larger economy would benefit enormously.

I met Leonard Santow in the early 1960s, when, following a stint as a research economist at the Federal Reserve Bank of Dallas, he came to New York to work for a dealer in U.S. government securities. I had just left the New York Fed to join Salomon Brothers. Although there were few serious *Fed watchers* in those days—indeed, the term itself had not yet been coined—the ranks of this special breed have now grown into a small army. It was a demanding task then and remains so today. The flow of information that one must monitor in order to effectively analyze Fed actions is so vast that few so-called Fed watchers perform the task well.

The training and experience needed to discern Fed actions range across a broad array of economic and financial fronts. Forecasting, of course, is an essential skill. What will the Federal Reserve do in the market during the trading week? Will it be a buyer or seller of securities? Will it conduct open market operations to offset seasonal factors in the market? Will it act through outright purchases, sales of securities, or repurchase agreements—or even, as has been the case during the past year, will the

Fed enter into longer-term funding arrangements? To answer these questions, a Fed watcher must project and correlate many factors that affect bank reserves. And he or she must always be on the lookout for any nuance in Fed operations that might hint of a shift in policy, the often-subtle signs that hint at monetary easing or tightening.

When I did this kind of work many years ago, I observed quickly that it was not difficult to make accurate projections because during most weeks, monetary policy remained unchanged. But such predictions had little value. The real test for a Fed watcher is to accurately forecast *shifts* in monetary policy. That great challenge involves tracking and projecting all the key economic and financial variables that influence the Fed's monetary decisions, domestic and international, and determining how they will influence monetary policy decision makers. Because monetary decisions are made by the twelve members of the Federal Open Market Committee (FOMC), the Fed watcher must judge how current conditions will affect the members of the FOMC both individually and as a group. That is a somewhat different task from making one's own judgments about current economic conditions. The astute Fed watcher must possess a rare combination of technical prowess and broad domestic and international vision as a professional economist, while at the same time setting his or her own political views on the sideline.

Do They Walk on Water? is rich with insights about Federal Reserve strategies, tactics, and behavior. Here is just a sample. Leonard Santow explains how, for all the riches of their data, monetary authorities do not possess perfect information. There are always gaps. For this reason and others, he concludes, Fed economic forecasts have been moderately accurate, at best. Indeed, the Fed's economic projections are only a compilation of estimates from the regional Federal Reserve banks and from other members of the FOMC. He reminds the reader that the primary objective of the Fed is not to get the economic *forecast* right, but rather to get monetary *policy* right.

Another insight in the book is that targets of monetary policy are continually in flux. In the forty-year span of the author's career, Fed targets have included net free or borrowed reserves, various definitions of money supply, and the federal funds rate. More recently, the inflation rate, as measured by the personal consumption deflator, has lurked in the background. Meanwhile, the value of the U.S. dollar in the foreign exchange markets has rarely commanded a high priority in Federal Reserve deliberations. Leonard Santow also shows that the Fed's methods for carrying out its objectives have been quite wide-ranging —from a "bills only" policy in the early post-World War II period, to purchasing securities all along the yield curve, to repurchase agreements, to, more recently, term loan facilities. The central bank's twin mission of containing inflation while maintaining economic growth remains a perennial challenge. According to the author, the Fed cannot correctly calibrate the Fed funds rate without changes in the inflation rate.

One of this book's strongest contributions is the author's examination and judgments about the chairmen of the Fed who served during the period of monetary ascendancy that followed World War II. Even though the chairman gets only one vote, he is clearly first among equals and wields enormous influence over monetary policy. In Leonard Santow's view, Paul Volcker ranks at the top of the performance scale among the five most recent Fed chairmen, followed by Alan Greenspan as number two, G. William Miller as number three, and Arthur Burns as number four. Current chairman Ben Bernanke's standing in the group must await the completion of his service.

Paul Volcker earns the top spot because of the extraordinarily daunting circumstances prevailing when he assumed the chairmanship in the summer of 1979. Stagflation had plagued the economy for years, and even Nixon's wage-and-price controls, followed by Carter's deregulation, had failed to end double-digit inflation or stimulate much economic growth. Volcker stayed the difficult monetary course, breaking the back of inflation and helping to launch an economic recovery. The author criticizes Alan Greenspan for his hands-off-the-market approach and occasional "roller-coaster approach to monetary policy," but gives him credit for an economy that was in better shape when he stepped down as chairman than when he took office.

G. William Miller's third-place ranking, ahead of Arthur Burns, will surprise many. The author readily acknowledges Mr. Miller's lack of background for the position of Fed chairman, yet also notes that when Bill Miller became Fed chairman in 1970, he too inherited a very difficult inflationary and financial situation. Chairman Miller responded by steadily raising the funds rate. Leonard Santow ranks Arthur Burns lowest in the group because "he talked tough about containing inflation and yet his policies created an inflation problem that was not brought under control until the early 1990s." Perhaps Chairman Bernanke should take note that a high ranking in the academic world, which Arthur Burns surely enjoyed, is not a necessary prerequisite for successful monetary leadership.

To that observation I will add that successful Fed chairmen should spurn celebrity status if possible. It is easy and tempting to become a hero of Wall Street and Main Street when accommodating monetary policies feed high stock prices and economic expansion. But it is often during such heady times that Fed chairmen need to make unpopular choices, that is (to paraphrase Chairman Martin) "take away the punch bowl when the party is about to get out of hand."

Few applaud such action; indeed, political pressure to let the good times roll can become intense. Chairman Martin was personally confronted by at least two presidents. President Truman reprimanded him at a gathering at the Waldorf Hotel in New York for not supporting a U.S. Treasury financing; and in the late 1960s President Johnson summoned the Fed chairman down to his Texas ranch and berated him for tightening monetary policy. With the passage of time, however, such courageous actions have earned the reputations they deserve. They exemplify the independence and long-term view to which the U.S. Federal Reserve and its leaders should remain loyal.

Henry Kaufman
President, Henry Kaufman & Co., Inc.
July 2008

SPECIAL ACKNOWLEDGMENT

For those who write books but do other things for a living, it takes a considerable amount of help from others. This is especially true for someone such as myself who is not a master of the King's English. I marvel at how well some of my economist friends, such as Henry Kaufman, Al Wojnilower, and Bill Griggs, can write.

Fortunately, at Griggs & Santow Inc., we have a colleague who has an ability to turn a phrase or two, and that is Joan Byrne. She has an unusual ability to take economic minutiae and make it sound almost interesting. Joan helped me in terms of the research, writing, and editing of this book, and also the three previous books that I wrote or coauthored. I am convinced that without Joan this book would never have seen the light of day.

1

SETTING THE STAGE

The approach in this book is unique, although I had to keep in mind that unique is not synonymous with worthwhile. That will be up to the critics, and I suspect there will be a considerable number waiting to get in line to take a crack at the analysis and the conclusions that I have drawn; I have stepped on many sensitive toes. My motivation, however, is not to be argumentative or to present what some may say is revisionist history. Rather, it is to write a book on monetary policy that would impart to others whatever wisdom I have accumulated in almost a half-century. My background is varied enough that I thought I could offer a balanced view of what happened to monetary policy in a period of more than four decades, and why it happened.

When I left the Federal Reserve in 1963—after a relatively short stay—and moved over to the private sector, it was a tough adjustment for a research economist. While at the Fed, I had a vast array of data and policy decisions available to me; all I had to do was check my inbox to get the information. In the private sector, no such luck; I had to spend hours, even days, trying to figure out what was happening. It is amazing how much more you learn about a subject when you have to do your own digging for information, ideas, and techniques and then put them in a meaningful and useful format. This same learning process takes place when you teach a course on a subject in which you think you are an expert, until a student asks a question that you never thought about—but should have.

One advantage of having been in a number of different positions in more than four decades is that you have a chance to be wrong many times over. In this business you learn from your mistakes or you will not have a job. No one will pay to listen to you if you keep making the same mistakes. As a matter of fact, no one will listen to you—period. That would be very frustrating for any economist.

When you err in your conclusions and your projections, you cost people money. When that happens—and it can happen all too frequently—you try to figure out what you missed in your analyses; which meant I had to continually fine-tune my methods and techniques in analyzing data and making forecasts. This has been a never-ending process, and I am amazed at how little I knew or understood in my earlier years.

It would be a shame to have all this knowledge and experience fall by the wayside by not providing others with the insights that I developed over almost a half century. By others, I am including Federal Reserve officials, market people, and academics, as well as readers generally interested in the economy and how it works. There is something in this book for all of them. There is information and analysis that you are not likely to find elsewhere, a good part of which is based on personal involvement or knowledge. Moreover, just maybe it might have an influence on public officials and how they conduct monetary policy. There are recommendations throughout the book that, even if they are not adopted, should at least be talked about.

This is the fourth book I have written. The first was on monetary policy, and the second was on the budget. The third, in collaboration with my son Mark, an American history professor, is entitled *Social Security and the Middle-Class Squeeze*. Although both of us were involved in all aspects of the book, I was the Social Security guru and he was the middle-class squeeze expert.

Each book contains what some might consider an excessive and burdensome amount of data and tables. When points are made, or conclusions drawn, I always try whenever possible to back up the ideas with large amounts of data. After all, numbers are my game. This attitude goes back to when I left the Fed and had to compile large amounts of data in order to make forecasts. This heavy reliance on numbers may be one of the reasons that my previous books did not exactly jump off the shelves, although the comments from my contemporaries tended to be quite positive.

It may seem to be a contradiction that my analysis relies heavily on numbers, and yet I view monetary policy as an art and not a science. These conclusions are not inconsistent. Most policies and objectives involve numbers, but they are no more than tools used to achieve objectives. Fed officials cannot avoid using mathematics and data, but they can overemphasize their importance. They are primarily a means to an end, not an end in itself. There are too many overly simplistic ideas floating around concerning monetary policy, and many are based on mathematical relationships that do not reflect the realities of the world. For example, some analysts believe there is a set time period for major changes in Fed policy to take hold, even though history has not shown that to be the case. Each time period is unique, and because of this, Fed policy makers need to be artists and not scientists.

Thus, with all these decades of being a Fed watcher who observed the "artists" at work, I decided that I wanted my swan-song performance to be about monetary policy and its evolution since 1970. But why this period?

The 1960s may have been the time when revolutionary changes in the markets and market instruments took place, but the 1970s ushered in the beginning of a new era of monetary policy, with the main problem being embedded inflation and how the Fed could combat it. For that reason, this book starts with Arthur Burns and when he took over at the Fed in 1970 and continues through the tenures of the next four chairmen into 2008. When Burns took over at the Fed, it was apparent that the new markets and financial instruments developed in the 1960s were making it more difficult for the Fed to sufficiently tighten policy by using such traditional measures as ratcheting up an overnight interest rate. Arthur Burns was an academic, and a good one at that, but he was not steeped in the knowledge of markets and the influence they could have on making it more difficult for monetary policy to become sufficiently restrictive.

As you may have already surmised, in this book I have relied heavily on my background and expertise in accumulating and crunching numbers. What I have tried to do is to present them in a way that is useful for those trying to understand monetary policy since 1970.

When I started doing the research for this book, I found my memory failing regarding the specifics of what happened to monetary policy as far back as 1970. As a matter of fact, I discovered I had forgotten things that occurred in the first few years of the twenty-first century. Thus, I decided to help myself—and by doing so, help the reader—by using a newspaper headline approach in a section that covers a variety of events (not just business and financial) that have taken place since 1970. This section, "A Flavor of the Times," is in the back of the book as an appendix.

Monetary policy and its changes do not take place in a vacuum. Economic and noneconomic events that take place around the world have had an important influence on U.S. monetary policy, with both international and domestic factors involved. Therefore, there is good reason to document many of the notable events. Especially important in this regard are political occurrences, military involvements, budget considerations, and energy and labor market events. Since 1970, the most notable impact on monetary policy from these sources has been in terms of inflation and the Fed's successes and failures in combating it. Realize that where the source of inflation comes from has a great deal to do with the Fed's success, or lack thereof, in combating it. It is much more difficult, for example, for the Fed to combat inflation that comes from abroad, and comes from the cost-side, and the flavor of the times section is replete with such instances.

EARLY RECOLLECTIONS

It was the spring of 1966 and my wife Sharon and I were looking to buy our first house. Alfred Johnson, a dear friend from Fed days, suggested that we look in an area just down the road from where he lived in Greenwich, Connecticut, where a reputable local builder was putting up a group of houses. We talked to the builder and he said he would build us a house with a base price of $35,000. That seemed like a lot of money, but we went forward and contracted to build the house. We financed it by taking out a 5.5 percent fixed-rate mortgage, which seemed very high at the time. We could remember when mortgage rates were down around 4 percent.

We moved in during 1967, but by 1969 a major problem developed. The builder was about to put up another house adjacent to ours—very adjacent. Adjacent enough that our dining room picture window would look out on the wall of the new house. However, luck was on our side and not the builder's. For those who are old enough to remember, this was a time when money became very tight and disintermediation (a term coined by Henry Kaufman at Salomon Brothers) was taking place.

For those who are unaware, disintermediation refers to the movement of funds out of deposit-type institutions into market instruments that pay a higher rate of interest. This movement was often triggered by interest rate ceilings imposed by the Federal Reserve on deposit-type institutions with the information presented in Regulation Q. Disintermediation was typically a problem when the Fed was tightening monetary policy and pushing interest rates higher. This brought about a substantial outflow of funds from deposit-type institutions and did considerable damage to the housing market. (Note: There is a glossary at the back of the book that defines technical terms and phrases—such as disintermediation, Regulation Q, and monetary policy.)

It was hard, and in some cases almost impossible, for a builder to get financing under such circumstances. It was a scary period for potential borrowers, because this led to a financing squeeze of the first order. We decided to approach the builder, who was having trouble getting financing, and make an offer for the adjacent building lot. He did not want to sell but said he would do so if the price was high enough to include a good part of the profit from building a house. Economists are not the smartest people in the world when it comes to dealing with real markets; therefore we said we would buy the lot for $27,500—not that much less than what we paid two years earlier for both our house and the lot. We felt that Jesse James was still alive and well and embarked on a new profession. But, sometimes it is better to be lucky than smart. Although we no longer own the house, we still own the empty lot. Supposedly, it is now worth about thirty times more than what we paid for it. Maybe someone above is looking out for economists and their families.

The purpose of this story is not to reminisce about our family history. Rather, it is to point out that in the late 1960s disintermediation had a very adverse and unexpectedly sharp impact on the economy in general, and housing and financial institutions in particular. A similar situation occurred in 2007 and 2008, and again a lack of ability to finance, as well as the cost of funding, were to blame. Yet there are important differences with respect to the two situations. In the late 1960s the problem was caused primarily by interest rate ceilings at depository institutions that made absolutely no sense, and once the Fed acted to limit the impact of Regulation Q ceilings, the problem subsided.

Unfortunately, the problems in housing in 2007 and 2008 were more fundamental and therefore ultimately more dangerous than what took place earlier. However, I am not minimizing the importance of what occurred in the late 1960s, when high interest rates and the inability of builders, individuals, and deposit-type institutions to borrow, created as close to a domestic financial crisis as I can remember. Many institutions, such as the savings and loan associations, were on the verge of bankruptcy.

In contrast, the weakness in the housing market that started in 2007 and became worse in 2008 was considerably different. The problems were much more fundamental than in the late 1960s, but this time they seemed to creep up on market participants and the regulatory authorities. The financing spigot in 2007 and 2008 was closed off gradually but never entirely. Thus, the recent situation did not create the same explosive fear factor as in the 1960s.

FEDERAL RESERVE CHAIRMEN AND THEIR TREATMENT IN DIFFICULT TIMES

In looking at U.S. monetary policy, one factor that struck me as being unusual is that over the years, and over difficult times such as in the 2007–2008 period and the disintermediation period in the late 1960s, the chairman of the Federal Reserve has been able to maintain an elevated position compared to other public servants, with the possible exception of the chief justice of the Supreme Court.

It was not that Federal Reserve chairmen had avoided criticism for their policies, but rather that the criticisms were usually done in a genteel manner. Perhaps it was the respect for the office they held, their background, or the capabilities they exhibited in previous positions; but whatever the reasons, they were treated with kid-gloves. This was especially evident when a Federal Reserve chairman testified before Congress.

During these Congressional appearances, chairmen were often asked questions on subjects for which they had little or no personal responsibility. It was as if they were viewed as the wise men who would help guide Congress in its legislative tasks. This was most obvious when they were asked questions on the budget, and particularly areas such as taxes, spending, and deficit financing. It made little difference whether the chairmen were Democrats, Republicans, or independents, or what their past economic philosophies seemed to be. After all, they were the chairmen of an august and independent body, one that was supposedly above politics.

Of course, some of the chairmen played their role to the hilt. They always seemed to be in favor of balancing the budget and controlling spending, and usually, they were against tax increases, even though these may not have been the right answers. When it came to areas outside their bailiwick, they were preaching to the choir and tried to impress Congress with their knowledge and independence. Consciously or not, they tried to come off as wise men, above and beyond any fray. The image they tried to portray was that they could walk on water.

Once they were anointed with the title "Chairman," their peers at the Fed were all distant seconds, thirds, and fourths when it came to how they were perceived. The chairman was the king among kings. Some might argue that the relationship between the chairman and the others was closer to that of the pope and the cardinals. While they were in office, their expertise and honesty were almost never questioned. They were rarely attacked either personally or with regard to their policies, and in general, they were usually given the benefit of the doubt. After all, they were *wise men* and should be treated as such. And yet, as this book will show, history does not support this thinking.

We begin with Arthur Burns and some of the major problems he inherited—and made worse. We then move forward to the cameo appearance by G. William Miller, who had policy heading in the right direction but at a snail's pace. He could hardly afford to move like a snail—and a cautious snail at that—when he had less than two years to make his mark. Paul Volcker, during his eight years as chairman, always seemed to be in the middle of a whirlwind of actions and reactions. There was no such thing as Volcker sitting back and getting a chance to study what his past policies had wrought, because he was on to the next set of problems. Of all the modern Fed chairmen, his achievements—and they are considerable—are probably the hardest to quantify and easiest to generalize.

Although all Fed chairmen have at one time or another taken advantage of their special exalted status, the one who seemed to perfect this role was Alan Greenspan. He was asked to pontificate on a wide variety of subjects, many of which had nothing to do with monetary policy. (Greenspan was professorial but not in an Arthur Burns domineering sort of way.) People generally were very impressed with his opinions; he had a way of saying one thing and then qualifying his statement, the result being that there were times when they were not quite sure what he said, but they liked the way he said it. He was the founder of "Fed speak." One might say—perhaps sarcastically and somewhat unfairly—that he was an advocate of words speaking louder than actions.

As for the current Fed chairman, Ben Bernanke, it is too early to tell how he will play his new role. Early appearances are that it will be an amalgamation of what some past chairmen have done. For example, he has been professorial like Burns but without talking down to people. His approach to the job has been closer to Greenspan's than to any of the others, but he has tried to be clearer, more concise, and more timely. His desire to be an educator, as well as a central banker, shows through. Unfortunately, in his attempt to be more "transparent" about the Fed and its policies, he may be understating the need to provide timely details of past and current policies, especially the misjudgments and mistakes that have been made. These can be viewed as part of his learning process.

Telling people what the Fed is trying to target and what it is trying to achieve is definitely worthwhile. However, transparency about the future and about desired outcomes may not be as useful as being transparent about what is happening now, what has happened in the recent past, and why these things happened. Transparency should also mean releasing information in such a manner that it will be neither misunderstood nor misinterpreted. Transparency and Fed-speak should be viewed as exact opposites. One thing for sure—the Fed should not use transparency as a public-relations tool, especially because actions ultimately speak louder than words, particularly when words and actions do not coincide.

The transparency issue is one that will not go away, and when policy mistakes are made, it will come to the forefront. So will the question of whether Chairman Bernanke is too academic and not flexible enough to make policy changes in a timely manner in the wake of unforeseen circumstances, or when events do not conform to what his models are telling him. How many of his academic shackles can he shake off in one of the most practical jobs a public servant can have? So far, he is no Arthur Burns—and that is meant as a compliment. So far, he is no Paul Volcker—and that is not meant as a compliment.

Only time will tell whether he will develop enough market and street smarts to balance his desire to rely on academic theory and modeling. Hopefully, he will realize that it is the policy decisions that count—not the sophistication of the approach used to arrive at the decisions. There is nothing wrong with Fed officials admitting that seat-of-the-pants judgments count, that mistakes are made, and that no public official can walk on water.

TOO MUCH CREDIT, TOO MUCH BLAME, AND SOME IMPORTANT EXCEPTIONS

When it comes to what happens in the economy, the importance of monetary policy is often overstated. This is especially true when, for an extended period of time, policy is neither at one extreme nor the other. Yet, many in the media seem to believe that when the Fed nudges policy in either direction, it is likely to have a major impact on economic growth or inflation. When watching some of the financial news shows, the impression is conveyed that every little twitch in the Fed funds target can make or break the economy, and that is simply not the case.

With regard to economic performance, what is going on in the private sector—regarding consumers and businesses in particular—is of much more importance. If the economy is healthy and doing well, it is the private sector that is primarily responsible. If the economy is sick and doing badly, it is the private sector that is primarily responsible. It is not that monetary or fiscal policies are unimportant, it is just that they are insufficient by themselves to carry the day for the economy.

Yet, there are some exceptions. When monetary policy is overly easy or overly tight for an extended period, it can influence the economy in an adverse way. For example, in mid-2007 the housing market, and ultimately the economy in general, started to pay the price for the excessive ease of monetary policy from late 2001 to late 2005. The problems created were numerous. There was excessive availability of funds, unsustainably low interest rates, regulatory policies that encouraged lending to those who were not creditworthy, and lending under terms that ultimately meant financial problems for borrowers once interest rates moved up. There were also problems with respect to the packaging of loans and then their being sold in order to package more loans, a lack of understanding by buyers of mortgage-backed instruments that the quality of the paper and the risks involved were not what they believed to be the case—and some government and quasi-government organizations that bought excessive amounts of packaged loans based on their capital limitations.

Monetary policy is not just interest rates and availability of funds. There is a regulatory side to monetary policy, and the Fed did little in the late 2001 to late 2005 period to dissuade lenders and to warn buyers about the risks involved. As a matter of fact, Chairman Greenspan made the statement that when short-term rates were near rock bottom, adjustable rate mortgages were attractive for those borrowing mortgage money. This was hardly moral suasion when it came to preaching financial caution.

From a professional economist's point of view, since late 2001 the Fed's policy mistakes have been obvious and consequential. Yet, a professional economist's opinion as to whether policy was appropriate really has little meaning. What counts is what price was paid in the real world as a result of inappropriate policies. One would have to be very optimistic to believe that the financial debacle that took place in 2007 and 2008 will be forgotten over the next few years. Too many people were adversely affected, and too much money was lost; the financial institutions will take a number of years to recover from their losses, and new and more restrictive legislation will surely be coming down the road—legislation that will no doubt be controversial and not to the liking of many commercial and investment banks.

Moreover, the breadth of the adverse impact was worldwide, and major losses are still to be uncovered. If there is any slight tinge of optimism in this picture, it is that write-offs and write-downs will probably ultimately be overstated, because in illiquid markets, the prices being quoted on assets are likely to be below what they are worth on a more fundamental long-term basis. This could be good news for some institutions, but the effects of that good news may not be felt until as far off as 2010.

MONETARY POLICY: DETERMINED BY AN INSTITUTION
BUT DOMINATED BY A CHAIRMAN

It is an institution that makes monetary policy, not just the person who sits on the top of the heap. Many seem to believe that the chairman of the Fed and the Federal Reserve are one and the same when it comes to monetary policy. Yet, that is not the case. There are other governors and district bank presidents who vote on monetary policy, and if enough of them feel strongly enough, they can influence the chairman's thinking. This may not show up in the official votes cast at Federal Open Market Committee (FOMC) meetings, where most of the monetary policy decisions are made. Even a vocal minority that votes against the chairman can be a major influence on his thinking about policy changes. In other words, the chairman does not make his policy recommendations in a vacuum. Paul Volcker, who was chairman from 1979 to 1987, can vouch for that.

What happens in the economic and monetary worlds is very complex, and it is often very difficult to determine cause and effect. That is one of the reasons the

Fed has so many economists and staff people, and the conclusions they reach influence those they report to, such as the seven governors and twelve district bank presidents. More often that not, what these economists and staff people say will have a noticeable impact on their bosses, who are responsible for making monetary policy.

Thus, if monetary policy is less important to economic performance than generally realized, and monetary policy is not a one-man show, then the chairman of the Fed often winds up getting more of the credit, or more of the blame, when things go very right or terribly wrong. If you think that monetary policy is a one-man operation, take a look at all the speeches made by various Fed officials; they do not necessarily mimic what the chairman is saying or what the Fed is doing.

That said, I am aware of only one occasion in recent decades where there was almost a palace revolt at the Fed when it came to decision making, and that was just prior to Volcker leaving office in 1987. Volcker was pushing for tough medicine when it came to fighting inflation, even if it meant unduly high interest rates, a major risk of a recession, and the loss of the White House in the next election. Needless to say, he was not the most popular person among politicians, whose long-run approach looks as far as what happens at the next election.

Adding to Volcker's woes were internal conflicts with a number of Board members rooted in part in policy differences and in part in egos. Volcker was viewed as a policy hawk because he was generally in favor of high interest rates and tight money, but other FOMC members were policy doves. It was unacceptable for Volcker to be outvoted on such an important issue as combating inflation. This internal conflict brought him to the edge of resigning, especially if he had lost control of monetary policy at a time when backing away from a strong anti-inflation policy ran the risk of undoing considerable gains made against what had been an embedded problem. Volcker won the battles, but it was not too many months before he resigned in frustration. Fortunately, the war against inflation was not lost, although there were times in future years where the control over inflation was challenged.

As we will see, William Martin, as chairman of the Fed, had a way of avoiding this loss-of-control problem. He had certain opinions on policy and he would check with other FOMC members to see whether they agreed with his views. If they did not, or if there was a considerable minority that would vote against him, he would not pursue his desires and would quietly slip in with the majority. Of course, his years at the Fed were quiet compared to what Volcker experienced. It is easy to compromise when the price for doing so is not all that great.

It should be clear from this analysis that monetary policy is not conceived and implemented by just one person—the chairman. Moreover, monetary policy decisions are not made in a vacuum, and there are forces outside the Fed that support or run counter to what the Fed wants to achieve. Thus, any statement that a Fed chairman has done a great job or a terrible job is not only overly simplistic, but in some cases may be incorrect. In many cases, you are as good, or as bad, as the information and analysis you are presented with by your advisors and fellow Fed members.

THE MODERN MONETARY ERA STARTED IN THE 1960s

In the early 1960s the financial world changed forever as new instruments and markets appeared on the scene. These changes in the financial world complicated monetary policy operations, although the objective remained the same. The stated objectives of monetary policy at that time were no inflation and no unemployment. Of course, this was impractical, but the belief was that if you accepted some inflation and unemployment, you were opening up a Pandora's box of potential problems, and that the Fed would be viewed as not being serious about these objectives. Eurodollars (a dollar deposit in a U.S. bank branch or in a foreign bank located outside the United States) and CDs (certificates of deposit—a time deposit with a specific maturity) came into being, and this was really the starting point for modern domestic and international financial markets as we know them today. I was fortunate enough to be on a Federal Reserve committee at that time whose charge was to figure out what was the market potential of that new instrument called a CD.

Being on the staff of the Dallas Federal Reserve Bank had its personal advantages. It had the smallest research department of any of the district banks and at one point, Bill Griggs and I were the only two financial economists in the bank. In other words, it was virtually impossible for us to do all the research work that was necessary, especially when it came to regional studies. This meant a heavy workload for the both of us, but there were also some advantages from a personal point of view.

In contrast, the district Federal Reserve banks today have large research staffs, but it seems as though they spend too much time analyzing the national economy, and not enough time on regional considerations. Not only does this approach create duplication of effort in studying the national economy, but it limits the benefits from having, so to speak, on-the-spot experts in each of the district economies. This personal history of my days at the Fed is important because both Bill and I were involved in system committees and studies that would not have happened if we had been in a large district bank such as New York. When there were system-wide committees, we were often given the opportunity (in other words, we were volunteered) to participate, and there were also opportunities to accompany the bank president to FOMC meetings. What makes this background information important is that I had a chance, although at a junior level, to be directly involved in committee discussions and recommendations. Thus, the following information is not second-hand. For example, I was fortunate to be on a committee of high-powered Federal Reserve System individuals brought together to study a new market instrument called CDs. These people were well above me in the Federal Reserve hierarchy and included Bob Lindsey, Bob Holland, and George Mitchell, who had overall responsibility for the project.

Frankly, I remember little about the meetings, or our conclusions, except that, based on what ultimately occurred with regard to the growth of CDs, we surely underestimated the future importance of this instrument, the market that it spawned, and the role that liability management has ultimately played in the banking system. Nevertheless, by being on the committee, I became more knowledgeable than most people at the Federal Reserve (an instant expert, if you will) about this fledgling instrument, its market, and how revolutionary this change was for markets in general. These are the kinds of insights you cannot get from reading historical documents.

The 1960s was a time of rapid growth in both CDs and Eurodollars. In the early 1960s these two financial instruments came into being. The Eurodollar deposit was started by a Soviet bank in London that did not want to be subject to regulations, especially by the American government (after all, there was a cold war going on). A small but emerging trading market began in the early 1960s for these deposits, and other banks besides the Soviet bank became involved. In the late 1960s, this market took off, and the rest is history.

Much of my knowledge about Eurodollar deposits and the Eurodollar market came from a friend and colleague, Claude Tygier. I met him in the mid-1970s, when he became the head foreign exchange trader at J. Henry Schroder Bank in New York. He wrote one of the earliest and most defining books on the topic of Eurodollar deposits and the Eurodollar market. His insights provided me with a leap forward in my understanding of international financial markets and transactions between markets.

In contrast, when I was at the Federal Reserve in the early 1960s, I kept a close eye on international arbitrage operations, which were about as rudimentary as one could get. A typical international arbitrage operation occurs when a higher return can be achieved in the money market for one currency by using another currency and swapping it on a fully hedged basis through the foreign exchange market. What was required on my part was primarily watching the relationship between U.S. Treasury bills and U.K. Treasury bills, although there were some operations outside the money market area between U.S. Treasury notes and British Gilts. This was like watching paint dry. Things changed, however, when the CD and Eurodollar markets came into being. It changed the whole picture of arbitrage and international money flows, and its influence on the foreign exchange market was monumental. International markets were just starting to come of age, and central banks were not always prepared to handle these changes.

The 1960s was an era of rapid growth in the domestic money and capital markets. It was also a time when Regulation Q was alive and well. This regulation put interest rate ceilings on various types of deposits, and when interest rates were at relatively high levels (for that time) and pressing on these ceilings, depository institutions could not compete for funds. Thus the money went outside the depository institutions, and with little money coming in and a great deal of money moving out, they could not make new loans. As a matter of fact, they had trouble rolling over already outstanding loans. If money coming into these financial institutions was intermediation between investors and lenders, then money reversing the process was disintermediation. Henry Kaufman, the king of the Wall Street gurus, coined the term "disintermediation," and it has stuck to this day.

Yet, this was not the entire story during the 1960s. The Fed's attitude with respect to bank borrowing at the discount window (the place at the Fed where banks go to borrow money) was that it was a privilege and not a right. In addition, the Fed also used as an intermediate policy target an item called *free reserves*, or its counterpart *net borrowed reserves*. Free reserves occurred when excess reserves in the banking system were greater than bank borrowings at the discount window; and net borrowed reserves occurred when window borrowings were larger than excess reserves.

When the Fed wanted money to be tight and wanted the banks to cut back on loans and investments, they put the banking system into a position of net borrowed reserves. To a large degree, the Fed had control over the size of net borrowed reserves. This amount could be several billion dollars, and it was only a matter of time before the banks would knuckle under because they were not allowed to be regular and frequent borrowers at the discount window.

At the other extreme, when the Fed was trying to stimulate the economy, it would move the banking system into substantial amounts of free reserves, which meant large amounts of excess reserves sloshing around in the banking system. There were times, however, when this approach was not always as effective as desired.

The Fed would push reserves into the banking system, and the banks would not always fully use the resources that were available to them. This brought about the term "pushing on a string," which in many ways is equivalent to the concept that you can lead a horse to water but cannot make it drink.

These were not the only tools of the Fed policy managers. There were required reserves on both demand and time accounts, and these could be moved up or down depending on how tight or easy the Fed wanted policy. Marginal changes in these requirements could have a considerable impact on the overall ease or tightness of monetary policy.

Thus, if an analyst looked back and studied monetary policy through much of the 1960s, looking at just interest rate levels as a measurement of Fed ease or tightness was misleading. Policy was much more than interest rates, and much, much more than just an overnight interest rate. Policy was an amalgamation of free reserves/net borrowed reserves, discount window borrowings, required reserves, Regulation Q ceilings, selective controls such as margin requirements on stocks, and bending the Treasury yield curve (called operation twist or operation nudge, whereby the Fed tried to push up short-term interest rates for dollar-support purposes and to push down long-term interest rates in order to help domestic economic growth). The importance of these items with respect to monetary policy has virtually disappeared. At present, Regulation Q covers only interest rate ceilings on deposits, and bending the yield curve was long ago abandoned.

The advent of Eurodollars, CDs, a broad array of policy tools that the Fed used, the Glass-Steagall Act of 1933 (which prohibited commercial banks from owning, underwriting, or dealing in corporate stock and corporate bonds) and interest rate ceilings such as Regulation Q, were all factors that had a major impact on monetary policy. Moreover, although inflation was always a concern for the Fed, this was a period during which unemployment was also a major concern. Implicit in the desire to limit unemployment was that there had to be sufficient real growth to achieve such an objective, although no specific target was stated. This is a far cry from the situation that eventually evolved, whereby the Fed's primary policy tool is adjusting an overnight interest rate in order to achieve a desired range of inflation rates that exclude food and energy. Thus, in a more sophisticated world, the Fed is now using a less sophisticated approach to policy.

THE STARTING POINT

Arthur Burns became chairman of the Federal Reserve in 1970, and many of the problems that the Fed has since encountered had their genesis during the 1970s. Burns's predecessor, William Martin, was chairman under a very different set of circumstances both in the 1950s and 1960s. Yet, although the book starts with Burns and 1970, background information presented with respect to Martin and the 1960s is included not only to indicate the circumstances that Burns inherited, but also to allow the reader to look back at a period when the Fed had available—and used—a broad array of policy tools. It is hoped that this approach will give current Fed officials some ideas as to how they could improve the management of monetary policy. One wonders how monetary policy and its impact might have been different through much of the last few decades, had the Fed been less one dimensional, and in some cases less conceptual, in its use of policy tools.

Many of the subsequent inflation concerns and fears—and how the Fed responded—were caused by what Burns did or did not do back in the 1970s. Burns's predecessor—William Martin—had little influence on the course of today's monetary policy. Not that the Martin period was unimportant, but rather that the monetary circumstances, both at home and abroad, were so different from what developed as time moved on. If there was a logical break between time periods and between chairmen, the end of the Martin era and the beginning of the Burns era was the most obvious.

Also, U.S. monetary policy in the 1960s concentrated primarily on domestic factors. Markets were so much simpler. On the international side, a relatively few industrial countries received most of the attention, and there was a clear distinction between developed countries and those that were developing or had yet to develop. And quite a few of those then-developing nations eventually became major players in the world's economic and financial markets, now exerting considerable influence on the U.S. economy, monetary policy, and interest rates.

Just think, in the 1960s, we were in the midst of a cold war with the USSR, and China had little in the way of financial resources and capabilities. Who would have imagined that by the end of 2007, these two formerly economically backward countries would have almost two trillion dollars of official reserves. As a matter of fact, Russian official reserves are growing so rapidly that in a few years they could rival China's in size! OPEC started in 1960 with eleven countries, but it was not until the 1970s that these countries felt their financial oats and became major players on the world financial scene. Their importance has increased exponentially. They are now dominant players when it comes to holding official reserves. The investments of China and OPEC (and down the road, probably Russia) help the United States finance its public and private sectors and recycle funds to offset its massive balance of payments deficit.

2

MONETARY POLICY AROUND THE WORLD

From 1973 to 1982, I was a senior vice president of J. Henry Schroder Bank & Trust Company in New York. My boss was James Wolfenson, who would go on to be the head of the World Bank. Schroder funded itself largely through foreign central bank deposits, and one of my jobs was to meet with central bankers around the world, give advice, and conduct seminars. Having formerly worked for the Federal Reserve, I was treated warmly by foreign central bank officials. Once you have worked for a central bank, other central bankers consider you a member of a large fraternity. Relationships between central banks are typically much more cordial than those between governments. For example, when the French moved their gold out of the United States, it was accomplished in a cordial and professional manner by the two central banks involved. Also, even when China and the United States had limited relationships, there was considerable contact between the Federal Reserve and the People's Bank of China.

When visiting these central banks, I became quite familiar with the various organizational structures and the way policy was implemented. Each was very different. This should not be surprising, given that each country's central bank evolved in different ways. Some were dominated and controlled by their governments, while others were a combination of official and private control. The relationships between central banks and finance ministries or treasuries were also very different depending on the country and, not surprisingly, so was the independence of the central banks.

The seminars I conducted tended to run from as little as a day to as long as a week. They covered a wide variety of topics, running the gamut from a U.S. and international economic outlook, to the areas that drove monetary policy in the United States, to how markets operated. The breadth of the discussions depended to a considerable degree on the sophistication of the people in the audience. For those central banks that were rich in foreign exchange reserves, there was considerable discussion as to how they could improve their investment portfolios. It was

quite common to receive a bank's investment portfolio and make recommendations as to how its investment performance might be improved. It was also not
unusual to be asked about the tools and techniques other banks were using and
how they might apply, in order to improve their investment performance.

After speaking at several dozens of these seminars over a period of almost a
decade, I realized that what worked for the Federal Reserve would not work for
other central banks. This meant that when making policy or technique recommendations, I had to take into consideration politics, economics, history, people's
capabilities, development of markets, the banking system, regulatory functions,
research sources, and abilities, among other things. I bring this up because this
book concentrates on U.S. monetary policy and those who have been in charge
since 1970. Realize that—except as background material that might prove to be
thought provoking—the analyses, critiques, and recommendations presented
here are for the Federal Reserve and its monetary policy, and are likely to have less
usefulness for other central banks.

For a better understanding of how central banks—all of which are in the same
business of managing monetary policy—can be different in so many ways, let us
consider some background information. Five major central banks—the Federal
Reserve, the European Central Bank, the Bank of England, the Bank of Japan, and
the People's Bank of China—all have very different histories; the countries involved
have different economic, geographical, and political backgrounds, and dealings with
their governments are very different. The European Central Bank is a special case. It
is a relatively new entity that operates monetary policy for fifteen countries, and
when it first came into being, many questioned whether it would survive.

After all, the differences among these countries can be just as great as their similarities and involve almost every aspect that one can think of, including politics, economics, demographics, education, immigration, foreign trade, fiscal policies, and the
role and structure of government. This means that a monetary policy stance that is
too easy for some countries may be too restrictive for others. Moreover, the primary
policy objective for most central banks is to hold down inflation, although in the case
of the Bank of Japan, in recent years it has had the opposite problem of deflation.

The problems with respect to the European Central Bank are especially complex
because it wants to hold the overall inflation rate at under 2 percent for the fifteen
member countries, even though the price performance of the members are all over
the lot. Nevertheless, up to this point, the monetary union has held together
because there have been economic advantages to breaking down economic and
political barriers that appear to offset mistakes, misjudgments, and questionable
approaches to monetary policy.

THE FEDERAL RESERVE

When I was a graduate student and taught at the University of Illinois, the bible
for studying the Federal Reserve was a book called *The Federal Reserve System:
Purposes and Functions*. Its first printing was in May 1939, and the ninth printing

was in June 2005. The book was generally updated about every ten years, which frankly was not often enough. It was published by the Federal Reserve Bank of New York, and one can get the information contained in the book online at the New York Federal Reserve Bank site. It covers every aspect of the Federal Reserve System.

There is another book published by the New York Federal Reserve Bank entitled: *U.S. Monetary Policy & Financial Markets.* Paul Meek wrote the first edition of this book in 1982 and it was updated in 1990. Because I had been involved in the government securities business, I was one of a number of people asked to read a draft and make comments and suggestions. Ann-Marie Meulendyke wrote the expanded and updated 1998 edition. This book was far more detailed than the *Purposes and Functions* book, but if you studied both, you had a solid background on the Federal Reserve, its history, and its operations.

Unfortunately, if you talk to most people who are currently involved in the debt markets in general, and the government market in particular, they are unaware of these two valuable sources of background information. Part of the reason is that in earlier days, government securities dealers were considered the centerpiece of the debt markets, and those involved in the markets wanted to know as much nitty-gritty about the Federal Reserve as possible. However, as time passed and independent government securities dealers were bought up, went out of business, or became only one division of a debt-market business, detailed information about the Fed seemed to be not as important.

As a matter of fact, many people in the financial markets today are not familiar with the Fed's weekly, monthly, and quarterly releases. However, recently there has been positive news in this regard, although this benefit was spawned out of adversity. When the Federal Reserve became very involved in helping to cushion the financial debacle in 2007 and 2008, many analysts began to look at Federal Reserve releases they knew nothing about, with titles such as "Factors Affecting Reserve Balances (H.4.1)," "Charge-Off and Delinquency Rates on Loans," "Aggregate Reserves of Depository Institutions and the Monetary Base (H.3)," "Assets and Liabilities of Commercial Banks in the United States (H.8)," and "Senior Loan Officer Opinion Survey on Bank Lending Practices."

BRIEF HISTORY OF THE FEDERAL RESERVE SYSTEM

In order to understand the present, and to make educated guesses as to the future, it is important to look at the history of the Federal Reserve. Here is a useful summary. The quotations come from the Fed's book *U.S. Monetary Policy and Financial Markets.* On December 23, 1913, the Federal Reserve was created by an act of Congress. Its purpose was to serve as the nation's central bank. I have quoted key items that show some of the history prior to the inception of the Fed, at the time of its inception, and changes that have occurred since its inception.

One way to break out the history of the country's approach to a national central banking system is to present it by time periods. The first period would be from 1791 to 1846, the second from 1846 to 1914, the third from 1914 to 1935, the fourth from 1935 to 1951, and the fifth from 1951 up to the present.

1791–1846: This was a period of rapid population and economic expansion in the United States. People immigrated to the United States primarily from Europe, and immigrants from one country often settled in the same locale; the skills and vocations they had acquired abroad were often carried on in the new country. In essence, the United States was a loose federation, and people in rural areas typically had little in common with those in cities. Thus, it is no surprise that the concept of a central or national bank was late in coming to the United States, as it was created against a background of long-standing distrust of centralized power. The First Bank of the United States was chartered by Congress on February 25, 1791. The charter was for twenty years, and when it expired, the Second Bank of the United States was granted a charter in 1816.

According to *U.S. Monetary Policy & Financial Markets*:

> [T]he United States had twice established central banks to stabilize the banking system through reserve and currency management activities. However, the charters of the First Bank of the United States (1791–1811) and the Second Bank of the United States (1816–32) were not renewed by Congress upon expiration, primarily because of political distrust of the Eastern financial establishment and a desire by Western farmers for inexpensive credit.

1846–1914: Upon the demise of the Second Bank of the United States, state governments supervised the banks. It very soon became clear that banking was running well behind the needs of the country. While this was generally recognized, it was difficult to get an agreement on what should be done. The national banking system was a patchwork affair and the country was subject to huge economic and financial swings, with events in the banking system often exacerbating or even causing the problem. Again, from *U.S. Monetary Policy & Financial Markets*:

> From 1846 until the establishment of the Federal Reserve in 1914, reserve management was effected through a "national banking system." Under this system, "country banks" were required to hold reserves at larger banks as well as in the form of cash. "Reserve city banks" were required to hold their reserves in cash and as deposits in "central reserve city banks." Central reserve city banks were required to hold their reserves in cash. The Treasury Department altered reserve levels by adding or draining funds that it kept on deposit at central reserve city banks. The large city banks were unable to respond adequately to seasonal and cyclical variations in the cash and credit requirements of the economy. The years were marked by periodic financial crises that were resolved primarily through emergency actions of private bankers.

In 1907, a banking panic was brought under control through extraordinary actions by a group of commercial banks, led by J. Pierpont Morgan. The panic inspired considerable interest in developing a better system to deal with future crises. A series of congressional studies, hearings, and proposals culminated in the passage of the Federal Reserve Act in December 1913.

1914–1935: World War I began in 1914, and while the United States was not initially involved, it brought to the fore the question of whether the country should continue to follow an isolationist approach. That was answered when the United States became militarily involved in the war. In the 1920s, an economic boom period occurred, with all of its excesses and imbalances, and the boom turned into a bust in 1929 with the stock market crash. This turned into a recession in the 1930s. The Federal Reserve, which was created by the Federal Reserve Act of 1913, was not set up in a way or given the necessary powers to combat all of the problems it encountered during this boom and bust period. The initial structure of the Federal Reserve was as follows, according to *U.S. Monetary Policy & Financial Markets*:

> The system . . . consisted of the Federal Reserve Board in Washington, D.C., and twelve regional Federal Reserve Banks with main offices and branches to serve the entire country. . . . The regional Reserve Banks were to have considerable authority to set the terms for credit provision in response to local developments and to regulate member banks in their districts. The Board in Washington was assigned responsibility for overseeing the activities of the Reserve Banks. The Board consisted of a governor and four other regular members, with the Secretary of the Treasury and the Comptroller of the Currency designated as ex officio members. The twelve regional banks were headed by governors, most of whom had been commercial bankers. . . .
>
> Beginning in 1920, Governor Strong sought to achieve better coordination of open market operations. He preferred to have all operations on behalf of the System conducted by the New York Federal Reserve. . . . The efforts to study and coordinate Reserve Bank operations led to the creation of the Open Market Investment Committee (OMIC) in 1923, consisting of the governors of the Federal Reserve Banks in New York, Boston, Philadelphia, Cleveland, and Chicago. A Trading Desk at the New York Federal Reserve Bank carried out operations for the Federal Reserve System as well as for the New York Bank.
>
> During the 1920s, the System's domestic securities portfolio did not grow significantly. Federal Reserve officials reportedly preferred to purchase short-term securities. Limited available supplies, however, led the Reserve Banks to purchase a mix of securities that spanned the maturity spectrum. . . . In 1930, the OMIC was replaced by the Open Market Policy Conference (OMPC), composed of all twelve Federal Reserve governors and the members of the Federal Reserve Board.

1935–1951: The Banking Act of 1935 was developed in the depths of the Great Depression. According to *U.S. Monetary Policy & Financial Markets,*

> [It] reorganized the Federal Reserve System, introducing the basic structure that exists today. The Board became the Board of Governors of the Federal Reserve System, with seven governors, one of whom was designated Chairman. The Treasury Secretary and the Comptroller of the Currency no longer sat on the Board. The act formally charged the Board with responsibility for exercising such powers as it possessed to promote conditions consistent with business stability. The Reserve Bank governors were redesignated as presidents, and membership of the renamed Federal Reserve Open Market Committee (FOMC) was limited to five presidents at any one time. The act also took away the power of individual Reserve Banks to buy or sell government debt without permission of the FOMC, thereby formally ending one of the major controversies of the 1920s. Finally, it made permanent the provision of deposit insurance.

The year 1951 was chosen as the end of this period because it was a time when the approach to monetary policy changed in a drastic way. From the start of World War II up to 1951, the Federal Reserve pegged yields on long-term government securities (bonds) at very low levels. This was not at the choice of the Fed, but was in essence a carryover from a War World II policy. Finally, in March 1951, after a major political skirmish between the Fed and the Treasury, the latter finally agreed to permit the Federal Reserve to pursue an independent interest rate and monetary policy. This was called the "Treasury-Federal Reserve Accord." The impact of this agreement was far reaching, especially for the debt markets and financial institutions. The rapid rate of expansion in these areas and the economy in general would never have taken place without the Accord. Interestingly, today, if you ask most people in the financial community about the Accord, they would not have the slightest idea of what you are talking about.

1951 to the Present: This period could easily be subdivided into the new instruments and markets of the 1960s, the embedded inflation problem, the use of monetary-aggregate targeting and high and volatile interest rates in much of the 1970s and 1980s, and major structural changes and reforms in the banking system and financial community in the 1990s. Since the turn of the century, the internationalization of markets and institutions, and the complexities of asset and liability products, have created both benefits and headaches for all of those concerned—and particularly for financial institutions and their regulators.

Due to the financial meltdown in the United States in 2007 and 2008, and the adversities that have been created around the world, it is highly likely that the powers and responsibilities of the Federal Reserve and other central banks will be expanded, with much greater emphasis placed on policy coordination. Yet, one should not jump to the conclusion that the financial meltdown was due primarily to a lack of power on the part of regulators in general and the Federal

Reserve in particular. The power was there, with the main problem being that the Fed, and others, did not act in a timely and forceful manner. Having power is important, but it does little good if it is not used in an appropriate and opportune way.

A brief history of central banking in the United States provides useful background information before delving into the whys and wherefores of Federal Reserve monetary policy. Yet, because of the internationalization of markets and institutions in recent years, it is also worthwhile to look at some of the history and structure of other major central banks. The first to be presented is the European Central Bank, followed by the Bank of England, the Bank of Japan, and the People's Bank of China.

THE EUROPEAN CENTRAL BANK

The firm Griggs & Santow has had several foreign governments and central banks as clients. When the European Central Bank (ECB) began operating, one of our major clients (a foreign government not in Europe) asked us to do a detailed study of the euro and the ECB, and whether it would succeed, or even last. Apparently, there were staff studies done inside this foreign government that suggested that both the euro and the ECB would fail. Much of their reasoning was based on the confederation history of Europe, or should I say the lack thereof. Moreover, significant differences among the countries ran the gamut from rich and successful to poor and aspiring. Moreover, ethnic differences were considerable to say the least, and new countries evolved while others disappeared.

The study took well over one month, and I worked on it almost full time. The conclusions I reached were that both the euro and the ECB would endure, but substantial problems would exist in the first few years because of lack of cooperation, jealousies, and a lack of leadership. To start with, there was a big battle as to who would be the first head of the ECB (not surprisingly, France and Germany were on opposite sides), and when that decision was made, from a monetary policy leadership point of view, the person selected was far from an optimum choice. In other words, some bumbling and stumbling were to be expected in the first few years, but in the long run, the overall advantages of one currency and one central bank would more than offset the nationalistic tendencies of each country. With respect to my forecasts, so far, so good.

In a sense, the euro and ECB fears were similar to the arguments surrounding the formation of NAFTA. In the case of NAFTA, it was clear there were overall benefits for the United States, Canada, and Mexico combined. For Canada and Mexico, the advantages were obvious and the disadvantages few, and this has since shown up in their economies in general and their foreign trade numbers in particular. As for the United States, the argument still rages as to how the pluses and minuses balance out. While these were similar to the discussions that originally occurred when the euro and the ECB were implemented—who would be better off and who would be worse off—they no longer seem to be major issues.

The ECB has now been in existence for about one decade, but the genesis of the organization goes back to June 1988, when the European Council stated as its objective an Economic and Monetary Union (EMU). A committee was formed to study and propose specific stages that would lead to such a union. The committee was made up of the governors of the then European Community (EC) central banks and the general manager of the Bank for International Settlements (BIS), a professor of economics, and the president of the central bank of Spain.

The commission recommended that the economic and monetary union should be achieved in three stages. The first stage started July 1, 1990, when member states abolished restrictions on capital movements among them. Stage two started on January 1, 1994. The main tasks here were to improve central bank cooperation and monetary policy coordination, start preparations for the establishment of the European System of Central Banks (ESCB), and to work towards the creation of a single currency in the third stage. On January 1, 1999, the third and final stage of the EMU began with the irrevocable fixing of the exchange rates of the currencies of the eleven nations that initially participated in EMU, and with formation of a single monetary policy under the ECB. As one might expect, there was some controversy as to the fixing of each currency into the new euro.

On January 1, 2001, the number of member states increased to twelve when Greece entered the third stage of the EMU. Slovenia was the thirteenth state to become a euro area member, and that occurred on January 1, 2007; in early 2008, Cyprus and Malta became members. The central banks that are members automatically become part of the Eurosystem.

Currently, the Governing Council is the main decision-making body of the ECB. It comprises six members of the Executive Board and the governors of the national central banks of the fifteen euro area nations. Its responsibilities are stated as follows:

> To adopt the guidelines and make the decisions necessary to ensure the performance of the task entrusted to the Eurosystem; To formulate monetary policy for the euro area. This included decisions relating to monetary objectives, to key interest rates, the supply of reserves in the Eurosystem, and the establishment of guidelines for the implementation of those decisions.

Yet in the real world, the primary objective of the ECB is to control price increases. The attempt is to keep the twelve-month consumer price index increase to less than 2 percent. However, because the central bank is very anti-inflation oriented, even if the twelve-month increase in prices is less than 2 percent, if the bank's forecast is for an increase of more than 2 percent down the road, that will be sufficient reason to keep a restrictive policy.

As for policy meetings, the Governing Council usually meets twice a month in Frankfurt. Obviously, during the financial market problems in 2007 and 2008 meetings were more frequent. Interestingly, although the origins of the meltdowns were generated in the United States, the ECB was earlier and more aggressive than the Federal Reserve in trying to head off financial difficulties. The main difficulty for the ECB and the Bank of England appeared to be a dysfunctional interbank market, in which some banks were unwilling to lend to other banks.

At the first meeting in any given month, the Governing Council evaluates monetary and economic factors and makes its monthly policy decision. At the second meeting, the Council talks mainly about issues related to other functions and responsibilities of the ECB and the Eurosystem. Minutes of ECB meetings are not published, but monetary policy decisions are presented at a press conference held after the first meeting of the month. The president, aided by the vice-president, conducts the conference.

THE BANK OF ENGLAND

The Bank of England was established in 1693 to act as the English government's banker. It was nationalized on March 1, 1946, and gained its "independence" in 1997. The bank is a state-owned institution; it acts as the central bank of the United Kingdom, and is responsible for managing the monetary policy of the country. "The current governance and accountability framework is set by the 1998 Bank of England Act, which provides for a Court of Directors, a Committee on Nonexecutive Directors within Court, and a Monetary Policy Committee (MPC)."

In terms of generalities, the bank lists and discusses its two core purposes—monetary stability and financial stability. Quoting from the Bank of England with respect to its core purposes:

Core Purpose 1—Monetary Stability
Monetary stability means stable prices and confidence in the currency. Stable prices are defined by the Government's inflation target, which the Bank seeks to meet through the decision on interest rates taken by the Monetary Policy Committee, explaining those decisions transparently and implementing them effectively in the money markets.

Core Purpose 2—Financial Stability
Financial stability entails detecting and reducing threats to the financial system as a whole. Such threats are detected through the Bank's surveillance and market intelligence functions. They are reduced by strengthening infrastructure, and by financial and other operations, at home and abroad, including, in exceptional circumstances, by acting as the lender of last resort.

However, generalized objectives of most central banks and their order of precedence can be misleading. In the real world, a lack of financial stability is given precedence over economic objectives such as price increases. Moreover, when a recession is near or occurring, that typically will take precedence over price containment. However, when financial instability is not a problem, and when a recession is not a problem, then most central banks such as the Bank of England will concentrate on acceptable price performance.

As for the decision-making process at the Bank of England, at least once a year, the British government specifies the price target (which is currently 2 percent), and its growth and employment objectives. According to the bank, the MPC, whose members comprise the governor and deputy governors, two of the bank's executive directors, and four members appointed by the chancellor, must meet at least monthly. MPC decisions are announced after each monthly meeting. Minutes of their meetings are published two weeks later. The quarterly inflation report includes the MPC projections of inflation and output. The bank performs all the functions of a typical central bank, such as maintaining price stability and supporting the economic policies of the U.K. government.

All of these guidelines and rules seem so clear cut, but when it comes to determining what monetary policy should be at any given time, that is not the case. For example, there is little doubt that the governor of a central bank is the kingpin, but the power of a governor can vary from one central bank to another. For example, at a Bank of England meeting held June 6–7, 2007, the governor (Mervyn King) and one of the two deputy governors, were outvoted five to four on whether the Bank should raise its official Bank rate. The governor voted on the side of raising the rate, and he lost. Yet, this did not create any crisis of confidence inside the Bank. If that had happened at some other central banks, I am not sure that would be the case.

Yet, it is hard to imagine this type of situation occurring at the European Central Bank, the Federal Reserve, the Bank of Japan, or the People's Bank of China. In the case of the European Central Bank, it is highly unlikely that Jean Claude Trichet would ever lose on an important vote; in the case of the Federal Reserve, while it is not unusual for one or two policymakers to vote against the majority, as far as I am aware, the chairman has not been on the losing side on any major issue. There have been a few cases of dissenting votes at the Bank of Japan, but nothing that placed in doubt who was in charge. As for the head of the People's Bank, it is hard to imagine the head of the bank (obviously a political appointee) being outvoted on a policy issue. In looking at the next two central banks, keep in mind that structure and methodology do not tell the entire story.

THE BANK OF JAPAN

Beginning in the 1970s, my consulting relationships took me to Japan, and these trips continue up to the present. Many of the individuals that I currently visit in Tokyo and also in Nagoya I had first met in the United States. Among this group is Shijuro Ogata, who was the representative of the Bank of Japan (BOJ) in the United States. He is a former deputy governor for international relations of the Bank of Japan and deputy governor of the Japan Development Bank. In one of my early trips to Japan, he asked me if I would be willing to conduct seminars on the U.S. economy and monetary policy for the Bank of Japan research staff. I accepted and that was the beginning of a close and long-term relationship with many senior officers of the BOJ.

I bring this up because, as a result of my meetings in Japan, I have gained considerable knowledge about how things really work in that country, including the political side. For example, the independence of the BOJ has always been limited, even when the laws were changed to give the central bank more independence. This is especially true with respect to who becomes the governor of the BOJ. If you think this comment is overstated, all one has to do is look at the political problems in 2008 when the prime minister attempted to appoint a new governor who had the backing of the Ministry of Finance, and was rebuffed by the upper house of the Diet. The information that follows with respect to the BOJ, however, is primarily boiler-plate so that you can see how the bank came into being and how it differs from other major central banks.

The BOJ was established by the Bank of Japan Act in 1882. Then, in 1942 during World War II, a new law was enacted to replace the Bank of Japan Act, with no major revisions implemented over the next fifty years. However, the world had changed so much during this time—especially with respect to the globalization of the economy, financial markets and their mechanisms—that it was clear that the laws enacted in 1942 were way out of date. After the war, the Allies made some changes that gave the BOJ somewhat more independence than had previously been the case. However, it was not until 1997 that the laws governing the BOJ were revised, based on the principles of greater independence and transparency. This was a step in the right direction, although there is more to be done regarding independence and transparency, especially the former.

Currently, the organization of the BOJ is as follows. The executives consist of six deliberative members, the BOJ's governor and two deputy governors, no more than three executive auditors, no more than six executive directors, and a few counselors. As for the Board, it comprises nine members consisting of six deliberative members, the governor, and the two deputy governors. The Board has a chairman elected by Board members, and the chairman exercises general control over Board business.

To indicate some of the limitations on the independence of the BOJ, the Ministry of Finance and the minister who is in charge of economic and fiscal policy are allowed to attend certain meetings as prescribed by Article 19 of the Bank of Japan Law. When attending Board meetings for monetary control matters, these outsiders may submit proposals about monetary control items or request that the Board postpone a vote on such matters until the next Board meeting of this type.

According to its current charter, the BOJ has six primary missions: the issuance and management of banknotes; implementation of monetary policy; providing settlement services and ensuring the stability of the financial system; treasury and operations related to government securities; international activities; and compilation of data, economic analyses, and research activities.

The BOJ has fifteen departments at its head office in Tokyo, thirty-two branches and fourteen local offices in Japan, and seven overseas representative offices. The bank is capitalized at 100 million yen in accordance with the law, with approximately 55 percent of the capital subscribed by the government. The law does not allow holders of subscription certificates the right to participate in the bank's management, which should be no surprise since this is a governmental organization. The holders do have some rights (at least on a theoretical basis) in the case of liquidation.

THE PEOPLE'S BANK OF CHINA

A number of years ago, I attended a reception at the Japanese consulate in New York celebrating the emperor's birthday. Many of the guests were foreign dignitaries, and I happened to get into a discussion with a representative from the People's Republic of China. Because a number of Griggs & Santow clients did business in China, or were significantly affected by what happened there, our firm was quite knowledgeable (at least on the surface) of what was happening in China, especially on the economic front.

I do not remember the specifics of our conversation, except that I was asked if I would like to meet with other Chinese government representatives. I accepted the invitation and the meeting took place several weeks later. I had hoped to develop some sort of consulting relationship similar to one that we previously had with the Monetary Authority of Singapore, but that did not happen.

Even though our firm did not develop a relationship with China, it did not limit our interest in what was happening in that country, and in particular, at the People's Bank of China. Although China is a communist country, do not assume that the People's Bank is operated in a communist fashion. The central bank is about as traditional as a central bank can be, except that, in many ways, it is more aggressive and capitalistic than other central banks. It aggressively manages the official reserves of the country, not only with respect to types of investments, but also with respect to its currency. When the official reserves of the country exceeded $1 trillion, the government realized that it could be more aggressive in investments, and new investment funds came on the scene. The hope here was to be more aggressive in taking on risks with the expectation of getting greater rewards.

The People's Bank has been far from passive when it comes to currency management. At one point, official foreign exchange reserves were almost all in dollar investments, but in recent years, greater diversification of currencies has taken place, and this trend has been accelerated because of the deterioration of the greenback. To be charitable, one can say that the currency in the foreign exchange market is *managed*; to be less than charitable, one can say the currency is *rigged*, which means purposely held down in price in order to stimulate exports and build foreign exchange reserves to help grow the country. (If a currency is cheap, then firms in other countries will invest more in China and foreign consumers will buy more. The undervalued Chinese currency also helps explain why so many U.S. companies have goods manufactured in China.)

A very important area in which the People's Bank has been involved, but obviously one that it talks little about, are the major capital problems of the banking system in China. Quietly in recent years, the People's Bank has made considerable capital injections to the Chinese banks. The main reason for this capital problem is that over the years many of the loans the banks made were at the "suggestion" of the government, even though many of the loans were far from creditworthy. Thus, the Chinese banks have a shockingly large percentage of loans that would be classified as nonperforming in the capitalist world.

Of course, six decades of communist rule has not done wonders for having creditworthy standards, let alone the data to make such judgments. If the Chinese financial institutions are ultimately going to prosper and become much more international, the financial institutions need more major injections of capital and improved methods of risk-measurement. In this regard, the Chinese have "borrowed" expertise from foreign firms that do business in China in order to help build a proper credit analysis system.

This may seem like an excessive introduction to a section that talks about the nuts and bolts of a central bank, but unless these comments are made, one might assume that this is just another communist institution run by a communist government. Obviously, this is not the case, and the People's Bank has been well accepted by the central bank community.

When it comes to history, responsibilities, institutional arrangements, and management and organization structure, information is readily available on the People's Bank of China Web site (www.pbc.gov.cn/english/) from which the following information is primarily drawn: The People's Bank started on December 1, 1948, and initially was primarily a combination of the Huabei Bank, the Beihai Bank, and the Xibei Farmer Bank. Beijing became the bank's headquarters in 1949 following the military defeat of the nationalist government. From 1949 to 1978, it was the only bank in the country and therefore had both central banking and commercial banking responsibilities.

As part of the economic reform in the 1980s, the commercial banking functions of the People's Bank were divided into four independent but state-owned banks. Then, in 1983 the State Council determined that it would be the central bank of China, and this was legally confirmed on March 18, 1995. Because of the rapidly changing economic landscape in China, in 1998 the bank was restructured in a major way. Provincial and local branches were done away with, and they were replaced by nine regional branches. In 2003 the Bank's role was strengthened and broadened with respect to monetary policy implementation, overall financial stability, and providing financial services.

The People's Bank, under the guidance of the State Council, formulates and implements monetary policy. It also has the responsibility for preventing and resolving financial risks and safeguards financial stability. The stated objective of monetary policy is to maintain the stability and the value of the currency and thereby promote economic growth. This is different from most other central banks that emphasize price objectives. Realize that China's primary economic objective is economic growth, and that is for both economic and political reasons. Price increases that seem excessive are tolerated as long as the situation does not get out of control. (One can argue that the government has the same attitude with respect to pollution.)

The monetary policy instruments that are used by the People's Bank include reserve requirement ratios, a central bank base interest rate, rediscounting, central bank lending, open market operations, and other policy instruments specified by the State Council.

Article 12 of the Law of the People's Republic of China is a guiding factor when it comes to monetary policy. This article states that "the People's Bank of China is to establish a monetary policy committee, whose responsibilities, composition, and working procedures shall be prescribed by the State Council." The Monetary Policy Committee (MPC) is designated as the consultative body for monetary policy. The MPC has an incredibly large number of members that is not traditional for most central banks.

It has as members the Bank's governor and two deputy governors, a deputy secretary-general of the State Council, a vice minister of the State Development of Reform Commission, a vice finance minister, the administrator of the State Administration of Foreign Exchange, the chairman of the China Banking Regulatory Committee, the chairman of the China Securities Regulatory Commission, the chairman of the China Insurance Regulatory Commission, the commissioner of the National Bureau of Statistics, the president of the China Association of Banks, and an expert from academia. (Only one expert from academia; the U.S. Federal Reserve has many more.)

AN EXPANDING PROFESSION—FED WATCHERS

In the 1960s and 1970s a select group of economists in the United States were called "Fed watchers." While there were monetary policy observers in other countries, they did not seem to have the same cult designation as those in the United States. Almost every Fed watcher understood the intricacies of monetary policy, and they often made suggestions to the private sector and to public officials through regular publications. The most noteworthy publications were from Salomon Brothers, Aubrey G. Lanston, and First Boston Corporation. Those who wrote the analyses and forecasts generally had PhDs, worked at one time at the Federal Reserve or the Treasury (or both), and had positions with dealers in government securities. They were educators as well as analysts, and their opinions were highly sought.

As time passed, the financial world became more compressed and interrelated, and those who analyzed and pontificated on U.S. monetary policy broadened their horizons. They were no longer just "Fed watchers;" they were international monetary policy watchers. Their analyses and forecasts took on a broader base and meaning. A big help in this regard were international financial conferences that various Federal Reserve District banks held, such as the Federal Reserve Bank of Kansas City and the Federal Reserve Bank of Boston. The Jackson Hole annual meetings conducted by the Kansas City Federal Reserve Bank are probably the most well known of the conferences, and it attracts central bankers from all over the world. I was fortunate enough to attend the Jackson Hole meetings for almost two decades.

It is clear from these meetings that while circumstances were very different among the various countries, many of the problems facing central banks around the world were similar, and thoughtful people from both the official and private sectors were meeting to discuss the problems and how policies could be improved. While comparable conferences continue to this day and are of great value, the world of so-called monetary policy experts seems to have expanded exponentially, and unfortunately not necessarily based on professional credentials. For many, their claim to fame is making interest rate forecasts, and such forecasts tend to be a dime a dozen.

These "experts" are not hard to find. Many of those now considered "Fed watchers" are regulars on the various twenty-four-hour business news channels. They are the ones in the expensive designer suits, and behind them in big letters, is the name of the firm they represent. This immediately raises the question, "Are these people marketers or economists?" When numbers or policy shifts are released, within a few seconds they have analyzed the information and then pontificate on what it all means for the benefit of their television audience, which numbers in the millions. This is how a vast majority of the public becomes educated about the Federal Reserve, its policies, and the data upon which policy judgments are made.

In an effort to deal with these circumstances, my business partner, Bill Griggs, and I keep one television station on all day—but with the sound off. Whenever any economic stats are released, the television station is nice enough to put up the headlines and the numbers, and frankly that is all we expect from them. There is no attempt by the media to educate the public about how the Federal Reserve works, why it does things in a certain way, and what the information means. Nor is there any attempt to give the analysts who appear on their programs a sufficient amount of time to study the newly released data before talking about what the numbers really mean.

The Federal Reserve publishes a wealth of information in its regular releases but the main media focus is on the dissecting of press releases, speeches, and testimonies of Fed officials, looking for hidden meanings. There are times when media pundits and their guests spend hours on end talking about whether the Fed will change its funds target by 25 or 50 basis points, and, supposedly, how important the difference is between these two alternatives. If an analyst makes it to the big time by speaking frequently on a business television network, then they are considered to be Fed watchers—analysts who should be listened to. I have trouble believing this is progress.

In the next chapter, we'll go beyond "Fed watching" to consider the Fed's policy levers, how they can be used, and what good—or evil—they can do.

3

THE FED AND ITS POLICIES

The main goal of this chapter is to impart some background information on the Federal Reserve and its policies that those in the media fail to provide. As you will see, there is much more to monetary policy than the Fed nudging an overnight rate by a token amount. **Note:** There is a glossary in the back of the book that will explain everything from monetary policy to yield curve, and I encourage you to refer to it frequently (see the sidebar).

THE STRUCTURE OF THE FEDERAL RESERVE SYSTEM

The Federal Reserve is subdivided into twelve districts, and the borders of each district do not follow state lines. For example, I live in Fairfield County, Connecticut; the western part of county is in the New York district and the eastern part is in the Boston district. The Federal Reserve has numbers for each district, and those who are at the Fed, or have worked there, are quite familiar with these numbers and the areas they represent.

The districts and their numbers are as follows: Boston (1); New York (2); Philadelphia (3); Cleveland (4); Richmond (5); Atlanta (6); Chicago (7); St. Louis (8); Minneapolis (9); Kansas City (10); Dallas (11); and San Francisco (12). The San Francisco district is responsible for Alaska, Hawaii, American Samoa, Guam, and the Northern Mariana Islands, while the New York district services Puerto Rico and the U.S. Virgin Islands. Washington D.C. is in the Richmond District, and that is where the Federal Reserve Board is located.

Ten of the twelve district banks have branches, and similar to the unusually drawn borders between districts, some of the branches are not where you might expect them to be. In the New York district there is a Buffalo branch; the Cleveland district has Cincinnati and Pittsburgh branches; the Richmond district has Baltimore and

THE MAKING OF A GLOSSARY

Before getting into the nitty-gritty of information and analysis in this chapter and beyond, I felt I should provide the reader with some definitions and explanations of many of the terms used in this chapter and the book in the form of a glossary.

Creating a glossary may sound like a rather simple project. However, that turned out not to be the case. There is no one source that provides anywhere near complete information with respect to explanations and definitions. Equally frustrating is that explanations and definitions can be different, depending upon the source and the markets being written about.

To make the situation even more complex, both "Fed watchers" and "market watchers" have their own terminology, and their own understanding of what certain words and terms mean. This meant considerable rewriting and modification of what others had presented. The list of items to be defined kept growing, and after a while I realized that the best way to handle this situation was to develop a glossary, which is what I did, and it is located in the back of the book.

The more I worked on the glossary, the more I realized that it could stand alone as something that was worthwhile for the reader to at least peruse. Some of the terms presented in the glossary are not specifically covered in the body of the book, but they will give the reader a more complete understanding of market and monetary-policy terminology. Logic would suggest at least glancing at the glossary early on in reading this book in order to provide you with assistance when you get to the more complex and analytical chapters.

Charlotte branches; and the Atlanta district has Birmingham, Jacksonville, Miami, Nashville, and New Orleans branches. Then there is the Chicago district which has a Detroit branch, the St. Louis district has Little Rock, Louisville, and Memphis branches; and the Minneapolis district has a Helena branch. Finally, the Kansas City district has Denver, Oklahoma City, and Omaha branches; the Dallas district has El Paso, Houston, and San Antonio branches; and the San Francisco district has Los Angles, Portland, Salt Lake City, and Seattle branches. The two remaining districts not listed above—Boston and Philadelphia—have no branches. The last time the Board of Governors revised branch boundaries was in February 1996.

THE FEDERAL OPEN MARKET COMMITTEE

The group inside the Federal Reserve that sets monetary policy is called the Federal Open Market Committee (FOMC). It establishes policy guidelines and targets, but it is not involved in actual open market operations, which are conducted by the trading desk at the Federal Reserve Bank of New York. Also, the FOMC is not directly involved in making loans to commercial banks, which is the responsibility of the district Federal Reserve banks.

There are twelve voting members of the FOMC, with vacancies quite common, especially when it comes to governors. The voting members of the FOMC are comprised of seven governors, the president of the Federal Reserve Bank of New York, and four of the remaining eleven district bank presidents. These last four serve one-year terms on a rotating basis. The rotating seats are divided into four bank group-ings with one member from each grouping. There is one voting member on the FOMC from each of the following groups: Boston, Philadelphia, and Rich-mond; Cleveland and Chicago; Atlanta, St. Louis, and Dallas; and Minneapolis, Kansas City, and San Francisco. This breakdown, with the Chicago and Cleve-land banks being voting FOMC members every other year rather than every third year, may not seem logical, but that is the way it was set up. Historical precedence is difficult to break.

Nonvoting presidents attend the FOMC meetings. They participate in the dis-cussions and have their say when it comes to analyzing the economy and the Fed's policy options. The FOMC determines its own organization, and it elects the chairman of the Board of Governors as its chairman. The president of the New York Bank is the vice-chairman.

Up until 1978 twelve regularly scheduled FOMC meetings took place every year. After that, the number of meetings was cut back, in good part because of logistical and time-conflict problems. There are now eight regularly scheduled meetings per year. Frankly, a good case can be made in this fast-paced modern world that the Fed should return to twelve meetings per year—eight held in per-son and four held via teleconferencing. Of course, irrespective of the frequency of the meetings, when unanticipated problems arise, there can be—and there are—special conference calls. For example, in 2001 when the Fed was in a rush to ease monetary policy, there were five special meetings.

A good case can be made that regularly scheduled meetings should be one-and-a-half days in length—a full first day, a partial second day, and then off to home. One-day meetings prove to be less than one day, and there is too much ground to be covered in such a short time. In 2005, when Alan Greenspan was chairman, two of the eight regularly scheduled meetings were held over two days (really a day and a half). In 2006, under Ben Bernanke, there were three two-day meetings; and in 2007 and in 2008, there were four two-day meetings.

One issue that has created a major controversy over the years has been the release of the FOMC meeting minutes. The pressure on the Fed for greater trans-parency on a timelier basis has increased, and the Fed has responded in a way that still does not satisfy most of its critics. However, there are some practical problems involved when it comes to a quick release of the minutes. For example, those who were involved in the meeting should have the right to check what they were reported to have said and what others were reported to have said, so that the record is accurate. It has always been my belief that if the FOMC meetings were held once a month, the minutes could be released with only a two-week time lag, half-way between regularly scheduled meetings.

On January 4, 2005, the Fed decided to expedite the release of the FOMC minutes. They are now released three weeks after the date of policy decisions. As for actual transcripts of the meetings, they are released for an entire year, but with a five-year time lag. This seems an overly long period, especially for someone who is trying to do a historical study of monetary policy.

THE BOARD OF GOVERNORS

The Board of Governors consists of seven members. They are nominated by the President of the United States and they have to be confirmed by the Senate. At times, the confirmation hearings have been testy, especially if they are held just prior to an election. A full term for a governor is fourteen years, but few have served the full term, often leaving for greener pastures (especially in the monetary sense). Thus, many governors have been appointed to fill the remainder of someone else's term. A member who serves a full fourteen-year term cannot be reappointed, but that is not the case for a member who completes an unexpired portion of a term. All terms end on their statutory date regardless of when the member is sworn into office.

The chairman and the vice-chairman are named by the President, from among Board members, and they can be reappointed. Their term of office is four years. A member's term on the Board is not affected by his or her status as chairman or vice-chairman. In choosing the Board members, only one is supposed to be selected from a Federal Reserve district. However, at times this has been loosely interpreted, such as for someone living part time in a district.

Unfortunately, it seems that more often than not, there is a lack of a full complement of seven governors. As a matter of fact, there have been times when there have been as few as five governors (through much of 2007 and into 2008). Because it seems as though there is often a lack of breadth in expertise when there is a full complement of governors, the situation becomes even direr when there is a shortage of members. For example, in 2007, there was a shortage of experts in bank regulation on the Board, which was not exactly a good time to lack such expertise (having staff members with such knowledge is not good enough).

If one wonders why there is not always a full complement of governors and why the best people are often not chosen to fill the Federal Reserve's needs, all one has to do is look at what happened in the middle of 2008. On June 27, 2008, the Senate confirmed Elizabeth A. Duke, a senior officer at TowneBank in Portsmouth, Virginia, to become a Federal Reserve governor. She will serve the remainder of a term that ends in January 2012. However, the Senate did not act on two other nominees: Larry Klane, a former Capital One Financial Corporation executive, and Randall Kroszner, a Federal Reserve governor whose term had expired, but who had been allowed to serve until being replaced.

The obvious question here is, Why was one person approved by the Senate when, in essence, the other two—one of whom is a sitting member—were turned down? The answer appears to be a mixture of practicality and politics. If the Senate did not approve either of the three, there was a likelihood of having only three governors out of a full complement of seven, at a time of major economic and financial problems. This situation would have severely limited Bernanke's power, especially because there are five voting district bank presidents.

It appears that the situation called for a political compromise—approve one of the three. This would still allow the Democrats to have several Federal Reserve Board appointments if they should win the national elections in November 2008. By approving Elizabeth Duke, the senate chose the safest nominee from a political standpoint.

Playing politics with Federal Reserve Board nominations and approvals is very detrimental to having a sound monetary policy. In the case at hand, there is a shortage of Board members and a dearth of expertise that is crucial to all central banks, especially when combating major financial crises.

The following is a list of the sitting governors as of late 2008, along with their backgrounds. This information is summarized and taken primarily from Federal Reserve sources. It allows the reader to study these individuals and ascertain their strengths and shortcomings:

Ben S. Bernanke, Chairman, was appointed to a full fourteen-year term that expires on January 31, 2020, and to a four-year term as chairman that expires on January 31, 2010 (he can be reappointed as chairman to additional terms). He was sworn in on February 1, 2006, as chairman and a member of the Board of Governors. Before his appointment, he was chairman of the President's Council of Economic Advisers from June 2005 to January 2006. Previous to that, he was a member of the Board of Governors of the Federal Reserve from 2002 to 2005. Dr. Bernanke's background is primarily in academia, with most of his time spent at Princeton University. He also has taught at Stanford University, New York University, and Massachusetts Institute of Technology. He has published many articles on a wide variety of economic issues, including monetary policy and macroeconomics, and is the author of several books, including two textbooks. Dr. Bernanke was born in December 1953 in Augusta, Georgia, and grew up in Dillon, South Carolina. He received a BA in economics in 1975 from Harvard University (summa cum laude) and a PhD in economics in 1979 from the Massachusetts Institute of Technology. He is married and has two children.

Elizabeth A. Duke was approved by the Senate on June 27, 2008 to be the new Federal Reserve governor. Her term will expire in January 2012. She received a BFA from the University of North Carolina and an MBA from Old Dominion University. She has been senior executive vice president of TowneBank, Portsmouth, Virginia, a member of the Federal Reserve Bank of Richmond, and in 2004–2005 was chairman of the American Bankers Association.

Donald Kohn, Vice-Chairman, originally took office on August 5, 2002, as a member of the Board of Governors for a full term ending January 31, 2016. On June 23, 2006, Dr. Kohn was sworn in as vice chairman of the Board of Governors for a four-year term ending June 23, 2010. He started his career at the Federal Reserve as a Financial Economist at the Federal Reserve Bank of Kansas City from 1970 to 1975. He then moved on to the Board of Governors where he held positions that included Economist, chief of Capital Markets, associate director, deputy staff director for Monetary and Financial Policy, director of the Division of Monetary Affairs, secretary of the Open Market Committee, and adviser to the Board for Monetary Policy, before being appointed as a governor. Dr. Kohn was born in November 1942 in Philadelphia and received a BA in economics in 1964 from the College of Wooster and a PhD in economics from the University of Michigan. He has written extensively on issues that relate to monetary policy and its implementation.

Randall S. Kroszner took office on March 1, 2006, to fill an unexpired term ending January 31, 2008. Before becoming a member of the Board, Dr. Kroszner was professor of economics at the Graduate School of Business at the University of Chicago (1999–2006). He was also assistant professor (1990–94) and associate professor (1994–99) at the University of Chicago. He was a member of the President's Council of Economic Advisers from 2001 to 2003. His research interests include conflicts of interest in financial services firms, international financial crises, corporate governance, debt restructuring and bankruptcy, and monetary economics. Dr. Kroszner was born in June 1962 in Englewood, New Jersey, and received a ScB in applied mathematics-economics from Brown University in 1984 and an MA (1987) and PhD (1990), both in economics, from Harvard University.

Kevin M. Warsh took office on February 24, 2006, to fill an unexpired term ending January 31, 2018. Prior to his appointment, he served as special assistant to the President for Economic Policy and as executive secretary of the National Economic Council. He participated in the President's Working Group on Financial Markets and served as the administration's chief liaison to the independent financial regulatory agencies. From 1995 to 2002, Mr. Warsh was a member of the Mergers and Acquisitions Department of Morgan Stanley, ultimately serving as vice president and executive director. He was born in April 1970 in Albany New York, and received an AB in public policy from Stanford University in 1992 and a JD in 1995 from Harvard Law School.

CHAIRMEN OF THE BOARD SINCE 1914

There have been only fourteen Federal Reserve chairmen since 1914. They tend to stay on until their terms as a governor and chairman are over. However, when it comes to the other governors or district bank presidents, they seldom stay on and complete their terms:

Charles S. Hamlin	August 10, 1914–August 10, 1916
William P.G. Harding	August 10, 1916–August 9, 1922
Daniel R. Crissinger	May 1, 1923–September 15, 1927
Roy A. Young	October 4, 1927–August 31, 1930
Eugene Meyer	September 16, 1930–May 10, 1933
Eugene R. Black	May 19, 1933–August 15, 1934

Marriner S. Eccles   November 15, 1934–February 3, 1948
Thomas B. McCabe   April 15, 1948–April 2, 1951
William McChesney Martin, Jr.   April 2, 1951–February 1, 1970
Arthur F. Burns   February 1, 1970–January 31, 1978
G. William Miller   March 8, 1978–August 6, 1979
Paul A. Volcker   August 6, 1979–August 11, 1987
Alan Greenspan   August 11, 1987–January 31, 2006
Ben S. Bernanke   February 1, 2006–

See Table 3-1 for a list of Governors during the terms of the past five chairmen.

Table 3-1
Governors during the Terms of Arthur F. Burns, G. William Miller, Paul A. Volcker, Alan Greenspan, and Ben S. Bernanke

Governor	Appointed	Term	Chairmen
J. L. Robertson	Feb 18, 1952	Reappointed 1964; resigned Apr 30, 1973	Martin and Burns
George W. Mitchell	Aug 31, 1961	Reappointed 1962; served until Feb 13, 1976	Martin and Burns
J. Dewey Daane	Nov 29, 1963	Served until Mar 8, 1974	Martin and Burns
Sherman J. Maisel	Apr 30, 1965	Served through May 31, 1972	Martin and Burns
Andrew F. Brimmer	May 9, 1966	Resigned Aug 31, 1974	Martin and Burns
William W. Sherrill	May 1, 1967	Reappointed in 1968; resigned Nov 15, 1971	Martin and Burns
Arthur F. Burns	Jan 31, 1970	Resigned Mar 31, 1978	Burns
John E. Sheehan	Jan 4, 1972	Resigned Jun 1, 1975	Burns
Jeffrey M. Bucher	Jun 5, 1972	Resigned Jan 2, 1976	Burns
Robert C. Holland	Jun 11, 1973	Resigned May 15, 1976	Burns
Henry C. Wallich	Mar 8, 1974	Resigned Dec 15, 1978	Burns, Miller, Volcker
Philip E. Coldwell	Oct 29, 1974	Served through Feb 29, 1980	Burns, Miller, Volcker
Philip C. Jackson, Jr.	Jul 14, 1975	Resigned Nov 17, 1978	Burns and Miller
J. Charles Partee	Jan 5, 1976	Served until Feb 7, 1986	Burns, Miller, Volcker
Stephen S. Gardner	Feb 13, 1976	Died Nov 19, 1978	Burns and Miller
David M. Lilly	Jun 1, 1976	Resigned Feb 24, 1978	Burns and Miller
G. William Miller	Mar 8, 1978	Resigned Aug 6, 1979	Miller
Nancy H. Teeters	Sep 18, 1978	Served through Jun 27, 1984	Miller and Volcker
Emmett J. Rice	Jun 20, 1979	Resigned Dec 31, 1986	Miller and Volcker
Frederick H. Schultz	Jul 27, 1979	Served through Feb 11, 1982	Miller and Volcker

(Continued)

Table 3-1
(Continued)

Governor	Appointed	Term	Chairmen
Paul A. Volcker	Aug 6, 1979	Resigned Aug 11, 1987	Volcker
Lyle E. Gramley	May 28, 1980	Resigned Sep 1, 1985	Volcker
Preston Martin	Mar 31, 1982	Resigned Apr 30, 1986	Volcker
Martha R. Seger	Jul 2, 1984	Resigned Mar 11, 1991	Volcker and Greenspan
Wayne D. Angell	Feb 7, 1986	Served through Feb 9, 1994	Volcker and Greenspan
Manuel H. Johnson	Feb 7, 1986	Resigned Aug 3, 1990	Volcker and Greenspan
H. Robert Heller	Aug 19, 1986	Resigned Jul 31, 1989	Volcker and Greenspan
Edward W. Kelley, Jr.	May 26, 1987	Reappointed 1990; resigned Dec 31, 2001	Volcker and Greenspan
Alan Greenspan	Aug 11, 1987	Reappointed 1992; served through Jan 31, 2006	Greenspan
John P. LaWare	Aug 15, 1988	Resigned Apr 30, 1995	Greenspan
David W. Mullins, Jr.	May 21, 1990	Resigned Feb 14, 1994	Greenspan
Lawrence B. Lindsey	Nov 26, 1991	Resigned Feb 5, 1997	Greenspan
Susan M. Phillips	Dec 2, 1991	Served through Jun 30, 1998	Greenspan
Alan S. Blinder	Jun 27, 1994	Term expired Jan 31, 1996	Greenspan
Janet L. Yellen	Aug 12, 1994	Resigned Feb 17, 1997	Greenspan
Laurence H. Meyer	Jun 24, 1996	Term expired Jan 31, 2002	Greenspan
Alice M. Rivlin	Jun 25, 1996	Resigned Jul 16, 1999	Greenspan
Roger W. Ferguson, Jr.	Nov 5, 1997	Reappointed 2001; resigned Apr 28, 2006	Greenspan and Bernanke
Edward M. Gramlich	Nov 5, 1997	Resigned Aug 31, 2005	Greenspan
Susan S. Bies	Dec 7, 2001	Resigned Mar 30, 2007	Greenspan and Bernanke
Mark W. Olson	Dec 7, 2001	Resigned Jun 30, 2006	Greenspan and Bernanke
Ben S. Bernanke	Aug 5, 2002	Resigned Jun 21, 2005	Greenspan
Donald L. Kohn	Aug 5, 2002		Greenspan and Bernanke
Ben S. Bernanke	Feb 1, 2006		Bernanke
Kevin M. Warsh	Feb 24, 2006		Bernanke
Randall S. Kroszner	Mar 1, 2006		Bernanke
Frederic S. Mishkin	Sep 5, 2006	Resigned Aug 31, 2008	Bernanke
Elizabeth A. Duke	Aug 5, 2008		Bernanke

MONETARY POLICY LEVERS: THE DISCOUNT RATE AND THE DISCOUNT WINDOW

So, what does the Fed actually do? It uses a variety of policies and tools to influence everything from interest rates, money supply, bank credit expansion, economic growth, and inflation (or deflation) to employment and unemployment.

Two key levers in setting monetary policy are the discount rate and the discount window policies. (See sidebar.) The Fed's approach to the discount window has changed a number of times, and this has had more of an impact than many seem to realize. Moreover, few so-called Fed watchers realize the importance of the discount window; instead, they concentrate on changes in the federal funds rate and what this means for either the tightness or ease of monetary policy.

The boards of directors of district Federal Reserve banks initiate changes in the discount rate, which is the interest rate on loans made by district banks to depository institutions. Discount-rate changes must be approved by the Board of Governors. It should be noted, however, that in the real world, pressure can come from the chairman and the Board of Governors to change the rate, and therefore the initiation process may not come from the district bank level.

Institutions that are subject to reserve requirements set by the Federal Reserve—commercial banks, mutual savings banks, savings and loan associations, and credit

---

ESSENTIAL MONETARY POLICY TERMS

Discount rate: The interest rate the Federal Reserve charges member banks for collateralized loans.

Discount window: Department at district Federal Reserve banks where members can borrow. Traditionally, borrowing from the Fed is considered a privilege and not a right, although this distinction is no longer clear cut.

Federal funds rate: The interest rate at which federal funds are traded. Rates charged by banks with excess reserves to other banks that need overnight money to meet reserve requirements. The rate tends to fluctuate, but typically by small amounts, since the Federal Reserve has a target rate which is publicly known.

Free reserves: Borrowings by banks at the discount window that are subtracted from excess reserves in the banking system. It is a measurement of the ease or tightness of the Fed's reserve policy. If borrowings are more than excess reserves, this difference is called net borrowed reserves.

Monetary policy: Policies that a central bank, such as the Federal Reserve, develop to influence such important items as interest rates, money supply, bank credit expansion, prices, real economic growth, employment, and unemployment. Monetary policy is different from fiscal policy, which is carried out primarily through government spending and taxation, and is not a responsibility of the Federal Reserve.

Reserve requirement: Federal Reserve rule mandating the financial assets that member banks must keep in the form of cash and other liquid assets as a percentage of demand deposits and time deposits. The money must be kept in the bank's own vaults or on deposit with its regional Federal Reserve bank.

unions—have access to the discount window. (The Federal Reserve is responsible for establishing the percentage of deposits that must be held by banks as backing for deposits, and the form these reserves must take to meet the mandated reserve-requirement rules of the Federal Reserve.)

Discount window policy has not changed frequently, but when it has changed, it can be of considerable importance from a policy point of view. From the mid-1960s until 2003, the basic discount rate frequently was below the prevailing federal funds rate. The Federal Reserve relied on administrative procedures to limit access to the window by restricting the frequency and amounts of borrowing. Despite the often attractive rates, the discount window was used very little, and borrowings diminished in importance as a policy tool. The Federal Reserve's administrative restrictions had been the primary factor that discouraged borrowing, but that changed as the banks themselves were responsible for much of the limitation.

Heavy borrowing in the 1980s by a few banks with financial difficulties caused others to avoid the window, for fear depositors might conclude that they were also in trouble. Those banks that borrowed at the window were concerned that it would also send a negative signal to the Federal Reserve, bank supervisors, and eventually to the market at large. Reluctance to borrow contributed to a seemingly contradictory result—namely, that increases in the amount of reserves in the banking system, when provided through the discount window, made reserve availability more restrictive on the margin, because such increases put banks under pressure to find other sources of reserves to repay the loans.

During the early 1990s, borrowing from the discount window fell significantly, averaging only $233 million on a daily basis, even though this was a period of banking system stress. Even when their financial conditions improved, banks remained reluctant to borrow at the window. In an attempt to rectify this situation, on January 9, 2003, the Federal Reserve made two important changes in the operation of the discount window in an effort to induce banks to borrow when circumstances dictated this was the proper approach. These changes were aimed at providing banks with a less burdensome source of short-term funding.

First, the Fed relaxed many restrictions, so that banks in good health and with adequate collateral no longer needed to seek alternative sources of funds before coming to the discount window; nor did they generally need to provide a reason for their desire to borrow. Second, the Fed set the rates it charged on primary and secondary borrowing at 100 and 150 basis points, respectively, over the Fed's target for the federal funds rate. These were initial values and the Fed indicated at the time that it could change them. Previous to this new approach, the Fed had offered short-term loans to banks at below-market rates of interest.

Thus, the Fed replaced its adjustment and extended credit programs with these new primary and secondary credit facilities. These changes supposedly allowed those banks that were willing to pay the higher explicit cost of borrowing from the Fed to be able to do so without being subject to considerable central bank scrutiny. Although the Fed has always offered a lending service, this change in discount window administration reflected, in part, an attempt to encourage banks to use the Fed as a source of short-term funds.

Supposedly, the changes were aimed at providing banks with a less burdensome source of short-term funding that would increase such funding. In fact, from 2003 to 2007, window borrowings, with few exceptions, have averaged less than $100 million per month. This small number is, to a large degree, due to the fact that the Federal Reserve had been very generous—as evidenced by the amount of free reserves (excess reserves after subtracting out discount window borrowings in the banking system). A typical free reserve level in this period was in excess of $1.5 billion. With so much in free reserves sloshing around in the banking system, there was little reason to borrow money from the discount window. Even after moving the federal funds target rate from 1 percent to 5.25 percent, there was still a substantial amount of money in the banking system. However, by concentrating on the size of a fed funds rate increase without looking at how the availability of funds has changed, analysts can misjudge how much the Fed has changed monetary policy.

One can argue that the discount window should have two primary functions: One is to allow banks that are having financial difficulties to obtain short-term borrowings. And two, the discount window should be used as a monetary policy tool that allows the Fed to ease or tighten policy. Yet, if there is little inducement or reason for the banks to borrow at the Federal Reserve, the usefulness of the discount window as a monetary policy tool is very limited.

If commercial banks want to continue to be overly aggressive in making loans and investments, they should have to borrow at rates that become progressively more punitive. Moreover, the punitive nature of the rates should take into consideration the quality of loans or investments that banks make.

The purpose of such a discount-rate approach would be to induce banks to cut back on the growth of bank credit expansion when the Fed deems it to be clearly excessive and especially in areas where excesses exist in high risk and other questionable sectors. This approach, if applied properly, would have limited the problems created by mortgage loans that brought about the bubble that burst in 2007 and 2008. Both Greenspan and Bernanke apparently believed that they could reach the same policy objectives by fine tuning the fed funds target rate rather than by using a more proactive discount rate policy. That proved to be a costly mistake on the part of both chairmen.

Having some flexibility in setting the discount rate—running the gamut from being punitive to being expansionary—could put some real teeth into the discount window as a policy tool. For example, if the Fed had reduced free reserves and made discount window borrowings more punitive, and made these changes on a more timely and aggressive basis, it could have relied less on adjusting a targeted federal funds rate. Compounding the Fed's mistake was that it inched up its funds target, rather than moving it up by more significant amounts over a shorter period of time (See Table 3-2). Frankly, it made little sense to have seventeen token

Table 3-2
Discount Rate Changes from 1970 to 2008

Discount Rate Changes – 1970 through 2008

Arthur F. Burns			G. William Miller			Paul A. Volker			Alan Greenspan			Ben S. Bernank		
01/01/70	6.00		05/11/78	7.00	+ .50	08/16/79	10.50	+ 50	09/04/87	6.00	+ .50	03/28/06	5.75	6.25
11/16/70	5.75	- .25	06/30/78	7.25	+ .25	09/18/79	11.00	+ .50	09/09/88	6.50	+ .50	05/10/06	6.00	6.50
12/04/70	5.50	- .25	08/18/78	7.75	+ .50	10/06/79	12.00	+1.00	02/24/89	7.00	- .50	06/29/06	6.25	6.75
01/07/71	5.25	- .25	09/22/78	8.00	+ .25	02/15/80	13.00	+1.00	12/18/90	6.50	- .50	08/17/07	5.75	6.25
01/18/71	5.00	- .25	10/13/78	8.50	+ .50	05/28/80	12.00	-1.00	02/01/91	6.00	- .50	09/18/07	5.25	5.75
02/12/71	4.75	- .25	11/01/78	9.50	+1.00	06/12/80	11.00	-1.00	04/30/91	5.50	- .50	10/31/07	5.00	5.50
07/15/71	5.00	+ .25	07/20/79	10.00	+ .50	07/25/80	10.00	-1.00	09/13/91	5.00	- .50	12/11/07	4.75	5.25
11/10/71	4.75	- .25				09/25/80	11.00	+1.00	11/06/91	4.50	- .50	01/22/08	4.00	4.50
12/10/71	4.50	- .25				11/14/80	12.00	+1.00	12/20/91	3.50	-1.00	01/30/08	3.50	4.00
01/12/73	5.00	+ .50				12/04/80	13.00	+1.00	07/02/92	3.00	- .50	03/16/08	3.25	3.75
02/23/73	5.50	+ .50				05/04/81	14.00	+1.00	05/17/94	3.50	+ .50	03/18/08	2.50	3.00
04/20/73	5.75	+ .25				10/30/81	13.00	-1.00	08/16/94	4.00	+ .50	04/30/08	2.25	2.75
05/10/73	6.00	+ .25				12/03/81	12.00	-1.00	11/15/94	4.75	+ .75	10/08/08	1.75	2.25
06/08/73	6.50	+ .50				07/09/82	11.50	- .50	02/01/95	5.25	+ .50			
06/29/73	7.00	+ .50				07/30/82	11.00	- .50	01/31/96	5.00	- .25			
08/13/73	7.50	+ .50				08/13/82	10.50	- .50	10/15/98	4.75	- .25			
04/24/74	8.00	+ .50-*				08/26/82	10.00	- .50	11/15/98	4.50	- .25			
12/06/74	7.75	- .25				10/08/82	9.50	- .50	08/24/99	4.75	+ .25			
01/03/75	7.25	- .50				11/19/82	9.00	- .50	11/16/99	5.00	+ .25			
02/04/75	6.75	- .50				12/13/82	8.50	- .50	02/02/00	5.25	+ .25			
03/07/75	6.25	- .50				04/06/84	9.00	+ .50	03/21/00	5.50	+ .25			
05/15/75	6.00	- .25				11/21/84	8.50	- .50	05/19/00	6.00	+ .50			
01/16/76	5.50	- .50				12/21/84	8.00	- .50	01/03/01	5.75	- .25			
11/19/76	5.25	- .25				05/17/85	7.50	- .50	01/04/01	5.50	- .25			

08/29/77	5.75	+ .50
10/25/77	6.00	+ .25
01/06/78	6.50	+ .50

03/07/86	7.00	- .50
04/18/86	6.50	- .50
07/10/86	6.00	- .50
08/20/86	5.50	- .50

01/31/01	5.00	- .50
03/20/01	4.50	- .50
04/18/01	4.00	- .50
05/15/01	3.50	- .50
06/27/01	3.25	- .25
08/21/01	3.00	- .25
09/17/01	2.50	- .50
10/02/01	2.00	- .50
11/06/01	1.50	- .50
12/11/01	1.25	- .25
11/06/02	.75	- .50

	Pri.	Sec.
01/09/03	2.25	2.75
06/25/03	2.00	2.50
06/30/04	2.25	2.75
08/10/04	2.50	3.00
09/21/04	2.75	3.25
11/10/04	3.00	3.50
12/14/04	3.25	3.75
02/02/05	3.50	4.00
03/22/05	3.75	4.25
05/03/05	4.00	4.50
06/30/05	4.25	4.75
08/09/05	4.50	5.00
09/20/05	4.75	5.25
11/01/05	5.00	5.50
12/13/05	5.25	5.75
01/31/06	5.50	6.00

funds-rate increases of 25 basis points each, especially when the increases started from an inordinately easy and stimulative monetary policy. Of course, the other policy alternative would have been larger increases in the fed funds rate, implemented on a timelier basis.

A HISTORY OF FEDERAL FUNDS RATE TARGETING

During most of the 1970s, the Fed had a desired range for the funds rate. Then, shortly after Paul Volcker took office in August 1979, the Fed shifted toward targeting a form of money supply and allowing the funds rate to move quite freely. It appears that this period of volatile fed funds rates with no target began around March 1980 and lasted through August 1982, after which a semblance of funds-rate targeting returned. Since then, the Fed has continued to rely on targeting a specific funds rate (See Table 3-3).

Beginning in 1994, the FOMC began announcing changes in its policy stance, and in 1995, it began to explicitly state its target level for the federal funds rate. Since February 2000, the statement issued by the FOMC at the close of each of its meetings usually includes the Committee's assessment of the risks involved in attaining its long-term goals of price stability and sustainable economic growth.

Unfortunately, many in the markets seem to believe that the fed funds target rate is the be-all and end-all when it comes to measuring and changing monetary policy. An overnight rate by itself can hardly be considered a measurement of ease or tightness in monetary policy. Interest rates out on the yield curve (which are interest rate levels plotted along a series of maturities), availability of funds for borrowers and lenders, and interest rates versus the rate of inflation, are several other policy factors that need to be considered. Many analysts, both inside and outside the Fed, are aware of the limitations in using the fed funds rate as a policy measurement. Nevertheless, because it is the one item that can be directly targeted, the Fed in its analysis has often incorporated the funds rate with an adjustment made for inflation—a so-called *real* fed funds rate.

Even though the ten-year Treasury yield measured against inflation is a better measurement of real interest rates, the Fed has little control over ten-year rates, but it does have considerable control over the overnight funds rate. Thus, it should not be surprising that in many of its studies, the Fed looks back to see when real fed funds rates were part of a policy that proved to be excessively easy, excessively tight, or just about right. For years, the approach that was taken by the Fed was to compare the consumer price index (CPI) rate with the federal funds rate. Generally speaking, when the real fed funds rate was about 3 percent or higher, it was generally viewed as tight money; when it was 1 percent or less, it was viewed as easy money; and when it was around 2 percent, it was viewed as accommodative, neither easy nor tight. Overly simplistic, yes—but useful.

This approach, however, has created measurement problems because in recent years, when targeting inflation, the Fed has moved from a CPI inflation approach

Table 3-3

Federal Funds Rates Discount Rate Changes from 1970–2008

	Federal Open Market Fed Funds Rate Objectives Monthly Averages - %									
Arthur F. Burns				G. William Miller				Paul Volcker		No Funds Rate Objective Paul Volcker
J-70	8.98	J-73	10.40	J-77	4.61	M-78	6.79	A-79	10.94	M-80	17.19
F	8.98	A	10.50	F	4.68	A	6.89	S	11.43	A	17.61
M	7.76	S	10.78	M	4.69	M	7.36	O	13.77	M	10.98
A	8.10	O	10.01	A	4.73	J	7.60	N	13.18	J	9.47
M	7.94	N	10.03	M	5.35	J	7.81	D	13.78	J	9.03
J	7.60	D	9.95	J	5.39	A	8.04			A	9.61
J	7.21			J	5.42	S	8.45	J-80	13.82	S	10.87
A	6.61	J-74	9.65	A	5.90	O	8.96	F	14.13	O	12.81
S	6.29	F	8.97	S	6.14	N	9.76			N	15.85
O	6.20	M	9.35	O	6.47	D	10.03			D	18.90
N	5.69	A	10.51	N	6.51	J-79	10.07			J-81	19.08
D	4.90	M	11.31	D	6.56	F	10.06			F	15.93
J-71	4.14	J	11.93	J-78	6.70	M	10.09			M	14.07
F	3.72	J	12.92	F	6.78	A	10.01			A	15.72
M	3.71	A	12.01			M	10.24			M	18.52
A	4.15	S	11.34			J	10.29			J	19.10
M	4.63	O	10.06			J	10.47			J	19.04
J	4.91	N	9.45							A	17.82
J	5.31	D	8.53							S	15.82
A	5.56	J-75	7.13							O	15.08

Table 3-3

(Continued)

Federal Open Market Fed Funds Rate Objectives
Monthly Averages - %

Arthur F. Burns				G. William Miller	Paul Volcker	No Funds Rate Objective Paul Volcker	
S	5.55	F	6.24			N	13.31
O	5.20	M	5.54			D	12.37
N	4.91	A	5.49			J-82	13.22
D	4.14	M	5.22			F	14.78
J-72	3.50	J	5.55			M	14.68
F	3.28	J	6.10			A	14.94
M	3.83	A	6.14			M	14.45
A	4.17	S	6.24			J	14.15
M	4.27	O	5.82			J	12.59
J	4.46	N	5.22			A	10.12
J	4.55	D	5.20				
A	4.80	J-76	4.87				
S	4.87	F	4.77				
O	5.04	M	4.84				
N	5.06	A	4.82				
D	5.33	M	5.29				
J-73	5.94	J	5.48				
F	6.58	J	5.31				
M	7.09	A	5.29				
A	7.12	S	5.25				
M	7.84	O	5.02				
J	8.49	N	4.95				
		D	4.65				

Table 3-4

Federal Open Market Committee

Return to Fed Funds Rate Target Objectives - %							
Paul A. Volcker		**Alan Greenspan**				**Ben S. Bernanke**	
9/27/82	**10.25**	**8/27/87**	6.75	**2/4/94**	**3.25**	**3/28/06**	**4.75**
10/1	10.00	9/3	6.88	3/22	3.50	5/20	5.00
10/7	9.50	9/4	7.25	4/18	3.75	6/29	5.25
11/19	9.00	9/24	7.31	5/17	4.25	**9/9/07**	**4.75**
12/14	8.50	11/4	6.81	8/16	4.75	10/31	4.50
3/31/83	8.63	**1/28/88**	**6.63**	11/15	5.50	12/11	4.25
5/25	8.75	2/11	6.50	**2/1/95**	**6.00**	**1/22/08**	**3.50**
6/24	9.00	3/30	6.75	7/6	5.75	1/30	3.00
7/14	9.25	5/9	7.00	12/19	5.50	3/18	2.25
8/11	9.44	5/25	7.25	**1/31/96**	**5.25**	4/30	2.00
8/17	9.56	6/22	7.44	**3/25/97**	**5.50**	6/25	2.00
9/15	9.50	7/1	7.50	**9/29/98**	**5.25**	10/08	1.50
3/29/84	**10.50**	7/19	7.69	10/15	5.50		
7/5	11.00	8/8	7.75	11/17	4.75		
7/19	11.25	8/9	8.13	**6/30/99**	**5.00**		
8/9	11.50	11/17	8.31	8/24	5.25		
9/20	11.25	11/22	8.38	11/16	5.50		
9/27	11.00	12/16	8.69	**2/2/00**	**5.75**		
10/11	10.50	**1/5/89**	**9.00**	3/21	6.00		
10/18	10.00	2/9	9.13	5/16	6.50		
11/8	9.50	2/14	9.31	**1/3/01**	**6.00**		
11/23	9.00	2/24	9.75	1/31	5.50		
12/6	8.75	5/17	9.81	3/20	5.00		
12/19	8.50	6/6	9.56	4/18	4.50		
12/24	8.13	7/7	9.31	5/15	4.00		
1/24/85	**8.25**	7/27	9.06	6/27	3.75		
2/14	8.38	10/19	8.75	8/21	3.50		
3/28	8.50	11/6	8.50	9/17	3.00		
4/25	8.25	12/20	8.25	10/2	2.50		
5/20	7.75	**7/13/90**	**8.00**	11/6	2.00		
7/11	7.69	10/29	7.75	12/11	1.75		
7/25	7.75	11/14	7.50	**11/6/02**	**1.25**		
8/21	7.81	12/7	7.25	**6/25/03**	**1.00**		
9/6	8.00	12/19	7.00	**6/30/04**	**1.25**		
12/18	7.75	**1/9/91**	**6.75**	8/10	1.50		
3/7/86	**7.25**	2/1	6.25	9/21	1.75		
4/2	7.32	3/8	6.00	11/10	2.00		
4/21	6.75	4/20	5.75	12/14	2.25		
4/22	6.81	8/6	5.50	**2/2/05**	**2.50**		
6/5	6.88	9/13	5.25	3/22	2.75		
7/11	6.38	10/31	5.00	5/3	3.00		
8/21	5.88	11/6	4.75	6/30	3.25		
1/5/87	**6.00**	12/6	4.50	8/9	3.50		

Table 3-4
(Continued)

Return to Fed Funds Rate Target Objectives - %						
Paul A. Volcker		Alan Greenspan				Ben S. Bernanke
4/30	6.50	12/20	4.00	9/20	3.75	
5/22	6.75	**4/9/92**	**3.75**	11/1	4.00	
7/2	6.63	7/2	3.25	12/13	4.25	
		9/4/92	3.00	**1/31/06**	**4.50**	

Source: Board of Governors of the Federal Reserve System. Dates from September 1982 to 1994 came from the working paper "A New Federal Funds Rate Target Series: September 27, 1982-December 31, 1993." (Thornton, Federal Reserve Bank of St. Louis 2005). Data from 1994 to 1997 are derived by the Federal Reserve from FOMC transcripts and meeting statements.

to a personal consumption expenditures (PCE) price approach and from a change in the total PCE to a change in the core, which excludes food and energy. The PCE approach is no more than a derivation of the CPI with somewhat different weightings of the various components, and a different approach when it comes to substituting a lower price product or service for another. The Fed has done this not so much because it believes a core is the best measurement, but because when food and energy are excluded, the numbers tend to be less volatile. Additionally, the Fed has little influence over food and energy prices. Nevertheless, it is the overall price performance that counts, irrespective of its sources. Because measuring inflation and the Fed trying to influence inflation are not the same thing when it comes to determining the ease or tightness of policy in a fed funds context, a better approach is to compare the fed funds target with the total (not the core) PCE price numbers.

The results derived are no more than an approximation of the ease or tightness of policy. Yet, in the second half of 2000, when the funds target was 6.5 percent and the total PCE price increase was somewhat over 2 percent, this supported the view that monetary policy was not just on the firm side, it was tight. Then from the middle of 2003 to the middle of 2004, when the funds target was 1 percent and the PCE price increase had moved up to between 2 and 3 percent, this negative real interest rate gave credence to the belief that policy was accommodative, very accommodative.

Finally, in the middle of 2006 when the funds target was elevated to 5.25 percent and the PCE price increase was around 3 percent, this suggested a policy that was neither easy nor tight.

4

Four Decades of Data that Tell a Story

Most of the books written on U.S. monetary policy in the last several decades concentrate on the individuals who were in charge at the Federal Reserve and the concepts and policies they followed. They highlight the difficulties that the Fed chairmen encountered and how they were addressed, and they heap both praise and criticism upon them. Further, authors of such books present cases that support or attack concepts and policies of the various chairmen and "explain" where they got it right and where they got it wrong. These books also emphasize the personal side of policy and the chairmen's relationships with others in dealing with the issues. Typically, they also overemphasize the importance of Fed policy in the performance of the U.S. economy. The Fed in general, and its chairmen in particular, are either given too much credit or bear too much blame for what happened in the economy, at financial institutions, and in the financial markets.

Not surprisingly, books about the Federal Reserve run the risk of engaging, unintentionally, in revisionist history. Former Fed officials often tend to emphasize those policies and events that are favorable for them, while policy decisions and events that are not so favorable are downplayed. In other words, history is more than what is written; it is also what is not written. Many younger market participants are forced to rely on books that supposedly present history in a complete sense. Unfortunately, they have little ability to judge whether a particular book presents a proper interpretation of what happened several decades ago or why it happened.

One might ask how this book might rectify the problem and why it might have a better lock on the truth. Living through a period does not mean that one fully understands what occurred: What were the causes and what were the effects? Yet, I thought I could make a meaningful contribution to a more balanced history of monetary policy in the United States.

The first approach I used was to develop a numerical picture of economic and financial events, one that would allow the reader to understand what was happening, and what a Fed chairman was looking at when he made his policy decisions. Eventually, I chose eighteen indicators to illustrate the story since 1970. The second approach is the appendix, "A Flavor of the Times." It presents a broad array of headlines, also beginning with 1970. As you will see, this method has been important in determining why inflation became so embedded, and why the inflation surge came to an end.

About the Tables

At the respective ends of chapters 6 through 10—the chapters on the last five Fed chairmen—are a series of tables such as the sample below (Table 4-1, for 1970). Again, these tables are designed to create a picture of the economic and financial events during a particular time period.

It should be noted that while the eighteen indicators present a picture of various areas, they are not the only ones scrutinized by the Fed. These numbers illustrate trends and changes, but tell us little about cause and effect, although if one studies the tables over a period of time, certain relationships will become evident. Realize that most of the indicators presented were not under the direct influence or control of the Federal Reserve. Thus, one cannot look at this numerical picture and make a judgment as to whether monetary policy at any point in time was appropriate, especially since the impact from monetary policy works with a time lag, and often a considerable one.

Let's take a closer look at what the tables reveal. You'll see four groupings of economic and financial data for each period. They are: financial markets, monetary policy, economic indicators, and commodity prices. The following are the items presented in each category:

Financial Markets

Federal funds—Overnight market rate. Banks with more deposits at the Fed than needed sell them to banks that have a need for such deposits.

Treasury bonds—Yields on treasury bonds, which are securities offered by the U.S. Treasury that have maturities of over ten years.

Corporate bonds (Aaa)—Yields on the highest-quality, long-term corporate debt. There are three private rating agencies of consequence and their measurement terminology differs.

Corporate bonds (Baa)—Yields on "investment grade" bonds of the lowest rating. Typically, this is the fourth rating down.

30-year mortgage—Interest rates on conventional mortgages with a 30-year maturity. Legally speaking, the borrower gives the lender a lien on the property as security for repayment of the loan.

Standard & Poor's 500 Stock Index—A composite index of 500 stocks. It is an index that shows changes in the market value of 500 stocks relative to a base period.

Foreign currencies—The deutschemark (DM) was the currency of Germany. The euro was created in 1999 and is used by the fifteen countries that are members

Table 4-1
Sample Table of 18 Indicators Detailing Financial and Economic Conditions

1970	Fed Funds	Treas 20-yr	Corporates Aaa	Corporates Baa	30-yr Mtge	S&P 500	DM	Monetary Base	Free Rsvs	Bank Credit Loans	Bank Credit Inv	Real GDP	Unemp Rate	CPI-% Total	CPI-% Core	Budget	Oil	Gold
					Financial Markets					Monetary Policy				Economic Indicators				Commodities Prices-$
Jan	8.98	6.92	7.91	8.86	8.16	85.02	.2713	$61.8b	-785	$292b	$111b		3.9%	+0.5	+0.5		3.35	34.94
Feb	8.98	6.67	7.93	8.78	8.23	89.50	.2711	61.9	-872	290	111	-0.7%	4.2	+0.5	+0.5		3.35	34.99
Mar	7.76	6.72	7.84	8.63	8.29	89.63	.2723	62.2	-735	291	112		4.4	+0.5	+0.8		3.35	35.09
Apr	8.10	6.85	7.83	8.70	8.24	81.52	.2746	62.7	-693	293	114		4.6	+0.5	+0.7		3.35	35.62
May	7.94	7.24	8.11	8.98	8.28	76.55	.2752	63.0	-811	293	115	+0.8	4.8	+0.3	+0.2	FY	3.35	35.95
Jun	7.60	7.34	8.48	9.25	8.31	72.72	.2753	63.2	-691	293	116		4.9	+0.5	+0.7	-$2.8b	3.35	35.44
Jul	7.21	6.92	8.44	9.40	8.32	78.05	.2754	63.4	-1194	297	118		5.0	+0.3	+0.2		3.31	35.32
Aug	6.61	7.07	8.13	9.44	8.35	81.52	.2754	63.7	-663	299	121	+3.6	5.1	+0.3	+0.5		3.31	35.38
Sep	6.29	6.88	8.09	9.39	8.31	84.30	.2754	64.1	-356	300	123		5.4	+0.5	+0.5		3.31	36.19
Oct	6.20	6.88	8.03	9.33	8.33	83.25	.2753	64.3	-258	303	125		5.5	+0.5	+0.5		3.31	37.52
Nov	5.60	6.58	8.05	9.38	8.26	87.20	.2754	64.6	-181	304	127	-4.2	5.9	+0.5	+0.7		3.31	37.44
Dec	4.90	6.28	7.64	9.12	8.20	92.15	.2744	65.0	-83	305	130		6.1	+0.5	+0.5		3.56	37.44
						+1.0%	+1.1%	+5.6%		+5.3%	+15.4%	-0.2%		+5.6%	+6.6%			
						D-D	D-D	D-D		D-D	D-D	4Q-4Q		D-D	D-D			

of the European Central Bank (ECB). These are presented in terms of their value relative to the U.S. dollar.

Monetary Policy

Monetary base—Closely watched derivation of the money supply. It consists of currency outside the Federal Reserve and required and excess reserve balances held at the Federal Reserve.

Free reserves—Excess reserves in the banking system above what is required, reduced by borrowings at the Federal Reserve.

Bank credit—The amount of loans and investments outstanding in the banking system.

Economic Indicators

Real GDP (gross domestic product)—The primary measurement of the value of goods and services produced inside the United States over a specified period of time, with the price or inflation factor eliminated.

Unemployment rate—The number of people unemployed divided by the number of people in the civilian labor force. The numbers are based on samples and the data are seasonally adjusted.

Consumer Price Index (CPI)—A measurement of changes in consumer prices as determined monthly by the U.S. Bureau of Labor Statistics. A sampling system is used and some of the items are imputed. One derivation of the CPI is to exclude food and energy from the computation; that is called the "core CPI."

U.S. budget deficit or surplus—A budget deficit occurs when revenues the U.S. government receives are less than its outlays. A budget surplus is when the revenues are more than the outlays. The U.S. Treasury publishes budget data monthly and annually.

Commodity Prices

Oil prices—The price of crude petroleum. Different countries have different prices. The most commonly used price in the United States is called West Texas intermediate. The price noted is for a barrel of oil that holds 42 gallons.

Gold prices—The price of gold is set by specialists and bank officials in London, Paris, and Zurich. The price per ounce is fixed twice a day in London at 10:30 a.m. and 3:30 p.m.

Table 4-2 shows the sources for the table data.

Financial Markets Indicators

Each of the items in the first grouping has a special reason for being included. The Federal Reserve has usually used the federal funds rate as a guide or target for

Table 4-2
Sources for Table Data

	Financial Markets							Monetary Policy				Economic Indicators					Commodities	
	Fed Funds	Treas 20-yr	Corporates		30-yr Mtge	S&P 500	DM	Monetary Base	Free Rsvs	Bank Credit		Real GDP	Unemp Rate	CPI - %		Budget	Prices - $	
			Aaa	Baa						Loans	Inv			Total	Core		Oil	Gold
1970																		

	Financial Markets							Monetary Policy				Economic Indicators					Commodities	
	Fed Funds	Treas 30-yr	Corporates		30-yr Mtge	S&P 500	Euro	Monetary Base	Free Rsvs	Bank Credit		Real GDP	Unemp Rate	CPI - %		Budget	Prices - $	
			Aaa	Baa						Loans	Inv			Total	Core		Oil	Gold
1999																		

Financial Markets:—Fed funds, 20- and 30-year Treasuries, Corporates Aaa and Baa from Federal Reserve Statistical Release H.15 Selected Interest Rates
    —S&P 500 from Yahoo! Finance, Monthly Price Average
    —DM and euro from Federal Reserve Statistical Release H.10 Foreign Exchange Rates 1971–2008 and Federal Reserve Bulletins 1971–1979

Monetary Policy:—Monetary Base and free reserves from Federal Reserve Statistical Release H.3 Aggregate Reserves of Depository Institutions and the Monetary Base
    —Bank credit, loans, and investments from Federal Reserve Statistical Release, H.8 Assets and Liabilities of Commercial Banks in the United States

Economic Indicators:—Real GDP from the Bureau of Economic Analysis, National Economic Accounts, U.S. Department of Commerce
    —Unemployment rate and CPI total and core from U.S. Department of Labor, Bureau of Labor Statistics, www.bls.gov
    —Budget from Monthly Treasury Statement www.fms.treas.gov

Commodities:—Oil from www.economagic.com: Economic Time Series, Price of West Texas Intermediate Crude; Monthly NSA, Dollars per Barrel
    —Gold from London Bullion Market Association, Gold P.M. Fixings, Monthly Average

monetary policy. Currently, it is used by the Fed as a target in order to achieve desired rates of inflation and economic growth. Long-term Treasury yields show what is happening to long-term rates in general. When long-term treasury yields are compared with the fed funds rate, it gives an indication of the slope to the yield curve, which shows the differences in interest rate levels along a series of maturities. The highest-grade corporate bond yields are useful because, by comparing these yields with those of long-term Treasury securities, they give some idea of the risk factor for those who purchase these securities. The lowest investment-grade corporate bonds can be compared with the yields on the highest grade issues in order to help determine how quality differences within the corporate sector are priced.

I include long-term mortgage rates because of the importance of housing in the economy. The Federal Reserve is quite aware that when it adjusts its overnight funds rate, it is setting in motion changes in other areas of the money and capital markets, such as the mortgage market. It realizes that the funds rate is just the starting point. When changes in the fed funds rate percolate through to other markets, such as the corporate and mortgage markets, the impact on businesses and housing can be meaningful. Thus the Fed tries to fine tune the funds rate in the hope it will attain desired levels of price increases and economic growth. Unfortunately, the linkages from the funds rate to other areas of the financial markets, and then to prices and economic growth, are not fully known or understood, and are subject to change.

What is important for the interest-rate categories in the financial market sector is not just levels, but also changes. Those not familiar with what happened in the United States in the 1970s and 1980s are likely to be shocked by the high rate levels and the volatility of the debt markets. This is very obvious when one studies the interest rate section of the tables over the years. The distinction between what happened in the 1970s and 1980s versus what has happened since is striking, and is of major importance in understanding Federal Reserve policy performance and the performances of the various chairmen.

Yet markets cover a much broader range than just debt market instruments and interest rates. The picture is incomplete unless we look at the stock market, the foreign exchange market, and in the commodity sector, oil and gold prices. All of these have at one time or another played an important role in determining Federal Reserve policy. This is evident when one sees the sharp movements in these areas. In the period of almost four decades beginning in the 1970s, stock markets typically had their primary influence on monetary policy in bubble-and-burst periods. The same can be said for oil and energy prices.

The foreign exchange market and gold have had much less of an influence on monetary policy in recent years. This is so even when their prices moved around substantially. It appears that when the foreign exchange market moved from fixed to floating rates, and from heavy official intervention to little intervention (with a few exceptions such as China), its importance as a U.S. monetary policy factor faded. With fewer crises in the foreign exchange market, with inflation much less of a problem compared with the 1970s and 1980s, with the

U.S. monetary system no longer tied to gold, and with the advent of economic and currency blocs, the foreign exchange market has become a much-reduced monetary policy factor. Whether it has been downplayed too much is another matter.

Monetary Policy Indicators

The second grouping consists of four items that are used to reflect what is happening in monetary policy. They are the monetary base, free reserves, bank loans outstanding, and total investments of banks (the federal funds rate obviously could also be included here). At times, all have had targets or at least desirable growth rates. The monetary base and bank loans and investments show the aggressiveness of the banks in providing grist for the economic mill. To avoid redundancy in the eighteen tabular categories, other monetary aggregates such as M-1, M-2, and M-3 are not presented.

I include free reserves, because they are especially important and targeted early in the period studied. Unfortunately, it is now more difficult to find and compute the data. Free reserves are excess reserves in the banking system excluding borrowings at the discount window. Thus, they were a measure at the margin of ease or tightness in the banking system. Typically, in a period of easy money, free reserves could be several billion dollars; in a period of tight money, free reserves could be a negative number of several billion dollars. When the number is negative, it is called net borrowed reserves. Free reserves (or net borrowed reserves) were often used by the Fed in conjunction with a federal funds target range in order to attain monetary aggregate targets, which in turn would hopefully attain desired real growth, unemployment, and price objectives.

Economic Indicators

The economic section consists of five categories: real gross domestic product (GDP); the unemployment rate; the total consumer price index (CPI); the core CPI; and the budget deficit or surplus. This does not mean that other items are unimportant, but again, the attempt is to look at five broad areas that often had an influence on monetary policy and at the same time avoid duplication. When these five items are looked at as a package, it is easy to see the major swings in the economy and which areas created a problem for the Fed. In studying these data, what seems clear is that beginning around 1992, the Fed's problems in many of these areas diminished considerably.

Commodity Price Indicators

Commodities cover a wide range of products, the most important of which are agriculture, energy, and metals. Each of these categories contains a variety of components. But, because this is a book that deals primarily with monetary policy, it makes sense to present those commodities that had the greatest influence on Federal Reserve policy, and they are gold and oil.

Gold has always had an influence on monetary policy around the world, especially when the international financial system was basically on a gold standard, which is where units of a currency are convertible into fixed amounts of gold. Moreover, gold was often viewed as a safe-haven investment, especially when there were inflation fears. Although the gold standard has disappeared from the scene, gold as a safe-haven investment surely has not. For these reasons, the price of gold adjustments beginning with 1970 is published in these tables.

Oil prices, however, tell a much different story than gold, especially since 1970. The advent of the Organization of the Petroleum Exporting Countries (OPEC) in 1960, and the organization's becoming an economic and political powerhouse in the 1970s, significantly increased the importance of oil to central banks such as the Federal Reserve. Petroleum now significantly exceeds gold in terms of economic and financial importance around the world. Oil supplies and prices strongly influence the strength of the world's economic performance and have major political and military repercussions. The accumulation of official foreign exchange reserves by oil-rich countries and how they invest the funds has a major influence on economic growth, inflation, and the state of many financial markets.

In short, it is necessary to look at these eighteen categories to determine what has happened in the economic and financial world since 1970 and how the Federal Reserve has responded.

Yet I offer a word of caution: The numbers are often a result of events that had already occurred and policies that had already been implemented. Also realize that the Federal Reserve and its policies are only one part of an overall economic and financial mosaic. The Fed gets too much of the blame when things go wrong in the economy, the financial system, and the markets, and too much of the credit when things turn out right. Although the chairman almost always gets his way when it comes to policy, realize that if the Federal Reserve role is often overstated in importance, then the chairman's role is also overstated.

THE BEST WAY TO TELL THE INFLATION STORY SINCE 1970

Here is how the tables, combined with the "Flavor of the Times" appendix, tell a story. For example, take the data history since 1970 as presented in the eighteen-item table, and combine this information with events as reflected in the appendix, and you can readily see what happened to price changes in general, and surging inflation problems in particular, since 1970.

Starting with the "Flavor of the Times," from 1974 up to 1982, there was an abundance of headlines dealing with labor strikes, length of contracts, and wage increases. It was the labor and wage factor that were primarily responsible for the embedded inflation problems that gripped the United States at that time. One example of large pay increases in the 1970s occurred in April 1974 when the steelworkers gained a pattern-setting three-year pact with a 40 percent increase in wages and benefits. In June 1976, General Electric agreed to a labor pact raising wages 33 percent over three years, with the agreement assuming a 6 percent annual increase in wages. In October 1976, Ford began to reopen plants after a thirty-day strike. Compensation per hour would rise 13 percent in the first year.

In April 1977, the steelworkers were back at the bargaining table and agreed to a package that included raising compensation more than 30 percent over three years, and in October 1977 there was a federal pay boost of 7.05 percent for civilian employees and the military. In October 1978, there was another pay increase for federal workers of 5.5 percent, plus step increases; in October 1979, there was another 7 percent cost-of-living increase above and beyond the step increases.

Moving into the 1980s, in May 1980, the aluminum workers won a 42 percent boost over three years, and this increase assumed an 11 percent inflation rate. In July 1980, the Labor Department reported that white-collar salaries were up 9.1 percent in the twelve months ending March 1980. Also in the same month, checks to 35.2 million Social Security recipients rose 14.3 percent based on the COLA (cost of living adjustment) formula. In August 1980, the AT&T labor contract gave a 34.5 percent pay boost over three years, and the increase assumed a 9.5 percent rise in the CPI. Finally, in October 1980, federal employees received a 9.1 percent general pay boost in addition to step increases. To say the least, 1980 was a busy year when it came to people trying to cope with a very rapid rate of inflation. However, while these increases were helping people deal with inflation, they also added to embedded inflation down the road.

The story in 1981 started out the same way. In February, western coal miners accepted a 37 percent increase in wages over a period of three years. In June, the United Mine Workers ratified a forty-month contract with the coal mining industry. It ended a strike that began in February. In October, federal employees received a 4.8 percent general pay increase plus regular step increases, while military pay jumped 14.3 percent. However, the increase for federal employees was considerably smaller than what had been achieved previously, and importantly, this appears to be the start of much more moderate advances of wages in general. For example, by October 1982, both federal employees and the military received increases of only 4 percent, plus the step adjustments.

The sources of embedded inflation started to crack in late 1981 as a painfully tight monetary policy began to work its magic. The implementation of a monetary aggregate approach to policy allowed interest rates to go to the moon. The objective was to contain the monetary aggregates and let the overnight funds rate go where market forces would take it. The result was a double-digit unemployment rate that reached 10.8 percent by November 1982, and with double-digit interest rates, they put the economy into a recession. Needless to say, very generous wage increases were stopped dead in their tracks.

Yet, there is more to this story. While inflation was embedded because of labor settlements from 1974 to 1981, another factor reared its head at roughly the same time. From the end of 1973 to the end of 1980, the price of oil literally exploded.

This surely added to U.S. inflation woes during this period, and one can argue that it also added to inflationary pressures that were coming from the labor-cost side.

At the end of 1973, oil prices were $4.31 per barrel. They moved up to $11.16 at the end of 1974 and into 1975; they were $13.90 at the end of 1976; $14.85 at the end of 1977 and 1978; $32.50 at the end of 1979, and $37.00 at the end of 1980. How much of the embedded inflation during this period came from oil price increases is difficult to determine, but it surely was a factor.

It is interesting to note that while the back of embedded labor-cost inflation was broken in 1982, oil prices also tumbled at about the same time. At the end of 1981, oil was $35.00 per barrel. The price then slipped to $31.72 at the end of 1982; $29.24 at the end of 1983; $25.43 at the end of 1984; then back up to $27.23 at the end of 1985, but then plummeted all the way down to $16.08 at the end of 1986. The obvious question here is, if oil price increases played a role in embedded labor cost increases from 1974 through 1981, did oil price declines help get rid of embedded inflation from 1982 to 1986?

Before the reader jumps to conclusions about the relationship between embedded labor costs and oil prices, realize that since 1986 oil prices have moved all over the place with some major swings (as low as $11.28 per barrel in December 1998 and above $147.00 per barrel on a day in July 2008), and yet that has not been the case with respect to labor costs or inflation in general. It can be argued that the cheaper labor-cost advantages of other countries and their ability to sell goods abroad offset, from an inflation perspective, the worldwide oil price surge in recent years. With cheap goods and cheap labor abroad, the jump in oil prices has been offset to a considerable degree, and therefore, the net impact on inflation in the United States and most of the rest of the developed world has also been limited.

What about the role of monetary policy when it came to embedded inflation? From 1982 to the present, the highest annual core CPI rate occurred in 1990 at only 5.3 percent. Yet, from 1982 to 2008, there have been periods when monetary policy has been unduly tight, unduly easy, and just about right. Nevertheless, there has been no major embedded inflation problem in the United States during this last quarter century. There were periods when inflation was undesirably high, but undesirably high and embedded are not the same thing.

Controlling the growth of the monetary aggregates, which allowed the Fed to be much tighter than if it were targeting just interest rates, took a while to work. Volcker moved to a monetarist-type approach in early 1980, and it took almost two years of oppressively high interest rates before embedded inflation began to crumble. The fact that it took severe medicine almost two years to work its magic was because of how embedded inflation had become.

This was the golden age for monetarists. The Fed *had* to switch to a monetarist approach to break the back of inflation. Politically speaking, it would have been impossible to target an overnight interest rate anywhere near 20 percent. Individuals and businesses would not have tolerated a policy that targeted ultrahigh interest rates, but if the rate levels were supposedly market driven and not the

result of a Federal Reserve policy objective, then the results were somewhat more tolerable, although still far from acceptable.

Now, the importance of monetary aggregates in policy has slipped back to the fringes. This is unfortunate, because monetary aggregates as a policy factor would probably have stopped the Fed from taking the funds rate down to unduly low levels (such as 1 percent) in 2003, staying there for an excessively long period, and then increasing the rate by token amounts. Although I am surely no monetarist, excessive monetary aggregate growth is unacceptable for a central bank that claims as its primary objective the containment of inflation.

A reasonable question the Fed should ask itself is, "Should the monetary aggregates play a more important role in determining a fed funds rate target?" The Fed has virtually no direct influence over consumer prices as reflected in the personal consumption expenditures (PCE) core. However, that is not the case with respect to monetary aggregate growth such as bank credit expansion. If the Fed can find a funds rate target range that can bring about a rate of growth for an aggregate such as bank credit, that in turn can achieve acceptable numbers with respect to real growth, prices, and the unemployment rate, then the quality of monetary policy would be improved. Thus, one can make a good case that containing monetary aggregate growth has more value than when it was simply used as an emergency policy tool after prices were already out of control.

Much of this previous analysis could not have been achieved without the "Flavor of the Times" section in this book. However, there are other periods when this background information will prove to be useful, such as when energy and energy prices (primarily oil) were important factors in the performance of the U.S. economy and therefore monetary policy.

In summary, breaking the back of inflation was no easy matter. It was time consuming and painful. It involved ultrahigh interest rates and ultrahigh unemployment, and those who lived through these difficult times paid a high price. However, the almost quarter century of substantial economic growth since the early 1980s could not have been achieved if the monetary aggregate approach to policy had not been a major factor in fighting embedded inflation. For those Fed chairmen who followed Paul Volcker, their lives have been made much easier—and so have their policies.

5

THE FIVE RECENT CHAIRMEN: AN OVERVIEW

The five individuals who have presided over the Fed since 1970 were quite different in terms of background, personality, policy preferences, the circumstances they encountered, and their performance on the job. Probably the best way to compare and contrast these people is to first write about their qualifications and next to write about their performance.

QUALIFICATIONS

Strictly on the basis of their qualifications as they entered the job, Paul Volcker would have the number one standing, and by a considerable amount. It seemed as though he had been in training for this job throughout his whole professional career. He had all of the bases covered. He was the best qualified not only by training, intellect, and personality, but he also had considerable street smarts. He had little trouble catching the attention of those who were listening to him.

Volcker did his undergraduate work at Princeton and his graduate work at Harvard. He also attended the London School of Economics. His private sector career helped him prepare for his days as Federal Reserve chairman. He was a financial economist at Chase Manhattan Bank, where he had a chance to see how markets operated first hand. He expanded his knowledge when he moved to the U.S. Treasury, and then expanded upon even more when he became president of the Federal Reserve Bank of New York. This is the part of the Federal Reserve that conducts open market and foreign exchange operations for the Federal Reserve System. Thus, there were no gaps to fill with respect to his qualifications as Fed chairman.

Alan Greenspan would rank second in qualifications because, although he was a good business economist and performed admirably in other government roles, his background in commercial and central banking and financial markets was lacking when he entered the Fed. In his early annual Jackson Hole meetings, where major central bankers from around the world were present, my personal observation was that Greenspan at first seemed somewhat in awe of his contemporaries, but that changed as he grew into his job as chairman.

Similar to Volcker, Greenspan's academic credentials were outstanding. He received a PhD in Economics from New York University. His private sector career took him down a different path than Volcker, who was always not far from the markets. Greenspan worked as an economic analyst at the Conference Board, which is a business-oriented organization, was the head of an economic consulting firm, and was the head of the president's Council of Economic Advisers. He would be classified as a business economist, while Volcker would be considered a financial economist.

Ben Bernanke is third in this group with regard to qualifications. Actually, because of his theoretical and practical background in monetary policy, he was close to being on a par with Greenspan. He had previously been both a college professor and a Federal Reserve governor. However, Greenspan had been associated with real-world economics during his entire career, which was not the case with Bernanke, and real-world experience trumps theoretical knowledge when it comes to qualifications for the job of Fed chairman.

Irrespective of Bernanke's earlier days as a Federal Reserve governor and chairman of the Council of Economic Advisers, he was through and through an academic economist. Concepts and models were his strong points. Not having some sort of financial market experience has proven to be a deficiency for someone who heads up a central bank. Bernanke's academic qualifications, as one might expect, were outstanding. He received a BA in economics from Harvard and a PhD in economics from Massachusetts Institute of Technology. He was a professor at Princeton and was known for his teaching, writing, and research capabilities.

Arthur Burns is ranked fourth in terms of qualifications. He may have had the strongest background on the academic side, but had the weakest background when it came to real-world experience. Some might say that of the five chairmen discussed here, he was last when it came to street and market smarts. The country paid a considerable price for these shortcomings.

Burns earned a BS and PhD from Columbia University. He was a professor at Columbia, president of the National Bureau of Economic Research, and like Greenspan and Bernanke, head of the president's Council of Economic Advisers. He was much more involved in politics than the other chairmen discussed here, and this proved to be a negative factor when it came to his performance as Fed chairman.

G. William Miller brings up the rear in terms of professional qualifications. He was totally out of his element when he was appointed as Federal Reserve chairman. Yet, having been the chief executive officer of a large corporation meant he had to make some tough managerial decisions. None of the other four had this type of experience. In fact, he was not shy about making tough policy decisions at the Fed (not always the right ones) despite being a "political" appointee. He is given short-shrift by most historians—often regarded as someone who simply occupied the Fed chairmanship for eighteen months between Burns and Volcker. One thing is certain, however, he was far from irrelevant in his short tour of duty, and his record at the Fed was not as bad as some make it out to be.

His academic background was considerably different from the other four chairmen discussed here. He graduated from the Coast Guard Academy with a BS in Marine Engineering and received a law degree from the University of California at Berkeley. Two advantages he had over the others were that first, he had major executive responsibilities as the chief executive officer of a large corporation, and second, the corporation that he headed—Textron—had important trading operations in the metals field.

PERFORMANCE

Measuring performance is much more difficult than measuring qualifications. There are so many ways of measuring performance, and in different circumstances, some are more important than others. There are times when major changes in policy are necessary, and there are times when staying out of trouble is the best approach.

Measuring performance is not confined to just one item. There is a package of factors to be looked at, such as what is achieved throughout one's tenure as chairman, the bumps in the performance record, and what is left for the new chairman versus what the old chairman inherited. What also needs to be considered is a chairman's claim to fame, either in a positive or negative sense, and his performance in areas that tend to receive inadequate attention, such as new regulatory policies, research improvements, and advancements in analytical techniques. A chairman's place in history should be an amalgamation of factors, with some standing above the rest.

One complication is the length of time that has passed in analyzing the performance of the person who held office. The shorter the time period since an individual has left the Fed, the more likely that near-term positive and negative performance will be emphasized. The longer the time period, the more that major turning points will be remembered, as near-term positives and negatives slip into oblivion. In the case at hand, the Burns, Miller, and Volcker periods are now distant enough so that both short-run and longer-run judgments can be made. In the case of Greenspan, because of his length of time in office and the fact that he left office as recently as early 2006, there are still some judgments that need to be made. Obviously, it is too early to make any meaningful judgments with respect to Bernanke.

Arthur Burns (February 1, 1970–January 31, 1978)

Of the five chairmen, Arthur Burns comes off as low man on the performance totem pole in virtually all respects. At the end of his eight years on the job, he left conditions far worse than he inherited; his policy ride was bumpy and filled with missteps; he left nothing of substance that he could be known for; he was active on the regulatory side, but not by choice and in an inconsistent way; and he added little value when it came to such things as research improvement and analytical techniques. He was the biggest disappointment compared with the other four chairmen. He was influenced by politicians more than he should have been, and at times changed his views based on political considerations. He talked tough and acted meek. What is even more disturbing in this assessment is that the farther we get from his time in office, the worse his record looks. In this regard, he was no Harry Truman.

G. William Miller (March 8, 1978–August 6, 1979)

G. William Miller's performance was one step removed from the bottom. He was in office only eighteen months, so his record is rather abbreviated. But 1978, when he took over, was a key period for the U.S. economy and monetary policy. Most historians have treated him with disdain because by background and professional training, he was not qualified to be Federal Reserve chairman. Nevertheless, he not only became chairman of the Fed, but also went on to become secretary of the treasury. He was an example of the Peter Principle—rising to his level of incompetence—not just once, but twice.

When President Carter announced that Miller would be the next Federal Reserve chairman, people were shocked and dumbfounded. Some had no clue who he was, and some wondered whether he was the same person who ran for vice president of the United States in 1964 (he was not). His claim to fame, aside from being chief executive of a good-size corporation, was that he had been on the board of directors of a district Federal Reserve bank. These credentials should have put him at the back of any credible list for the job of chairman—way back.

Yet, when he took over at the Fed, he did have one thing going for him. Not much was expected of him, and surely less than in the case of Arthur Burns. He was expected to live down to his capabilities for the job. Yet there are positive things to say about Miller. This is one of those cases where the more distant the analysis, the better he looks as a Fed chairman.

He was consistent in his policy approach during his eighteen months in office. He moved policy in the right direction and by much more than a token amount in an effort to combat the inflation that was becoming embedded, thanks mainly to double-digit wage increases. One of his main problems was that he thought he was doing more to fight inflation than really was the case. As a matter of fact, at the time he was pushing up the funds rate and tightening the availability of funds, he was criticized for doing too much when in fact he did too little. Early on in his term, he was not lacking in political courage, although later on, he was less aggressive in firming policy. What he was short of was the type of policy background that would have enabled him to realize that ratcheting up an overnight interest rate was not severe enough to break the back of embedded inflation.

There is always an advantage in having training and experience before taking a job, but it is possible to do a good job without having such an advantage. Even so, there is no guarantee of success, whatever one's background and training. These were abnormal and difficult times, and how would Miller know that using what were considered traditional techniques would prove to be inadequate medicine? How would he know that in a period of hyperinflation and embedded inflation, the Fed needed to use a different policy-tightening technique: a clamp on the growth of the monetary aggregates that would take interest rates to painfully high levels—levels that would not have been politically possible if the Fed had been targeting the fed funds rate?

Miller recognized the main problem—inflation—but he did not understand that his remedy was neither creative enough nor tough enough. Also, late in his eighteen-month term as chairman, some of his aggressiveness began to fade. Yet, realize that under Miller, the Fed moved the federal funds rate from 6.75 percent in March 1978 to about 11 percent by August 1979—hardly a token increase by past standards. Unfortunately, most of the increase occurred in 1978, and if he had kept cranking up the funds rate through the first half of 1979, he would have had a better chance of cutting back on the degree of embedded inflation. A few hundred basis points more and he might have been the inflation fighter he thought he was, and he would have gotten at least some share of the credit for helping knock off embedded inflation. Instead, he wound up taking considerable political heat for raising the funds rate to a double-digit level and wound up getting no credit for having made such a move.

The space devoted to G. William Miller may seem excessive for a man who held office for such a short length of time. Yet, there are some periods, even though abbreviated, that are especially important because they can have a significant impact on the future course of events. Think about the United States's involvement in wars in recent decades, in which there were turning points regarding what direction U.S. policy would take. Key turning-point decisions were made in the post-World War II period, during the Korean War, the war in Vietnam, the Gulf War, and in the current wars in Afghanistan and Iraq. While no one should equate the importance of killing off inflation versus killing off people, it does point up that key decisions at one point in time can set the course of events for an extended period. Both Miller and Volcker ran the Fed at key turning points in history.

Paul Volcker (August 6, 1979–August 11, 1987)

In contrast to Burns and Miller, Paul Volcker was the man for the times. Under ordinary circumstances, he may not have excelled. Have him carry forward what others had already set in motion, and his record as chairman might not have been as distinguished. If he had been chairman during a period where everything was quiet and copacetic, he would have had little chance to exercise his abilities, and his achievements might have been more modest. But when it came to stepping in during a crisis and making painful decisions in both the political and economic worlds, his abilities came to the fore. It is hard to think of anyone who was as well qualified in virtually every conceivable way to take over at the Fed at a time of economic crisis. He should have been made chairman in 1970, and U.S. politicians should not have waited until 1979 to do the right thing.

Although no one knows how an earlier Volcker appointment would have changed the course of U.S. economic history, the situation would surely have been better than during the Burns-Miller era. Even if Volcker had taken over after Burns in 1978, it no doubt would have been an improvement, because he probably would have attacked the inflation problem more aggressively than Miller. What can be said with some conviction (based on what he did when he ultimately took over at the Fed) is that Volcker would have better recognized the depth of the inflation problem and would have moved more aggressively in 1978 and in 1979 to tighten monetary policy.

Yet, let us also be realistic. It is highly unlikely that Volcker would have been able to halt embedded inflation dead in its tracks in 1978 and 1979. If he had taken over the Fed in 1970, the story would have been different, but by 1978, inflation was already out of control and embedded, especially in the labor cost area. Moreover, the situation was getting worse. One should realize that while Miller tightened policy by an inadequate amount, he surely could not be accused of sitting on his hands in 1979. But at that time it would have taken a large amount of additional political courage on his part to push up the overnight rate by several hundred basis points—into the middle teens.

It is almost impossible to measure Volcker's achievements and shortcomings during his eight years in office (1979–1987) in some sort of organized way. That is not the case for the other four chairmen analyzed in this book. It is foolish to look with microscopic intensity at his short-run policy movements, or the tools he used, because he was always trying to put out major fires with whatever seemed to work the best. It was the time for a pragmatist, and he was surely that. He used policy tools and targets that served his overall policy needs. It was not a time for decisions based on theory or concepts.

How can one measure Volcker's performance with respect to economic growth when, in essence, he knowingly helped send the economy into a tailspin in an attempt to break the back of inflation? How can one measure his performance with respect to major U.S. international and dollar problems when the Fed needed to use unsustainably high interest rates to create a short-term subpar economic performance? How can one measure his performance with respect to influencing the budget when the high interest rates and weak economic growth enhanced the size of the budget deficit?

Moreover, during his term as chairman, Volcker faced major international problems, many of which were structural and therefore difficult to eliminate. It was a time when fixed exchange rates were king, and they tended to be counterproductive to world economic stability. There was a cold war going on, and emerging countries were facing major economic and financial problems. These factors made Volcker's job at the Fed more difficult and more complex.

In contrast, both Greenspan and Bernanke were the beneficiaries of better times. The cold war ended in 1991 and since then, many emerging countries have become important economic players. These countries, by selling their products abroad, have helped hold down worldwide inflation. Many of these same countries accumulated massive amounts of wealth that helped finance U.S. trade deficits and made major investments in U.S. industries. Regional international organizations such as the European Community and North American Free Trade Agreement have helped most of their members prosper, have brought additional economic stability to their regions, and at the same time have helped limit inflationary pressures. These factors made life much easier for Greenspan and Bernanke than for the previous three chairmen.

Of the last five chairmen, Burns allowed the inflation problem to get out of hand; Miller attacked the problem but in an inadequate way; and Volcker was the Fed chairman who, by far, did the most to help kill off embedded inflation. During their inflation battles, all three of these chairmen had to deal with outside factors and circumstances that made their jobs especially difficult. Greenspan and Bernanke (so far) have helped hold inflation in check, but they have been aided by domestic and international factors that made their task easier than it was for the three previous chairman. Greenspan and Bernanke have had the luxury of controlling inflation by fine-tuning monetary policy. The others did not have that option.

Alan Greenspan (August 11, 1987–January 31, 2006)

Alan Greenspan was chairman of the Federal Reserve from August 11, 1987, to January 31, 2006. Anyone who is in a position whereby it is perceived that he can walk on water is going to have, over an eighteen-year period, an extensive list of positives and negatives. But, as with Volcker, it is misleading to merely make a list and tally up the positives versus the negatives. Obviously, some results are much more important than others. Some results are transitory, while others have long-term importance. Nevertheless, presenting a rough idea of the pluses and minuses for Greenspan can be a worthwhile exercise so long as there is an explanation that goes along with it.

On the positive side, when Greenspan left office at the end of January 2006, the economy was performing reasonably well. Real growth was respectable and there were no signs of embedded inflation. During most of Greenspan's eighteen years, the economy experienced solid growth, with no major recessions. The state of financial institutions was reasonably good, although problems were emerging, and the financial markets, on balance, showed depth, breadth, and resilience. However, a strong case can be made that his policies sowed the seeds for financial difficulties later on, although Bernanke has to shoulder part of the blame because he did not deal with impending problems in an aggressive and timely manner.

The status of the Fed, both at home and abroad, remained high during those eighteen years, and the public had considerable confidence in the Fed and in

Greenspan. Foreigners viewed him as an excellent and astute central banker, and this not only helped the dollar, but made foreigners comfortable with investing in the United States. There were no major scandals at the Fed during his extended period, and he came off clean as a whistle, although some questioned his statements on Fed policies and actions he made after he left, and for which he was paid handsomely by private organizations. His statements clearly made life more difficult for his successor, something that Volcker avoided when Greenspan took over at the Fed.

On the negative side, there was often a roller-coaster approach to his monetary policy; there seemed to be policy cycles where the Fed tightened too much and stayed too long; eased too much and stayed too long; and then tightened too much and stayed too long. The fed funds rate, on a nominal basis, was given too much importance as a policy tool and market rates were used excessively to measure inflation expectations. Too many policy tools gathered dust on the back shelf during the Greenspan period, and there were times when using tools such as margin requirements on equities, reserve requirements on deposits, and discount window policies could have made the cutting edge of monetary policy much more effective. When considering whether policy was too easy or too tight, more emphasis could have been placed on the growth in monetary aggregates and specifically the expansion in bank credit.

The Fed had the capability to minimize or offset many of the major problems that arose, but Greenspan tended to favor a hands-off approach. He did not seem interested in using preventive medicine. Moreover, he was not forceful when making comments such as "irrational exuberance" when talking about the rise of the stock market indices in late 1996, and gave little indication as to whether or not the Fed would act if the stock market upswing did not moderate. His approach was to let the markets take care of the situation and let events play out. Not a bad policy for transitory problems; not a good policy for fundamental problems that could reach epidemic proportions.

The following should be of some help in recalling the policy roller-coaster under Greenspan: When he took over as Fed chairman in August 1987, federal funds were targeted at about 6.75 percent; by April 1989 funds were at almost 10 percent; they were down to near 3 percent by October 1992, and back up to 6 percent in February 1995. Funds were still subject to some volatility over the next few years, but to a considerably lesser degree. Then, starting in early 1999, the degree of volatility increased substantially, and from that point on, the swings in the funds rate were more severe.

From about 4.75 percent in early 1999, the funds rate was moved up to 6.5 percent by the middle of 2000 and, unfortunately, stayed there through the end of the year. It then dropped like a stone and reached 1 percent by the middle of 2003. Beginning in the middle of 2004, the funds rate started an upward trek. Increases of 25 basis points each occurred at seventeen consecutive meetings (fourteen under Greenspan). The funds rate was at 4.5 percent when Greenspan left office.

One can argue that implicit in the magnitude of these policy swings and changes in policy direction was that Greenspan and the Fed were not on top of changes in economic conditions. They often seemed to be late in catching economic trends, and there were times when, pure and simple, they got it wrong. For example, the deflation fears in late 2003 and 2004 were misguided, incorrect, and frankly had little chance of happening in the United States. Moreover, only a year or two later, the fears had shifted to inflation. This was despite the fact that the degree of change in price between these two periods hardly justified a 180-degree swing in attitude.

Greenspan also seemed to have a blind spot with respect to policy tools. He did not seem to realize that the fed funds rate was not as powerful a monetary policy tool as he thought, especially when changes were made in very small increments. In the world of interest rates, the greatest cutting edge of monetary policy comes from the longer end of the Treasury market, not from an overnight rate where commercial banks trade reserves. Long Treasury security rates dominate long rates in the mortgage and corporate bond markets—not the federal funds rate.

Under his leadership, Greenspan and the Fed used some questionable reasoning that did not help them pursue a correct monetary policy, and some of these problems are in evidence today. The Fed paid too much attention to real fed funds rates as an indicator of whether monetary policy was on the easy or restrictive side. In this regard, the Fed should have paid more attention to indicators such as bank credit expansion and the availability of funds to both lenders and borrowers. In the real world, from late 2001 to late 2005, monetary policy was much easier than Greenspan seemed to realize, and this was the genesis of many of the problems in the mortgage and housing markets that arose a few years later.

Greenspan also seemed to place too much emphasis on the yield difference between full coupon Treasury securities and Treasury inflation-protected securities (TIPS). The Fed seemed to presume that changes in the differential reflected how concerned investors were with respect to inflation down the road. This was naïve. The TIPS market has much less breadth, depth, and resilience than the full-coupon market. Thus, the TIPS market is much less liquid, many investors are restricted in the purchases they can make, the tax treatment is different, and dealers have discovered that financing these securities can be unprofitable. Also, when the Treasury increased its emphasis on TIPS financing, the relationship between the floating supply of TIPS and the full-coupon market changed. Thus, when there was a shift in the yield differentials between these markets, it was difficult to determine what caused the change. It is a mistake to assume that it was due entirely to changes in the inflation outlook. Yet Fed officials keep referring to this relationship when they talked about measuring changes in inflation expectations.

Further, while it is important to know how investors feel about inflation, it is even more important to determine how the consumer feels about the subject. Measuring investor concerns and consumer concerns are not the same. Realize that when it comes to price measurements and targets, the Fed uses consumer prices as measured by personal consumption expenditures (excluding food and energy). Would not the Fed be better off canvassing consumer expectations directly rather than using a questionable approach measuring investor expectations of inflation?

There was also a reluctance on Greenspan's part when it came to nipping problems in the bud. He was willing to talk about problems that existed, but would not allow the Fed to get involved until the problems were full-blown. This was evident in stock market excesses where he talked about, but did nothing about, irrational exuberance, the problems that developed with respect to the Long-Term Capital Management implosion, and most recently, the questionable bank lending practices in the mortgage market. Many of the problems that developed in the mortgage market had their genesis in an overly easy monetary policy, and this started on Greenspan's watch. The Fed's willingness to use regulatory pressures took a back seat during his tour of duty. Increased regulatory pressures on those lending in the subprime market were several years late in coming and would have been a worthwhile dose of preventive medicine.

Greenspan could also have been more aggressive in taking advantage of the Fed's research talents, which could have helped in improving its forecasting capabilities. The Fed has highly qualified research people at the Board and at the district banks, which gives them a unique insight as to what is happening around the country. District banks could spend more time analyzing what is happening in their regions and analyzing industries that are the most important in their region. Results of the Fed's studies and surveys could be put together in a much more comprehensive manner and provide a much more detailed economic outlook than what appears in the *Beige Book,* which provides not much more than snippets of information. In this regard, the Fed could put together by districts, and then in total, a timely survey similar to those done by the Institute for Supply Management, the Conference Board, and the University of Michigan, but on a much broader and more policy-useful basis. The Bank of Japan Tankan survey approach would also be a useful addition to the Fed's research arsenal.

Greenspan was an active advocate of policy transparency, and that is all to the good. However, he did not deliver the information in the clearest and most useful manner. Being a wordsmith seemed to be something that he enjoyed, but his comments were often misunderstood, and markets experienced excessive movements based on the interpretation by participants of what they thought was the Greenspan message. And when it came to Treasury rate levels and the slope of the yield curve, his "conundrum" comment indicated that he did not fully understand the nitty-gritty factors in the Treasury market that brought about such results. There was no conundrum, only a lack of understanding of the details that caused long Treasury rates to be conceptually lower than he thought should be the case.

While this list of negatives is long, and considerably longer than the positives, it should be pointed out that several of the positives were of great importance. Of his positive contributions, the most important by far was that relatively early in his tenure at the Fed, he played a major role in bringing financial institutions back to health—health in terms of both balance sheets and income statements. In the early 1990s, he eased monetary policy by an appropriate amount at an appropriate time, which allowed financial institutions to make substantial profits in terms of both capital gains and carry profits (the rate of return on an investment after subtracting the cost of financing the investment), and rebuild their capital. He was also involved in reducing regulations that restricted banks and other financial institutions in the types of products and services they could offer. This broadened their earnings base.

Consider this: If the Fed and Greenspan had not helped bring back prosperity to financial institutions in the early 1990s, there is no way the economy could have had a major and sustained economic recovery. From 1992 to 2000, there was only one small blip in economic performance, and that occurred late in 1994 and early 1995; and, if it were not for some questionable fine tuning of policies on the part of the Fed, there would have been eight straight years of considerable and sustained real growth with no inflation problems of consequence. Even in the 2000 through 2005 period when Greenspan had monetary policy on a fed-funds rate rollercoaster, his mistakes were not of a sufficient magnitude to derail the economic performance during that period.

One can say that while Greenspan made his share of policy mistakes, they were not of a magnitude that offset the underlying positives that were taking place in the private sector of the economy. Many of the positives were not of the Fed's doing, but the Fed did nothing to limit their effectiveness. Underlying improvements in productivity, a labor picture that was much more conducive to economic growth than was previously the case, the rapid growth of computers, the Internet, and other communication devices and techniques all helped to improve business knowledge and efficiency. And, competition from abroad made many companies run a tighter ship. These changes were not just at the mega corporation level. They filtered down to small enterprises, and this brought productivity improvements to the "little guy" that could never have been imagined a decade or so earlier.

Ben Bernanke (From February 1, 2006)

Regarding Ben Bernanke, it is too early to tell what his legacy will be, although he surely has not gotten off to a good start and in some cases seems overwhelmed by events. His background is in academia, and that can be both good and bad. Good because he is steeped in understanding monetary concepts, but bad if he relies too much on theory to make pragmatic decisions. Being chairman of the Federal Reserve is a job for pragmatists. Only time will tell if he can develop enough street smarts and market expertise to balance what initially appears to be too much emphasis on concepts and theory. Burns was a theoretician and a model builder; we do not need another theoretician and model builder to run the Fed.

In judging each of the five chairmen's performance since 1970, what appears to make the greatest difference in results is a combination of pragmatism, political courage, strong leadership, good advisers, well-versed governors, a sixth sense, a willingness to admit mistakes, the ability to make timely changes, and not presenting an attitude that suggests the chairman can walk on water. When it comes to these attributes, Volcker is at the top of the list, Burns is at the bottom of the list, and Miller is next to the bottom of the list.

The Greenspan story has not been entirely written, and most of Bernanke's story is still to be written. As is true for each chairman, the successor can have a great deal to do with how history treats the predecessor. In this regard, Bernanke's performance during his first three years at the helm of the Federal Reserve did not do Greenspan any favors.

In his early days as chairman, Bernanke appeared to pride himself on continuing Greenspan's policies. Yet, by early 2006, the financial situation in the U.S. was in the process of changing, and not for the better. Regulatory inadequacies and market problems were emerging, although it would have taken considerable foresight to realize how bad things were going to get. Greenspan, Bernanke and the Fed are only partially to blame for recent financial debacles, but the both should have blown the whistle on a more timely and aggressive basis.

6

Arthur Burns
(February 1, 1970–January 31, 1978)

Arthur Burns became chairman of the Federal Reserve on February 1, 1970, and his tour of duty lasted until January 31, 1978. He was a highly regarded professor who fell far short of what was expected of him as Fed chairman. When he left, both the economy and monetary policy were in far worse shape than when he took over the stewardship eight years earlier. His major shortcoming was that he talked tough about containing inflation, and yet, his policies created an inflation problem that was not brought under control until the early 1990s.

To show how much he underestimated the inflation problem, about a half year after he took office as Fed chairman, he gave a presentation to the Joint Economic Committee on July 23, 1970. One does not have to read too much between the lines in the following quotes to determine that he believed he had inherited a serious inflation problem—in other words, one not of his doing—and that in his first half year in office, substantial progress had been made in alleviating that problem. It is too bad that history has proven him wrong on both counts; the problems he inherited were small potatoes compared with what ultimately occurred on his watch, and he grossly overestimated the progress he made against inflation early in his term. His overoptimism was evident from his testimony:

> As we are all well aware, the performance of the economy thus far in 1970 has left much to be desired. I believe, however, that the available evidence indicates that our economy is basically sound and resilient, and that we are making progress in resolving the inflationary problems that have plagued us over the past five years. . . . The process of wringing out the inflationary excesses of the past has not been painless, but the alternative of letting inflation run rampant would have been utterly disastrous. . . .
>
> Thus far, our success in moderating inflationary pressures has been disappointingly small. . . . The unwinding from the inflationary excesses of the past is proving a longer and more difficult process than we had anticipated.

However, while economy is still some distance from the stability of costs and prices that we seek, progress is being made in this area—more progress, perhaps, than is generally realized. We are now witnessing some clear signs of reduced upward pressure on prices.

Yet, it was more than bad estimates that got Burns into trouble, both inside and outside the Fed. He had a very elevated opinion of his talents as a monetary policy expert, and he had a tendency to talk down to people. He never had a good feel for what was happening in either the markets or the economy. He pontificated as if he were still teaching at Columbia University, and often what he said and the policies the Fed followed were not consistent. He talked tough about combating inflation, but he did not act tough. He talked about the importance of a free-market economy, and yet, when inflation got out of control, he was in favor of price controls. He believed that running monetary policy was a science, not an art, and that models were a very important factor in this endeavor. Ultimately—and unfortunately—he found out differently. (In 2006, when Ben Bernanke was being considered for the chairman's job, there were some fears among those in the financial community that he might be the second coming of Arthur Burns. After all, they did have some similarities in their academic backgrounds.)

When Burns took over the helm of the Fed in 1970, he was not short of policy tools that could help contain inflation. There was an elaborate (and punitive) reserve requirements system; Regulation Q, which provided a ceiling on interest rates that banks and other saving institutions could pay; a relatively strict approach for banks borrowing at the discount window at penalty rates, and a multitude of monetary aggregate and bank credit expansion targets. In addition, there were margin requirements, which are limitations on the percentage that customers can borrow from a broker when buying securities. There were also short-term interest rate objectives that were all available to help the Fed contain inflation. Thus, the arsenal of useable constraints was considerable. Although some of these tools needed to be changed and ultimately eliminated (which they were), the fact was that they were in place at a time when the Fed needed to use restraints, and thus they were available to Burns at that time.

As for some of the details when Burns took office in early 1970, the economy was weak, but prices and costs were continuing to rise at a rapid pace. There was a small decline in real growth, the CPI was increasing at about 0.5 percent per month (6 percent at an annual rate); the fed funds rate was about 9 percent; U.S. Treasury long-bond yields were running between 6.5 and 7 percent; borrowings at the discount window were running at a very large $1 billion; net borrowed reserves (the opposite of free reserves) were also a very large, $800 million; and M-1 (the narrowest form of money supply) and bank credit were showing little growth. In other words, this was a case of stagflation—slow or no economic growth combined with significant inflation.

ARTHUR BURNS 75

Turning to the international side, the circumstances were best expressed in regular Treasury-Federal Reserve joint reports that were published in the Federal Reserve Bulletins. They present a flow of events and deterioration that would have been a challenge to any central banker, no matter how well that person had been prepared. The international financial system was flawed, and inappropriate U.S. domestic policies were making a bad situation worse.

The following two Federal Reserve Bulletin articles show how quickly international financial conditions can change. First, there was an improvement, but shortly thereafter, there was a major deterioration and a debacle that adversely affected the economic and financial situation of all major countries.

From the March 1970 Federal Reserve Bulletin

The recurrent speculative storms that had swept across the foreign exchanges during the first 9 months of 1969 were succeeded during the fall and winter months by a general clearing-away of market fears and tensions. . . . The activation of the special drawing rights (SDR's) agreement, together with the abrupt decline in the free market price of gold, contributed to a strong revival of confidence in the continuing viability of the international financial system.

From the October 1971 Federal Reserve Bulletin

[In early 1971,] the international financial markets began to sense an impending crisis of the dollar. As interest rate differentials between the United States and Europe widened out still further, outflows of short-term funds to the European markets accelerated and forced most European currencies hard against their ceilings. Despite Federal Reserve and Treasury efforts to slow down or offset the repayment of U.S. bank debt to the euro-dollar deposit market, several billion dollars more was repaid during the first quarter of 1971. Even more ominous, the severe slump of the U.S. trade surplus during late 1970 persisted into early 1971 and aroused increasing apprehension of a loss of U.S. competitive strength in world markets. . . .

In July and early August events moved inexorably toward their climax as speculative anticipation reached throughout the full range of trade and investment decisions in the market. On Friday, August 6, a congressional subcommittee report asserted that the dollar had become overvalued and called for corrective action through a general realignment of exchange rates. That same day the U.S. Treasury reported a loss of gold and other reserve assets totaling more than $1 billion, mainly as a consequence of British and French repayment of debt to the IMF. Over the following week, the flight from the dollar accelerated sharply. . . .

On Sunday, August 15, 1971, President Nixon announced a major new program of domestic and international economic measures. Using powers available under the Economic Stabilization Act of 1970, the President ordered a 90-day freeze on wages and prices, and in order to stimulate a more rapid expansion of production and employment, recommended new tax measures. With respect to international payments, the President introduced a 10 percent temporary surcharge on dutiable imports into the United States and announced a temporary suspension of convertibility of the dollar into gold and other reserve assets.

The major European governments kept their exchange markets closed all of the following week, as they sought to develop some joint policy response to the U.S. measures. These negotiating efforts failed, and on Monday, August 23, European governments reopened their exchange markets on an uncoordinated basis. While each government continued to adhere to its pre-August 15 parity, all but the French Government suspended their commitments to defend the previous upper limits of their exchange rates. . . .

The Japanese Government initially sought to maintain the rate for the yen by continuing to intervene at the ceiling, but it was swamped by an inflow of dollars, which by month-end, had swollen official reserves. On August 28, official intervention at the ceiling for the yen was suspended, and the yen immediately rose 4.7 percent; in subsequent weeks the yen moved gradually higher. By October 8, the rates of the major trading currencies of the world had moved to . . . premiums over their former official ceilings.

The exchange rate structure thus emerging after August 15, 1971, was, in most instances, the product of controlled rather than free-floating currencies. Many central banks continued to intervene on an ad hoc basis, while the market was further strongly influenced by a wide variety of new exchange controls, the U.S. import surcharge, and sharply conflicting official appraisals of an appropriate realignment of parities.

Despite heavy swap drawings by the Federal Reserve during the period under review, the U.S. stocks of gold and other reserve assets were severely eroded by the flow of dollars into foreign central banks.

DOMESTIC DECISIONS

Upon arrival at the Fed in early 1970, Burns had to make a policy choice: Does the Federal Reserve try to stimulate the economy or should it continue to try to limit inflation? The answer was that it tried to stimulate the economy, and this was especially evident with respect to the fed funds rate, which was only about 4 percent by January 1971, or less than half of what it was twelve months earlier. This could hardly be considered a fine-tuning operation. Yet, during this same period, the long Treasury rate declined by only about 100 basis points to somewhat under 6 percent, which suggested that the government bond market still had some inflation concerns.

Of course, both the economy and the monetary aggregates responded to the large amount of Fed easing. After bottoming out in 1970 with a flat performance, the economy showed an increase of about 4.5 percent in 1971 and almost 7 percent in 1972. This rapid real-growth advance, combined with an oil-price bubble, brought about massive increases in CPI prices. After slowing in 1971 and 1972 to an annual increase of somewhat over 3 percent, the CPI moved sharply higher, rising by about 9 percent in 1973 and about 12 percent in 1974. Thus, the Fed was paying the price for the excessive amount of easing that took place in 1971.

Yet, this is only part of the story. After only a few months in office, in May 1970, Burns decided that he would support a wage-price review board. It would have only persuasion powers with respect to major wage-price increases. This strongly indicates that he was unwilling to keep monetary policy as tight as necessary to curtail potential inflation pressures. Then, in the middle of August 1971, with the Fed having already eased substantially, and with upward inflationary pressures sitting in the wings, the Nixon administration came up with the New Economic Policy, which would freeze wages and prices for a ninety-day period in order to check inflation. The Cost of Living Council was to be at the controls.

After the initial ninety days, the controls were gradually relaxed. This allowed bottled-up inflation to be uncorked. Yet, it was not only the excessively easy monetary policy that took hold; there were also wage and price increases that had been delayed by the controls. Adding to the inflationary pressures were strength in the international economy, crop failures in the Soviet Union, and increases in oil prices. These factors caused a reimposition of a freeze in June 1973, which did not work. It was just more of the same bad medicine. By April 1974, against a background of out-of-control inflation and a CPI that was running at a double-digit rate of advance, most of the controls system was finally abolished.

Thus, early in his term of office, Burns's standing as a central banker was already damaged beyond repair. There was little he could do to rectify the situation, and to this day his reputation remains tarnished. Yet, as bad a job as Burns did, it should be pointed out that he appears to have inherited stagflation; he was not responsible for what happened to energy prices and events such as a possible run on the U.S. gold stock. And he was the victim of some bad judgment and excessive influence by the Nixon administration.

Further, fiscal policy (federal government taxation, spending, and debt management policies) was of no help to Burns during his first four years in office. With inflation out of control, one might have hoped for a budgetary policy designed to rein in federal spending. Yet, in looking at fiscal years 1970, 1971, 1972, 1973, and 1974, the budget deficits were $2.8 billion, $23.0 billion, $23.4 billion, $14.9 billion, and $6.1 billion, respectively. In these same years, U.S. government spending was up 6.5 percent, 7.5 percent, 9.7 percent, 6.5 percent, and 9.6 percent. In a period when fiscal policy needed to lean against the wind and provide restraint, that was not being done.

Even though there was an explosion of inflationary pressures from 1970 to 1974, the Fed was both late and slow in raising the funds rate. It had cut its fed funds target by an unduly large amount, from about 9 percent in early 1970 to about 3.75 percent by early 1971. Obviously, from the Fed's perspective, moving the economy out of a moderate recession was far more important than holding down major inflationary pressures. This was a mistake of the first order.

Then, when it was clear that the Fed had eased too much and stayed too long, it began to eliminate some of the ease. However, the firming moves were short-lived, and in August 1971, the movement towards a higher fed funds rate ground to a halt at about 5.5 percent. This was a tragic mistake. Instead of continuing to push up the funds rate, the Fed headed in the other direction. By February 1972, it had moved the funds rate back down to 3.25 percent. At that point, the funds target was probably about half of what it should have been. It was at about zero in real interest rate terms, and this was with inflation starting to pick up.

In looking at the CPI, by December 1972, the twelve-month rate of inflation stood at 3.4 percent; by December 1973 it was 8.9 percent, and by December 1974 it was 12.1 percent. There may be nothing in modern times in the United States that com-pares with this massive misjudgment on the part of the Fed. Thus, it is little wonder that ever since, Fed chairmen have almost always talked tough about containing inflation, and rather than higher-than-desired unemployment or disappointing real economic growth, it is inflation concerns have dominated the policy scene.

Moreover, not only did the Fed move in the wrong direction up to early 1972, but it was also painfully slow in raising the funds rate, especially when compared with what was happening to inflationary pressures. By the end of 1972, the funds rate had been increased to only about 5.5 percent. It was not until the spring of 1973 that the Fed began to get serious with respect to raising the funds rate. Then, it moved the funds rate up sharply, and by the third quarter of 1973, the rate was more than 10 percent, and by the third quarter of 1974, it had moved up to around 13 percent.

Thus, in a period of two and one-half years, the Fed had moved from an exces-sively and unsustainably low funds rate to an excessively and unsustainably high funds rate. In this situation, confidence in the Fed and confidence in the economic outlook were both unduly low. If you were a CEO, how would you like to make forecasts for your company's outlook under such volatile circumstances? Fed pol-icy was dominated by attempts to offset past mistakes.

With monetary policy unsustainably tight by the middle of 1974, the Fed was under considerable pressure to cut the funds rate—and sharply. That is in fact what happened, and by early 1976, the funds target was down to less than 5 per-cent. The good news was that the unsustainably and excessively high funds rate that prevailed in the middle of 1974 had helped bring about a considerable slow-ing of the inflation rate; the bad news was that coming from a 12-percent CPI increase by the end of 1974 to an inflation rate somewhat below 6 percent was nowhere near good enough.

Inflation had wound down from "rampant" to merely "excessive," and the funds rate had gone from being too high to being too low. The funds rate—at slightly under 5 percent—was on the low side, compared with an inflation rate of some-what over 5 percent. This meant the policy roller coaster ride was alive and well. By the time that Burns left office, the funds rate was up to 6.75 percent, and would head higher under the next chairman (G. William Miller).

Table 6-1 shows the incredible volatility of the federal funds rate under Arthur Burns. It also shows the path the CPI followed during the same period:

Table 6-1

Months	Fed Fund Rates - % Interim Highs and Lows	Consumer Price Index - % 12-Month Increase
March 1971	3.71	4.4
August 1971	5.56	4.4
February 1972	3.29	3.8
August 1973	10.78	7.4
February 1974	8.97	11.8
July 1974	12.92	11.5
February 1976	4.77	6.3
January 1978	6.70	6.8

In conclusion, in looking at Table 6-1, at first glance you might think that major progress had been made in cutting back on inflation. The high CPI rate over a twelve-month period had been 11.8 percent for the year ended February 1974, and by February 1976, the yearly increase was down to a semi-respectable 6.3 percent. However, this would prove to be false optimism. Not only did the yearly inflation rate move up to 6.8 percent by January 1978, but the underlying forces that caused the double-digit rate of inflation were still embedded, and the handwriting was on the wall that it was only a matter of time before double-digit inflation returned. The return to greater inflation adversity is reflected in Table 6-2.

Table 6-2
Arthur Burns, Chairman-Federal Reserve Board of Governors February 1, 1970—January 31, 1978

	Financial Markets							Monetary Policy					Economic Indicators				Commodities	
			Corporates							Bank Credit				CPI - %			Prices - $	
1970	Fed Funds	Treas 30-yr	Aaa	Baa	30-yr Mtge	S&P 500	DM	Monetary Base	Free Rsvs	Loans	Inv	Real GDP	Unemp Rate	Total	Core	Budget	Oil	Gold
Jan	8.98	6.92	7.91	8.86	8.16	85.02	.2713	$61.8b	−785	$292b	$111b		3.9%	+0.5	+0.5		3.35	34.94
Feb	8.98	6.67	7.93	8.78	8.23	89.50	.2711	61.9	−872	290	111	−0.7%	4.2	+0.5	+0.5		3.35	34.99
Mar	7.76	6.72	7.84	8.63	8.29	89.63	.2723	62.2	−735	291	112		4.4	+0.5	+0.8		3.35	35.09
Apr	8.10	6.85	7.83	8.70	8.24	81.52	.2746	62.7	−693	293	114		4.6	+0.5	+0.7		3.35	35.62
May	7.94	7.24	8.11	8.98	8.28	76.55	.2752	63.0	−811	293	115	+0.8	4.8	+0.3	+0.2	FY	3.35	35.95
Jun	7.60	7.34	8.48	9.25	8.31	72.72	.2753	63.2	−691	293	116		4.9	+0.5	+0.7	−2.8b	3.35	35.44
Jul	7.21	6.92	8.44	9.40	8.32	78.05	.2754	63.4	−1194	297	118		5.0	+0.3	+0.2		3.31	35.32
Aug	6.61	7.07	8.13	9.44	8.35	81.52	.2754	63.7	−663	299	121	+3.6	5.1	+0.3	+0.5		3.31	35.38
Sep	6.29	6.88	8.09	9.39	8.31	84.30	.2754	64.1	−356	300	123		5.4	+0.5	+0.5		3.31	36.19
Oct	6.20	6.88	8.03	9.33	8.33	83.25	.2753	64.3	−258	303	125		5.5	+0.5	+0.5		3.31	37.52
Nov	5.60	6.58	8.05	9.38	8.26	87.20	.2754	64.6	−181	304	127	−4.2	5.9	+0.5	+0.7		3.31	37.44
Dec	4.90	6.28	7.64	9.12	8.20	92.15	.2744	65.0	−83	305	130		6.1	+0.5	+0.5		3.56	37.44
						+1.0%	+1.1%	+5.6%		+5.3%	+15.4%	−0.2%		+5.6%	+6.6%			
						D-D	D-D	D-D		D-D	D-D	4Q-4Q		D-D	D-D			

80

1971

Jan	4.14	6.18	7.36	8.74	8.03	95.88	.2754	$65.5b	-130	$309b	$133b		5.9%	+0.3	+0.2		3.56	37.87
Feb	3.72	6.14	7.08	8.39	7.74	96.75	.2750	66.0	-78	310	136	+11.6%	5.9	0.0	+0.2		3.56	38.74
Mar	3.71	5.94	7.21	8.46	7.52	100.31	.2755	66.4	-124	312	137		6.0	+0.3	0.0		3.56	38.87
Apr	4.15	6.00	7.25	8.45	7.31	103.95	.2753	66.7	+15	315	139		5.9	+0.3	+0.5		3.56	39.01
May	4.63	6.32	7.53	8.62	7.43	99.63	.2818	67.3	-65	318	140	+2.3	5.9	+0.5	+0.5	FY	3.56	40.52
Jun	4.91	6.38	7.64	8.75	7.53	98.70	.2860	67.7	-291	321	141		5.9	+0.5	+0.5	-23.0b	3.56	40.10
Jul	5.31	6.38	7.64	8.76	7.60	95.58	.2890	68.2	-639	324	144		6.0	+0.2	+0.2		3.56	40.95
Aug	5.56	6.27	7.59	8.76	7.70	99.03	.2942	68.4	-613	327	143	+3.2	6.1	+0.2	+0.2		3.56	42.73
Sep	5.55	6.05	7.44	8.59	7.69	98.34	.3016	68.8	-306	330	144		6.0	+0.2	0.0		3.56	42.02
Oct	5.20	5.92	7.39	8.48	7.63	94.23	.2996	68.6	-194	333	145		5.8	+0.2	+0.2		3.56	42.50
Nov	4.91	5.86	7.26	8.38	7.55	93.99	.3020	68.9	-147	336	146	+1.1	6.0	+0.2	+0.2		3.56	42.86
Dec	4.14	6.00	7.25	8.38	7.48	102.09	.3059	69.1	+56	338	148		6.0	+0.2	+0.2		3.56	43.48
						+10.8%	+11.5%	+6.3%		+10.8%	+13.7%	+4.5%		+3.3	+3.1		0	+16.1%
						D-D	D-D	D-D		D-D	D-D	4Q-4Q		D-D	D-D			

(Continued)

Table 6-2
(Continued)

1972	Financial Markets							Monetary Policy				Economic Indicators					Commodities	
	Fed Funds	Treas 30-yr	Corporates Aaa	Corporates Baa	30-yr Mtge	S&P 500	DM	Monetary Base	Free Rsvs	Bank Credit Loans	Bank Credit Inv	Real GDP	Unemp Rate	CPI - % Total	CPI - % Core	Budget	Prices - $ Oil	Prices - $ Gold
Jan	3.50	6.01	7.19	8.23	7.44	103.94	.3116	$69.9b	+185	$344b	$149b		5.8%	+0.2	+0.5		3.56	45.75
Feb	3.29	6.06	7.27	8.23	7.33	106.57	.3143	70.4	+119	346	150	+7.3%	5.7	+0.5	+0.2		3.56	48.26
Mar	3.83	6.06	7.24	8.24	7.30	107.20	.3157	70.8	+92	351	152		5.8	0.0	0.0		3.56	48.33
Apr	4.17	6.16	7.30	8.24	7.29	107.67	.3145	71.0	+39	356	153		5.7	+0.2	+0.5		3.56	49.03
May	4.27	6.07	7.30	8.23	7.37	109.53	.3149	71.5	+28	361	155	+9.8%	5.7	+0.2	+0.2	FY	3.56	54.62
Jun	4.46	6.01	7.23	8.20	7.37	107.14	.3174	71.8	+103	364	155		5.7	+0.2	+0.2	−23.4b	3.56	62.09
Jul	4.55	6.01	7.21	8.23	7.40	107.39	.3150	72.2	−45	371	156		5.6	+0.2	+0.2		3.56	65.67
Aug	4.80	5.94	7.19	8.19	7.40	111.09	.3134	72.6	−200	375	157	+3.9%	5.6	+0.2	+0.5		3.56	67.03
Sep	4.87	6.05	7.22	8.09	7.42	110.55	.3122	73.0	−329	379	159		5.5	+0.5	0.0		3.56	65.47
Oct	5.04	6.00	7.21	8.06	7.42	111.58	.3120	73.6	−344	385	159		5.6	+0.2	+0.2		3.56	64.86
Nov	5.06	5.79	7.12	7.99	7.43	116.67	.3132	74.4	−254	391	160	+6.7%	5.3	+0.5	0.0		3.56	62.91
Dec	5.33	5.96	7.08	7.93	7.44	118.05	.3123	75.2	−766	395	161		5.2	+0.2	+0.5		3.56	63.91
						+15.6%	+2.1%	+8.8%		+16.9%	+8.9%	+6.9%		+3.4	+3.0		0	+47.0%
						D-D	D-D	D-D		D-D	D-D	D-D	4Q-4Q	D-D			D-D	D-D

82

1973

Month																		
Jan	5.94	6.78	7.15	7.90	7.44	116.03	.3170	$75.9	−902b	$403b	$163b		4.9%	+0.5	0.0		3.56	65.14
Feb	6.58	6.88	7.22	7.97	7.44	111.68	.3529	76.2	−1396	415	161	+10.6	5.0	+0.7	+0.4		3.56	74.20
Mar	7.09	6.91	7.29	8.03	7.46	111.57	.3518	76.7	−1615	425	159		4.9	+0.9	+0.4		3.56	84.37
Apr	7.12	6.86	7.26	8.09	7.54	106.97	.3524	77.0	−1484	430	159		5.0	+0.7	+0.2		3.56	90.50
May	7.84	6.99	7.29	8.06	7.65	104.95	.3708	77.4	−1673	437	160	+4.7%	4.9	+0.5	+0.4	FY	3.56	101.96
Jun	8.49	7.06	7.37	8.13	7.73	104.26	.4115	77.8	−1547	443	161		4.9	+0.7	+0.2	−14.9b	3.56	120.12
Jul	10.40	7.29	7.45	8.24	8.05	108.22	.4305	78.5	−1515	450	162		4.8	0.0	+0.2		3.56	120.17
Aug	10.50	7.61	7.68	8.53	8.50	104.25	.4063	78.8	−1804	457	163	−2.1%	4.8	+1.8	+0.4		4.31	106.76
Sep	10.78	7.25	7.63	8.63	8.82	108.43	.4141	79.3	−1446	459	164		4.8	+0.4	+0.7		4.31	102.97
Oct	10.01	7.18	7.60	8.41	8.77	108.29	.4087	80.2	−1082	463	166	+3.9%	4.6	+0.9	+0.7		4.31	100.08
Nov	10.03	7.30	7.67	8.42	8.58	95.96	.3812	80.5	−1084	466	168		4.8	+0.7	+0.4		4.31	94.82
Dec	9.95	7.29	7.68	8.48	8.54	97.55	.3697	81.1	−953	470	168		4.9	+0.9	+0.4		4.31	106.72
						−17.4	18.4%	+7.9%		+19.1%	+4.9%	+4.2%		+8.9	+4.7		+21.1%	+67.0%
						D-D	D-D	D-D		D-D	D-D	4Q-4Q		D-D	D-D		D-D	D-D

(Continued)

Table 6-2
(*Continued*)

| 1974 | Financial Markets | | | | | | | Monetary Policy | | | | Economic Indicators | | | | | Commodities | |
	Fed Funds	Treas 30-yr	Corporates Aaa	Baa	30-yr Mtge	S&P 500	DM	Monetary Base	Free Rsvs	Bank Credit Loans	Inv	Real GDP	Unemp Rate	CPI - % Total	Core	Budget	Prices - $ Oil	Gold
Jan	9.65	7.47	7.83	8.48	8.54	96.57	.3635	$81.9b	−868	$475b	$170b		5.1%	+1.1	+0.4		10.11	129.19
Feb	8.97	7.46	7.85	8.53	8.46	96.22	.3739	82.3	−990	480	171	−3.4%	5.2	+1.1	+0.6		10.11	150.23
Mar	9.35	7.73	8.01	8.62	8.41	93.98	.3948	82.8	−1148	487	172		5.1	+1.1	+0.8		10.11	168.42
Apr	10.51	8.01	8.25	8.87	8.58	90.91	.4073	83.6	−1502	498	172		5.1	+0.6	+0.6		10.11	172.24
May	11.31	8.14	8.37	9.05	8.97	87.28	.3964	84.4	−1671	504	172	+1.2%	5.1	+1.0	+1.3	FY	10.11	163.27
Jun	11.93	8.10	8.47	9.27	9.09	86.00	.3925	84.9	−1448	510	172		5.4	+0.8	+1.0	−6.1b	10.11	154.10
Jul	12.92	8.26	8.72	9.48	9.28	79.31	.3886	85.4	−1560	516	172		5.5	+0.6	+1.0		10.11	142.98
Aug	12.01	8.60	9.00	9.77	9.59	72.15	.3756	86.0	−1447	521	173	−3.8%	5.5	+1.2	+1.4		10.11	154.64
Sep	11.34	8.59	9.24	10.18	9.96	63.54	.3767	86.4	−1334	524	172		5.9	+1.4	+1.0		10.11	151.77
Oct	10.06	8.37	9.27	10.48	9.98	73.90	.3878	86.5	−1090	526	172	−1.6%	6.0	+0.8	+1.0		11.16	158.78
Nov	9.45	7.98	8.89	10.60	9.79	69.97	.4044	87.0	−820	527	172		6.6	+1.0	+0.8		11.16	181.66
Dec	8.53	7.91	8.89	10.63	9.62	68.56	.4150	87.5	−290	528	174		7.2	+0.8	+0.8		11.16	183.85
						−29.7	+12.3%	+8.0%		+12.3%	+3.2%	−1.9%		+12.1	+11.3		+159%	+72.0%
						D-D	D-D	D-D		D-D	D-D	4Q-4Q		D-D	D-D		D-D	D-D

84

1975

Jan	7.13	7.88	8.83	10.81	9.43	76.98	.4274	$87.8b	-102	$528b	$174b		8.1%	+0.8	+0.6		11.16	176.27
Feb	6.24	7.71	8.62	10.65	9.11	81.57	.4391	88.2	+110	526	175	-4.7%	8.1	+0.6	+1.0		11.16	179.59
Mar	5.54	7.99	8.67	10.48	8.90	83.36	.4262	88.9	+138	525	179		8.6	+0.4	+0.4		11.16	178.16
Apr	5.49	8.36	8.95	10.58	8.82	87.30	.4203	89.1	+66	522	183	+3.0%	8.8	+0.4	+0.6		11.16	169.84
May	5.22	8.22	8.90	10.69	8.91	91.15	.4267	89.6	+102	520	187		9.0	+0.2	+0.4	FY	11.16	167.39
Jun	5.55	8.04	8.77	10.62	8.89	95.19	.4247	90.8	+1	520	191		8.8	+0.8	+0.6		11.16	164.24
Jul	6.10	8.17	8.84	10.55	8.89	88.75	.3894	91.4	-76	519	195	+6.9%	8.6	+0.9	+0.4	-53.2b	11.16	165.17
Aug	6.14	8.50	8.95	10.59	8.94	86.88	.3874	91.7	+33	518	198		8.4	+0.4	+0.4		11.16	163.00
Sep	6.24	8.57	8.95	10.61	9.13	83.87	.3777	92.1	-130	520	202		8.4	+0.7	+0.6		11.16	144.09
Oct	5.82	8.35	8.86	10.62	9.22	89.04	.3910	92.4	+93	522	204	+5.4%	8.4	+0.5	+0.6		11.16	142.76
Nov	5.22	8.28	8.78	10.56	9.15	91.24	.3809	93.4	+257	522	205		8.3	+0.7	+0.7		11.16	142.42
Dec	5.20	8.23	8.79	10.56	9.10	90.19	.3817	93.9	+162	526	207		8.2	+0.5	+0.5		11.16	139.30
						+31.5	-8.0%	+7.3%	-0.3%	+18.9%	+2.5%			+7.1	+6.7		0	-24.2%
						D-D	D-D	D-D	D-D	D-D	4Q-4Q			D-D	D-D		D-D	D-D

(Continued)

Table 6-2
(*Continued*)

1976	Financial Markets							Monetary Policy				Economic Indicators					Commodities	
	Fed Funds	Treas 20-yr	Corporates		30-yr Mtge	S&P 500	DM	Monetary Base	Free Rsvs	Bank Credit		Real GDP	Unemp Rate	CPI - %		Budget	Prices - $	
			Aaa	Baa						Loans	Inv			Total	Core		Oil	Gold
Jan	4.87	8.01	8.60	10.41	9.02	100.86	.3863	$94.3b	+182	$524b	$208b		7.9%	+0.4	+0.7		11.16	131.49
Feb	4.77	8.03	8.55	10.24	8.81	99.71	.3893	95.0	+158	526	209	+9.3%	7.7	+0.2	+0.5		12.03	131.07
Mar	4.84	7.97	8.52	10.12	8.76	102.77	.3938	95.8	+181	530	211		7.6	+0.2	+0.5		12.10	132.58
Apr	4.82	7.86	8.40	9.94	8.73	101.64	.3943	96.5	+121	531	214		7.7	+0.2	+0.4		12.17	127.94
May	5.29	8.13	8.58	9.86	8.77	100.18	.3857	97.3	+107	534	217	+3.0%	7.4	+0.5	+0.5	9mo	12.17	126.94
Jun	5.48	8.03	8.62	9.89	8.85	104.28	.3883	97.7	+107	539	218		7.6	+0.5	+0.4	-73.7b	12.17	125.71
Jul	5.31	8.00	8.56	9.82	8.93	103.44	.3933	98.2	+126	540	218		7.8	+0.5	+0.7		12.17	117.76
Aug	5.29	7.91	8.45	9.64	9.00	102.91	.3956	98.9	+135	544	220	+1.9%	7.8	+0.5	+0.5	3mo	12.17	109.33
Sep	5.25	7.78	8.38	9.40	8.98	105.24	.4107	99.5	+170	547	221		7.6	+0.5	+0.5	-14.7b	13.90	114.15
Oct	5.02	7.70	8.32	9.29	8.93	102.90	.4167	100.1	+157	553	224		7.7	+0.5	+0.5		13.90	116.14
Nov	4.95	7.64	8.25	9.23	8.81	102.10	.4158	100.9	+208	557	226	+2.9%	7.8	+0.3	+0.3		13.90	130.48
Dec	4.65	7.30	7.98	9.12	8.79	107.46	.4237	101.5	+234	562	229		7.8	+0.5	+0.3		13.90	133.88
						+19.1%	+11.0%	+8.1%		+6.8%	+10.6%	+4.2%		+5.0	+6.1		+24.6%	-3.9%
						D-D	D-D	D-D		D-D	D-D	4Q-4Q		D-D	D-D		D-D	D-D

86

1977

1977																	
Jan	4.61	7.59	7.96	9.08	8.72	102.03	.4154	$102.2b	+208	$566b	$229b		7.5%	+0.5	+0.7		13.90	132.26
Feb	4.68	7.75	8.04	9.12	8.67	99.82	.4186	102.7	+139	572	231	+4.9%	7.6	+1.0	+0.7		13.90	136.29
Mar	4.69	7.80	8.10	9.12	8.69	98.42	.4183	103.3	+48	579	233		7.4	+0.5	+0.5		13.90	148.22
Apr	4.73	7.73	8.04	9.07	8.75	98.44	.4248	104.1	+133	585	234		7.2	+0.7	+0.5		13.90	149.16
May	5.35	7.80	8.05	9.01	8.82	96.12	.4239	104.6	+31	592	236	+8.1%	7.0	+0.3	+0.5		13.90	146.60
Jun	5.39	7.64	7.95	8.91	8.86	100.48	.4272	105.2	-62	598	237		7.2	+0.5	+0.7		13.90	140.77
Jul	5.42	7.64	7.94	8.87	8.94	98.85	.4366	106.4	+12	605	237		6.9	+0.5	+0.3		13.90	143.39
Aug	5.90	7.68	7.98	8.82	8.94	96.77	.4314	107.2	-746	614	237	+7.4%	7.0	+0.5	+0.5	FY	14.85	144.95
Sep	6.14	7.64	7.92	8.80	8.90	96.53	.4331	107.9	-304	620	236		6.8	+0.3	+0.5	-53.7b	14.85	149.52
Oct	6.47	7.77	8.04	8.89	8.91	92.34	.4442	108.8	-983	627	236		6.8	+0.5	+0.3		14.85	158.86
Nov	6.51	7.85	8.08	8.95	8.92	94.83	.4500	109.6	-527	635	236	0.0%	6.8	+0.6	+0.5		14.85	162.10
Dec	6.56	7.94	8.19	8.99	8.96	95.10	.4767	110.3	-324	640	236		6.4	+0.5	+0.6		14.85	160.45
						-11.5	+12.5%	+8.7%		+13.8%	+3.4%	+5.0%		+6.7	+6.5		+6.8%	+19.8%
						D-D	D-D	D-D		D-D	D-D	4Q-4Q		D-D	D-D		D-D	D-D

(Continued)

Table 6-2
(*Continued*)

| 1978 | Financial Markets | | | | | | | Monetary Policy | | | | Economic Indicators | | | | | Commodities | |
	Fed Funds	Treas 30-yr	Corporates Aaa	Corporates Baa	30-yr Mtge	S&P 500	DM	Monetary Base	Free Rsvs	Bank Credit Loans	Bank Credit Inv	Real GDP	Unemp Rate	CPI - % Total	CPI - % Core	Budget	Prices - $ Oil	Prices - $ Gold
Jan	6.70	8.18	8.41	9.17	9.02	89.25	.4735	$111.4b	–185	$649b	$236b		6.4%	+0.6	+0.6	6.70	14.85	173.17
Feb	6.78	8.25	8.47	9.20	9.16	87.04	.4960	112.5	–113	656	238	+1.3%	6.3	+0.5	+0.5	6.78	14.85	178.15
Mar																		
Apr																		
May																		
Jun																		
Jul																		
Aug																		
Sep																		
Oct																		
Nov																		
Dec																		

7

G. WILLIAM MILLER
(MARCH 8, 1978–AUGUST 6, 1979)

In contrast to Arthur Burns, who was well known prior to his appointment as Fed chairman, hardly anything was known of G. William Miller. As a matter of fact, when it came over the tape that President Carter had appointed Miller, quite a few people wondered why. They thought he had appointed William E. Miller, the failed vice-presidential candidate from 1964; and that hardly seemed like sufficient credentials to be appointed as Fed chairman. Of course, this was the wrong Miller.

The Miller who was appointed was the chief executive officer and chairman of Textron, was a director of the Federal Reserve Bank of Boston, and was on the board of several corporations. He may have been important in some corporate circles, but he was totally unknown in the economic and financial world. Given all of the problems that the economy and the Fed faced at that time, it was shocking that a relative unknown in monetary policy circles would be chosen for such an important position at such an important time. He was perceived as the wrong person for the wrong position at the wrong time.

Miller's chairmanship ran from March 8, 1978, to August 6, 1979, and during this period he tried to run the Fed as if he were still in charge of a corporation. That did not go over well with other Board members who, in many cases, had more distinguished careers, and in almost all cases were far more knowledgeable about monetary policy. He became famous in financial circles for taking ash trays out of the Board's meeting room without consulting the other members—some of whom were smokers.

In a cruel twist of fate, Miller passed away at the age of 81 from idiopathic pulmonary fibrosis, a relatively rare hardening and deterioration of the lungs. He was a non-smoker who had been in good health his entire life until the lung disease was diagnosed in June 2004. He passed away on March 17, 2006.

Unfortunately, public figures are often remembered for things said or done that have little to do with their performance. In the case of Miller, he was known for being a political appointee with few credentials and for removing ash trays from FOMC meetings without asking other members of the committee if it was all right to do so. This was followed by a confrontation over his unilateral nonsmoking decision with the highly regarded and mild-mannered Henry Wallach, a fellow Board member and previously a prominent professor at Yale University.

The feeling of many FOMC members was that Miller had overstepped his bounds by making a unilateral decision without canvassing members of the committee. Miller, thinking about his bygone days as a CEO of a large corporation, probably never realized this would create so much bad blood. His colleagues at the Fed surely did not believe that he could walk on water. Moreover, with so much at stake in the monetary policy arena, this was not a good time to have backbiting among FOMC members on nonpolicy issues.

Although Miller's accomplishments at the Fed proved to be limited, he ended up smelling like a rose compared with Burns's tenure, where virtually everything came out on the negative side. Miller moved policy in the right direction, and was aggressive by past standards. The United States was fortunate to have Miller at the helm for eighteen months rather than Burns. This may not be much of a legacy for Miller, especially because it would have been far better to have had Volcker in charge during these eighteen months. Nevertheless, he deserves both more attention and better treatment from those analysts who tended to skip over Miller in the history of Fed chairmen and who view him as not much more than a footnote. He came on the scene at a crossroads period for monetary policy, and he inherited a deteriorating situation. Miller took moderate steps towards combating inflation; Paul Volcker took giant steps.

Interestingly, despite his problems and shortcomings, Miller was treated by Congress and the executive branch with respect. It was obvious that the respect was primarily for his position as Fed chairman. In any case, they did not embarrass him or talk down to him. As a matter of fact, not only was he treated with a reasonable degree of deference, but upon leaving the Federal Reserve, he was appointed secretary of the Treasury by President Jimmy Carter and confirmed by the Senate. In the wacky world of politics, he achieved the special distinction of being the head of both the Treasury and the Federal Reserve despite a lack of job qualifications. Volcker, on the other hand, never headed the Treasury, although he was especially well qualified for that job.

Let us turn to some of the specifics that confronted Miller when he took over as Fed chairman. In March 1978, the economy had just finished a half year with little economic growth and an inflation rate (CPI) of about 6.5 percent and heading higher. With the funds rate at roughly 6.75 percent, it was clear that Miller had to do something to take the steam out of the high and rising inflation rate without doing more damage to economic growth.

During his tour of duty of almost one and one-half years, he steadily advanced the funds target—by July 1979 it stood at 10.5 percent—which resulted in some analysts dubbing him an inflation fighter. Yet the fed funds rate is not the only measurement of monetary ease or tightness, and in this case, the increase in the funds target overstated the degree of anti-inflation medicine that he provided.

In the tables at the end of the chapter, the data for 1978 showed an increase in the monetary base of 9.2 percent and an increase in bank loans of 16.8 percent. These are huge amounts by any standard and do not suggest that monetary policy was anywhere near as restrictive as the funds rate suggested. In addition, real economic growth was clearly excessive and unsustainable, and the same could be said for the CPI performance. From the fourth quarter of 1977 to the fourth quarter of 1978, real growth was 6.7 percent, and it was little wonder that the CPI increase for 1978 was a clearly excessive 9.0 percent. Even the core CPI (excluding food and energy) rose 8.5 percent for the year. Gold prices in 1978 jumped by 29.5 percent, and one can argue that much of this jump was a belief on the part of investors that the work on combating inflation was far from successful. Thus, the message in the economic and financial data, and in market reactions, was that Miller's anti-inflation policy was inadequate.

Of course, one could argue that when he came into office, he was continuing the approach of a rising fed funds rate that the monetary policy expert Arthur Burns had followed. How did Miller know as a monetary policy neophyte that the Burns anti-inflation approach was inadequate and too narrow in scope? As Chairman Bernanke has found out, also the hard way, if you decide to follow the policy approach of your predecessor, who is viewed by many as an icon, in an effort to make the public and market participants feel comfortable with you, it can have some dangerous consequences. If a previous chairman was an icon and could walk on water, what was wrong with following the policy of your predecessor?

Unfortunately, by the time that Miller left office in August 1979, increases in the CPI had hardly skipped a beat, and the twelve-month performance was approaching 12 percent. Of course, it was only a matter of time before a hyper rate of inflation finally took its toll on real economic growth. While it had surged for several quarters in 1978, GDP growth had declined to a token rate of advance by the time Miller left office.

The real story here is that once inflation and inflation expectations become embedded, it is extremely difficult to turn matters around. What, on the surface, seemed like a very large amount of firming during his short tenure proved to be inadequate. If the Fed had acted more quickly and firmly in raising its funds target, and had used other policy tools such as increases in reserve requirements, Miller no doubt would have been more successful in moderating inflation. However, he also probably would have put the economy back into a tailspin before he left office. Actually, what happened was that by the second quarter of 1980, the economy had moved into a recession.

It is interesting to note that one of the most famous academic economists (Arthur Burns) had been chairman of the Fed for eight years, had done a miserable job, and had turned over massive problems to his successor (G. William Miller), who lacked the background and expertise to be the head of a central bank and handle these problems. Yet in a Fed fraught with considerable infighting, and

Table 7-1
G. William Miller, Chairman—Federal Reserve Board of Governors March 8, 1978–August 6, 1979

| | Financial Markets | | | | | | | Monetary Policy | | | | | Economic Indicators | | | | Commodities | |
| | | | Corporates | | | | | | | Bank Credit | | | | | CPI - % | | Prices - $ | |
1978	Fed Funds	Treas 30-yr	Aaa	Baa	30-yr Mtge	S&P 500	DM	Monetary Base	Free Rsvs	Loans	Inv	Real GDP	Unemp Rate	Total	Core	Budget	Oil	Gold
Jan																		
Feb																		
Mar	6.79	8.23	8.47	9.22	9.20	89.21	.5004	112.8b	-82	665	239		6.3	+0.6	+0.6		14.85	183.66
Apr	6.89	8.34	8.56	9.32	9.36	96.83	.4822	113.4	-366	674	240		6.1	+0.8	+0.8		14.85	175.27
May	7.36	8.43	8.69	9.49	9.58	97.24	.4783	114.4	-901	685	241	+16.7	6.0	+0.9	+0.6		14.85	176.30
Jun	7.60	8.50	8.76	9.60	9.71	95.53	.4826	115.4	-796	694	242		5.9	+0.8	+0.8		14.85	183.75
Jul	7.81	8.65	8.88	9.60	9.74	100.68	.4907	116.3	-977	705	243		6.2	+0.8	+0.6		14.85	188.72
Aug	8.04	8.47	8.69	9.48	9.78	103.29	.5029	116.9	-783	711	243	+4.0%	5.9	+0.6	+0.8	FY	14.85	206.30
Sep	8.45	8.47	8.69	9.42	9.76	102.54	.5158	118.1	-676	720	244		6.0	+0.9	+0.9	-59.2b	14.85	212.07
Oct	8.96	8.67	8.69	9.59	9.86	93.15	.5701	119.0	-892	729	244	+5.4%	5.8	+0.9	+0.7		14.85	227.39
Nov	9.76	8.75	9.03	9.83	10.11	94.70	.5187	119.7	-295	740	243		5.9	+0.6	+0.6		14.85	206.07
Dec	10.03	8.88	9.16	9.94	10.35	96.11	.5495	120.4	-502	747	242		6.0	+0.6	+0.6		14.85	207.83
						+1.1%	+15.3%	+9.2%		+16.8%	+2.5%	+6.7%		+9.0	+8.5		0	+29.5%
						D-D	D-D	D-D		D-D	D-D	4Q-4Q		D-D	D-D		D-D	D-D

Table 7-1
(Continued)

1979	Financial Markets							Monetary Policy				Economic Indicators					Commodities	
	Fed Funds	Treas 30-yr	Corporates Aaa	Baa	30-yr Mtge	S&P 500	DM	Monetary Base	Free Rsvs	Bank Credit Loans	Inv	Real GDP	Unemp Rate	CPI - % Total	Core	Budget	Prices - $ Oil	Gold
Jan	10.07	8.94	9.25	10.13	10.39	99.93	.5339	121.3b	−683	758	246		5.9	+0.9	+0.7		14.85	227.27
Feb	10.06	9.00	9.26	10.08	10.41	96.28	.5399	121.5	−650	766	246	+0.8%	5.9	+1.0	+1.0		15.85	245.67
Mar	10.09	9.03	9.37	10.26	10.43	101.59	.5355	122.1	−713	776	248		5.8	+1.0	+0.9		15.85	242.04
Apr	10.01	9.08	9.38	10.33	10.50	101.76	.5266	122.8	−608	787	250	+0.4%	5.8	+1.0	+0.7		15.85	239.16
May	10.24	9.19	9.50	10.47	10.69	99.08	.5238	123.5	−1450	797	251		5.6	+1.1	+0.7		18.10	257.61
Jun	10.29	8.92	9.29	10.38	11.04	102.91	.5444	124.6	−1005	808	251		5.7	+1.1	+0.7		19.10	279.06
Jul	10.47	8.93	9.20	10.29	11.09	103.81	.5454	125.8	−778	819	252		5.7	+1.1	+0.8		21.75	294.73
Aug	10.94	8.98	9.23	10.35	11.09	109.32	.5480	127.1	−684	827	253	+2.9%	6.0	+1.0	+1.1		26.50	300.81
Sep																		
Oct																		
Nov																		
Dec																		

with a chairman who was not well respected by other senior members, Miller did a far better job than his predecessor.

Despite Miller's lack of credentials, in August 1979 he was appointed by President Carter to be Secretary of the Treasury, replacing Michael Blumenthal. He served in that position until January 1981, and left office when Carter was defeated for the presidency by Ronald Reagan. The state of the economy surely had something to do with the political rout of Jimmy Carter, and Miller had to shoulder part of the blame.

8

PAUL VOLCKER
(AUGUST 6, 1979–AUGUST 11, 1987)

Paul Volcker became chairman of the Federal Reserve in 1979, but as early as the 1960s, many in the financial community could see this appointment coming. It was as if he were preordained for that job. Every career decision he made seemed to move him along the path towards the top position at the Fed. This made him unique among all Fed chairmen, none of whom had either the background or the expertise to prepare them for the job.

William Martin had been a former chairman of the New York Stock Exchange; Arthur Burns was an academic whose primary expertise was business cycles; G. William Miller was a businessman; Alan Greenspan had a strong economics background in the private sector; and Ben Bernanke was an academic with strong theoretical credentials in the monetary sphere. All had solid backgrounds in specific areas, but not on a broad basis. An optimum background for being Fed chairman requires more than just being an expert in one or a few areas. Volcker more than met all the requirements needed to be the head of the most powerful central bank in the world.

If you think that this is an overstatement, think again. Volcker's academic background was Princeton and Harvard, he had been an economist at the New York Federal Reserve Bank and at Chase Manhattan Bank, he had held a position at the U.S. Treasury as director of financial analysis, and later as deputy-undersecretary for monetary affairs. Then he returned to Chase Manhattan Bank as vice-president and director of planning, went back to the Treasury as undersecretary for international monetary affairs, and returned to the New York Federal Reserve Bank as president. Thus, three institutions dominated his background, and in each case, when he returned to an organization, it was in a more responsible position, which added to his reputation and knowledge. Nor did he neglect the academic side during his meteoric rise in the financial world. In 1975, he became a senior fellow in the Woodrow Wilson School of Public and International Affairs at Princeton. Again, he returned to familiar ground, but at a much higher and more prestigious level.

It is important to go into the details of Volcker's background because, when he took over the Fed in 1979, financial conditions and the U.S. economy were both in bad shape. This was no time for on-the-job training; he had to hit the ground running. In the last half century, no chairman inherited problems as serious as Volcker faced when he took office in 1979. He was clearly the right man at the right time for the Federal Reserve job.

The problems Volcker inherited were far worse than any that had arisen in the post-World War II period. Thus, it is difficult to compare his performance with those of other Fed chairmen. He had many major policy decisions to make during his eight years in office, as one crisis was quickly followed by another, and situations arose whereby trying to alleviate the problems in one area added to the problems in other areas. For those who have forgotten, or were not around at the time, Volcker had to deal with inflation, recessions, international crises, dollar crises, the soundness of the U.S. financial system, and painfully high interest rates. He had little time to consider such things as trying to attain optimum real growth rates and optimum rates of inflation. If this was not enough to be concerned about, he also had to handle some very difficult political problems, both inside and outside the Fed, which appear to have hastened his return to the private sector in 1987.

The results of many of the decisions Volcker had to make when he was chairman were painful for many Americans, and there were those who were calling for his head. But history has been kinder to him as it became clear that the pain suffered by many when he was in office was a major positive for the United States in later years. In some ways, his story is akin to how the public felt about Harry Truman when he was president, and how they view him after many decades have passed.

BREAKING THE BACK OF EMBEDDED INFLATION

In the first three years of Paul Volcker's eight-year chairmanship, fighting inflation was the main battle. This was a tough-love period. Interest rates of almost all types and all maturities traded at double-digit levels, and, as one might expect, it wreaked havoc on the economy. For example, in August 1979 when Volcker took over at the Fed, the unemployment rate was 6 percent; by August 1982, it was 9.8 percent, and four months later it peaked at 10.8 percent.

Of all the economic indicators, the one that has the most meaning to the man on the street is the unemployment rate. There is nothing academic or conceptual about this number. It signifies real-world pain, and no official who has helped bring about a double-digit rate of unemployment can last long in his job if he does not help alleviate the problem. The key here was to do enough in roughly three years to break the back of embedded inflation, so that in the following years a more accommodative monetary policy would lead to an economic recovery. Volcker was successful in that regard, although it should be pointed out that while the Fed's policy stance was more accommodative in the last five years of his term, it was not on the easy side.

When Volcker took over at the Fed, CPI increases had entered double-digit land. Over the previous twelve months, the CPI had risen to 11.8 percent. Worse yet, the rate of advance was increasing. By March 1980, the CPI growth rate was 14.6 percent—the peak for the cycle. In August 1979, the funds rate was 10.9 percent and was moving higher. Yet, it was clear that the very high Fed funds rate was nowhere near high enough to quell inflation pressures. Part of the problem was that these pressures were, to a considerable extent, outside of the direct control of the Fed. Thus, in order to take the steam out of inflation, and with no help from other sources, the Fed had to push up funds rate to shockingly high levels. By April 1980, the average Fed funds rate was 17.6 percent.

Despite a very noticeable decline in real economic growth, the Fed was firming policy when Volcker took office in August 1979. In the first quarter of that year, the economy had slowed significantly since the second quarter of 1978 and showed virtually no growth. In early 1979, the unemployment rate had leveled off at about 6 percent, and based on the lack of economic growth in late 1978 and early 1979, it was only a matter of time before the rate would begin to increase. Moreover, because it was clear that Volcker would need to tighten monetary policy much more aggressively than what had previously occurred, this would add to the increase in the unemployment rate. What ultimately occurred was that a 6 percent unemployment rate in August 1979 increased to 7.2 percent by the end of 1980, to 8.5 percent by the end of 1981, and to 10.8 percent by the end of 1982. In August 1979, the number unemployed was 6.3 million; by the end of 1982 it was 12.1 million. These are numbers that can bring about a lynch mob.

Of all the early speeches and testimonies that Volcker made immediately after he took the reins at the Fed, the one that best sets out his objectives, how he wanted to achieve them, and what others needed to do to help him, was his testimony before the Joint Economic Committee of Congress on October 17, 1979. He had been in office for only a little over two months when he made the following comments:

> An entire generation of young adults has grown up since the mid-1960s knowing only inflation, indeed inflation that has seemed to accelerate inexorably. In the circumstances, it is hardly surprising that many citizens have begun to wonder whether it is realistic to anticipate a return to general price stability and have begun to change their behavior accordingly. Inflation feeds in part on itself, so part of the job of returning to a more stable and more productive economy must be to break the grip of inflationary expectations.
>
> The Federal Reserve actions announced on October 6 were part of a continuing effort to maintain control over money and credit expansion. Our basic targets were not changed, But the new measures, which involved among other things a change in operating procedures, should provide added assurance that those objectives will be reached. Above all, the new measures should make abundantly clear our unwillingness to finance a continuing inflation process. . . .

The doubts about the dollar in exchange markets in recent months have been one factor increasing uncertainties faced by businessmen and consumers alike. Given the dollar's central position in the international financial system, we must recognize that its external value is particularly sensitive to perceptions and expectations about economic policy and especially to concern about our ability to deal with inflation. I see no fundamental conflict, indeed no meaningful "trade-off" between our domestic and international economic objectives in this respect. . . .

Finally, we should not rely on monetary policy alone, critical as disciplined monetary policy is, to solve our economic problems. We also need a sustained, disciplined fiscal policy; we need an effective energy policy, commanding the support of all segments of our society, that will put us more surely in control of our destiny; we need regulatory and tax policies that will help stimulate investments, cut costs, and increase productivity; and we need international cooperation and understanding.

The previous statement is not just important for what Volcker said, but how he said it. The statements were clear, concise, and straightforward. This was not Fed-speak; there were no conundrums and no transparency problems. There was no reference to theory and concepts, and there was no attempt to dazzle the audience with his intellect or his background in economics. It is hard to imagine any of the other Fed chairman, beginning with Burns, making a similar statement and then backing it up.

Equally important with respect to this testimony is that it set out publicly Volcker's objectives for his term as chairman. It was something his performance could be measured against. In this regard, he helped break the back of hyper-inflation, but he did not bring inflation under control. Part of the reason he fell short was not of his doing. He did not get the help on the budget side that he hoped for, and international financial events became a major complicating force. Nor did he get the full support of many inside the government or inside the Fed. He stepped on a lot of toes, and he paid a price.

As for what was happening on the international side when Volcker took office, there appeared in the September 1979 *Federal Reserve Bulletin*, a very enlightening article entitled "Treasury and Federal Reserve Foreign Exchange Operations." Realize that this article (the 35th joint report published by the Treasury and the Fed) is about as factual as one can get, and, if anything, it understates rather than overstates the problems. It was bad enough for Volcker to have to confront domestic problems when he took office, but the international situation during the first seven months of 1979 made circumstances far worse. The following are quotes from the article:

Market participants and policymakers had to contend with new shocks to the international economy. A shortfall in world oil supplies emerged abruptly in early 1979, following the political upheavals in Iran, which temporarily cut off crude oil exports from that country. The ensuing scramble for spot crude pushed spot market prices to astronomical highs and prompted individual members of the Organization of Petroleum Exporting Countries to jack up their posted prices.

The surge in world oil prices aggravated inflation pressures generally, since it came at a time when a number of important international commodity prices were also advancing. The economies of Japan and continental Western Europe were no longer shielded from these price increases as they had been earlier when their currencies were appreciating against the dollar. Consequently, wholesale and consumer prices abroad jumped sharply. Since inflation had also accelerated in the United States, this jump raised concern over the possibility of a renewed worldwide price spiral such as that in the early 1970s. . . .

In these highly unstable market conditions, the U.S. authorities intervened forcefully to check the decline [in the dollar]. . . . Nevertheless, . . . [t]he dollar came under repeated bouts of selling pressure, especially following the President's energy speech on July 15 and over subsequent days during which the President made several changes in the Cabinet.

The U.S. authorities intervened vigorously in German marks to head off a possible generalized decline of the dollar, which might exacerbate inflationary pressures in the United States. Those operations, conducted both in New York and in the overnight markets in the Far East, were coordinated with those of the German Federal Bank in Frankfurt and helped to blunt the immediate pressures on the dollar.

Volcker's successes accrued because he was a realist and a pragmatist. Say what you have to say, and do what you have to do, to make monetary policy work. He was not a monetarist, but he was smart enough to realize that there are certain things that work at certain times, and hitching his policy train to a monetarist approach was the one chance he had to break the back of inflation.

Under Volcker, the Fed began targeting the growth rate of the monetary aggregates, indicating that it was excessive money supply growth that was a driving force in inflation. What happens to interest rates was considered a by-product of supply-and-demand factors, therefore the rates were not dominated by the Fed. Let the rates go where the markets take them, and in the case of the funds rate and the prime loan rate, they touched 21 percent, and the 30-year mortgage rate moved up over 18 percent. How many public officials, let alone a Fed chairman, would have had the combination of guts and smarts to pull this off?

Interestingly, this was a period when there were many academics who considered themselves monetarists, who gave considerable credibility to Volcker and his policies. Help from any source was of paramount importance so long as it would contribute toward maintaining the ultratight monetary policy course that was needed to fight inflation.

Without getting into the academic side of the appropriateness of such a policy approach, one can argue that when there is excessive inflation or deflation, and the problem seems to be embedded and not due to just cyclical considerations, a monetarist approach, in combination with the use of other tools—such as reserve requirements and margin requirements on stocks—makes sense. Let interest rates rise or fall where they may because in periods of undue inflation or deflation, how does the central bank know what the proper interest rates should be?

When Volcker took office in August 1979, the main policy tool the Fed used was targeting the federal funds rate (the overnight rate at which banks buy and sell reserves). The problem here was that the funds rate target the Fed had chosen, while high from a historical basis, was unduly low based on what was needed to quell inflation.

In October 1979, the funds rate was allowed to move much more freely and the Fed concentrated on containing the growth of the money supply, irrespective of where it took the funds rate. In other words, the funds rate was dominated by basic supply and demand factors and not just a Federal Reserve decision (or guess) on what the proper level should be. When this change occurred, the funds rate exploded. Along with this change in policy approach came large amounts of interest rate volatility, not only in the funds market, but in other debt markets as well.

The monetary aggregate targeting approach lasted until October 1982, when its importance was downgraded by the Fed. However, monetary aggregates were still significant, in part because Congress expected the Fed to report to it about monetary aggregate growth rates and desirable targets. In hindsight, using monetary aggregate targeting had served a useful purpose in holding down inflation by making money less available and keeping interest rates higher than otherwise would have been the case. However, a continuation of such an approach ran the risk of an unacceptable weakening of the economy and the political problems that would create.

From then on, monetary aggregate targeting lost importance as a policy tool and the Fed returned to targeting the federal funds rate. In October 1986, targeting monetary aggregate growth rates had moved into the background of policy decision making. By that time, the fed funds rate stood at a relatively reasonable 6 percent, and embedded inflation had moderated considerably. Thus, Federal funds rate targeting became dominant once the need for a very tight monetary policy and ultrahigh interest rates were no longer necessary.

What a funds-rate-volatility ride it was from October 1979 to October 1986, when controlling the monetary aggregates was a dominant factor in policy considerations. A look at the monthly averages in the tables at the end of the chapter show that two factors dominated Fed funds rates during this period: first, they fluctuated substantially and in some cases wildly; and second, all of this took place in period of ultrahigh interest rates that might not have been politically attainable if the Fed had set a target rather than letting market forces set the rate.

As a matter of fact, from October 1979 through September 1982, there wasn't a single month when the funds rate averaged less than 10 percent. Then, from October 1982 to early 1986, the funds rate generally stayed above 8 percent, although the degree of volatility was considerably less than it what was from October 1979 to September 1982. This monetarist approach, which was in full bloom for three years, and in partial bloom for four years, had a great deal to do with bringing inflation under control, although there were other things that were involved.

In looking at the "Flavor of the Times" appendix, notice that from 1974 to 1982, labor strikes, contracts that lasted several years, and generous and extended wage increases were among the important factors that contributed to the problem of embedded inflation. In April 1974, the steel workers gained a pattern-setting three-year pact with a 40 percent increase in wages and benefits. Increases of similar magnitude and duration continued into the early 1980s. For example, in August 1980, the AT&T labor contract provided for a 34.5 percent pay boost over three years; the increase assumed a 9.5 percent rise in the CPI. In October 1980, federal employees received a 9.1 percent general pay boost in addition to step increases.

In 1981 and the first three quarters of 1982, the Fed funds rate was solidly at double-digit levels, and it was only a matter of time before the economy slipped into a recession. By the fourth quarter of 1982, the unemployment rate had increased to an economic and politically unacceptable rate of 10.8 percent. Volcker could not ignore these downward cyclical pressures, and, fortunately for him, a meaningful reduction in inflation in 1982 allowed the Fed to move to a somewhat less restrictive monetary policy.

Of course, everything is relative. It was not until late 1984 before the Fed funds rate regularly broke below a double-digit level. As a matter of fact, in September 1984, the average funds rate level was still an ultrahigh 11.30 percent. Then, the Fed began to guide the funds rate lower, and it would not return to an ultrahigh level during the rest of Volcker's term, which ended in August 1987. From 1985 through Volcker's departure from the Fed in August 1987, he gradually took his foot off the policy brake, and by August 1987, the funds rate averaged a mere 6.73 percent.

One might presume, based on this description, that economic and financial events in the United States and around the world from early 1985 through August 1987 were favorable enough that Volcker could bring monetary policy back to something that one might consider more normal and relatively sustainable. However, conditions were far from favorable, and one can argue that the return to a more moderate policy came about despite a rash of problems and swings in circumstances that Volcker and the Fed encountered during this period.

As an aside, Greenspan also guided a funds rate surge fairly early in his term as chairman. For seven months—from January 1990 through July 1990—the funds rate averaged over 9 percent. This proved to be unfortunate, because the rates were excessively high and monetary policy unduly restrictive, and while inflation was a problem, it was a small-potatoes problem compared with what Volcker had encountered in the 1979–1981 period. Fortunately, Greenspan and the Fed realized their policy mistake in a relatively timely manner, and by late 1992, the Fed had pushed down its funds rate target to 3 percent. It stayed at 3 percent through early 1994, when it began to rise again.

VOLCKER TAKES HIS FOOT OFF THE BRAKES

From early 1985 through mid-1987, the Griggs & Santow Report often addressed the problems Paul Volcker encountered in trying to maintain the gains that he and the Fed had made against inflation, while at the same time dealing with other difficulties. The quotes are rather detailed, but their purpose is to convey the complex nature of the crises he confronted, many aspects of which were not under his control or direct influence.

In this regard, one should notice that Volcker's job was complicated by international economic and financial considerations, especially in the foreign exchange market. In addition to fixed exchange rate bands, some governments (including our own) had policies which did not allow their currencies to trade where underlying economic forces suggested they should. This led to problems that the Fed could not ignore and had considerable difficulty combating.

Further, a central bank is not primarily responsible for its country's currency. Rather, it is the treasury or the finance ministry that establishes overall currency policies, which in turn conveys to the heads of the various central banks when to intervene in the foreign exchange market and what is to be achieved. It is not unusual for a treasury secretary or finance minister not to see eye-to-eye with the central bank with regard to monetary policies and objectives. Volcker had problems in the international sphere throughout his term at the Fed; Alan Greenspan also faced some similar problems, but they were not of the magnitude that would significantly influence monetary policy. International considerations played a smaller role in policy deliberations in the early stages of Ben Bernanke's chairmanship.

Finally, one advantage in using quotes from past Griggs & Santow Reports is that there is little chance of employing revisionist history. The comments were written as events unfolded, and they expressed analyses and opinions that were as close to real time as possible. That does not mean these analyses were always correct, but they surely were timely. This approach is much different from trying to recollect events that occurred several decades ago; such recollections often make the authors appear more discerning than was actually the case.

February 4, 1985: In the last two months or so, monetary policy may have been as accommodative as it has been since Paul Volcker became Chairman. The objective evidence for such a view includes the recent rapid growth in total reserves and in all the monetary aggregates, the low level of borrowing at the discount window, the significant and sustained level of free reserves and, up until the last few days, a determination to err on the easy side.

March 4, 1985: The behavior of the U.S. dollar has become a critical factor in the outlook for the U.S. economy, for the behavior of interest rates and, without exaggeration, for the fortunes of the entire world. This is by no means a new perception, but it seems to be something of a revelation to many in the United States. It is certainly a new consideration for our money and capital markets. . . . There is no evidence that the recent weakness of the

dollar reflects a fundamental change in the supply/demand situation. . . .
The dollar gained its strength from a demand/supply relationship which
produced a dollar shortage.

April 22, 1985: In the last month or two . . . while the economy has
clearly been the major concern, and remains so, the behavior of the monetary aggregates, which was so important throughout the second half of
1984, appears to have been displaced from its number two spot by concerns
about domestic financial problems. This shifting in relative position . . .
is a product of the well-publicized problems among financial institutions.

May 28, 1985: The Fed's rationale (for cutting the discount rate) was not
the weak behavior of the overall economy but rather the weakness of a
particular sector. In the Fed's words, its concern is that the output of the
"industrial sector" had been relatively unchanged for some time. This rep-
resents a striking departure from the usual Fed focus in formulating policy.

September 16, 1985: Fed policy in 1985 has had two characteristics
which distinguish it from 1984—first, policy this year is more stable and
second, it is more accommodative. These differences are no accident. Using
20/20 hindsight, Fed policy seemed tighter than it should have been in the
first half of 1984, and only a substantial and rapid decline in interest rates
in the second half avoided a recession. Perhaps because of that experience,
the Fed has behaved differently this year. There seems, for example, to be a
clear desire this year to err on the accommodative side, irrespective of what
technique one uses to measure the degree of accommodation.

September 30, 1985: The G-5 international package announced a week
ago appears to have had two primary purposes—to head off highly restrictive
(and unwise) legislation in Congress and to move the dollar lower. While the
two are clearly related, it would appear that it is the restrictive legislation that
was the most pressing. After all, the dollar had been much higher earlier in
the year and yet no international package had been forthcoming.

December 30, 1985: In the second half of 1985, the Fed's accommodative
policy was continued, with only slight adjustments. However, the (Treasury)
market responded positively to the modest pace of the economic recovery, the
failure of inflation to accelerate, the G-5 announcement which seemed to
require lower interest rates, the prospect of action to reduce the budget deficit,
the expectation of another cut in the discount rate and, most fundamentally,
by the market's more favorable reassessment of the long-term inflation
outlook. In this latter regard, the market has for some years sustained a real
rate of return that contemplated a much higher rate of inflation than the
economy was actually experiencing.

March 16, 1986: The relationship between the U.S. dollar and other
currencies has recently been elevated to a level of such importance in the
formulation of economic policy, and in the behavior of U.S. markets, that
it behooves all of us to give the matter serious attention. . . . The dollar has
been in a continuous downtrend since early 1985. Indeed, since reaching a
peak in late February of last year, the dollar has lost about one-third of its
value against the world's major currencies. (Over one-half of that fall has

occurred since the G-5 announcement of September 22). This decline has effectively eliminated the dollar's gains over the last four years. . . . One striking feature that sets this dollar decline apart from that of 1978 is that this time, the fall has not been associated with a loss of confidence in the United States.

April 7, 1986: The initial stage of the current bull market in bonds began in mid-1984 when long Treasury issues approached 14%. This first stage lasted until early 1985 when the long rates declined to the 11% area. At that point, the previous excessive deterioration in the bond market was eliminated. The second phase of the bull market took place from early 1985 to early 1986; there was substantial bullish news throughout the period and investors perceived that long-term values existed.

July 14, 1986: The Fed cut the discount rate last Thursday night by one-half percent, bringing the rate to 6 percent. This was the third reduction in a period of a little over four months, and it was widely anticipated, although it came a bit sooner than had been expected. . . . Chairman Volcker, and perhaps one or two others, might have preferred to wait a bit longer before acting to reduce the rate. However, both the economic and political realities suggested that this was not a good time to have a split decision coming from the Fed.

September 8, 1986: The long bond market participant has looked at a continuing recovery, the prospect of worsening inflation, the risk of reduced foreign participation in our debt markets and the certainty that Treasury financing will remain huge, and has concluded that the better part of valor is to take a defensive view and run for higher rate ground to see how things unfold.

September 22, 1986: Comments from the U.S. Treasury concerning the need for a lower dollar appear to have antagonized both the Germans and the Japanese. The odds of getting multi-lateral cooperation to lower interest rates now look less likely and will not be a positive force for U.S. debt markets. . . . While it may be appropriate (for the Treasury) to ask major trading partners to stimulate their economies, it is highly questionable whether we should tell them what techniques should be used.

November 3, 1986: The latest cut in the Japanese discount rate was not solely dictated by domestic considerations, although the Japanese economy appears to have stalled in recent months. Its announcement was coupled with the release of a surprise statement by Treasury Secretary Baker and Finance Minister Miyazawa indicating that they had reached agreement to cooperate on a number of economic issues and noting that the current level of the dollar/yen relationship is now consistent with present underlying fundamentals. This statement is significant in that it marks the first time in months that these two major industrial powers have reached an agreement on exchange rate matters.

January 26, 1987: The insistence of U.S. officials that the dollar move still lower and that we not engage in any support activities has become counterproductive. The more disappointing the trade numbers, the more the U.S. tries to induce the dollar to move lower. The rationale for U.S. policy seems to be to head off restrictive trade legislation and force the Germans and Japanese to adopt more expansionary economic policies.

February 23, 1987: It was hard not to feel that if Volcker still dominated policy to the extent he did for so many years, policy would not be as accommodative as it is currently. However, the corollary reality one sensed was that his was a minority view.

March 16, 1987: Inflation concerns have been very much on the mind of Chairman Paul Volcker. This is readily apparent in all of his recent public pronouncements. . . . Since last August/September there has been a clear firming in the price picture. The increases are far from explosive, but with energy prices no longer showing sustained weakness, the chances of translating these price pressures into the broader price indexes have been enhanced.

March 30, 1987: The major central banks of the world—the Fed, the Bank of Japan, the Bundesbank, the Bank of England and the Banque de France—all intervened last week to reverse the dollar's slide against the yen. Such intervention is presumed to be dictated by the understanding reached at the February G-6 meeting.

April 13, 1987: The Treasury continues to believe that a lower dollar is acceptable, if not beneficial, while the Fed seems to be of the opinion that further dollar declines are risky, and potentially dangerous. The behavior of the debt market would seem to indicate that it agrees with the Fed. Thus, every time officials talk about the general level of the dollar being acceptable, and the fluctuations reasonable and not chaotic, interest rates rise and holders liquidate positions.

June 8, 1987: It was announced that Chairman Volcker was leaving the Fed. In Volcker, the markets knew they had not only an inflation fighter, but a champion of a strong currency and of halting the slide of the dollar. In this, Volcker has been something of a voice in the wilderness, but he has been there. The market does not know how Greenspan feels on this matter. Further, it does not know whether, or to what extent, Greenspan's views might be tempered if they are in conflict with the administration's views in this area.

One thing about Volcker's days as Fed chairman—from Wall Street to Main Street, virtually everyone seemed to have strong opinions about him. This was because in his eight years as chairman of the Fed, his policies had a direct impact on almost everyone, in either their jobs or their personal financial circumstances. No Fed chairman—either before or since—created the same degree of interest and controversy. This should not be surprising, because during Volcker's tour at the Fed, there had been bouts of inflation, recession, ultrahigh interest rates, tight money, unacceptably high unemployment rates, and major swings in the stock market, the dollar, and other financial markets.

Table 8-1

Paul A. Volcker, Chairman—Federal Reserve Board of Governors August 6, 1979–August 11, 1987

	Financial markets							Monetary policy					Economic indicators				Commodities	
			Corporates							Bank credit				CPI - %			Prices - $	
1979	Fed funds	Treas 30-yr	Aaa	Baa	30-yr mtge	S&P 500	DM	Monetary base	Free rsvs	Loans	Inv	Real GDP	Unemp rate	Total	Core	Budget	Oil	Gold
Jan																		
Feb																		
Mar																		
Apr																		
May																		
Jun																		
Jul																		
Aug	10.94	8.98	9.23	10.35	11.09	109.32	.5480	127.1b	−684	827	253	+2.9%	6.0	+1.0	+1.1	FY	26.50	300.81
Sep	11.43	9.17	9.44	10.54	11.30	109.32	.5742	128.3	−976	840	257		5.9	+0.9	+0.8	−40.7b	28.50	355.11
Oct	13.77	9.85	10.13	11.40	11.64	101.82	.5543	129.5	−191	844	258		6.0	+1.1	+1.0		29.00	391.65
Nov	13.18	10.30	10.76	11.99	12.83	106.16	.5780	130.4	−1518	845	259	1.2%	5.9	+1.1	+1.1		31.00	391.99
Dec	13.78	10.12	10.74	12.06	12.90	107.94	.5794	131.1	−948	851	261	+1.3%	6.0	+1.2	+1.2		32.50	455.08
						+12.3%	+5.4%	+8.9%		+13.9%	+7.6%	+1.3%		+13.3	+11.3		+118.9	+119.0%
						D-D	D-D	D-D		D-D	D-D	4Q-4Q		D-D	D-D		D-D	D-D

1980

Month																	
Jan	13.82	10.60	11.09	12.42	12.88	114.16	.5735	132.0b	−916	858	261		6.3	+1.4	+1.3		32.50	675.30
Feb	14.13	12.13	12.38	13.57	13.04	113.66	.5628	132.8	−1347	867	263	+1.3%	6.3	+1.3	+1.0		37.00	665.32
Mar	17.19	12.34	12.96	14.45	15.28	102.09	.5124	133.6	−2389	875	264		6.3	+1.4	+1.4		38.00	553.58
Apr	17.61	11.40	12.04	14.19	16.33	106.29	.5556	134.7	−1551	872	265		6.9	+1.0	+1.1		39.50	517.41
May	10.98	10.36	10.99	13.17	14.26	111.24	.5623	135.0	−34	863	269	−7.8%	7.5	+1.0	+0.8		39.50	513.82
Jun	9.47	9.81	10.58	12.71	12.71	114.24	.5669	135.7	+142	860	272		7.6	+1.0	+1.1		39.50	600.71
Jul	9.03	10.24	11.07	12.65	12.19	121.67	.5616	136.6	+148	862	277		7.8	+0.1	−0.2		39.50	644.28
Aug	9.61	11.00	11.64	13.15	12.56	122.38	.5586	138.0	−106	870	283	−0.7%	7.7	+0.7	+0.6	FY	38.00	627.14
Sep	10.87	11.34	12.02	13.70	13.20	125.46	.5517	139.2	−940	876	286		7.5	+0.8	+1.0	−73.8b	36.00	673.62
Oct	12.81	11.59	12.31	14.23	13.79	127.47	.5247	140.2	−1038	886	289	+7.6%	7.5	+1.0	+1.1		36.00	661.14
Nov	15.85	12.37	12.97	14.64	14.21	140.52	.5190	141.6	−1442	900	294		7.5	+1.1	+1.1		36.00	623.46
Dec	18.90	12.40	13.21	15.14	14.79	135.76	.5067	142.0	−2085	910	297		7.2	+0.9	+1.2		37.00	594.92
	+25.8%					−12.5		+8.3%		+7.0%	+13.8%	0.0%		+12.4	+12.2		+13.8%	+30.7%
	D-D					D-D		D-D		D-D	D-D	4Q-4Q		D-D	D-D		D-D	D-D

(Continued)

107

Table 8-1
(Continued)

1981	Financial markets							Monetary policy				Economic indicators					Commodities	
	Fed funds	Treas 30-yr	Corporates Aaa	Baa	30-yr mtge	S&P 500	DM	Monetary base	Free rsvs	Bank credit Loans	Inv	Real GDP	Unemp rate	CPI - % Total	Core	Budget	Prices - $ Oil	Gold
Jan	19.08	12.14	12.81	15.03	14.90	129.55	.4690	141.5b	−830	916	300		7.5	+0.9	+0.6		38.00	557.38
Feb	15.93	12.80	13.35	15.37	15.13	131.27	.4693	142.3	−784	918	302	+8.4%	7.4	+0.9	+0.6		38.00	499.76
Mar	14.70	12.69	13.33	15.34	15.40	136.00	.4738	143.0	−509	924	303		7.4	+0.7	+0.6		38.00	498.76
Apr	15.72	13.20	13.88	15.56	15.58	132.81	.4524	143.9	−999	930	304		7.2	+0.6	+0.7		38.00	495.80
May	18.52	13.60	14.32	15.95	16.40	132.59	.4292	144.6	−1692	941	306	−3.1%	7.5	+0.7	+0.9		38.00	479.69
Jun	19.10	12.96	13.75	15.80	16.70	131.21	.4177	145.0	−1402	949	307		7.5	+0.9	+0.9		36.00	464.76
Jul	19.04	13.59	14.38	16.17	16.83	130.92	.4047	145.8	−1089	953	306		7.2	+1.1	+1.4		36.00	409.28
Aug	17.82	14.17	14.89	16.34	17.29	122.79	.4086	146.5	−813	960	307	+4.9%	7.4	+0.8	+1.0	FY	36.00	410.15
Sep	15.87	14.67	15.49	16.92	18.16	116.18	.4301	146.9	−519	967	307		7.6	+1.0	+1.2	−79.0b	36.00	443.58
Oct	15.08	14.68	15.40	17.11	18.45	121.89	.4457	147.1	−313	972	309		7.9	+0.3	+0.3		35.00	437.75
Nov	13.31	13.35	14.22	16.39	17.83	126.35	.4517	147.7	−59	979	310	−4.9%	8.3	+0.4	+0.4		36.00	413.36
Dec	12.37	13.45	14.23	16.55	16.92	122.55	.4468	149.0	−103	992	311		8.5	+0.3	+0.5		35.00	410.09
						−9.7%	−11.8	+4.9%		+8.9%	+4.8%	+1.2%		+8.9	+9.5		−5.0%	−31.1%
						D-D	D-D	D-D		D-D	D-D	4Q-4Q		D-D	D-D		D-D	D-D

1982

Jan	13.22	14.22	15.18	17.10	17.40	120.40	.4317	150.0b	−827	1004	312		8.6	+0.3	+0.3	33.85	384.38
Feb	14.78	14.22	15.27	17.18	17.60	113.11	.4188	150.5	−1122	1014	314	−6.4%	8.9	+0.3	+0.5	31.56	374.13
Mar	14.68	13.53	14.58	16.82	17.16	111.96	.4137	150.7	−711	1023	315		9.0	0.0	+0.1	28.48	330.04
Apr	14.94	13.37	14.46	16.78	16.89	116.44	.4290	151.6	−883	1032	317		9.3	+0.3	+0.9	33.45	350.34
May	14.45	13.24	14.26	16.64	16.68	111.88	.4260	152.9	−347	1040	318	+2.2%	9.4	+0.9	+0.7	35.93	333.82
Jun	14.15	13.92	14.81	16.92	16.70	109.61	.4066	153.9	−651	1048	318		9.6	+1.1	+0.7	35.07	314.98
Jul	12.59	13.55	14.61	16.80	16.82	107.09	.4055	154.4	−106	1053	319		9.8	+0.5	+0.6	34.16	338.97
Aug	10.12	12.77	13.71	16.32	16.27	119.51	.4005	155.5	+11	1057	322	−1.5%	9.8	+0.2	+0.4 FY	33.95	364.23
Sep	10.31	12.07	12.94	15.63	15.43	120.42	.3954	156.6	−329	1065	325		10.1	0.0	+0.1 −128.0	35.63	435.76
Oct	9.71	11.17	12.12	14.73	14.61	133.72	.3906	157.7	+153	1071	328		10.4	+0.4	+0.3	35.68	422.15
Nov	9.20	10.54	11.68	14.30	13.83	138.53	.4057	158.7	+18	1070	331	+0.4%	10.8	−0.1	−0.2	34.15	414.91
Dec	8.95	10.54	11.83	14.14	13.62	140.64	.4205	160.1	+85	1074	339		10.8	−0.3	−0.1	31.72	444.30
	+14.8%					−5.9%		+7.5%		+8.3%	+8.8%	−1.4%		+3.8	+4.5	−9.4%	+8.3%
	D-D					D-D	D-D	D-D		D-D	D-D	4Q-4Q		D-D	D-D	D-D	D-D

(Continued)

Table 8-1
(*Continued*)

1983	Fed funds	Treas 30-yr	Corporates Aaa	Corporates Baa	30-yr mtge	S&P 500	DM	Monetary base	Free rsvs	Loans	Inv	Real GDP	Unemp rate	CPI - % Total	CPI - % Core	Budget	Oil	Gold
Jan	8.68	10.63	11.79	13.94	13.25	145.30	.4057	161.1b	+209	1080	347		10.4	+0.2	+0.4		31.19	481.29
Feb	8.51	10.88	12.01	13.95	13.04	148.06	.4109	163.2	+171	1081	352	+5.0%	10.4	+0.1	+0.4		28.95	491.96
Mar	8.77	10.63	11.73	13.61	12.80	152.96	.4114	165.1	+11	1086	360		10.3	+0.1	+0.2		28.82	419.70
Apr	8.80	10.48	11.51	13.29	12.78	164.43	.4054	166.5	−47	1088	367		10.2	+0.7	+0.4		30.61	432.93
May	8.63	10.53	11.46	13.09	12.63	162.39	.3961	167.8	+108	1090	375	+9.3%	10.1	+0.4	+0.3		30.00	438.08
Jun	8.98	10.93	11.74	13.37	12.87	167.64	.3936	169.4	−76	1099	381		10.1	+0.2	+0.3		31.00	412.84
Jul	9.37	11.40	12.15	13.39	13.42	162.56	.3776	170.1	−197	1109	384		9.4	+0.4	+0.6		31.66	422.72
Aug	9.56	11.82	12.51	13.64	13.81	164.40	.3708	171.2	−411	1120	386	+8.1%	9.5	+0.3	+0.3	FY	31.91	416.24
Sep	9.45	11.63	12.37	13.55	13.73	166.07	.3800	172.4	−238	1127	390		9.2	+0.3	+0.4	−207.8	31.11	411.80
Oct	9.48	11.58	12.25	13.46	13.54	163.55	.3800	173.6	+59	1139	396		8.8	+0.4	+0.5		30.41	393.58
Nov	9.34	11.75	12.41	13.61	13.44	166.40	.3705	174.6	−249	1151	401	+8.4%	8.5	+0.3	+0.5		29.84	381.66
Dec	9.47	11.88	12.57	13.75	13.42	164.93	.3670	175.5	−85	1163	404		8.3	+0.3	+0.3		29.24	389.36
						+17.3	−12.7	+9.6%		+8.3%	+19.3	+7.7%		+3.8	+4.7		−7.8%	−12.4%
						D-D	D-D	D-D	D-D	D-D	D-D	4Q-4Q	D-D	D-D	D-D		D-D	D-D

1984

Jan	9.56	11.75	12.20	13.65	13.37	163.41	.3551	176.9b	−13	1171	407		8.0	+0.7	+0.7		29.69	370.90
Feb	9.59	11.95	12.08	13.59	13.23	157.06	.3849	177.8	+446	1190	407	+8.1%	7.8	+0.5	+0.3		30.15	386.33
Mar	9.91	12.38	12.57	13.99	13.69	159.18	.3855	178.9	−123	1201	408		7.8	+0.3	+0.4		30.76	394.33
Apr	10.29	12.65	12.81	14.31	13.65	160.05	.3674	179.9	−578	1216	407		7.7	+0.4	+0.5		30.62	381.36
May	10.32	13.43	13.28	14.74	13.94	150.55	.3661	180.7	−2187	1233	405	+7.1%	7.4	+0.2	+0.4		30.52	377.40
Jun	11.06	13.44	13.55	15.05	14.42	153.18	.3595	182.0	−405	1247	401		7.2	+0.2	+0.4		29.97	377.67
Jul	11.23	13.21	13.44	15.15	14.67	150.66	.3441	183.0	+22	1261	402		7.5	+0.4	+0.5		28.75	347.45
Aug	11.64	12.54	12.87	14.63	14.47	166.68	.3461	183.8	+52	1269	404	+3.9%	7.5	+0.3	+0.4	FY	29.25	347.70
Sep	11.30	12.29	12.66	14.35	14.35	166.10	.3255	184.7	+184	1283	405		7.3	+0.3	+0.4	−185.4	29.31	341.09
Oct	9.99	11.98	12.63	13.94	14.13	166.09	.3300	185.2	−43	1295	405		7.4	+0.4	+0.4		28.77	340.17
Nov	9.43	11.56	12.29	13.48	13.64	163.58	.3215	186.1	+129	1310	406	+3.3%	7.2	+0.2	+0.2		28.10	341.19
Dec	8.38	11.52	12.13	13.40	13.18	167.24	.3170	187.2	+366	1327	407		7.3	+0.2	+0.4		25.43	320.14
						+1.4%	−13.6	+6.7%		+14.1%	+0.7%	+5.6%		+4.0	+4.9		−13.0	−17.8%
						D-D	D-D	D-D	D-D	D-D	D-D	4Q-4Q		D-D	D-D		D-D	D-D

(Continued)

Table 8-1
(*Continued*)

1985	Financial markets							Monetary policy				Economic indicators					Commodities	
	Fed funds	Treas 30-yr	Corporates Aaa	Baa	30-yr mtge	S&P 500	DM	Monetary base	Free rsvs	Bank credit Loans	Inv	Real GDP	Unemp rate	CPI - % Total	Core	Budget	Prices - $ Oil	Gold
Jan	8.35	11.45	12.08	13.26	13.08	179.63	.3162	188.1	+459	1335	411		7.3	+0.2	+0.3		25.64	302.74
Feb	8.50	11.47	12.13	13.23	12.92	181.18	.2980	189.6	+435	1348	415	+3.8%	7.2	+0.6	+0.6		27.27	299.10
Mar	8.58	11.81	12.56	13.69	13.17	180.66	.3244	190.3	+229	1362	415		7.2	+0.5	+0.4		28.24	304.17
Apr	8.27	11.47	12.23	13.51	13.20	179.83	.3228	191.4	+416	1372	414		7.3	+0.2	+0.3		28.81	324.74
May	7.97	11.05	11.72	13.15	12.91	189.55	.3269	192.7	+118	1380	420	+3.5%	7.2	+0.2	+0.4		27.62	316.64
Jun	7.53	10.45	10.94	12.40	12.22	191.85	.3301	194.8	+533	1395	425		7.4	+0.3	+0.3		27.14	316.83
Jul	7.88	10.50	10.97	12.43	12.03	190.92	.3572	195.9	+407	1404	428		7.4	+0.2	+0.3		27.33	317.38
Aug	7.90	10.56	11.05	12.50	12.19	188.63	.3558	198.0	+552	1412	428	+6.4%	7.1	+0.2	+0.4	FY	27.76	329.33
Sep	7.92	10.61	11.07	12.48	12.19	182.08	.3733	199.3	+267	1426	432		7.1	+0.2	+0.2	−212.3	28.29	324.25
Oct	7.99	10.50	11.02	12.36	12.14	189.82	.3813	200.7	+358	1433	434		7.1	+0.4	+0.5		29.54	325.93
Nov	8.05	10.06	10.55	11.99	11.78	202.17	.3980	202.1	−186	1449	443	+3.1%	7.0	+0.5	+0.5		30.81	325.22
Dec	8.27	9.54	10.16	11.58	11.26	211.28	.4087	203.6	+300	1466	456		7.0	+0.5	+0.3		27.23	320.81
						+26.3	+28.9	+8.7%		+10.5	+12.1	+4.2%		+3.8	+4.3		+7.1%	+0.2%
						D-D	D-D	D-D		D-D	D-D	4Q-4Q		D-D	D-D		D-D	D-D

1986

Jan	8.14	9.40	10.05	11.44	10.88	211.78	.4188	204.2b	+844	1484	467		6.7	+0.4	+0.4		22.95	345.38
Feb	7.86	8.93	9.67	11.11	10.71	226.92	.4483	205.3	+679	1492	469	+3.9%	7.2	−0.2	+0.3		15.44	338.89
Mar	7.48	7.96	9.00	10.50	10.08	238.90	.4264	206.9	+709	1510	463		7.2	−0.5	+0.3		12.62	345.71
Apr	6.99	7.39	8.79	10.19	9.94	235.52	.4619	208.1	+587	1511	461	+1.6%	7.1	−0.4	+0.4		12.85	340.44
May	6.85	7.52	9.09	10.29	10.14	247.35	.4301	210.2	+680	1514	465		7.2	+0.3	+0.2		15.44	342.56
Jun	6.92	7.57	9.13	10.34	10.68	250.84	.4543	212.8	+755	1522	467		7.2	+0.4	+0.3		13.47	342.57
Jul	6.56	7.27	8.88	10.16	10.51	236.12	.4777	213.4	+627	1530	480		7.0	+0.1	+0.4		11.58	348.54
Aug	6.17	7.33	8.72	10.18	10.20	252.93	.4913	215.3	+477	1539	492	+3.9%	6.9	+0.1	+0.4	FY	15.09	376.60
Sep	5.89	7.62	8.89	10.20	10.01	231.32	.4933	216.8	+389	1551	504		7.0	+0.4	+0.4	−221.2	14.91	417.73
Oct	5.85	7.70	8.86	10.24	9.97	243.98	.4852	218.6	+472	1556	503	+2.0%	7.0	+0.2	+0.3		14.85	423.51
Nov	6.04	7.52	8.68	10.07	9.70	249.22	.5068	220.7	+638	1567	505		6.9	+0.2	+0.3		15.21	398.81
Dec	6.91	7.37	8.49	9.97	9.31	242.17	.5199	223.4	+687	1597	510		6.6	+0.4	+0.3		16.08	391.23
						+14.6%	+27.2	+9.8%	+8.9%	+11.9%		+2.8%		+1.2	+3.8		−40.9	+22.0%
						D-D	D-D	D-D	D-D	D-D	4Q-4Q			D-D	D-D		D-D	D-D

(Continued)

Table 8-1
(*Continued*)

1987	Financial markets							Monetary policy				Economic indicators					Commodities Prices - $	
	Fed funds	Treas 30-yr	Corporates Aaa	Corporates Baa	30-yr mtge	S&P 500	DM	Monetary base	Free rsvs	Bank credit Loans	Bank credit Inv	Real GDP	Unemp rate	CPI - % Total	CPI - % Core	Budget	Oil	Gold
Jan	6.43	7.39	8.36	9.72	9.20	274.08	.5456	225.3b	+749	1625	510		6.6	+0.5	+0.3		18.66	408.26
Feb	6.10	7.54	8.38	9.65	9.08	284.20	.5472	226.6	+991	1627	515	+2.7%	6.6	+0.4	+0.3		17.73	401.12
Mar	6.13	7.55	8.36	9.61	9.04	291.70	.5549	227.1	+749	1635	514		6.6	+0.4	+0.3		18.31	408.91
Apr	6.37	8.25	8.85	10.04	9.83	288.36	.5560	229.0	+254	1651	516		6.3	+0.4	+0.6		18.64	438.35
May	6.85	8.78	9.33	10.51	10.60	290.10	.5483	230.5	+515	1657	521	+4.5%	6.3	+0.3	+0.3		19.42	460.23
Jun	6.73	8.57	9.32	10.52	10.54	304.00	.5476	231.3	+990	1668	520		6.2	+0.4	+0.2		20.03	449.59
Jul	6.58	8.64	9.42	10.61	10.28	318.66	.5379	232.0	+664	1672	522		6.1	+0.3	+0.3		21.36	450.52
Aug	6.73	8.97	9.67	10.80	10.33	329.80	.5522	233.5	+815	1685	528	+3.7%	6.0	+0.4	+0.3		20.27	461.15
Sep																		
Oct																		
Nov																		
Dec																		

Opinions about Volcker were either very positive or very negative; they were seldom neutral. Many wanted him to stay on indefinitely as Fed chairman, whereas others believed he should have not had the job in the first place. People had such strong feelings about Volcker because in his eight years as Fed chairman he was the second most powerful person in the United States, and there were even times when he was number one. When you are running the institution that is in charge of the financial punchbowl, you become a lightening rod for both praise and criticism.

In recent years, Volcker's stock as a Fed chairman has risen significantly. Over two decades have passed since he was in charge of the Fed, and many individuals who were adversely affected by his policies have mellowed in their criticism. Some now realize that the financial pain the Fed inflicted during the Volcker era was necessary and helped bring about better times later on.

ALAN GREENSPAN
(AUGUST 11, 1987–JANUARY 31, 2006)

For more than four decades, my partner, Bill Griggs, and I have written an economic report; the previous chapter contained quotes from past editions. Our
expertise has always been focused on monetary and fiscal policies. Like many
economists, we try to keep everything we have ever written, which of course is
impossible, especially since over the years a lot of our records have been lost,
beginning with the first World Trade Center attack, several moves, excessive house
cleaning, and water damage from a recent fire in our present building. However,
among the surviving copies of *The Griggs & Santow Report* is the June 8, 1987,
issue that talks about Paul Volcker and Alan Greenspan. What makes these comments so important is that they were written as Volcker was on his way out and
Greenspan was on his way in:

> Paul Volcker will shortly leave the Federal Reserve Chairmanship, a position
> he has held since August 1979. Through his many accomplishments, Chair-
> man Volcker has secured a prominent place in central banking history.
> Those of us who have been privileged to know him will remember the
> man—his character, morality, intellectual honesty, and good humor. In his
> role as Chairman, as in other official positions, he has been a forceful leader,
> an independent thinker, and a public servant par excellence. The esteem in
> which he is widely held is well deserved—a testament to the man rather
> than the position he occupied. Paul Volcker will be missed.
>
> There may be something to be learned from the premature departure of
> a public servant of Volcker's caliber. For a Federal Reserve Chairman to be
> most effective, he must not only be a strong character, he must also enjoy
> the strong public support of the administration with which he works—
> including the support of the President. The Chairman's views and advice
> should be sought on all issues that directly affect monetary policy, dollar
> policy, deregulation strategies, and appointments to the Federal Reserve

Board. Consultation on Board appointments is particularly important to
the development of a harmonious and credible monetary policy. These
appointments should be as free as possible from political considerations.
Finally, there is need for a serious rethinking of the compensation paid to
Board members in general, and the Fed Chairman. Indeed, considering his
responsibilities, the Chairman may be the most underpaid public servant in
the country.

GREENSPAN'S ARRIVAL

Writing about Greenspan and his arrival at the Fed proved to be a bigger problem than writing about Volcker. We obviously wished the new chairman good luck
in his endeavors and had no preconceived notions as to how he would perform.
We were concerned, as were many others, about anyone taking over from Volcker
because there were still major economic and financial problems to be addressed.
Again, quoting from our June 8, 1987, report:

> Alan Greenspan has a large pair of shoes to fill, in more ways than one. He
> is an excellent economist who is highly regarded by the professional com-
> munity and widely respected in Washington mainly as a business econo-
> mist, although he does have good credentials in a number of financial areas.
> One glaring difference between Greenspan and Volcker occurs in the area of
> financial deregulation. The Chairman designate is much more in tune with
> the administration's pro-deregulation thinking than is Chairman Volcker.
> In all other areas, Greenspan's likely policy views are an open issue. What
> one says as a private economist, or even as an official or unofficial advisor
> to a president, is not necessarily what one would advocate as Chairman of
> the Federal Reserve. Thus, Mr. Greenspan's past comments on the economy,
> inflation and dollar provide little reliable guidance as to what his views
> might be as the sitting Fed Chairman.
>
> Greenspan's relationship with the other Federal Reserve governors is
> another uncertainty. The Board is much different in many ways than Boards
> of the past. The individual members seem to have strong and often con-
> flicting views on Fed matters and show no reluctance to differ in public
> about monetary policy issues. This may induce the incoming Chairman to
> take the William McChesney Martin consensus approach. Every chairman
> seeks consensus, of course, but in Chairman Martin this consensus style was
> truly striking. Chairman Martin would count noses on individual policy
> questions, determining who was on his side, who was on the other side, and
> who was on the fence. The Chairman tried to persuade the fence sitters to
> move toward his view, stating the consensus in such a way that it would
> attract the broadest possible support. If the consensus did not coincide with
> his own view, and if it was a strong consensus, Martin tended to join it.
>
> Yet, the Board in the last two years has often been sharply split, fre-
> quently leaving the Chairman in the position of not being sure whether he

can speak for the Board. Whether Mr. Greenspan can develop a consensus policy remains to be seen, but he does have a better chance for success than Volcker. After all, he is the current President's appointee, and since his views are likely to be more in line with those of the administration on several major issues, the consensus approach may well work. This is particularly so if, as seems likely, Greenspan enjoys more official encouragement and support from senior public officials of this administration than Volcker did.

These changes in Fed leadership, and style, are likely to create major near-term problems for those trying to make forecasts of Fed policy. Knowing the governors, their philosophies, and history, and knowing how policy decisions are made is important to Fed watching. It will be months after Greenspan assumes authority before a clear picture of the new Fed Board will emerge. It will also take quite a while to tell whether or not there has been any reordering of the goals and guides to policy. Keep in mind that the goals of policy are many and the Fed is rarely single minded about achieving any one goal. Rather, it is the relative importance attached to economic growth, inflation, the dollar, money supply, Third World debt, and the health of the banking system, which is the key to policy. Thus in the weeks ahead one can probably expect to see Fed watchers making frequent use of words such as "could," "might," and "may" in their economic, interest rate, and policy forecasts.

When Volcker joined the Fed, embedded labor-cost inflation, combined with large increases in oil prices, were more than a match for monetary policy, especially where the funds rate was the primary tool and it was increased in a very deliberate manner. This may explain why Burns and Miller were so frustrated by their lack of success in combating inflation. To his credit, Volcker seemed to better understand the depth of the inflation problem and that it could not be fought without using a broad array of policy tools and, in essence, taking the risk of crushing the economy. It was way too late for preventive medicine.

From Greenspan's perspective, the situation he found himself in had a good-news–bad-news quality. The good news was that he did not have to combat embedded inflation; the bad news was that the primary inflation-crushing achievement had been done before he arrived on the scene. While he correctly can claim that, on balance, during the eighteen years of his chairmanship, his policies tended to contain inflation, it is also true that events abroad, productivity at home, and the reduced bargaining power of labor played major roles in such containment. Yet bad things do not have to happen and then be combated in order for a Fed chairman to have done an excellent job in containing prices. It is just that breaking the back of inflation did not occur on his watch.

GREENSPAN'S PAINFUL LEARNING EXPERIENCE

The early Greenspan years do not get the attention they deserve. He hit the ground running when he took over the helm of the Fed in August 1987, even though he had no central bank experience. In the first few years, some mistakes occurred. Yet, most authors who write about Greenspan pay little attention to his early policy decisions and the events that confronted him. Some analysts start the discussion of Greenspan at the Fed with the 1990–91 recession and how the Fed responded, and it is not unusual for some to start with 1994–95, when the economy confronted a housing meltdown.

However, the early Greenspan years were more important than many seem to realize. They were quite hectic, and what occurred had a definite influence on how Greenspan conducted policy and reacted to events later in his term at the Fed. On-the-job training means learning while on the job. From when he took over in August 1987 to the end of 1990, there were many shifts in Fed policy as economic and financial events changed rapidly. Since this is a period that has not received the analytical attention it deserved, it seemed worthwhile to look at some quotes from various issues of *The Griggs & Santow Report* published during that period.

Some of the quotes are extensive, because they explained what happened, why things happened, and where correct calls and incorrect misjudgments were made. Remember, these excerpts are real-time, and we called them as we saw them. As previously stated, the benefit of timely analyses is that no one can accuse us of writing revisionist history; and, of course, some of these analyses may ultimately have been proven to be wide of the mark.

You will notice that in this period from 1987 through 1990, at no time did the Fed stand still. Policy seemed to be in constant motion. Early on, some of the changes—including the direction of policy—seemed inappropriate; later on, the Fed was slow to react. One of the most interesting aspects of Fed policy at that time was that it took until late 1990 before Greenspan used many of the tools available to him to influence policy. Unfortunately, they were not all heading in the same direction.

In availability and interest-rate terms, the Fed was easing while the regulators at the Fed wanted banks to be cautious in extending credit in order to protect capital positions. The availability and interest-rate approach was based on cyclical and special factors; the regulatory side was based primarily on longer-term safety and capital considerations. The problems Greenspan faced with his regulators at that time may have resulted in his becoming overly cautious when it came to regulators and monetary policy, especially in his later years at the Fed when there was a need—but little pressure from Greenspan—for regulators to be tough on loans, especially mortgage loans in general, and subprime loans in particular.

If inflation was the Fed's main problem whenever a new Fed chairman took over, it seemed as though he felt obligated to prove his mettle as an inflation fighter. Miller tried to do so after Burns; Volcker followed that same course after Miller; Greenspan did so after Volcker, and Bernanke took that approach after Greenspan. In each of these cases, the initial thrust toward firmness could not be sustained, and all of them had to take a step back—with one exception—and that was Burns, who eased after taking office and had to reverse course later on. The early years of Greenspan's rough policy ride are shown in statements from selected *Griggs & Santow Reports:*

September 7, 1987: The Fed discount rate increase took the market by surprise.... It is a shot across the bow, if you will, intended to indicate that additional tightening of policy can be expected if the dollar and inflation worsen.... The fact that the change was announced early on a Friday morning (which is unusual), and not right after an FOMC meeting, suggests the Fed felt some urgency about this matter. This is hard to square with the Fed's announcement that the change was made because of concerns over future inflation. Indeed, we are satisfied that this move is intended in good part as a message—that the Fed would hope to see the dollar stabilize near current levels.

By the middle of October 1987, it was clear that the Fed and Greenspan had made a policy mistake. When long-term treasury rates rise, it is not always a reflection of inflation fears on the part of investors. Higher long-term rates can be caused by a number of factors:

October 12, 1987: Fed policy has a singular rationale these days. The Fed seems to be operating on the theory that a backup in long-term bond rates indicates heightened inflation psychology and to counter that inflation concern, the Fed must firm policy. To say this is simplistic is being charitable. Long-bond rates can rise for many reasons as the events of the last two months clearly indicate. The recent backup in rates was prompted by many concerns; disappointing trade numbers that led to a reassessment of the U.S. trade outlook; fears that the dollar would move lower; domestic business indicators that were stronger than expected; concerns about reduced interest in U.S. markets on the part of foreign investors; rising interest rates abroad; and, nervousness over the rate impact of a Fed policy that was growing tighter in both rate and reserve terms.

By late October, the financial markets, and in particular the equity market, had changed drastically, and not in a positive way. The Fed was caught unprepared for what happened:

October 26, 1987: With a panic atmosphere in the stock market, the Fed's objective was to ensure that liquidity was more than sufficient to meet any need that might develop. Flooding the banking system with reserves was viewed as the proper policy to take under the circumstances, and there was a realization that if the stock market were to falter again, a discount rate reduction would have to be considered as well.

November 2, 1987: The Fed has had a crisis to deal with in the last two weeks and this has led to some misconceptions about monetary policy. Some analysts have concluded that the Fed's generous provision of reserves over the last two weeks reflects a policy decision aimed at preventing a recession no matter what the cost. To see events that way is to miss the point. The issue which the Fed suddenly found itself confronted with was a threat to the functioning of the entire financial system. Since the first responsibility of a central bank is to ensure the continuing viability of the financial system, the Fed had no choice but to aggressively flood the system with much needed liquidity.

By December 1987, we took a look back how the economic story for the year played out, and how it proved to be considerably different from what many—including the Fed and Greenspan—had expected. The mistakes were far reaching and consequential, as we pointed out in our December 21, 1987 *Report* where we stated the following:

December 21, 1987: It became clear in the early months of 1987 that the economy was considerably stronger and inflation considerably higher than it had been in 1986, and throughout the spring and summer of 1987 the debt markets were adjusting to this and other realities. This adjustment was associated with increased market instability, although by the end of the summer, a consensus emerged that the economy would continue to grow at a significant pace, inflation would not accelerate from current levels, the dollar would not deteriorate significantly and foreign investors would remain interested in the U.S., the trade picture would soon improve, our budget problems were being brought under control, oil prices would remain stable, and stock prices would continue to rise. Unfortunately, this consensus had no sooner become widespread than it began to unravel. This unraveling process first became apparent in September, and in the aftermath of the stock market crash of October 19, it became total.

Fast-forward to April 1988, about eight months after Greenspan took office. We presented a summary of his policy changes since he became chairman. Unfortunately, this period was not one of his finest. It appeared that he had been in too much of a hurry to make changes during his early months as chairman, and these changes created problems in terms of both direction and magnitude:

April 11, 1988: Alan Greenspan has been chairman of the Federal Reserve for approximately eight months. During that period there have been an unusual number of adjustments in policy. When he assumed the chairmanship in August, the funds target was 6.625–6.75 percent. By late August, the first policy change was made under his chairmanship. It was slight, and it was a move toward firming—raising the funds target to 6.75–6.875 percent. Shortly thereafter the discount rate was raised to 6 percent and the funds target was pushed up to 7.375–7.5 percent, and in mid-October it was increased to 7.625–7.75 percent. Thus, in a period a bit longer than two months, the Fed made four modest firming moves, the combined effect of which was to raise the average Fed funds rate 1 percent and the discount rate one-half percent.

After the stock market crash, the Fed's only concern was with providing adequate liquidity for the banking system, and the funds average fell sharply, erasing the recent rise. Weekly targeting of Fed funds lost its importance during this period, but when the dust settled, the underlying trading range was back at 6.625–6.75 percent—where it had been when Greenspan came aboard. Fed funds held in this target range for about three months. In early February, however, the Fed moved once again, easing the funds target down to 6.5–6.625 percent. This slight adjustment was made in response to concerns that the economy was weakening dramatically—a concern which proved to be exaggerated. Thus, at the beginning of April, the Fed, responding to the stronger-than-expected economic performance, some upward movement in commodity prices, and a softening of the dollar raised its funds target by one-quarter percent to 6.75–6.875 percent.

There is a message in this story: When the Fed acts on the basis of early-warning signals and projections in order to move more promptly to counter an apparent trend, this approach carries with it a risk that policy will be moved prematurely or in the wrong direction. In this case, both the Fed and Greenspan paid a price for some impetuous policy changes.

Over the next year or so, the Fed raised its funds rate target by a considerable and excessive amount. From an average of 6.58 percent in March 1987, the rate had been pushed up to 9.85 percent by March 1989. By mid 1989, the fed began to realize that it had overdone its firming of policy. And, indirectly, Greenspan had admitted as much during his July Congressional testimony.

July 24, 1989: In his (Greenspan's Humphrey-Hawkins testimony), he outlined the considerations that had shaped Fed policy in the past, and provided as clear an idea as he could of what would shape policy in the future. The key points he made were these: risk of recession had replaced inflation as the Fed's number one concern, this shift in priorities had prompted the Fed to ease policy in the last few weeks and could prompt still further easing moves in the future, inflation remained a serious problem, however, so any subsequent moves toward ease would be modest and measured as the previous two easing moves had been—one-quarter percent each in the Fed funds target.

Greenspan's unduly modest attempt to ease policy proved to be inadequate and this was clearly evident by mid October 1989:

October 16, 1989: Late Friday. . . everything else that happened during the week lost its significance because the stock market plummeted in response to concerns about junk bonds and leveraged balance sheets. Stocks began to move lower around noon and dropped dramatically after 3 p.m. New York time. At 4 p.m., the Dow Jones Industrial average was off 190.58. This produced a rush to quality which moved Treasury yields sharply lower.

October 23, 1989: The stock market did stabilize and, in fact, regained much of the ground lost during the week. . . . The Fed let it be known on the weekend following the sharp stock price fall that it would provide all the liquidity that was required to assure the ongoing integrity of the financial markets. This pledge was given expression on Monday and the two days that followed by the Fed doing customer RPs during a period in which it would have been draining money.

Also on the market's mind was the fortunes of junk bonds. Since it was concerned about the ability to finance high credit risk borrowing, which prompted the stock market to retreat so sharply, the markets were wondering how investors would react to such financing this week. The fact is that a number of these financings were postponed and, in general, investors showed considerably less enthusiasm for such paper—a potentially positive development.

Needless to say, the Fed had not only taken the funds rate too high by March 1989—to an average rate of 9.85 percent—but it was not until October 1989 that it had edged the funds rate to below 9 percent. This was a totally inadequate change as policy was still overly restrictive. However, the Fed's subsequent easing moves were slow and gradual. By December 1989, the funds target was 8.45 percent, but by October 1990, the average funds rate was still unduly high at 8.11 percent. Only then did the Fed start to get serious in its easing moves, and by December 1990, the average funds rate was 7.31 percent; by December 1991, it was 4.43 percent, and by December 1992, it was 2.92 percent. The numbers speak for themselves.

During this period of reducing the funds rate, Greenspan's February 26, 1990, Congressional testimony stands out. In February 1990 the funds rate averaged a relatively high 8.24 percent. Greenspan was proved wrong on both his economic and monetary policy forecasts. His comments were made at a time when the economy was already slipping:

February 26, 1990: Chairman Greenspan made his first Humphrey-Hawkins appearance of the year on Tuesday morning. . . . The chairman expressed the view that a recession seemed unlikely and appeared to dwell on the potential inflation risks in the current situation, although he forecast that inflation would moderate in 1990. The chairman's comments were interpreted by the market as meaning that he welcomed the slowdown in the economy, would do nothing much to enhance the rate of growth and might even be willing to firm, if necessary, to limit inflation. The (Treasury) market took all this badly and prices retreated sharply.

As April 1990 drew to a close, the Fed still had done only a modest amount of easing, even though evidence seemed clear that further weakness was in store for the economy:

April 30, 1990: The Fed is in a difficult position with respect to inflation because it has stated it wants inflation down to zero and yet has little control over the results. All the Fed can do is try to help steer a real growth rate of 1.5 to 2 percent versus an underlying growth capability of 2.5 percent, and hope the difference will gradually bleed inflation out of the system. The

Fed's zero-inflation target may well stand alongside the government's zero-deficit budget target as the height of optimism.

By July 1990, the funds rate was averaging 8.15 percent and the economy was slipping into a recession. In the second quarter of 1990, real GDP grew by only 1.0 percent; in the third quarter it showed no growth at all, and by the fourth quarter, real GDP had slipped to the minus side at a negative 3 percent. By themselves, these circumstances were more than sufficient to cause an aggressive easing. Yet, it appeared that Greenspan needed to be prompted, or pushed, to do anything meaningful. This situation is similar to that of late 2000, when the Fed maintained excessively high interest rates for an unduly long period of time:

> **July 16, 1990:** Chairman Greenspan created quite a stir last Thursday with his comment that the Fed was considering easing policy in response to reports that the banks were imposing tougher lending standards and were moving up loan rates relative to the cost of money. The latter suggested to Greenspan that markets were tightening independently of Fed actions. . . . If that were the case (and he said the Fed was monitoring the matter on a day-to-day basis), it would have such undesirable effects on the economy that the Fed might have to consider offsetting through monetary policy.
>
> **July 23, 1990:** The Fed now seemed to feel that the balance of risk had shifted in such a way that there was less concern about inflation and more concern about the economy. Some saw this shift as a sign the Fed was giving in to political pressure from the administration. Despite what seemed to be a shift in Fed thinking, Greenspan once again indicated that it was not the behavior of the economy or prices which propelled the Fed to ease, but "credit tightening" that was not of the Fed's doing. . . . The Fed concluded that creditworthy borrowers were feeling the effects of this greater selectivity and the Fed ease to offset the tightening.

In August 1990, we tried to explain the Fed's reasoning about the need for high interest rates and a restrictive monetary policy, although we did not agree with what the Fed was doing—or should we say, not doing:

> **August 6, 1990:** Fed policy faces a serious dilemma. The weakness in the economy indicates a need to ease policy. Yet, the state of the budget, inflation, and the dollar suggest monetary policy should hold its current stance. An already soft economy will be further weakened by this latest oil shock.
>
> **August 27, 1990:** The Fed is clearly in a very difficult situation. There is no way policy can be correct—because what is needed is two policies, one to deal with the weakness in the economy, and one to deal with the inflation problem. The Fed is trying to walk a narrow line between these problems, leaning towards one or the other as events seem to dictate.

It appeared to us that the key factor that finally pushed the Fed towards an aggressive easing of policy was the weak real estate market. Finally, the size and speed of the easing moves were consequential. In November 1990, the funds rate averaged 7.81 percent; by April 1991 it was below 6 percent; by November 1991; it was below 5 percent and still heading south.

> **December 17, 1990:** The weakness in real estate appears to be spreading. What was primarily a New England and Mid-Atlantic problem appears to be moving to other parts of the country. Reports from the Middle West and California are not encouraging, especially the latter. The most serious problem appears to be in commercial real estate, although residential housing is not doing well either.
>
> **December 24, 1990:** The reduction in the Fed's discount rate last week caught the market by surprise. It was the first reduction in the discount rate in over four years and the Fed accompanied the adjustment with another easing of the fed funds rate. . . . Last week's actions by the Fed suggest it has adopted a somewhat more aggressive posture in attempting to deal with the slowdown in economic activity and the credit availability issues. . . . The Fed, disappointed that the banks had not responded to previous easing moves and declines in interest rates, hoped that this more aggressive approach would "force" the banks to lower their lending rates. So far, that hope has not been realized. Although a few banks have announced reductions in their prime rates, most have not.
>
> With the actions of last week, the Fed has now used all the tools of monetary policy it possesses. It has lowered the discount rate by 50 basis points, it has reduced the fed funds rate by 100 basis points in the last few weeks, and by 150 basis points since mid-year and is in the midst of a substantial reduction in reserve requirements, the first since 1983. One can always argue about whether the Fed should have acted sooner, or been more aggressive in its actions, but there can be no denying that the Fed mounted a broad-based attack to deal with our economic and financial difficulties.

While it was clear that the Fed should have eased sooner, and might have avoided the recession if it had, it is also clear that by 1992, the Fed had finally arrived at a reasonably appropriate policy. It should be obvious from reading the previous analysis—which covers about three and a half years of Greenspan's chairmanship—that there was a great deal more going on than many analysts currently seem to realize, and that the timing and magnitude of Fed policy changes left much to be desired. Equally important is the fact that similar problems seemed to haunt the Greenspan Fed through much of his eighteen years as chairman.

A PAST POLICY APPROACH THAT ADVERSELY AFFECTS POLICY TODAY

By the end of his term, Greenspan's primary policy objective was to be within the target range set for the personal consumption expenditures (PCE) core inflation rate; his primary market tool was a specific and announced fed funds target rate. It appears as if the academics who emphasized overly simplistic models and techniques had gained increased influence with Greenspan and his policies. It almost appears as if Greenspan was looking for the simplest techniques and solutions to deal with the most complex of problems. The farther he got away from making policy an art—and a flexible one at that—the greater his policy problems seemed to be.

Anyone who emphasizes one policy objective such as consumer prices, uses a system to measure prices that excludes food and energy, and uses a narrow target band that is on the low side of history, is asking for policy and credibility problems.

When Bernanke took over from Greenspan in early 2006, that would have been an opportune time to make changes in price targeting and apply a more realistic and flexible approach. Unfortunately, that did not happen, because it appears that Bernanke may have thought that if he deviated from the Greenspan approach, he ran the risk of being viewed as softer on inflation than Greenspan. It was an unfortunate set of circumstances where the Fed chairman appears to have followed a policy approach in an effort to appease others.

Taking this analysis a step further, if a Fed chairman is afraid of how market participants will react to his policy decisions, it is likely that when policy decisions are made, excessive weight will be given to what the market reactions might be. There were times under Greenspan, and now under Benanke, where such concerns on their part appear to have been excessive and have influenced policy decisions. Yet, traders being disappointed or surprised by a Fed policy move is a small price to pay for getting policy right. For example, when the Fed and Greenspan jumped the funds target by an excessive 50 basis points, to an excessive 6.5 percent, in May 2000, one wonders whether market expectations had played a role in this rate increase.

GREENSPAN'S GREATEST SUCCESS FLEW UNDER THE RADAR

The late 1980s through the mid 1990s was a period of substantial bank deregulation. Banks enjoyed large profit increases in the early 1990s as interest rates plummeted under the direction of Chairman Greenspan, and carry profits from an upslope to the yield curve were substantial. The ability of banks to operate in a more realistic and beneficial regulatory climate, when combined with profits that stemmed from a bank's investment portfolio, added substantially to the capital in the banking system.

Without these improvements, the eight-year economic recovery from 1992 to 2000 probably would not have materialized. The Fed played a major role in this improved health of the banking system specifically and financial institutions in general, and while Greenspan may not have been involved in the nitty-gritty of some of the regulatory changes, it happened under his leadership and guidance. If he is to get the blame for some of his regulatory mistakes during his eighteen years, he surely should get the credit in this important area.

The best analysis of the changes in bank regulation in recent decades was part of a speech presented by Fed Governor Laurence Meyer to the Ohio Bankers Association on November 21, 1996. He broke out the history of banking regulation into several time periods and indicated major turning points. The first period began during the depression.

> From the 1930s through most of the 1970s, regulators focused on keeping the banking industry safe and sound by protecting banks from competition and by limiting the activities in which they could participate. This meant, for example, prohibiting interstate banking, restricting the rates that banks could pay on deposits, and preventing commercial banks from competing in other product markets, such as investment banking. During this period, the financial services industry was segmented into separate entities providing commercial banking, investment banking, insurance services, etc. This separation was largely due to legislative and regulatory decisions. A consequence of the separation was that firms in each segment of the financial services industry were protected from competition from firms providing the other services.

Even as early as the 1960s, there was evidence that suggested a need for changing and reducing the regulation of the banking system. It was clear that economic growth was being hindered by overly restrictive limitations on what financial institutions could do with respect to servicing businesses and individuals. In essence, bank regulation had not kept up with the economic times. But fear of the unknown, and still-vivid memories of banking problems during the Depression, were reasons enough to cause regulators to act very cautiously when it came to deregulation. However, as Meyer pointed out, attitudes finally changed:

> Starting in the late 1970s, the changed economic environment along with advances in technology, financial innovations, and globalization resulted in increased competition to U.S. banks, by thrifts, nondepository financial institutions, foreign banks, and the capital markets. . . . Banks responded to the challenge by expanding in ways that they could, also taking advantage of improvements in technology and applied finance. They expanded their roles as intermediaries through off-balance-sheet activities such as securitization, back-up lines of credit and derivatives, and in the process, substituted fee income for some of the income lost through competition with other financial intermediates. In addition, banks sought expanded powers to help them compete, including being able to cross state borders, set their own deposit rates and account types, and by the late 1980s—expand into securities underwriting activities.

The movement towards deregulation continued in the 1990's but on an accelerated basis:

> Regulators responded to the new environment by reducing the regulatory burden on banks and allowing them to compete on a more level playing field with nonbanking firms. That is, the new market realities required a

reorientation in emphasis from protecting banks from competition to giv-ing banks the opportunity to compete not only with other banks but with nonbank competitors as well. By allowing banks to enter other states, set their own prices, and engage in other-than-traditional banking activities, the orientation of regulators evolved toward protecting the safety net while allowing banks to deliver financial services to the public efficiently, prof-itably, and with sufficient capital to be protected against unforeseen events.

As a result of this process of structural change, the banking industry of the mid-1990s in many ways hardly resembles that of the late 1970s and early 1980s. Some of the major changes . . . are the increased consol-idation of the industry, the decline in traditional banking services as a result of increased outside competition, the expansion in bank powers, including the move into nontraditional activities to offset the competi-tion for their traditional products, the increased emphasis on risk man-agement in response to the increased complexity of financial instruments and practices, and the evolution of capital standards and capital positions to keep abreast of the changing risk profiles of banking organizations.

Greenspan and the Fed deserve a great deal of credit for helping restructure and rebuild financial institutions, which in turn, propelled the U.S. economy forward. Yet one might also argue that in recent years, there was a price to be paid for too much deregulation. It may have been taken too far, and therefore became a factor of consequence in the banking and financial crisis of 2007 and 2008. Surely, one can argue that the greater the deregulation, the broader and more comprehensive financial reporting should be. This is something that Greenspan—and now Bernanke—should have seriously considered as a weapon against excessive risk and financial mismanagement.

GREENSPAN'S OVERRELIANCE ON FED FUNDS TARGETING TO ACHIEVE A PRICE OBJECTIVE

During his career at the Fed, Greenspan—for some reason that is beyond understanding—moved to a point where targeting a specific fed funds rate became more and more important, and other monetary considerations became less and less important. Greenspan took the Fed from where the funds rate was one of several monetary-policy tools to where it was the primary tool; and from using an acceptable fed funds range that was not announced, to using a specific rate that was announced. Making this announcement in a press release after every FOMC meeting was not only too narrow a focus for what monetary policy entailed, it also led both the media and the public to believe that the fed funds tar-get and monetary policy were synonymous.

For someone like Greenspan who conceptually believes in free markets and min-imum regulation, it is hard to understand why he wanted the Fed to determine a specific rate that it would target, without letting underlying supply/demand factors play a role. This proved to be more than a technical problem for Greenspan because it made it difficult for him to realize where monetary policy had been, where it was, and where it should have been heading.

One can argue that a transmission device that uses an overnight rate, such as fed funds, to strongly influence or control other interest rates out on the yield curve, will lead to questionable results. The relationships are ever changing, and there are other factors in the supply and demand for securities besides the Fed's influence on an overnight rate. The difference between short and long rates is not merely an expectation factor; there are many other forces involved. Thus, while the funds rate may be the best indicator of the Fed's policy intentions, it may not be a good indicator of what is actually happening in monetary policy.

The cutting edge of monetary policy, with respect to easing or tightness, is better reflected in other ways besides a fed funds rate. If an interest rate is to be used as a guide to the cutting edge of monetary policy, the yield on the ten-year Treasury is more important than an overnight rate, because of its impact on other debt markets such as the corporate, mortgage, agency, and municpal markets. The same is true when adjusting interest rates for inflation. In an overnight market, real interest rates have little meaning to either investors or issuers, but that is not the case when a ten-year Treasury yield is compared with the consumer price index. Greenspan, not having experience in trading markets before his days at the Fed, did not seem to fully understand this distinction.

Also, interest rates are not the only cutting edge of monetary policy. Availability of money in the financial system, the willingness of financial institutions such as banks to lend money or buy securities, and the growth of monetary aggregates such as bank credit, are also a major part of the mix. Simply put, during the Greenspan era, the Fed placed an excessive amount of emphasis on changing the funds target because it believed that it was changing monetary policy, along with the ease or tightness in policy. What was especially disturbing is that the trend in measuring and using policy tools became narrower and more simplistic during Greenspan's tour of duty as chairman of the Fed.

Fortunately for Greenspan and the Fed, the wide swings in the funds target from August 1989 to January 2006 tended to overstate the swings in interest rates in general, the availability of funds in particular, and the changes in the ease or tightness of monetary policy in general. In other words, the swings in the funds target overstated the degree of the swings in monetary policy, and Greenspan was lucky in that regard.

The best example of this overstatement of the importance of a funds target occurred in the middle of 2006. The Fed had just completed seventeen straight 25 basis point increases in its funds target over a period of a little more than two years. At the end of June 2006, the funds rate was 5.25 percent. This is in sharp contrast to a funds rate that was only 1 percent in the middle of 2004. On the surface, it looks as if money was tight in the middle of 2006, and easy in the middle of 2004. The problem with this conclusion is that it overstates the case.

Despite a fed funds rate target of 5.25 percent in the middle of 2006, money was readily available at an attractive price. If you do not think that was the case, take a look at the rapid and excessive growth in bank credit expansion, substantial corporate financing, and most importantly, an unduly large volume of mortgage lending to subprime borrowers at relatively low rates. Virtually no borrowers got pushed to the sidelines; nor were any borrowers crowded out.

The 1 percent funds rate was in place relatively early in the economic recovery, but the demand for money at the banks and in the capital markets was not all that great. In the middle of 2006, with the funds rate at 5.25 percent, monetary policy was not only accommodative, it was almost as accommodative as two years earlier when the funds target was 1 percent. Thus the ease or tightness of monetary policy is dependent on much more than a funds rate that, in essence, is fixed by the Fed and not determined by market forces. Policy is much more a function of the availability and the demand for money and the cutting edge of interest rates out on the yield curve. The bottom line is that the increase in the funds target from 1 percent to 5.25 percent grossly overstated the increase in monetary policy firmness, and it was amazing how many economists and those in the media did not understand this situation.

If other policy tools had been used in conjunction with a fed funds rate that would have firmed policy, the story might have been different. For example, if reserve requirements had been increased and the Fed had used regulatory pressures on banks to limit their loans to poorly qualified borrowers, then the increase in the firmness of monetary policy would have been much greater than merely taking up an overnight rate from an unduly low level to a moderate level.

In one sense, it was probably fortunate that the Fed relied almost entirely on a policy tool that was nowhere near as effective in changing policy as the Fed believed to be the case. If the funds rate had been as important as the Fed thought it was, we would probably have seen excessive swings in real economic growth. Under most conditions, monetary policy has less influence on economic growth, and even less influence on inflation, than is generally believed to be the case. And the Fed fixing an overnight interest rate as a primary monetary policy tool has much less of an impact on the ease or tightness of policy than many, both inside and outside the Fed, seem to realize.

Speaking about overreactions, in the middle of 2000, the Fed was concerned about inflation. By late 2003 and early 2004, the pendulum had swung and the Fed was then concerned about deflation. By 2005, the pendulum had swung again to where inflation was the primary concern. As of late 2008, the Fed's near-term concentration about inflation had waned and weak economic growth had temporarily become the greater concern.

Yet, if one looks at the Fed's primary measurement for price increases—the PCE core—from 2000 to 2007 on a twelve-month basis, the changes have been negligible. At its low point, the annualized rate was slightly less than 1.5 percent and at its high point was roughly 2.5 percent, and by the middle of 2008 it was somewhat over 2 percent. It is hard to understand how such a narrow swing could cause such major changes in opinion as to what the Fed needs to combat.

RESEARCH DEFICIENCIES AT THE FED

If the Federal Reserve System had optimized its practical research capabilities, especially when it came to economic forecasting, would this have led to an improvement in monetary policy? There has been a research deficiency in the entire period studied in this book. It almost appears as though those at the Fed had too many other things on their minds, but a breakthrough in practical research was not one of them. It is not that the central bank did a bad job in this area, but looking at its potential capabilities, the Fed surely could have done a better job.

The Fed holds a unique position in the research world since it consists of twelve districts with numerous branches, as well as the staff at the Federal Reserve Board, that can monitor economic and financial situations around the country. These districts employ numerous economists with a variety of backgrounds. Since the federal government does not have these same capabilities, one wonders why the Federal Reserve does not do much more detailed regional analyses and arrive at a timely and detailed forecast as to what is likely to happen in both the districts and in the economy as a whole?

Do not assume that the Beige Book in any way achieves this objective. Each district conducts a survey in the private sector; results are combined into one national survey. The Fed provides no analysis; it merely presents some overall conclusions as to what the information shows. Frankly, the Fed is capable of doing much more than this in the way of quality research. Greenspan had eighteen years to add to and fine-tune the Fed's forecasting skills; unfortunately, little was achieved. In this regard, more time and effort could have been spent on practical research, such as where the key areas of the economy are heading, rather than on academic research emphasizing overly simplistic models that do not reflect the real world.

If this sounds too harsh, compare some recent Fed forecasts to what actually happened. In its February 2006 semi-annual report to Congress, the Fed projected real GDP growth between 3 percent and 3.5 percent from the fourth quarter of 2006 to the fourth quarter of 2007. In its July 2006 presentation, that forecast was lowered; it was lowered again at the February and July 2007 presentations. In its February 2007 presentation, the Fed projected real growth from the fourth quarter of 2007 to the fourth quarter of 2008 at between 2.7 percent and 3 percent. (Needless to say, that forecast has been substantially lowered. See Table 9-1, page 148.) All of the projections were too high, and much of these were the result of major misestimates of the problems in the housing and mortgage markets where, in essence, the Fed was blindsided.

Perhaps the Fed should be more concerned with the quality of its forecasts rather than the transparency of what it thinks is likely to happen. Extending the length of its forecasts by a year out to three years, which it adopted in late 2007, is not a step in the right direction, since it is already having a considerable amount of difficulty getting its shorter-term forecasts right. Actually, the Fed might be more successful in a third year of a forecast because it is has a better chance for compensating errors.

THE LACK OF A "FEEL" FOR THE MARKETS

Four of the five chairmen studied in this book did not have a good "feel" for the markets. "Feel" cannot be learned, it has to be experienced. Paul Volcker was fortunate that in his earlier years, he worked for a firm that was active in the markets and he benefited from his market background at the Treasury. There were times when the performance of the four other chairmen was hurt by not having a feel for the financial markets, especially when they were an important determinant of economic and financial events. Chairman Bernanke is, finding this out the hard way.

In the case of Greenspan, his market shortcomings were evident when in a speech he mentioned "irrational exuberance" in passing, and then did nothing about it, and when he talked about an "interest rate conundrum" that did not exist. This may help explain why he seemed timid when it came to regulatory policies and reluctant when it came to strong medicine, especially on the preventive side. If one does not fully understand what is happening in the markets and is reluctant to use regulatory tools, this combination can lead to not addressing major market problems in a timely manner. In this regard, there were instances from 1991 to 1998 when the Fed was asleep at the regulatory switch.

To better understand this situation, there was a series of four occurrences that deserve special attention. The first is what was really said and what happened when it came to the term "irrational exuberance;" the second involved a series of adverse domestic and international financial situations in 1997 and 1998; third was the financial debacle at Long Term Capital Management and how it relates to the financial problems that arose in 2007 and 2008, and fourth was Greenspan's famous "conundrum" which was in fact no conundrum at all.

Irrational Exuberance

On December 5, 1996, Chairman Greenspan made a speech at the annual dinner of The American Enterprise Institute for Public Policy Research, entitled "The Challenge of Central Banking in a Democratic Society." The printed copy of the speech was seven pages, and on page six there was one statement that caught the attention of listeners and readers alike, and that was the use of the term "irrational exuberance."

Neither the term "irrational exuberance" nor the tone of its delivery gave any indication that it was meant to be a centerpiece of the speech. The phrase was mentioned only once, and it was not part of Greenspan's conclusions; rather, it was contained in a series of questions and generalities. The following is the paragraph where the statement is made. As one can see, he was already starting to perfect an art which we now call Fed-speak. Quoting from the speech:

Clearly, sustained low inflation implies less uncertainty about the future, and lower risk premiums imply higher prices of stock and other earning assets. We can see that in the inverse relationship exhibited by price/earnings ratios and the rate of inflation in the past. But how do we know when irrational exuberance has unduly escalated asset values, which then become subject to unexpected and prolonged contractions as they have in Japan over the past decade? And how do we factor that assessment into monetary policy? We as central bankers need not be concerned if a collapsing financial asset bubble does not threaten to impair the real economy, its production, jobs, and price stability. Indeed, the sharp stock market break of 1987 had few negative consequences for the economy. But we should not underestimate or become complacent about the complexity of the interactions of asset markets and the economy. Thus, evaluating shifts in balance sheets generally, and in asset prices particularly, must be an integral part of the development of monetary policy.

This paragraph was hardly a shot across the bow, implying that irrational exuberance was a problem. Supporting this conclusion is the extensive table at the end of this chapter, which contains eighteen economic and financial measurements. In the middle of 1995, the Fed had stopped firming monetary policy. In June 1995, the average funds rate was 6.00 percent and the S&P 500 index was 544.75. By December 1995, the funds rate average was down to about 5.60 percent and the S&P was up to 615.93. Then, in 1996, 1997, and 1998, monetary policy, at least measured by the funds rate, was accommodative and the S&P was on an upward binge. In December 1996, at the time of the speech, it was 740.74, in December 1997 it was 970.43 and in December 1998, it was 1,229.23. Moreover, this happened despite several major domestic and international financial debacles. If it was not for these debacles, the S&P index would have been even higher by the end of 1998.

Despite this analysis, the term "irrational exuberance" has had considerable legs. It made much more of an impression on market participants than it did on Greenspan, the Fed, and monetary policy. Many traders around the world jumped on the phrase and ignored the context in which it was used. The Japanese stock market fell 3.2 percent in one day, the Hong Kong market dropped 3 percent, the German market 4 percent, and the London market 2 percent. When the New York Stock Exchange opened the next morning, the Dow Jones industrial average fell 145 points within 30 minutes. Yet, as days and weeks passed, the stock markets began to take off again, and it became clear that investors and analysts had initially read way more into these two words, buried on the sixth page of a seven-page speech, than Greenspan had intended.

The bottom line is that when Greenspan used the phrase in December 1996, there was little evidence of irrational exuberance at that time. However, by the end of 1998, the story was different. By late 1998, investors were hoping—and expecting—that the 30 percent annual advance in the stock market would continue. Yet, the Fed had said little and done nothing to moderate the surge in this run-up of stock prices. This analysis supports the view that on December 5, 1996, there was no attempt on Greenspan's part to give a warning in his speech. If that had been his intention, there surely would have been actions by the Fed somewhere along the line from December 1996 to December 1998.

Further supporting the view that this was not intended to be an "irrational exuberance" message was the title of Greenspan's speech, "The Challenge of Central Banking in a Democratic Society," and his wrap-up comments, which were as follows:

> This evening I have tried to put current central banking issues in historical context. Monetary arrangements, including central banks, naturally are under constant scrutiny and criticism. This is no less true of the Federal Reserve in 1996 than of the gold standard in 1896. Central banks need to respond patiently and responsibly to the commentary and we need to adapt to changing circumstances in markets and the economy.
>
> A democratic society requires a stable and effectively functioning economy. I trust that we and our successors at the Federal Reserve will be important contributors to that end.

Domestic and International Financial Problems in 1997–1998

Irrational exuberance survived not only through 1998, but continued into August 2000 when the S&P 500 reached 1,517.68. This performance was despite some ugly worldwide financial events that occurred in 1997 and 1998. International financial problems emerged in July 1997 in response to the Asian currency crisis, which started in Thailand with the collapse of the baht. The problems then spread to currencies, stocks markets, and other assets in other Asian countries. Indonesia and South Korea were significantly hit by the crisis, and Hong Kong, Malaysia, Laos, and the Philippines were not spared. While at this point, an international crisis had yet to develop, it was clearly a signal that major international financial problems were percolating. Yet U.S. monetary policy was virtually unchanged. For the first three months of 1997, the fed funds target stood at 5.25 percent; on March 25 it was raised to 5.50 percent, where it stayed for the rest of the year. The regulatory picture at the Fed was basically unchanged throughout the year.

After the Asian crisis, many foreign investors were reluctant to lend to developing countries. Real economic growth moderated throughout much of the world, especially in developing nations. These circumstances tended to reduce the price of oil, which led to a financial squeeze on OPEC and other oil exporting countries, including Russia. This meant a sharp reduction in Russian oil revenues and a considerable deterioration in the international financial situation. This was the beginning of events that contributed to the Russian financial crisis and to the Long-Term Capital Management misfortunes in 1998.

The Fed should have been aware of the banks involvement when it came to financing high-risk positions, and who could be left holding the financial bag if investment positions went terribly wrong. If the Fed was not obtaining timely financial data from the banks, that could have been rectified by asking for it. Moreover, at a minimum, moral suasion could have been used by the Fed to induce banks to rein in their financial exposure.

Long-Term Capital Management

History can repeat itself, and sometimes in unfortunate and costly ways. In the financial world, the best example of "three strikes and you're not out" is John Meriwether. The first strike was the problems at Salomon Brothers in 1991 that ultimately led to his departure from the firm; then in 1998, the Long-Term Capital Management (LTCM) debacle was strike two; and in 2008, the losses at JWM Partners LLC was strike three. On March 27, 2008, *The New York Times* published an article entitled "A Decade Later, John Meriwether Must Scramble Again." Quoting from that article:

> Mr. Meriwether's biggest fund, a bond portfolio, has plunged 28% this year; another broader market fund is down 6%. Both had subpar performances last year. Some investors in the funds are seeking to get their money out. Mr. Meriwether and his colleagues at JWM Partners LLC—which he launched in 1999 with LTCM alumni—are trying to reassure investors in the two funds that they have slashed risk and will use their experience to survive this market crisis, preserving about $1.4 billion in assets.

The first of Meriwether's missteps occurred in 1991, and involved collusion and a squeeze in the Treasury market. I was one of two experts hired by the plaintiffs in the legal proceeding that followed, with the defendants being Salomon Brothers and several hedge funds. My responsibilities dealt with everything that had to do with the trading and financing operations of the defendants in the Treasury market and how the squeeze came about. The responsibilities of the other expert (a professor from Stanford University) were primarily on the mathematics side.

To this day, few people realize that what happened in the spring of 1991 was the closest the Treasury market ever came to a financial debacle—and remember, the Treasury market is the centerpiece of the debt markets in general. The case was very complicated, and I spent thousands of hours trying to explain all of the ins and outs of the Treasury market to a team of lawyers who had to become quick learners.

In the spring of 1991, interest rates were heading lower and Salomon Brothers and several hedge funds decided that even more money could be made on the long side by having a dominant position in two-year Treasury notes. In essence, they had a plan to squeeze the market. To understand how this can happen, after the announcement of a Treasury financing auction, but before the payment date, the new issue is traded on a when-issued basis. The time span for this process was often close to two weeks between the announcement and payment dates, with the auction taking place near the middle of the period.

This system of when-issued trading in new securities was used in order to help the dealers in government securities distribute new issues to investors before they were actually auctioned. Normally, that would be no problem, because dealers could pick up the securities in the auction in order to cover their when-issued short positions. In the case of one two-year auction in particular in the spring of 1991, the system did not operate the way it was supposed to work.

In the April 1991 two-year note auction, a pure and simple squeeze took place. Those involved in the squeeze bid very aggressively for the new issue and cornered the market. In other words, they bid well above the price that was expected by others in the auction and closed out the other bidders. The dealers who were closed out in the auction had already sold massive amounts of two-year notes on a when-issued basis. The amounts they sold were so large that they exceeded by many billions of dollars the amount of actual securities that were auctioned.

As the payment date for the two-year note approached, the Fed and the Treasury realized that they had a problem of massive proportions, one that *would*—not merely *could*—create a disaster in the U.S. debt markets. Dealers had not only sold more than the entire size of the new issue, but almost all the dealers had been closed out of buying securities in the auction to cover what in essence were short positions. A massive delivery failure problem was about to ensue and with it, an almost impossible-to-handle ripple effect throughout the debt markets as a whole.

Although those at the New York Fed were naïve about government dealers being involved in a planned Treasury market squeeze with others, to their credit they acted aggressively and correctly when the stark reality of the situation became clear. They strongly "suggested" to those who had cornered the market that they lend out the securities when the settlement date came due. This would allow those dealers who had sold the securities without having them in hand to make their deliveries and complete their contracts. Even then, there was still a huge problem because the when-issued sales were more than the size of the entire issue. There was a need to make more out of less. Fortunately, the securities were freed up, and then recycled in such a manner that the problem was ultimately limited, and then resolved.

Meriwether was in charge of government securities operation at Salomon Brothers, and while he was never directly implicated in the squeeze itself, he did not go out of his way to inform the regulatory authorities about Salomon's role in the squeeze. Thus, while his general reputation was tarnished, his reputation as a trader was not adversely affected, and perhaps, in a convoluted way, it may even have added to his reputation as one sharp trader. This allowed him to go on his merry way and start a new firm called Long Term Capital Management.

There is a message in this three-strikes-and-you're-not-out scenario. Investors have short memories, and it is not much of a leap to say that, as the importance of reward overtook the importance of risk, those who lost a great deal of money in 2007 and 2008 will make the same mistakes again, and probably not as far down the road as you might think. This will be the case no matter how many improvements are made on the regulatory side. Greed never goes out of style; it just gets moderated in trying times.

The LTCM situation was different from the Salomon episode in a lot of ways. In the Salomon case, those involved did not lose a great deal of money, even after the legal settlements. However, that obviously was not the case with respect to LTCM. There are three sources of information that I consider quite reliable when it comes to understanding what happened to LTCM. One is a book by Roger Lowenstein entitled *When Genius Failed: The Rise and Fall of Long-Term Capital Management.* The second is a *Fortune* magazine article published on October 26, 1998, by Carol J. Loomis, with the headline "A House Built on Sand: John Meriwether's once-mighty Long-Term Capital has all but crumbled. So why did Warren Buffett offer to buy it?" The third source is a *Wall Street Journal* story published on September 24, 1998, written by Anita Raghavan and Mitchell Pacelle. The headline is "A Hedge Fund Falters." I found all three sources useful, especially when it came to the nitty-gritty details of the events that brought down LTCM.

Yet, these details, while important, only tell part of the story. Two Nobel Prize winners—Myron Scholes and Robert Merton—were shareholders in LTCM. They relied on a trading model called the Black-Scholes option pricing model. The model relies heavily on an efficient market philosophy where it is believed that markets react on a rational basis. History, however, has proven that while this is often the case, it is not always the case.

What can happen using this approach is that investors will make a considerable amount of money for an extended period—until something goes wrong; and when it goes wrong, it can go terribly wrong, especially when the liquidity in a firm or in markets dries up. In essence, you can lose control of your investment positions. I frequently remind our clients that when you are on a roll and are making money hand over fist, you will be rewarded by a promotion, a bigger payday, or both. However, when you lose a great deal of money and lose control over your positions as liquidity and investors dry up, you have a good chance of losing your job. These outcomes are hardly symmetrical on a risk-reward basis.

Initially LTCM's main strategy was to make trades that were carefully hedged, which would allow them to be successful irrespective of general market trends. However, they started to get away from this approach and got much more involved in directional trades (based on the direction that interest rates were expected to take) and spread-product trades (based on expected changes in yields between investments of different qualities). When they did so, they also added to their leverage when taking positions. A major problem with these more aggressive approaches was that the depth, breadth, and resilience of markets are not constants, and neither are the actual and perceived liquidity and financial capability of the investment manager. Trading models have a problem, to say the least, in coping with this lack of other things remaining equal. The world is more dynamic than the models.

Given the trend of events, red flags should have gone up at the Fed well before everything seemed to fall apart at LTCM as to the involvement of banks in general, and U.S. banks in particular, with regard to the huge amount of funding of LTCM in what was a highly leveraged situation. Additional warning lights should have gone on with respect to credit derivatives and who would be left holding the bag if failures took place. The regulators at the Fed should have been even more concerned when Salomon Brothers left the arbitrage business, since they were a major player in the market. More handwriting on the wall, and yet, the best that can be said is that the Fed—finally and belatedly—started to monitor these events. However, it was not until August 1998, when Russia was embroiled in a financial crisis, devalued its currency, and declared a moratorium on about $13.5 billion of its Treasury debt, that U.S. regulators at last began to realize that an international financial crisis was occurring, and a U.S. hedge fund was right in the middle of the problem.

As these events unfolded, investors tried to move out of risky markets and securities, and into U.S. Treasury issues. This resulted in a liquidity crisis of major proportions. Investors sold Japanese and European bonds to buy U.S. Treasuries. LTCM had expected differences in yield between Japanese and European bonds on one side and yields on U.S. Treasury securities on the other side to narrow. Instead they did the opposite; LTCM lost a huge amount of money, and so did many other investors.

In summary, both the Fed and Greenspan were a day late and a dollar short in not seeing this financial train wreck coming. The banks were over their heads in loans to LTCM, and neither the Fed nor the banks fully understood the risks involved, especially with respect to counterparties. When Bernanke took office in 2006, he would have been far better off if he had studied, in great detail, the financial situations that were especially difficult for Greenspan, such as the LTCM episode, when an excessively easy monetary policy ultimately brought about financial problems and meltdowns. If he had done so, Bernanke may have saved himself, and many others, a great deal of grief.

The Greenspan "Conundrum"

Greenspan's lack of feel for, and understanding of, the markets was indicated in his famous "conundrum" speech made on February 16, 2005 during his semi-annual monetary report to Congress. Bill Griggs and I commented in considerable detail on his testimony in our May 19, 2005, daily report. We stated the following:

> Greenspan is an outstanding business economist, and a good financial economist, but he seems to fall short as a market analyst. We have found over the years that having a good feel for what is happening in the markets does not require a PhD, and at times, a strong theoretical background is often a disadvantage when it comes to analyzing what is moving markets.

One statement in his February 16 testimony shows his excessive reliance on concepts, and not what is happening in the real world. We quote from that testimony:

Other things being equal, increasing short-term rates are normally accompanied by a rise in long-term yields. The simple mathematics of the yield curve governs the relationship between short- and long-term interest rates. Ten-year yields, for example, can be thought of as an average of ten consecutive one-year forward rates. A rise in the first-year forward rate, which correlates closely with the federal funds rate, would increase the yield on ten-year U.S. Treasury notes even if the more-distant forward rates remain unchanged. Historically, though, even these distant forward rates have tended to rise in association with monetary policy tightening.

In the current episode, however, the more-distant forward rates declined at the same time that short-term rates were rising. Indeed, the tenth-year tranche, which yielded 6.5 percent last June, is now at about 5.25 percent. During the same period, comparable real forward rates derived from quotes on Treasury inflation-indexed debt fell significantly as well, suggesting that only a portion of the decline in nominal forward rates in distant tranches is attributable to a drop in long-term inflation expectations.

When the chairman first made his conundrum comment, there was in fact no conundrum, and there has been no conundrum since then. The factor that has dominated the supply/demand equation for Treasuries has primarily come from the demand side, and it has produced submarkets in various maturity sectors. Thus, the ten-year market for Treasuries is often not driven by the same forces that drive the behavior of the two-year issues. Again, from *The Griggs & Santow Report:*

To help in understanding why yields have behaved as they have, let's first consider how the 2-year note has traded. The yield on 2-year notes is currently trading between 3.5% to 3.625 percent. Yet, the funds target is currently 3 percent, and the general expectation in the market is that by August 9th, it will be at 3.5 percent.

The obvious question is how can the yield on the 2-year note be so low? The obvious answer is that when bond and stock markets are not especially attractive to investors, and when at the same time investors desire to be flexible and hold readily tradable assets, the 2-year Treasury note is a good resting place. In short, because the 2-year enjoys a very liquid market in which new issues become available every month, it is an excellent place to park money on a temporary basis. Those investors who put money here are not considering the entire yield curve, nor are their investment decisions based on the behavior of forward contracts well out on the yield curve.

Turning to the 10-year Treasury yield, late last year there were many investors who decided to upgrade the quality of their portfolios. They chose to do this because they felt that down the road, credit spreads would have to widen to accommodate what were expected to be downgrades by the credit rating agencies, especially in key industries, such as automobiles and airlines. For pension funds, there was a fear that some of their security holdings would be downgraded to such an extent that they would fall below investment grade, a development which had the potential to adversely impact their regulatory status.

Also, the 10-year Treasury was the longest full-coupon Treasury now being regularly auctioned. Thus the 10-year was doing the duration work that the 30-year Treasury previously did. Many of these investors would have preferred to buy 30-year Treasuries, but auctions in that maturity were cancelled in 2001, and major investors are reluctant to buy off-the-run issues. Note, the yield differentials between the short- and long-term areas of the Treasury market were not an important consideration in the investment decision, and neither were the spreads driven by credit considerations.

Finally, in the middle of 2004, the market jumped on the bandwagon that the Fed was going to tighten by large, but unknown amounts, and that within a year the funds target would rise to between 4 and 5 percent. This rapid funds-rate increase was supposedly going to occur because of unsustainable strength and a jump in inflation. Those presumptions pushed the ten-year yield to 4.875% in a relatively short period of time.

THE FED IS NOT THE ONLY GAME IN TOWN

The previous analysis is very detailed about the problems that Greenspan faced. Yet, this concentration on Greenspan, his problems, and how he handled them must be kept in perspective, because it can lean toward placing excessive importance on one man and one institution. The Fed is only one slice of the economic pie, and when troubles arise in the economy, the financial markets, or at major financial institutions, the central bank often gets either too much credit or too much blame. Moreover, the Fed is more than just one person. It is also comprised of staff and operating people. Remember, the Fed is also a regulator, and that role is often more important than fine-tuning a funds rate target. Finally, the Fed can be significantly helped or hindered in its policy decisions by outside forces.

The Fed operates in an economy where many sectors are not under its control or even its influence. When Greenspan took over at the Fed, the international economy was just starting to bloom, and a management revolution was taking place in the domestic economy. The growth of foreign economies allowed them to sell goods in the United States at relatively low prices, and the money they accumulated allowed them to reinvest the funds abroad, such as in the United States. Productivity in the United States went from an increase of around 1.5 percent per year to over 2 percent. This held down prices in the United States and helped to limit inflation problems.

Other factors proved to be of considerable importance in helping the Fed in its management of monetary policy during Greenspan's era:

- The change from fixed to floating exchange rates, where the hiccups in the foreign exchange market no longer tended to reach crisis proportions.
- The creation of international treaties and organizations such as NAFTA (The North American Free Trade Agreement).
- The end of the cold war and the growth of countries that were under the mantle of the old Soviet Union.
- The growth in size and importance of multi-national corporations, and how they helped spread wealth around the world in terms of both production and sales.

This was a good time to be the head of the Federal Reserve. Fed officials were riding a tailwind; they were making short-run and cyclical policy mistakes, but generally, these mistakes could be handled without creating major problems. In contrast, Paul Volcker spent most of his eight years trying to get rid of gut-wrenching problems such as double-digit inflation, unsustainably high interest rates, and financial instability caused by the foreign exchange market. Volcker's primary task was to eliminate as much of the economic and financial adversity as possible, and to bring back creditability to the central bank that had been lost under Burns and Miller.

The most telling difference between the problems encountered by Volcker and Greenspan is the consumer price index story. When Greenspan took over from Volcker in August 1987, the CPI was running at a little over 4 percent, and when he left office in January 2006, it was somewhat over 3 percent—not a bad performance. When Volcker took over at the Fed in August 1979, the CPI was at more than 13 percent, and by the time he left office eight years later, it was somewhat over 4 percent. Both did a good job in this regard, but by far Volcker had the greater challenge and therefore, had the opportunity to achieve the greatest improvement.

SUBDIVIDING THE GREENSPAN ERA

The Greenspan era's eighteen years can be divided into six periods. The first, which was extensively discussed in the previous section, began in August 1987 when he took office. The initial period we will call *A Learning Process*. It was punctuated by about as wide a set of circumstances as one can imagine, with the Fed not shy about changing policy—not always by an appropriate amount, and at times, not even in the right direction.

The next period occurred when the Fed was either smart enough, or lucky enough, or some combination of the two, to have eased monetary policy more than what made sense from a cyclical point of view, but which made the greatest amount of sense from a fundamental, longer-term economic growth perspective. The Fed moved policy from very tight to very easy. From close to a 10 percent funds rate target in early 1989, by the fall of 1992, the funds rate target was down to 3 percent. This period allowed financial institutions to regain their health, with the Fed in good part responsible. This period, called *Greenspan at his Best,* is when both he and the Fed distinguished themselves. The return to health of various financial institutions and the easing of monetary policy helped set the stage for an extended economic recovery that began in 1992, which, with only a few blips, continued into the new century.

The third period began in 1993 when the Fed began to firm monetary policy. As was typical of much of Greenspan's term in office, he took the right approach too far, stayed too long with the new policy, and initially was too slow in moving policy in the other direction. For example, instead of ending the firming in the third quarter of 1994, the Fed made several excessive firming moves in late 1994 and early 1995, and paid for it by contributing to problems in the housing market that came close to causing a recession. This period I call *A Firming of Policy Too Far.* Fortunately, the underlying strength of the economy was sufficient enough that a mistake in Fed policy only created a pause in the economic advance.

The fourth period is one where it can be argued that both the Fed and Greenspan fell asleep at the regulatory switch. This is *The Snooze Period.* Greenspan believed in free markets and apparently believed if things went haywire, it was the Fed's job to come in after the fact to try to limit systemic risk. He had a personal belief that selective controls do not work, and for that reason he did not use them. In this snooze period, two events stand out.

In December 1994, the S&P 500 stock index was at 466. This was the starting point of a major upward movement in the stock market. In December 1995, the index was 616, and in December 1996 it was 741. These increases seemed quite rational given the economic and corporate-profit performance. However, after that point, "irrational exuberance" set in, and the index was at 970 in December 1997, 1,229 in December 1998, and 1,469 in December 1999.

The other time the Fed snoozed was when the LTCM crisis caused chaos in the international financial markets, and contributed to a financial calamity that had an impact as far away as Russia. Bank lending to LTCM allowed them to take excessively large positions. By the second quarter of 1998, the company was already in financial difficulty, but the regulators did little or nothing to influence the banks that were lending them the money. It was in the third quarter of 1998 when the feathers hit the fan.

The fifth period for Greenspan began in early 1999, when the Fed decided to edge towards a firmer policy. Again, similar to late 1994 and early 1995, the Fed moved too far and stayed too long. Not only did the Fed move too far, but in May 2000, when the economy was already softening (1 percent growth in the first quarter of 2000), it decided once again to firm policy. This was not a token move, as the Fed raised the funds target from 6 percent to 6.5 percent. Despite the signs of further weakness, and monthly core CPI numbers that were running at a reasonable 0.2 percent, the Fed stayed with that inappropriate policy through the rest of the year. The markets were indicating to the Fed that its policy stance was way too tight, and that it had stayed with it way too long. Stock prices began to plummet and there was a strong rally in the Treasury market. To be charitable, this period is called *Greenspan Not at His Best*.

The sixth and final period is called *Take another Ride on the Funds Rate Roller-Coaster*. At the beginning of 2001—and not waiting for a regular FOMC meeting—the Fed began major and aggressive easing. This continued throughout 2001, and by the end of the year, the fed funds target stood at 1.75 percent. It stayed at that level until late in 2001, when the Fed lowered the funds target to 1.25 percent, and by the middle of 2003, it was moved down to 1 percent and stayed at that level for a year.

In June 2004, a firming trend began in the overnight funds rate, but the changes were token in amount and late in coming. The year when the funds rate target was 1 percent (the middle of 2003 to the middle of 2004), with the regulators on stand-by, proved to be the genesis of the financial debacle of 2007 and 2008. On the lead in this debacle was housing, where too many mortgages loans were made to people who supposedly got a good deal by temporarily paying low floating rates. Then, excessive amounts of mortgages were packaged and sold to investors who did not understand the creditworthiness, or the lack thereof, of the securities they bought. Many of the underlying investments proved to be of questionable quality.

As of January 2006, the funds rate had been raised fourteen times, in 25 basis point increments, from a target rate of 1 percent to a target level of 4.5 percent. That 4.5 percent rate should have been reached at least a year earlier. After Greenspan departed in February 2006, Bernanke increased the funds target in three 25 basis point increments to 5.25 percent. However, a little over a year later, Bernanke and the Fed had cut the funds rate target, and by the second quarter of 2008, it was down to 2 percent. The funds rate roller-coaster that Greenspan had perfected and Bernanke inherited was alive and well.

COMPARING VOLCKER WITH GREENSPAN

An analysis of Fed chairmen would not be complete without comparing the two most prominent U.S. central bankers of our time—Volcker and Greenspan. In the United States, people like to rate one person against another. Who did a better job? Who was the best of the best? DiMaggio or Williams? Mays or Mantle? Russell or Chamberlain? Unitas or Graham? Or for really old-time football fans, Sid Luckman versus Sammy Baugh? (I saw both of them play.) Thus, it is not surprising that there are analysts who want to compare Volcker versus Greenspan. Of course, the venue of sports versus central banking is different. The problem is that in sports, the common denominator for comparison can be personal statistics. That is not possible when it comes to comparing one Fed chairman against another.

In the case of Paul Volcker versus Alan Greenspan, there is another problem. Enough time has passed where one can make a judgment about Volcker and his legacy. It is now two decades since he left the Fed and there have been two chairmen since he served. We are not likely to find out anything to add to or detract from the Volcker record.

Greenspan's situation is different. At this writing, he has been out of office for almost three years, and has had only one successor. The Greenspan story is still being written, and specifically one has to see how the financial market debacles which had their origins in the Greenspan era and reached fruition in 2007 and 2008 play out. Greenspan clearly is not blameless, but only time will tell whether the 2007 and 2008 financial calamities do considerable damage to his reputation. When he was in office, Greenspan was fortunate in that most all of his policy mistakes were temporary and had short legs.

We already know that Volcker inherited a mess of incredible proportions. When he left office, he had made exceptional progress in dealing with many problems, but there was still a ways to go. Eight years was not enough time for him to finish the job. While he left Greenspan with a situation where there were still problems, they were not of the crisis proportions that Volcker faced when he took office. This situation allowed Greenspan to have some time to learn on the job, and while he made some mistakes early in his tenure, he was able to reverse course without creating a crisis situation.

If Greenspan had taken over the Fed in 1979 and Volcker had taken over in 1987 (the opposite of what actually happened), the results in both cases may not have been as good. Greenspan probably would not have been innovative or aggressive enough to quell embedded inflation at the beginning of his days at the Fed. On the other hand, if Volcker had been chairman in the early 1990s, he may not have been as willing to free up the regulatory climate and ease policy as much as Greenspan did. Timing can be everything. There is such a thing as the right person at the right time, and we appear to have been lucky enough to have Volcker and Greenspan at the right times in these key economic and financial turning points.

However, whether the same can be said with respect to the financial system is open to debate. In better shape when he left office in February 2006—maybe; but how much of the blame should he shoulder for the financial disasters of 2007 and 2008? During Greenspan's term in office, there were only a few crises of major proportions, and he handled them adequately, although not always timely. The 2007–2008 financial markets crisis is one item that will tarnish his record, and in this regard, Greenspan's reputation as a central banker will depend to a considerable degree on how Chairman Bernanke performs. Bernanke has Greenspan's reputation in his hands. Yet, in measuring Greenspan's performance, staying out of trouble over much of an eighteen-year period is worth something, since there were are all kinds of opportunities to make major mistakes. Also, given that he did not inherit a period dominated by crises, do not blame Greenspan for not having had the opportunity to shine.

Where Greenspan did have an opportunity to shine in a major way was in dealing primarily with the financial health of depository institutions. Since this happened early in his term, he probably will not get the full credit for what he and the

Fed achieved in the early 1990s with regard to regulatory and interest rate policies. As a matter of fact, there is a good chance that in the next few years, those writing about Greenspan's years at the Fed will dwell primarily on what happened after he left office. This means that his later years at the Fed will receive much more attention than his early years, and this would be a shame, because it was in those earlier years when his achievements were very substantial.

Nor will history be kind to Greenspan for his roller-coaster policy ride when viewed in terms of fed funds rates. He will to be criticized for what appears to have been an over tightening in 1994 and early 1995, an over tightening again in 2000, an over easing in 2003, and then an agonizingly slow increase in the funds target that took over two years before getting it back to what would be considered a more proper level. Yet one hopes this overemphasis on short-term policy mistakes will fade as history has a chance to let long-term factors play out.

In contrast, Volcker was not blessed with enough time to achieve all he wanted to attain. During his eight-year chairmanship, his problems were so large and pressing that Fed policy always seemed to be fighting off impending crises; there were brush fires all over the place. Thus, he was seldom in a position where he could fine-tune or make small adjustments. When all was said and done, the Volcker legacy will be that of a big-time player who made the correct major policy decisions and left the economy and the financial system far better off over the long run.

Volcker's type-A personality helped him in getting through often unpopular policy decisions. He is impressive both physically and intellectually. He is six feet seven inches tall, with a deep voice, with a way of looking at—and through—people. He had a direct hands-on approach when it came to getting things done, and he made it clear who was the boss. All of these traits were a major help in allowing him to deal forcefully with the problems he inherited when he became Fed chairman. After all, he needed to beat the tar out of the economy in order to break the back of embedded inflation.

In contrast, all of the other chairmen since 1970—Burns, Miller, Greenspan, and Bernanke—have not had Volker's forceful personality. This is important because if these other chairman had been in Volcker's shoes in the 1979–1987 period, one wonders whether they would have been direct and persuasive enough to contend with the people and the problems that faced the country and the Fed. It was not the time for collegial discussions about monetary policy, and it was not the time for a chairman to talk a good game and try to impress people with his intellectual smarts.

Of all the Fed chairmen since 1970, Volcker may have been the only one capable of driving through a hard-nosed policy approach. It is difficult to believe, for example, that when the overnight funds rate soared to more than 20 percent, the other Fed chairman could have taken the heat for such a policy move. It is unlikely that the others could have pulled off what Volcker was able to achieve. This is not meant to be a knock against the other chairmen, because frankly, I am not aware of any other person who could have implemented such a painful policy stance in such difficult times.

Unfortunately, it was politics—both inside and outside the Fed—that ultimately did in Volcker. He fought a good fight, but in an organization where there is only one policy, you cannot have people inside the Fed speaking their minds publicly about what they think policy should be. Privately yes; publicly no. In his early years at the Fed, Greenspan also ran into difference-of-opinion problems, but he was not as confrontational as Volcker. In Greenspan's later years at the Fed, many of the differences with colleagues within the Fed seemed to disappear, and even if they did not, apparently they were not handled in a confrontational manner.

GREENSPAN'S FULL LEGACY HAS YET TO BE WRITTEN

As of February 2006, when Greenspan left office, the comparison between his accomplishments and Volcker's was slightly in Volker's favor. However, as events have unfolded in the last three years, the gap has widened and it is not because of Volcker.

Greenspan left Bernanke with a burgeoning regulatory problem, although there was still time for the new chairman to use preventive medicine. Using the Fed's regulatory arm, Bernanke could have been tougher on those banks that were already making questionable loans in the mortgage market. Bernanke had most of 2006 and early 2007, to rectify growing financial problems. He did not do so until the middle of 2007, and then in an inadequate manner when events began to spin out of control.

In weighing the pluses and minuses Greenspan was a good chairman, and we were lucky to have him in that position. In such a long period of eighteen years, it is no surprise that he had his share of good days and bad days, good years and bad years. What he brought to the job was creditability, and while he did not walk on water, he had the confidence of the American people and most of those in government. This is no small achievement, because in recent decades, it has been hard to find public officials who have been viewed in such a positive way for such a long period of time. In difficult times, it is valuable to have someone whom people trust, and to whom people will listen.

Table 9-1
Alan Greenspan, Chairman—Federal Reserve Board of Governors August 11, 1987–January 31, 2006

| 1987 | Financial Markets | | | | | | | Monetary Policy | | | | | Economic Indicators | | | | Commodities | |
	Fed Funds	Treas 30-yr	Corporates Aaa	Corporates Baa	30-yr Mtge	S&P 500	DM	Monetary Base	Free Rsvs	Bank Credit Loans	Bank Credit Inv	Real GDP	Unemp Rate	CPI - % Total	CPI - % Core	Budget	Prices - $ Oil	Prices - $ Gold
Jan																		
Feb																		
Mar																		
Apr																		
May																		
Jun																		
Jul																FY		
Aug	6.73	8.97	9.67	10.80	10.33	329.80	.5522	233.5b	+815	1685	528	+3.7%	6.0	+0.4	+0.3	−149.7	20.27	461.15
Sep	7.22	9.59	10.18	11.31	10.89	321.83	.5427	234.7	+484	1703	531		5.9	+0.3	+0.4		19.53	460.20
Oct	7.29	9.61	10.52	11.62	11.26	251.79	.5786	237.1	+784	1715	528		6.0	+0.3	+0.5		19.85	465.36
Nov	6.69	8.95	10.01	11.23	10.65	230.30	.6096	238.8	+835	1716	531	+7.2%	5.8	+0.3	+0.3		18.92	467.57
Dec	6.77	9.12	10.11	11.29	10.65	247.08	.6366	239.8	+818	1720	535		5.7	+0.2	+0.2		17.24	486.31
						+2.0%	+22.4%	+7.3%		+7.7%	+4.9%	+4.5%		+4.3	+4.2		+7.2%	+24.3%
						D-D	D-D	D-D	D-D	D-D	D-D	4Q-4Q		D-D	D-D		D-D	D-D

1988

Jan	6.83	8.83	9.88	11.07	10.43	257.07	.5958	241.8b	+601	1737	537		5.7	+0.3	+0.4		17.16	476.58
Feb	6.58	8.43	9.40	10.62	9.89	267.82	.5923	242.8	−1022	1749	538		5.7	+0.2	+0.2		16.77	442.07
Mar	6.58	8.63	9.39	10.57	9.93	258.89	.6039	243.7	+791	1762	541	+2.0%	5.7	+0.3	+0.4		16.22	443.61
Apr	6.87	8.95	9.67	10.90	10.20	261.33	.5972	245.8	+661	1779	545		5.4	+0.6	+0.5		17.88	451.55
May	7.09	9.23	9.90	11.04	10.46	262.16	.5784	247.4	+822	1798	548	+5.2%	5.6	+0.3	+0.3		17.44	451.01
Jun	7.51	9.00	9.86	11.00	10.46	273.50	.5504	249.2	+677	1814	552		5.4	+0.4	+0.4		16.53	451.33
Jul	7.75	9.14	9.96	11.11	10.43	272.02	.5333	251.0	+365	1825	553		5.4	+0.4	+0.3		15.50	437.63
Aug	8.01	9.32	10.11	11.21	10.60	261.52	.5323	252.1	+806	1836	554	+2.1%	5.6	+0.4	+0.3	FY	15.52	431.31
Sep	8.19	9.06	9.82	10.90	10.48	271.91	.5339	253.4	+657	1839	554		5.4	+0.4	+0.6	−155.2	14.47	412.79
Oct	8.30	8.89	9.51	10.41	10.30	278.97	.5612	254.6	+867	1851	554		5.4	+0.3	+0.4		13.80	406.78
Nov	8.35	9.02	9.45	10.48	10.27	273.70	.5765	255.7	+821	1860	558	+5.4%	5.3	+0.3	+0.3		13.98	420.17
Dec	8.76	9.01	9.57	10.65	10.61	277.72	.5639	256.9	+719	1872	562		5.3	+0.3	+0.3		16.27	418.49
	+12.4%					−11.4%		+7.1%		+8.8%	+5.0%	+3.7%		+4.4	+4.7		−5.6%	−13.9%
	D-D					D-D		D-D		D-D	D-D	4Q-4Q		D-D	D-D		D-D	D-D

(Continued)

149

Table 9-1
(Continued)

1989	Fed Funds	Treas 30-yr	Aaa	Baa	30-yr Mtge	S&P 500	DM	Monetary Base	Free Rsvs	Loans	Inv	Real GDP	Unemp Rate	Total	Core	Budget	Oil	Gold
			Corporates							Bank Credit				CPI - %			Prices - $	
Jan	9.12	8.93	9.62	10.65	10.73	297.47	.5323	257.9b	+609	1879	561		5.4	+0.4	+0.4		17.98	404.01
Feb	9.36	9.01	9.64	10.61	10.65	288.86	.5486	258.3	+814	1906	560	+4.1%	5.2	+0.3	+0.3		17.83	387.78
Mar	9.85	9.17	9.80	10.67	11.03	294.87	.5273	259.1	+579	1915	564		5.0	+0.5	+0.4		19.45	390.15
Apr	9.84	9.03	9.79	10.61	11.05	309.64	.5319	259.6	+444	1925	563		5.2	+0.7	+0.3		21.04	384.06
May	9.81	8.83	9.57	10.46	10.77	320.52	.5061	260.3	+865	1939	565	+2.6%	5.2	+0.5	+0.4		20.03	371.00
Jun	9.53	8.27	9.10	10.03	10.20	317.98	.5116	261.1	+766	1951	564		5.3	+0.3	+0.4		20.01	367.60
Jul	9.24	8.08	8.93	9.87	9.88	346.08	.5360	262.2	+891	1970	564		5.2	+0.3	+0.3		19.64	375.04
Aug	8.99	8.12	8.96	9.88	9.99	351.45	.5107	262.9	+749	1986	565	+2.9%	5.2	0.0	+0.2	FY	18.52	365.37
Sep	9.02	8.15	9.01	9.91	10.13	349.15	.5341	263.7	+726	1997	565		5.3	+0.2	+0.3	−152.6	19.59	361.75
Oct	8.84	8.00	8.92	9.81	9.95	340.36	.5431	264.9	+836	2011	575		5.3	+0.5	+0.5		20.09	366.88
Nov	8.55	7.90	8.89	9.81	9.77	345.99	.5618	265.6	+754	2017	580	+1.0%	5.4	+0.4	+0.4		19.82	394.26
Dec	8.45	7.90	8.86	9.82	9.74	353.40	.5919	267.8	+779	2018	585		5.4	+0.3	+0.4		21.09	409.39
						+27.3%	+5.0%	+4.2%		+7.8%	+4.1%	+2.7%		+4.6	+4.4		+29.6%	−2.2%
						D-D	D-D	D-D		D-D	D-D	4Q-4Q		D-D	D-D		D-D	D-D

1990

Jan	8.23	8.26	8.99	9.94	9.90	329.08	.5924	269.6b	+675	2022	595		5.4	+1.0	+0.4		22.64	410.11
Feb	8.24	8.50	9.22	10.14	10.20	331.89	.5875	271.1	+137	2032	604	+4.7%	5.3	+0.4	+0.5		22.11	416.83
Mar	8.28	8.56	9.37	10.21	10.27	339.94	.5923	273.1	+786	2044	607		5.2	+0.5	+0.6		20.42	393.07
Apr	8.26	8.76	9.46	10.30	10.37	330.80	.5956	275.2	+769	2054	610		5.4	+0.2	+0.4		18.58	374.27
May	8.18	8.73	9.47	10.41	10.48	361.23	.5886	276.8	+739	2062	613	+1.0	5.4	+0.2	+0.3		18.24	369.19
Jun	8.29	8.46	9.26	10.22	10.16	358.02	.6003	278.9	+563	2072	621		5.2	+0.6	+0.5		16.87	352.33
Jul	8.15	8.50	9.24	10.20	10.04	356.15	.6299	281.0	+780	2082	624		5.5	+0.5	+0.5		18.64	362.53
Aug	8.13	8.86	9.41	10.41	10.10	322.56	.6345	284.1	+507	2102	628	0.0	5.7	+0.8	+0.6	FY	27.17	394.73
Sep	8.20	9.03	9.56	10.64	10.18	306.05	.6384	287.3	+714	2102	631		5.9	+0.7	+0.4	−221.0	33.69	388.41
Oct	8.11	8.86	9.53	10.74	10.18	304.00	.6598	289.2	+783	2108	634		5.9	+0.7	+0.4		35.92	380.74
Nov	7.81	8.54	9.30	10.62	10.01	322.22	.6667	291.1	+884	2108	634	−3.0	6.2	+0.2	+0.3		32.30	381.73
Dec	7.31	8.24	9.05	10.43	9.67	330.22	.6680	293.3	+1437	2114	635		6.3	+0.4	+0.4		27.34	378.16
						−6.6%	+12.9%	+9.5%		+4.8%	+8.5%	+0.7%	+6.3	+5.3			+29.6%	−7.6%
						D-D	D-D	D-D		D-D	D-D	4Q-4Q	D-D	D-D			D-D	D-D

(Continued)

Table 9-1
(Continued)

1991	Financial Markets							Monetary Policy				Economic Indicators					Commodities	
	Fed Funds	Treas 30-yr	Corporates		30-yr Mtge	S&P 500	DM	Monetary Base	Free Rsvs	Bank Credit		Real GDP	Unemp Rate	CPI - %		Budget	Prices - $	
			Aaa	Baa						Loans	Inv			Total	Core		Oil	Gold
Jan	6.91	8.27	9.04	10.45	9.64	343.93	.6764	297.8b	+1668	2111	642	−2.0%	6.4	+0.4	+0.6		24.96	383.64
Feb	6.25	8.03	8.83	10.07	9.37	367.07	.6553	300.9	+1624	2124	646		6.6	+0.1	+0.5		20.52	363.83
Mar	6.12	8.29	8.93	10.09	9.50	375.22	.5891	302.7	+1051	2124	657		6.8	0.0	+0.2		19.86	363.33
Apr	5.91	8.21	8.86	9.94	9.49	375.34	.5819	303.0	+960	2122	660	+2.6%	6.7	+0.2	+0.3		20.82	358.39
May	5.78	8.27	8.86	9.86	9.47	389.83	.5748	304.2	+969	2119	666		6.9	+0.4	+0.3		21.24	356.82
Jun	5.90	8.47	9.01	9.96	9.62	371.16	.5513	305.5	+883	2121	675		6.9	+0.3	+0.4		20.20	366.72
Jul	5.82	8.45	9.00	9.89	9.57	387.81	.5726	307.2	+659	2111	684	+1.9%	6.8	+0.1	+0.4		21.42	367.68
Aug	5.66	8.14	8.75	9.65	9.24	395.43	.5719	309.3	+954	2109	692		6.9	+0.1	+0.4	FY	21.69	356.23
Sep	5.45	7.95	8.61	9.51	9.01	387.86	.6015	310.7	+874	2107	704		6.9	+0.3	+0.3	−269.2	21.86	348.74
Oct	5.21	7.93	8.55	9.49	8.86	392.45	.5995	312.7	+1017	2107	721		7.0	+0.1	+0.2		23.23	358.69
Nov	4.81	7.92	8.48	9.45	8.71	375.22	.6146	314.9	+872	2106	735	+1.9%	7.0	+0.4	+0.3		22.47	360.17
Dec	4.43	7.70	8.31	9.26	8.50	417.09	.6579	317.6	+836	2108	748		7.3	+0.3	+0.3		19.52	361.06
						+26.3%	−1.5%	+8.3%		−0.3%	+17.8%	+1.1%		+3.0	+4.4		−28.6	−4.5%
						D-D	D-D	D-D		D-D	D-D	4Q-4Q		D-D	D-D		D-D	D-D

152

1992

Jan	4.03	7.58	8.20	9.13	8.43	408.78	.6221	319.6b	+775	2113	756		7.3	+0.1	+0.3	18.82	354.45
Feb	4.06	7.85	8.29	9.23	8.76	412.70	.6108	322.6	+1000	2117	761	+4.2%	7.4	+0.2	+0.2	19.00	353.89
Mar	3.98	7.97	8.35	9.25	8.94	403.69	.6074	324.4	+967	2120	766		7.4	+0.4	+0.3	18.92	344.35
Apr	3.73	7.96	8.33	9.21	8.85	414.95	.6051	326.7	+1086	2119	773		7.4	+0.2	+0.3	20.24	338.50
May	3.82	7.89	8.28	9.13	8.67	415.35	.6225	328.8	+947	2112	783	+3.9%	7.6	+0.2	+0.3	20.94	337.23
Jun	3.76	7.84	8.22	9.05	8.51	408.14	.6562	330.2	+843	2112	791		7.8	+0.3	+0.2	22.38	340.80
Jul	3.25	7.60	8.07	8.84	8.13	424.21	.6754	333.2	+893	2101	803		7.7	+0.3	+0.3	21.76	353.05
Aug	3.30	7.39	7.95	8.65	7.98	414.03	.7134	336.9	+911	2104	817	+4.0%	7.6	+0.2	+0.2 FY	21.35	342.96
Sep	3.22	7.34	7.92	8.62	7.92	417.80	.7069	340.8	+918	2110	823		7.6	+0.2	+0.1 −290.3	21.90	345.55
Oct	3.10	7.53	7.99	8.84	8.09	418.68	.6481	344.6	+1032	2110	831		7.3	+0.4	+0.5	21.69	344.38
Nov	3.09	7.61	8.10	8.96	8.31	431.35	.6276	347.7	+978	2110	838	+4.5%	7.4	+0.3	+0.3	20.34	335.87
Dec	2.92	7.44	7.98	8.81	8.22	435.71	.6174	350.9	+1049	2111	842		7.4	+0.1	+0.3	19.41	334.80
					+4.5%	−6.2%	+10.5%	+0.1%	+12.6%	+4.1%			+3.0	+3.4	−5.6%	−7.3%
					D-D	D-D	D-D	D-D	D-D	4Q-4Q			D-D	D-D	D-D	D-D

(Continued)

Table 9-1
(Continued)

1993	Fed Funds	Treas 30-yr	Aaa	Baa	30-yr Mtge	S&P 500	DM	Monetary Base	Free Rsvs	Loans	Inv	Real GDP	Unemp Rate	Total	Core	Budget	Oil	Gold
			Corporates							Bank Credit				CPI - %			Prices - $	
Jan	3.02	7.34	7.91	8.67	8.02	438.78	.6207	353.7b	+1108	2111	847		7.3	+0.4	+0.3		19.08	329.01
Feb	3.03	7.09	7.71	8.39	7.68	443.38	.6089	355.4	+1065	2110	858	+0.5%	7.1	+0.2	+0.3		20.05	329.35
Mar	3.07	6.82	7.58	8.15	7.50	451.67	.6209	357.8	+1167	2116	872		7.0	+0.1	+0.1		20.35	330.08
Apr	2.96	6.85	7.46	8.14	7.47	440.19	.6299	360.9	+1072	2113	876	+2.0%	7.1	+0.3	+0.4		20.27	342.07
May	3.00	6.92	7.43	8.21	7.47	450.19	.6297	364.9	+959	2133	880		7.1	+0.3	+0.3		19.94	367.18
Jun	3.04	6.81	7.33	8.07	7.42	450.53	.5862	367.9	+852	2148	888		7.0	+0.1	+0.2		19.07	371.89
Jul	3.06	6.63	7.17	7.93	7.21	448.13	.5746	371.4	+1033	2160	894		6.9	+0.1	+0.1		17.87	392.19
Aug	3.03	6.32	6.85	7.60	7.11	463.56	.5960	374.6	+834	2164	902	+2.1%	6.8	+0.2	+0.3	FY	18.01	378.84
Sep	3.09	6.00	6.66	7.34	6.92	458.93	.6120	378.3	+891	2167	905		6.7	+0.1	+0.1	−255.1	17.51	355.27
Oct	2.99	5.94	6.67	7.31	6.83	467.83	.5963	381.6	+985	2175	904		6.8	+0.4	+0.3		18.15	364.18
Nov	3.02	6.21	6.93	7.66	7.16	461.79	.5822	384.1	+1103	2188	909	+5.5%	6.6	+0.3	+0.3		16.70	373.83
Dec	2.96	6.25	6.93	7.69	7.17	466.45	.5749	386.6	+1019	2195	916		6.5	+0.2	+0.3		14.51	383.35
						+7.1%	−6.9%	+10.2%		+4.0%	+8.8%	+2.5%		+2.8	+3.1		−25.2%	+14.5%
						D-D	D-D	D-D		D-D	D-D	4Q-4Q		D-D	D-D		D-D	D-D

1994

1994																		
Jan	3.05	6.29	6.92	7.65	7.06	481.61	.5748	390.2b	+1398	2199	945		6.6	0.0	+0.1		15.00	386.88
Feb	3.25	6.49	7.08	7.76	7.15	467.14	.5869	393.3	+1091	2208	941	+4.1%	6.6	+0.3	+0.2		14.78	381.91
Mar	3.34	6.91	7.48	8.13	7.68	445.77	.5995	396.0	+950	2221	957		6.5	+0.3	+0.3		14.66	384.13
Apr	3.56	7.27	7.88	8.52	8.32	450.91	.6021	398.9	+1072	2230	967		6.4	+0.1	+0.1		16.38	377.27
May	4.01	7.41	7.99	8.62	8.60	456.50	.6080	401.4	+799	2241	962	+5.3%	6.1	+0.2	+0.3		17.88	381.26
Jun	4.25	7.40	7.97	8.65	8.40	444.27	.6309	404.4	+1007	2251	966		6.1	+0.3	+0.3		19.07	385.64
Jul	4.26	7.58	8.11	8.80	8.61	458.26	.6299	407.8	+1017	2277	973		6.1	+0.3	+0.2		19.65	385.49
Aug	4.47	7.49	8.07	8.74	8.51	475.49	.6331	409.6	+980	2301	965	+2.3	6.0	+0.4	+0.3	FY	18.38	380.35
Sep	4.73	7.71	8.34	8.98	8.64	462.71	.6448	411.8	+1003	2314	962		5.9	+0.2	+0.3	−203.2	17.46	391.58
Oct	4.76	7.94	8.57	9.20	8.93	472.35	.6648	414.0	+749	2332	957		5.8	+0.1	+0.2		17.71	389.77
Nov	5.29	8.08	8.68	9.32	9.17	453.69	.6376	416.7	+902	2349	948	+4.8%	5.6	+0.3	+0.3		18.10	384.39
Dec	5.45	7.87	8.46	9.10	9.20	459.27	.6454	418.3	+1050	2375	940		5.5	+0.2	+0.1		17.16	379.29
						−1.5%	+12.3%	+8.2%		+8.2%	+2.6%	+4.1%		+2.6	+2.6		+18.3%	−1.1%
						D-D	D-D	D-D		D-D	D-D	4Q-4Q		D-D	D-D		D-D	D-D

(Continued)

155

Table 9-1
(Continued)

| 1995 | Financial Markets | | | | | | | Monetary Policy | | | | Economic Indicators | | | | | Commodities | |
| | Fed Funds | Treas 30-yr | Corporates | | 30-yr Mtge | S&P 500 | DM | Monetary Base | Free Rsvs | Bank Credit | | Real GDP | Unemp Rate | CPI - % | | Budget | Prices - $ | |
			Aaa	Baa						Loans	Inv			Total	Core		Oil	Gold
Jan	5.53	7.85	8.46	9.08	9.15	470.42	.6565	421.0b	+1254	2399	940		5.6	+0.3	+0.4		17.99	378.55
Feb	5.92	7.61	8.26	8.85	8.83	487.39	.6865	421.6	+935	2423	934	+1.1%	5.4	+0.3	+0.3		18.53	376.64
Mar	5.98	7.45	8.12	8.70	8.46	500.71	.7254	424.7	+797	2447	948		5.4	+0.2	+0.3		18.55	382.12
Apr	6.05	7.36	8.03	8.60	8.32	514.71	.7217	427.9	+725	2473	1001	+0.7%	5.8	+0.4	+0.3		19.87	391.03
May	6.01	6.95	7.65	8.20	7.96	533.40	.7072	430.5	+861	2507	988		5.6	+0.2	+0.2		19.74	385.12
Jun	6.00	6.57	7.30	7.90	7.57	544.75	.7228	430.2	+882	2530	984		5.6	+0.2	+0.2		18.42	387.56
Jul	5.85	6.72	7.41	8.04	7.61	562.06	.7219	430.7	+963	2552	987	+3.3%	5.7	+0.1	+0.2		17.30	386.23
Aug	5.74	6.86	7.57	8.19	7.86	561.88	.6813	431.3	+980	2566	994		5.7	+0.2	+0.2	FY	18.03	383.81
Sep	5.80	6.55	7.32	7.93	7.64	584.41	.6996	431.9	+943	2584	997		5.6	+0.1	+0.2	−164.0	18.23	383.05
Oct	5.76	6.37	7.12	7.75	7.48	581.50	.7105	432.6	+1039	2591	995	+3.0%	5.5	+0.3	+0.3		17.44	383.14
Nov	5.80	6.26	7.02	7.68	7.38	605.37	.6912	432.9	+823	2605	990		5.6	+0.1	+0.2		17.99	385.30
Dec	5.60	6.06	6.82	7.49	7.20	615.93	.6971	434.6	+1073	2613	984		5.6	+0.1	+0.1		19.04	387.44
						+34.1%	+8.0%	+3.9%		+10.0%	+4.7%	+2.0%		+2.5	+3.0		+11.0%	+2.1%
						D-D	D-D	D-D		D-D	D-D	4Q-4Q		D-D	D-D		D-D	D-D

1996

Jan	5.56	6.05	6.81	7.47	7.03	636.02	.6714	434.8b	+1433	2638	983		5.6	+0.5	+0.4		18.88	400.27
Feb	5.22	6.24	6.99	7.63	7.08	640.43	.6801	432.6	+829	2645	996	+2.9%	5.5	+0.2	+0.2		19.07	404.79
Mar	5.31	6.60	7.35	8.03	7.62	645.50	.6772	435.9	+1128	2654	990		5.5	+0.3	+0.2		21.36	396.25
Apr	5.22	6.79	7.50	8.19	7.93	654.17	.6535	437.0	+1066	2674	991		5.6	+0.4	+0.1		23.57	392.83
May	5.24	6.93	7.62	8.30	8.07	669.12	.6551	437.5	+883	2675	998	+6.7%	5.6	+0.2	+0.2		21.25	391.86
Jun	5.27	7.06	7.71	8.40	8.32	670.63	.6575	440.1	+914	2689	991		5.3	+0.2	+0.2		20.45	385.27
Jul	5.40	7.03	7.65	8.35	8.24	630.95	.6791	442.6	+934	2704	990		5.5	+0.2	+0.2		21.32	383.47
Aug	5.22	6.84	7.46	8.18	8.00	651.99	.6756	444.7	+933	2708	982	+3.4%	5.1	+0.1	+0.2	FY	21.96	387.46
Sep	5.30	7.03	7.66	8.35	8.23	687.33	.6549	446.0	+986	2728	974		5.2	+0.3	+0.3	−107.4	23.99	383.14
Oct	5.24	6.81	7.39	8.07	7.92	705.27	.6605	446.9	+932	2740	981		5.2	+0.3	+0.2		24.90	381.07
Nov	5.31	6.48	7.10	7.79	7.62	757.02	.6503	448.8	+947	2752	987	+4.8%	5.4	+0.3	+0.2		23.71	377.85
Dec	5.29	6.55	7.20	7.89	7.60	740.74	.6499	452.1	+1329	2769	985		5.4	+0.3	+0.1		25.39	369.00
						+20.3%	−6.8%	+4.0%		+6.0%	+0.1%	+4.4%		+3.4	+2.6		+33.4%	−4.8%
						D-D	D-D	D-D		D-D	D-D	4Q-4Q		D-D	D-D		D-D	D-D

(Continued)

Table 9-1
(Continued)

1997	Financial Markets							Monetary Policy					Economic Indicators					Commodities	
	Fed Funds	Treas 30-yr	Corporates Aaa	Corporates Baa	30-yr Mtge	S&P 500	DM	Monetary Base	Free Rsvs	Bank Credit Loans	Bank Credit Inv	Real GDP	Unemp Rate	CPI - % Total	CPI - % Core	Budget	Prices - $ Oil	Prices - $ Gold
Jan	5.25	6.83	7.42	8.09	7.82	786.16	.6112	453.5b	+1198	2787	1005	+3.1%	5.3	+0.2	+0.2		25.17	354.11
Feb	5.19	6.69	7.31	7.94	7.65	790.82	.5927	454.5	+1010	2806	1024		5.2	+0.2	+0.2		22.21	346.58
Mar	5.39	6.93	7.55	8.18	7.90	757.12	.5996	456.2	+1046	2832	1023		5.2	+0.1	+0.2		20.99	351.81
Apr	5.51	7.09	7.73	8.34	8.14	801.34	.5770	457.9	+ 836	2856	1040	+6.2%	5.1	+0.1	+0.3		19.72	344.47
May	5.50	6.94	7.58	8.20	7.94	848.28	.5851	459.5	+1192	2882	1026		4.9	0.0	+0.2		20.83	343.97
Jun	5.56	6.77	7.41	8.02	7.69	885.14	.5735	462.2	+1190	2904	1025		5.0	+0.2	+0.1		19.17	340.76
Jul	5.52	6.51	7.14	7.75	7.50	954.31	.5441	464.7	+1137	2924	1049	+5.1%	4.9	+0.1	+0.2		19.63	324.10
Aug	5.54	6.58	7.22	7.82	7.48	899.47	.5540	467.0	+1042	2939	1049		4.8	+0.2	+0.1	FY	19.93	324.01
Sep	5.54	6.50	7.15	7.70	7.43	947.28	.5659	469.2	+1231	2957	1051		4.9	+0.2	+0.2	−21.9	19.79	322.82
Oct	5.50	6.33	7.00	7.57	7.29	914.62	.5807	471.8	+1373	2977	1067	+3.0%	4.7	+0.2	+0.2		21.26	324.87
Nov	5.52	6.11	6.87	7.42	7.21	955.40	.5666	475.9	+1631	2985	1096		4.6	+0.1	+0.1		20.17	306.04
Dec	5.50	5.99	6.76	7.32	7.10	970.43	.5558	479.9	+1440	2998	1100		4.7	+0.1	+0.2		18.32	288.74
						+31.0%	−14.5	+6.1%		+8.3%	+11.7%	+4.3%		+1.7	+2.3		−27.8%	−21.8%
						D-D	D-D	D-D		D-D	D-D	4Q-4Q		D-D	D-D		D-D	D-D

1998

Jan	5.56	5.81	6.61	7.19	6.99	980.28	.5460	482.1b	+1601	3024	1124		4.6	+0.1	+0.2		16.71	289.15
Feb	5.51	5.89	6.67	7.25	7.04	1049.34	.5512	483.2	+1487	3053	1125	+4.5%	4.6	0.0	+0.2		16.06	297.49
Mar	5.49	5.95	6.72	7.32	7.13	1101.75	.5405	484.9	+1332	3080	1139		4.7	0.0	+0.2		15.02	295.94
Apr	5.45	5.92	6.69	7.33	7.14	1111.75	.5573	486.9	+1357	3099	1130		4.3	+0.1	+0.2		15.44	308.29
May	5.49	5.93	6.69	7.30	7.14	1090.82	.5605	488.8	+1214	3107	1141	+2.7%	4.4	+0.2	+0.2		14.86	299.10
Jun	5.56	5.70	6.53	7.13	7.00	1133.84	.5545	491.9	+1524	3130	1140		4.5	+0.1	+0.2		13.66	292.32
Jul	5.54	5.68	6.55	7.15	6.95	1120.67	.5621	494.7	+1328	3142	1145		4.5	+0.2	+0.2		14.08	292.87
Aug	5.55	5.54	6.52	7.14	6.92	957.28	.5687	497.9	+1502	3177	1168	+4.7%	4.5	+0.1	+0.3	FY	13.36	284.11
Sep	5.51	5.20	6.40	7.09	6.72	1017.01	.5987	502.6	+1622	3207	1186		4.6	+0.1	+0.1	+69.3	14.95	288.98
Oct	5.07	5.01	6.37	7.18	6.71	1098.67	.6037	506.9	+1505	3258	1235		4.5	+0.2	+0.1		14.39	296.22
Nov	4.83	5.25	6.41	7.34	6.87	1163.63	.5894	510.4	+1572	3285	1239	+6.2%	4.4	+0.1	+0.2		12.85	294.77
Dec	4.68	5.06	6.22	7.23	6.72	1229.23	.5999	513.9	+1413	3293	1240		4.4	+0.2	+0.3		11.28	291.62
						+26.7%	+7.9%	+7.1%	+9.8%	+12.7%	+4.5%		+1.6	+2.5		-38.4%	+1.0%
						D-D	D-D	D-D	D-D	D-D	4Q-4Q		D-D	D-D		D-D	D-D

(Continued)

Table 9-1
(Continued)

1999	Fed Funds	Treas 30-yr	Corporates Aaa	Corporates Baa	30-yr Mtge	S&P 500	Euro	Monetary Base	Free Rsvs	Bank Credit Loans	Bank Credit Inv	Real GDP	Unemp Rate	CPI - % Total	CPI - % Core	Budget	Oil	Gold
Jan	4.63	5.16	6.24	7.29	6.79	1279.64	1.1371	516.4b	+1287	3294	1230		4.3	+0.2	+0.1		12.47	287.07
Feb	4.76	5.37	6.40	7.39	6.81	1238.33	1.0995	520.3	+1090	3289	1218	+3.4%	4.4	0.0	0.0		12.01	287.22
Mar	4.81	5.58	6.62	7.53	7.04	1286.37	1.0808	524.6	+1222	3287	1200		4.2	+0.1	+0.1		14.66	285.96
Apr	4.74	5.55	6.64	7.48	6.92	1335.18	1.0564	528.3	+1032	3295	1205		4.3	+0.7	+0.3		17.34	282.62
May	4.74	5.81	6.93	7.72	7.15	1301.84	1.0422	533.2	+1183	3305	1204	+3.4%	4.2	+0.1	+0.1		17.75	276.88
Jun	4.76	6.04	7.23	8.02	7.55	1372.71	1.0310	537.0	+1277	3324	1221		4.3	0.0	+0.1		17.89	261.37
Jul	4.99	5.98	7.19	7.95	7.63	1328.72	1.0694	540.5	+1041	3308	1236		4.3	+0.4	+0.3		20.07	256.08
Aug	5.07	6.07	7.40	8.15	7.94	1320.41	1.0581	544.8	+1088	3328	1248	+4.8%	4.2	+0.2	+0.1	FY	21.26	256.70
Sep	5.22	6.07	7.39	8.20	7.82	1282.71	1.0643	550.3	+1154	3349	1253		4.2	+0.4	+0.3	+125.6	23.88	266.60
Oct	5.20	6.26	7.55	8.38	7.85	1362.93	1.0518	557.8	+1099	3369	1267		4.1	+0.2	+0.2		22.64	310.72
Nov	5.42	6.15	7.36	8.15	7.74	1388.91	1.0077	571.7	+1173	3428	1268	+7.3%	4.1	+0.2	+0.2		24.97	293.18
Dec	5.30	6.35	7.55	8.19	7.91	1469.25	1.0070	593.9	+1118	3479	1286		4.0	+0.2	+0.2		26.08	283.34
						+19.5%	−14.7	+15.6%		+5.6%	+3.7%	+4.7%		+2.7	+1.9		+131.2%	−2.8%
						D-D	D-D	D-D		D-D	D-D	4Q-4Q		D-D	D-D		D-D	D-D

2000

Jan	5.45	6.63	7.78	8.33	8.21	1394.46	.9757	590.9b	+1724	3505	1284		4.0	+0.3	+0.3		27.18	284.32
Feb	5.73	6.23	7.68	8.29	8.32	1366.42	.9643	572.5	+1067	3548	1278	+1.0%	4.1	+0.4	+0.1		29.35	299.94
Mar	5.85	6.05	7.68	8.37	8.24	1498.58	.9574	571.2	+1108	3590	1289		4.0	+0.6	+0.3		29.89	286.39
Apr	6.02	5.85	7.64	8.40	8.15	1452.43	.9089	572.0	+973	3623	1303		3.8	−0.1	+0.2		25.74	279.86
May	6.27	6.15	7.99	8.90	8.52	1420.60	.9328	573.5	+886	3669	1319	+6.4%	4.0	+0.2	+0.2		28.78	275.31
Jun	6.53	5.93	7.67	8.48	8.29	1454.60	.9545	575.7	+1027	3710	1314		4.0	+0.6	+0.2		31.83	285.73
Jul	6.54	5.85	7.65	8.35	8.15	1430.83	.9266	577.1	+1083	3746	1320		4.0	+0.3	+0.2		29.77	281.55
Aug	6.50	5.72	7.55	8.26	8.03	1517.68	.8878	577.7	+993	3776	1325	−0.5%	4.1	0.0	+0.2	FY	31.22	274.47
Sep	6.52	5.83	7.62	8.35	7.91	1436.51	.8837	578.4	+1069	3807	1341		3.9	+0.5	+0.2	+236.2	33.88	273.68
Oct	6.51	5.80	7.55	8.34	7.80	1429.40	.8486	580.5	+1031	3818	1326		3.9	+0.2	+0.2		33.08	270.00
Nov	6.51	5.78	7.45	8.28	7.75	1314.95	.8694	582.5	+1184	3836	1326	+2.1%	3.9	+0.2	+0.3		34.40	266.01
Dec	6.40	5.49	7.21	8.02	7.38	1320.28	.9388	585.0	+1329	3868	1351		3.9	+0.2	+0.1		28.46	271.45
						−10.1%	−6.8%	−1.0%	+11.2%	+5.1%	+2.2%			+3.4	+2.6		+9.1%	−4.2%
						D-D	D-D	D-D	D-D	D-D	4Q-4Q			D-D			D-D	D-D

(Continued)

Table 9-1
(Continued)

| 2001 | Financial Markets | | | | | | | Monetary Policy | | | | Economic Indicators | | | | | Commodities | |
	Fed Funds	Treas 30-yr	Corporates Aaa	Baa	30-yr Mtge	S&P 500	Euro	Monetary Base	Free Rsvs	Bank Credit Loans	Inv	Real GDP	Unemp Rate	CPI - % Total	Core	Budget	Prices - $ Oil	Gold
Jan	5.98	5.54	7.15	7.93	7.03	1366.01	.9308	587.9b	+1345	3885	1374		4.2	+0.6	+0.3		29.58	265.49
Feb	5.49	5.45	7.10	7.87	7.05	1239.94	.9212	589.5	+1477	3901	1362	−0.5%	4.2	+0.2	+0.3		29.61	261.86
Mar	5.31	5.34	6.98	7.84	6.95	1160.33	.8794	592.2	+1361	3927	1360		4.3	+0.1	+0.2		27.24	263.06
Apr	4.80	5.65	7.20	8.07	7.08	1249.46	.8874	595.4	+1262	3935	1375	+1.2%	4.4	+0.2	+0.2		27.41	260.48
May	4.21	5.78	7.29	8.07	7.15	1255.82	.8455	598.7	+885	3937	1380		4.3	+0.5	+0.1		28.64	272.35
Jun	3.97	5.67	7.18	7.97	7.16	1224.38	.8474	602.1	+1253	3932	1393		4.5	+0.2	+0.4		27.60	270.73
Jul	3.77	5.61	7.13	7.97	7.13	1211.23	.8752	608.0	+1299	3928	1395	−1.4%	4.6	−0.2	+0.2		26.45	267.53
Aug	3.65	5.48	7.02	7.85	6.95	1133.58	.9090	615.5	+15725	3914	1426		4.9	0.0	+0.2	FY	27.47	272.39
Sep	3.07	5.48	7.17	8.03	6.82	1040.94	.9099	639.7	+1266	3967	1446		5.0	+0.4	+0.2	+128.2	25.88	283.42
Oct	2.49	5.32	7.03	7.91	6.62	1059.78	.8993	630.3	+1266	3933	1476	+1.6%	5.3	−0.3	+0.2		22.21	283.06
Nov	2.09	5.12	6.97	7.81	6.66	1139.45	.8958	630.2	+1391	3944	1491		5.5	−0.1	+0.4		19.67	276.16
Dec	1.82	5.48	6.77	8.05	7.07	1148.08	.8901	635.5	+1616	3932	1490		5.7	−0.1	+0.2		19.33	275.85
						−13.0%	−5.2%	+8.6%		+1.7%	+10.3%	+0.2%		+1.6	+2.8		−32.1%	+1.6%
						D-D	D-D	D-D		D-D	D-D	4Q-4Q		D-D	D-D		D-D	D-D

162

2002

2002																		
Jan	1.73	5.45	6.55	7.87	7.00	1130.20	.8594	641.1b	+1362	3917	1491		5.7	+0.2	+0.2		19.67	282.65
Feb	1.74	5.40	6.51	7.89	6.89	1106.73	.8658	646.0	+1359	3932	1489	+2.7%	5.7	+0.2	+0.2		20.74	295.50
Mar	1.73	5.93	6.81	8.11	7.01	1147.39	.8717	649.7	+1362	3934	1488		5.7	+0.3	+0.1		24.42	294.05
Apr	1.75	5.85	6.76	8.03	6.99	1076.92	.9002	653.7	+1190	3945	1501		5.9	+0.4	+0.3		26.27	302.68
May	1.75	5.81	6.75	8.09	6.81	1067.14	.9339	657.7	+1254	3962	1528	+2.2%	5.8	+0.1	+0.2		27.02	314.49
Jun	1.75	5.65	6.63	7.95	6.65	989.82	.9856	663.0	+1232	3982	1557		5.8	+0.1	+0.1		25.52	321.18
Jul	1.73	5.51	6.53	7.90	6.49	911.62	.9796	668.6	+1361	3994	1590		5.8	+0.2	+0.2		26.94	313.29
Aug	1.74	5.19	6.37	7.58	6.29	916.07	.9806	670.3	+1460	4031	1631	+2.4%	5.7	+0.3	+0.3	FY	28.38	310.25
Sep	1.75	4.87	6.15	7.40	6.09	815.28	.9879	671.4	+1426	4073	1648		5.7	+0.2	+0.1	−157.8	29.67	319.16
Oct	1.75	5.00	6.32	7.73	6.11	885.76	.9881	674.0	+1512	4104	1649		5.7	+0.2	+0.1		28.85	316.56
Nov	1.34	5.04	6.31	7.62	6.07	936.31	.9932	677.3	+1428	4135	1685	+0.2%	5.9	+0.2	+0.2		26.27	319.15
Dec	1.24	5.01	6.21	7.45	6.05	879.82	1.0485	681.7	+1974	4166	1725		6.0	+0.2	+0.1		29.42	332.43
						−23.4%	+17.8	+7.3%	+6.0%	+15.8%		+1.9%		+2.5	+2.0		+52.2%	+20.4%
						D-D	D-D	D-D	D-D	D-D		4Q-4Q		D-D	D-D		D-D	D-D

Note: 20-year offered from Mar 2002 to Feb 2006

(Continued)

Table 9-1
(Continued)

2003	Fed Funds	Treas 30-yr	Corporates Aaa	Corporates Baa	30-yr Mtge	S&P 500	Euro	Monetary Base	Free Rsvs	Bank Credit Loans	Bank Credit Inv	Real GDP	Unemp Rate	CPI Total	CPI Core	Budget	Oil	Gold
Jan	1.24	5.02	6.17	7.35	5.92	855.70	1.0739	685.0b	+1706	4161	1727	+1.2%	5.8	+0.3	+0.1		32.94	356.86
Feb	1.26	4.87	5.95	7.06	5.84	841.15	1.0779	690.2	+1946	4199	1766		5.9	+0.5	+0.1		35.87	358.97
Mar	1.25	4.82	5.89	6.95	5.75	848.18	1.0900	694.5	+1620	4229	1776		5.9	+0.4	0.0		33.55	340.55
Apr	1.26	4.91	5.74	6.85	5.81	916.92	1.1180	697.9	+1535	4266	1778	+3.5%	6.0	-0.4	0.0		28.25	328.18
May	1.26	4.52	5.22	6.38	5.48	963.59	1.1766	701.2	+1619	4320	1830		6.1	-0.1	+0.2		28.14	355.68
Jun	1.22	4.34	4.97	6.19	5.23	974.50	1.1502	703.7	+1959	4351	1854		6.3	+0.1	+0.1		30.72	356.53
Jul	1.01	4.92	5.49	6.62	5.63	990.31	1.1231	705.5	+1915	4383	1816		6.2	+0.2	+0.2		30.76	351.02
Aug	1.03	5.39	5.88	7.01	6.26	1008.01	1.0986	709.8	+3600	4406	1780	+7.5%	6.1	+0.4	+0.1	FY	31.59	359.77
Sep	1.01	5.21	5.72	6.79	6.15	995.97	1.1650	711.1	+1488	4403	1789		6.1	+0.3	+0.1	-377.6	28.29	378.95
Oct	1.01	5.21	5.70	6.73	5.95	1050.71	1.1609	715.1	+1463	4367	1806		6.0	-0.1	+0.2		30.33	378.92
Nov	1.00	5.17	5.65	6.66	5.93	1058.20	1.1995	718.3	+1467	4376	1829	+2.7%	5.8	-0.1	0.0		31.09	389.91
Dec	0.98	5.11	5.62	6.60	5.88	1111.92	1.2597	720.5	+1026	4407	1852		5.7	+0.3	+0.2		32.15	407.59
						+26.4%	+20.1%	+5.7%		+5.8%	+7.4%	+3.7%		+1.9	+1.1		+9.3%	+22.6%
						D-D	D-D	D-D		D-D	D-D	4Q-4Q		D-D	D-D		D-D	D-D

164

2004

Jan	1.00	5.01	5.54	6.44	5.74	1131.13	1.2452	721.7b	+799	4465	1860		5.7	+0.4	+0.2		34.27	413.99
Feb	1.01	4.94	5.50	6.27	5.64	1144.94	1.2441	723.4	+1168	4510	1931	+3.9%	5.6	+0.3	+0.2		34.74	405.33
Mar	1.00	4.72	5.33	6.11	5.45	1126.21	1.2292	726.1	+1784	4539	1978		5.8	+0.4	+0.3		36.76	406.67
Apr	1.00	5.16	5.73	6.46	5.83	1107.30	1.1975	730.0	+1779	4585	1951		5.6	+0.2	+0.2		36.69	403.02
May	1.00	5.46	6.04	6.75	6.27	1120.68	1.2217	733.6	+1677	4620	1927	+4.0%	5.6	+0.6	+0.2		40.28	383.45
Jun	1.03	5.45	6.01	6.78	6.29	1140.84	1.2179	738.6	+1893	4657	1932		5.6	+0.4	+0.2		38.02	391.99
Jul	1.26	5.24	5.82	6.62	6.06	1101.72	1.2032	746.3	+1677	4696	1910		5.5	0.0	+0.2		40.69	398.09
Aug	1.43	5.07	5.65	6.46	5.87	1104.24	1.2183	748.0	+1565	4719	1918	+3.1%	5.4	+0.1	+0.1	FY	44.94	400.48
Sep	1.61	4.89	5.46	6.27	5.75	1114.58	1.2417	752.5	+1558	4781	1927		5.4	+0.2	+0.3	−412.7	45.95	405.27
Oct	1.76	4.85	5.47	6.21	5.72	1130.20	1.2746	755.5	+1741	4801	1920		5.4	+0.6	+0.2		53.13	420.46
Nov	1.93	4.89	5.52	6.20	5.73	1173.82	1.3259	760.0	+1678	4840	1921	+2.6%	5.4	+0.3	+0.2		48.46	439.39
Dec	2.16	4.88	5.47	6.15	5.75	1211.92	1.3538	759.7	+1898	4859	1936		5.4	0.0	+0.1		43.33	441.76
						+9.0%	+7.5%	+5.4%	+10.3%	+4.5%	+3.4%		+3.3	+2.2		+34.8%	+8.4%
						D-D	D-D	D-D	D-D	D-D	4Q-4Q		D-D	D-D		D-D	D-D

(Continued)

165

Table 9-1
(*Continued*)

2005	Financial Markets							Monetary Policy					Economic Indicators				Commodities	
	Fed Funds	Treas 20-yr	Corporates Aaa	Baa	30-yr Mtge	S&P 500	Euro	Monetary Base	Free Rsvs	Bank Credit Loans	Inv	Real GDP	Unemp Rate	CPI - % Total	Core	Budget	Prices - $ Oil	Gold
Jan	2.28	4.77	5.36	6.02	5.71	1181.27	1.3049	760.4b	+1701	4897	1996		5.2	0.0	+0.3		46.84	424.15
Feb	2.50	4.61	5.20	5.82	5.63	1203.60	1.3274	762.7	+1468	4955	2039	+3.4%	5.4	+0.4	+0.3		47.97	423.35
Mar	2.63	4.89	5.40	6.06	5.93	1180.59	1.2969	765.0	+1767	5025	2056		5.2	+0.5	+0.3		54.31	434.24
Apr	2.79	4.75	5.33	6.05	5.86	1156.85	1.2919	766.0	+1619	5065	2041		5.1	+0.5	+0.1		53.04	428.93
May	3.00	4.56	5.15	6.01	5.72	1191.50	1.2349	766.9	+1530	5092	2067	+3.3%	5.1	+0.1	+0.1		49.83	421.87
Jun	3.04	4.35	4.96	5.86	5.58	1191.33	1.2098	770.6	+1657	5164	2052		5.0	0.0	0.0		56.26	430.66
Jul	3.26	4.48	5.06	5.95	5.70	1234.18	1.2129	773.6	+1611	5218	2063		5.0	+0.6	+0.1		58.70	424.48
Aug	3.50	4.53	5.09	5.96	5.82	1220.33	1.2230	776.0	+1546	5293	2069	+4.2%	4.9	+0.6	+0.1	FY	64.97	437.93
Sep	3.62	4.51	5.13	6.03	5.77	1228.81	1.2058	779.8	+1989	5332	2078		5.1	+1.2	+0.1	–318.3	65.57	456.04
Oct	3.78	4.74	5.35	6.30	6.07	1207.01	1.1995	782.1	+1863	5357	2073		5.0	+0.3	+0.3		62.37	469.90
Nov	4.00	4.81	5.42	6.39	6.33	1249.48	1.1790	785.3	+1762	5390	2060	+1.8%	5.0	–0.7	+0.2		58.30	476.67
Dec	4.16	4.73	5.37	6.32	6.27	1248.29	1.1842	788.1	+1806	5450	2052		4.9	–0.1	+0.2		59.43	509.76
						+3.0%	–12.5%	+3.7%		+12.2%	+6.0%	+3.1%		+3.4	+2.2		+37.2%	+15.4%
						D-D	D-D	D-D		D-D	D-D	4Q-4Q		D-D	D-D		D-D	D-D

2006

Jan	4.29	4.65	5.29	6.24	6.15	1280.08	1.2158	791.8b	+1506	5491	2068	4.7	+0.6	+0.1	65.51	549.86
Feb																
Mar																
Apr																
May																
Jun																
Jul																
Aug																
Sep																
Oct																
Nov																
Dec																
D-D																

10

BEN S. BERNANKE
(FROM FEBRUARY 1, 2006)

Ben Bernanke is an academic, but one with some previous Federal Reserve experience. And that, at least, sets him apart from the academic Arthur Burns, whose performance at the Fed left a great deal to be desired. During his previous time at the Fed, Bernanke had an opportunity to learn from his positive and negative experiences, especially the latter. In late 2003 and early 2004, Bernanke developed an excessive fear of deflation, although there were no signs that it was either occurring or was likely to.

The personal consumption expenditure (PCE) core price index was running at slightly over 1 percent, and there were no indications anywhere in the economy that deflation was on the horizon. Yet Bernanke felt so strongly about the deflation risk that he discussed it in public. He did not use the word "deflation" in the title of one of his most important speeches; instead he talked about the possibility of an unwelcome decline in inflation. This may have been Fed-speak at its worst. Had some of Greenspan's bad habits rubbed off on Bernanke? The following are some of Bernanke's comments made before the Economics Roundtable at the University of California at San Diego on July 23, 2003. The speech was entitled "An Unwelcome Fall in Inflation?" and can be read in its entirety on the Board of Governors Web site:

Today, I would like to share my own thoughts on the prospect of an "unwelcome substantial fall in inflation"—in particular, why a substantial fall in inflation going forward would indeed be unwelcome; why some risk of further disinflation, though "minor," should not be ignored; and what such a fall would imply for the conduct of monetary policy. Obviously, the opinions I will express are strictly my own and are not necessarily those of my colleagues on the Federal Open Market Committee or the Board of Governors of the Federal Reserve System. . . .

I hope we can agree that a substantial fall in inflation at this stage has the potential to interfere with the ongoing U.S. recovery, and that in conceivable—though remote—circumstances, a serious deflation could do significant harm. Thus, avoiding a further substantial fall in inflation should be a priority of monetary policy.

The only country of consequence worldwide that was experiencing deflation was Japan, and its circumstances were entirely different from what was transpiring in the United States. The Japanese consumer was not in a spending mood and had not been for quite some time. There were a variety of reasons contributing to this situation, many of which were unique to Japan. It is a country of savers; the population is old and getting older; many had little confidence in the government; many vividly remembered the stock market and real estate bubbles that burst and are not close to getting even in their investments; the lifetime employment concept started to unravel; there were financial problems and bankruptcies that made people even more nervous; and competition from abroad meant Japan was losing ground economically. These were not the circumstances facing the United States in the middle of 2003, when economic growth was putting in a solid performance.

Sometime in early 2004, it appears that Bernanke changed his mind and backtracked on his undue concerns about deflation, although the exact timing of his change of heart is difficult to tell. For example, on April 22, 2004, in a speech entitled "The Economic Outlook and Monetary Policy" made before the Bond Market Association of New York, he made the following statement:

Based on the information currently available, my own best guess is that core inflation has stopped falling and appears to be stabilizing in the vicinity of 1.5 percent, comfortably within my own preferred range of 1 to 2 percent.

Over the next year, he did not significantly change these newfound views and seemed quite content with the price picture. For example, on March 25, 2005, in a speech before the Executives' Club of Chicago, entitled "The Economic Outlook," he made the following comment:

My own guess is that core PCE inflation in 2005 will be slightly higher than its 2004 rate of 1.6 percent, though likely remaining within what I think of as the "comfort zone" of 1 to 2 percent.

As a result, when Bernanke was nominated as Federal Reserve chairman in late 2006, there were some questions as to whether he would be tough on inflation. His previous record at the Fed seemed to suggest otherwise. This also brought up the question as to whether he would be as tough on inflation as Greenspan had been. Of course, Greenspan was nowhere the inflation fighter he made himself out to be, although because underlying pressures on prices had been relatively moderate in recent years, he did not need to be.

During his nomination hearings on November 15, 2005, Bernanke went out of his way to convince the Senate Banking Committee that he was an inflation fighter. After all, was that not what they wanted to hear? And because they had his future in their hands, it made sense to preach to the choir. The following are quotes from that testimony:

> I believe that the Federal Reserve's success in reducing and stabilizing infla-tion and inflation expectations is a major reason for this improved eco-nomic performance. If I am confirmed, I am confident that my colleagues on the Federal Open Market Committee (FOMC) and I will maintain the focus on long-term price stability as monetary policy's greatest contribution to general economic prosperity and maximum employment.
>
> One possible step toward greater transparency would be for the FOMC to state explicitly the numerical inflation rate or range of inflation rates it considers to be consistent with the goal of long-term price stability, a practice currently employed by many of the world's central banks. I have supported this idea in my academic writings and in speeches as a Board member. Providing quantitative guidance about the meaning of "long-term price stability" could have several advantages, including further reducing public uncertainty about monetary policy and anchoring long-term infla-tion expectations even more effectively.
>
> I view the explicit statement of a long-run inflation objective as fully consistent with the Federal Reserve's current policy approach, including its appropriate emphasis on the role of judgment and flexibility in policymaking. . . . In any case, I assure this Committee that, if I am con-firmed, I will take no precipitate steps in the direction of quantifying the definition of long-run price stability.

However, in its questioning of Bernanke during his nomination hearings, Congress definitely missed the boat. They should have emphasized not what he thought about inflation and what he would do about it, but rather, how he arrived at the incorrect conclusions he did with respect to deflation as recently as late 2003 and early 2004. Was there something wrong with the techniques that he used to arrive at his conclusions? Whatever influence he might have had on Greenspan and the other FOMC members at that time with respect to deflation was unfor-tunate. Did Bernanke's opinion play a role in the Fed reducing its funds target to an unduly low level of 1 percent and staying there for an unduly long time?

When Bernanke finally took over as chairman in February 2006, he apparently believed he needed to continue to put up a tough-on-inflation front. Thus he and his colleagues at the Fed jacked up the funds target by 25 basis points on three occasions, and by the middle of 2006, it stood at 5.25 percent. The question arises: In implementing these three firming moves, was he trying to ride the Greenspan anti-inflation legacy? After all, he was constantly being compared with Greenspan and what Greenspan might have done if he was still running monetary policy.

Following these three firming moves in the first half of 2006, there were no changes in Fed policy until the implementation of a 50 basis point cut in the discount rate (but not the funds rate) in August 2007, from 5.75 percent to 5.25 percent. In September 2007, the funds target was lowered by 50 basis points, from 5.25 percent to 4.75 percent; in October it was again lowered, but this time by 25 basis points to 4.5 percent, and in December this was followed by another 25 basis point cut to 4.25 percent. These easing moves had little to do with the performance of inflation data in general, or PCE core prices in particular. Rather, they were due to problems in the financial markets, and considerable difficulties in the housing market.

For some background on the PCE core, in recent decades, this price measurement has tended to run at an annual rate of between 1.5 percent and 2.5 percent (not 1 percent to 2 percent), with the central tendency at about 1.75 percent. Moreover, seldom has it moved below the 1.5 percent midpoint, and it has yet to fall below the bottom end of the 1 to 2 percent range. In the second half of 2007 and so far in 2008, the monthly increases in the PCE core price index tended to average slightly less than 0.2 percent. This meant an annualized advance of about 2 percent, which was supposedly the top end of the Fed's target range. Yet, in this period, the Fed cut its fed funds target by 100 basis points. In other words, in a period of economic weakness and financial stress, these factors trumped an inflation rate that was, presumably, on the border of being unacceptably high.

Perhaps Bernanke believes he has more policy flexibility than being a slave to a 1 to 2 percent PCE core range. Or perhaps he realizes that the 1 to 2 percent band is unduly low, but believes he would be viewed as being soft on inflation if he raised the band. Whatever the answer, the Fed appears to be acting as if a 1.75 percent to 2.25 percent PCE core range is acceptable, and the ceiling could be as high as 2.5 percent if the Fed is concerned about subpar economic growth or financial market problems. But if that is the case, then say so. Transparency and Fed-speak are in conflict with each other. Less than three years on the job is not enough time for analysts to figure out the full range of Bernanke's policy tendencies. However, economic weakness and financial adversities appear to make him more pragmatic than what his verbiage suggests.

Experience can be a wonderful teacher, especially when it comes to what Bernanke learned during his earlier years at the Fed. For example, what did he really think about monetary policy under Greenspan in the 2000 to 2005 period, when the Fed was involved in some excessive and ill-timed changes in policy that may have done more harm than good with respect to economic growth and price performance? He may believe that there is such a thing as excessive fine-tuning of monetary policy. Or he may be searching for a policy "sweet spot," irrespective of whether price changes are running exactly the way he would like to see them. Or he may realize that changing an overnight interest rate has only a very indirect and uncertain influence over inflation and, therefore, one has to be more flexible in using an acceptable price range.

It is also possible that perhaps—following his transition period when his three firming moves were employed in order to gain the confidence of market participants—he wanted to gradually move away from the Greenspan legacy and become his own man with regard to policy. If this is the case, less fine-tuning of policy would be expected on his part. After all, Bernanke had not changed the funds target for over a year (the last change was in April 2008, from 2.25 to 2 percent), and seldom in his eighteen years at the Fed did Greenspan sit that long without changing policy. However, Bernanke's slow and inadequate response to financial problems, especially in the second half of 2007, seems to be reminiscent of the Greenspan era.

This brings up an interesting hypothetical. If Greenspan had still been running monetary policy, what adjustments would he have made in the 2006 and 2007 period? Strictly as a guess, in the second half of the 2006, he may have taken the funds rate above its midyear level of 5.25 percent, to somewhere between 5.5 and 6 percent. Then, sometime in 2007, he could have begun to steadily cut the funds rate. This presumption is based on how Greenspan acted in his last years as chairman, on his nervousness over inflation when he left office in early 2006, and his fears of a recession starting in 2007.

WHERE WERE THE REGULATORY WHISTLE-BLOWERS?

Irrespective of what Bernanke has done with regard to fed funds targeting, or what Greenspan might have done, it should be pointed out that neither seemed to be looking at monetary policy and its tools in a broad enough sense. When Greenspan left office in early 2006, problems were emerging in the mortgage and housing markets. Mortgage lenders were coming up with new ways for people who could not afford to buy a house to buy one. The amount of mortgage lending kept increasing, because those who created the mortgages felt that they could package them and sell them ad infinitum. After all, there were several federal agencies that were gobbling up these securities. When a financial institution is a seller and not a holder of assets, this does not induce them to do their credit-quality homework. Where were the regulatory whistle-blowers?

Credit rating agencies should also have been whistle-blowers, and in this regard, they came up a day late and many dollars short. Packages of mortgage-backed securities were rated Aaa, signifying "investment grade" securities, even though there were portions of these packages that did not deserve such a rating. Off-balance sheet items became more commonplace, which is usually a leading indicator of financial problems ahead. Many organizations borrowed short term—often off balance sheet—and used the proceeds to buy longer-term, higher-risk assets. The game was to take advantage of several factors—the high credit rating of the parent organization, an upslope to the yield curve, and assets having higher yields than liabilities because of credit-quality differences. The rollover risk for short-term liability funding was substantial and grossly understated as a risk because if a cloud came over the name of an issuer and it could not roll over its current liabilities, let alone raise new money, it had to sell off investments that were of questionable quality in a market that had little liquidity.

This was a situation where banks around the world that were involved in these operations—either directly or indirectly—needed to pull in their oars. The Fed in particular had primary responsibility because most of the problems originated in U.S. institutions. All of this began on Greenspan's watch, and continued to worsen on Bernanke's watch. Greenspan's Fed was remiss because it did not understand the depth of the financial problems, and Greenspan seemed to be averse to using preemptive regulatory medicine. It was too late for Bernanke to nip the problems in the bud, but under his leadership, the Fed did have the opportunity to limit the scope of the financial crisis.

The Fed had one regulator of note on its Board of Governors in 2006—Susan Schmidt Bies. In 2006, Ms. Bies made several speeches about the regulatory side of policy in which she fired warning shots across the bow. Unfortunately, neither the Fed nor the markets paid any heed to her comments. Worse yet, she left the Fed in March 2007. Ms. Bies was the only real expert on the Board when it came to regulation, and when the subprime mortgage problem broke in the third quarter of 2007, her seat on the Board had not been filled.

On June 14, 2006, Ms. Bies made a presentation before the Mortgage Bankers Association. Unfortunately, the media did not give her speech the attention it deserved. On that day, the consumer price index for May and the Fed's Beige Book were released, and the media deemed these items of far more importance than a speech indicating that major financial problems were in the offing. This speech was delivered more than one year before the debacle in the subprime mortgage market emerged and then spread to other asset-backed markets. The first part of the speech discussed risks that those who borrowed mortgage money took on without fully realizing the problems that it could create for them and others down the road:

> Nontraditional mortgages have been offered to a wider spectrum of consumers, including subprime borrowers, who may be less suited for these types of mortgages and may not fully recognize their embedded risks. These borrowers are more likely to experience an unmanageable payment shock during the life of the loan, meaning that they may be more likely to default on the loan. Further, nontraditional mortgage loans are becoming more prevalent in the subprime market at the same time risk tolerances in the capital markets have increased. Banks need to be prepared for the resulting impact on liquidity and pricing if and when risk spreads return to more "normal" levels and competition in the mortgage banking industry intensifies.

Although Bies talked about how underwriting standards of mortgage lenders had declined, she did not say this in a very forceful manner. Thus, it was not interpreted as a shot-across-the-bow from a regulator. Who makes a statement, and the tone in which it is delivered, can be just as important as the content of the statement.

Supervisors have also observed that lenders are increasingly combining non-traditional mortgage loans with weaker mitigating controls on credit exposures—for example, by accepting less documentation in evaluating an applicant's creditworthiness and not evaluating the borrower's ability to meet increasing monthly payments when amortization begins or when interest rates rise. The "risk layering" practices have become more and more prevalent in mortgage originations. Thus, although some banks may have used some elements of nontraditional mortgage products successfully in the past, the recent easing of traditional underwriting controls and the sale of nontraditional products to subprime borrowers may contribute to these products.

One indication of how this was a missed opportunity on the part of a Fed official was the use of the words "may" and "seems to show" (emphasis added) in the following paragraph:

> Supervisors are concerned that banks **may** not be fully aware of the potential risks of using risk-layering practices with nontraditional mortgage products. These practices **may** have become more widespread over the past couple of years as competition for borrowers and declining profit margins **may** have forced lenders to loosen their credit standards to maintain their loan volume. In the Federal Reserve Board's most recent Senior Loan Officer Survey, conducted this past April, more than 10 percent of the surveyed institutions reported having eased their underwriting standards for residential mortgage loans. Only one of the surveyed lenders reported having tightened standards. Additionally, information from other sources **seems to show** continued growth in the number of borrowers purchasing real estate with no equity using simultaneous second liens.

In 2007, it was the monetary authorities who allowed the housing and mortgage-market crises to occur. Yet, the primary blame falls on the institutions and individuals in the private sector that made the mistakes. Too much of a good thing ultimately becomes too much of a bad thing. Yet, the regulators cannot be let off the hook. They did not step up in a timely manner—in either word or deed—to stop the excesses and improprieties from developing. The Fed is one of those regulators.

A good case can be made that instead of concentrating on price targets and its funds rate target, the Fed should have spent more time concentrating on its research and regulatory functions in order to nip financial problems in the bud. This would be groundbreaking, because frankly, none of the Fed chairmen studied here placed enough emphasis on elevating the research and regulatory functions. That is, when it comes to Federal Reserve policy, there should have been better research on a timely basis, and preventive medicine from the regulatory side. This would have been a far better approach than allowing things to go terribly wrong, letting the chips fall where they may, and then coming in late in the game and bailing out people who did not deserve to be bailed out. This is one area where transparency by the Fed before things got out of hand would have been especially useful—far more useful than transparency about such items as fed funds targeting, and where the Fed *thinks* the economy and policy might be heading.

It is easy to talk in generalities when it comes to criticizing others; it is more difficult to talk in terms of specifics, to make recommendations about what should have been done, and then make suggestions as to what should be done in the future. For example, the Fed conducts a quarterly survey called "Senior Loan Officer Opinion Survey on Bank Lending Practices." There are questions in this survey that deal directly with the mortgage market, and there is an obvious need to improve the questionnaire. The Fed asks questions that pertain to three types of mortgage borrowers—prime, nontraditional, and subprime. The word prime is understandable and so is subprime, but the category nontraditional does not seem to fit. To be blunt, the term makes absolutely no sense.

Prime is a strong credit, subprime is a weak credit, but what is nontraditional? It is *not* a middle ground. The Fed defines nontraditional as residential mortgages that include but are not limited to "adjustable-rate mortgages with multiple payment options, interest-only mortgages, and 'Alt-A' products such as mortgages with limited income verification and mortgages secured by non-owner occupied properties." This classification does not sound like a grouping that measures the credit quality of a borrower. Moreover, should there not be a suspicion that an interest-only loan or a limited-income-verification loan is more likely to be in the subprime and not the prime category, especially if the economy deteriorates by an unexpected amount?

You might ask, So what? After all, this is only a questionnaire. The problem with this line of reasoning is that in mid 2007, the then-current quarterly results of the survey overstated the credit quality of the borrowers and therefore understated the credit risks involved. The Fed could well have been misled by the fact that the subprime category was not all that large; but when the nontraditional category was added to it, impending credit problems were considerably larger than thought to be the case.

What could have been done here was to have three categories—prime, marginal, and subprime—with the Fed concentrating on the combination of marginal and subprime categories as indicating credit risks, and then having a forward-looking approach to some of the questions that deal with how well potential borrowers might be able to handle adversity.

Of course, if all the Fed does is change its verbiage when classifying mortgage loans and their borrowers, that does little good. What is needed is for the regulators to monitor the percentage of marginal and subprime mortgage loans in a bank's portfolio and determine whether the numbers have moved up to disturbing levels. If that is the case, then the regulators would meet with a bank's representatives, indicate their displeasure with such a performance and "suggest" that quality standards be raised. If that had been done in 2005 and 2006, there is a good chance that the subprime problem would not have mushroomed in 2007.

There is another approach that the Fed could have taken to make the subprime mortgage problem more obvious and transparent. It should review its regular data releases and surveys and provide more detailed information with respect to loans in general and subprime mortgage loans in particular. This is the kind of transparency that is necessary, not how the Fed "feels" about data or how it "sees" events evolving. One suggestion: in the Fed's weekly H.8 release, why not have items that present the dollar amount of delinquencies and foreclosures? A nuisance for the banks and for the Fed to accumulate such information, to be sure; but it would definitely be a better approach than waiting for the regulators to get blind-sided and then realize after the fact that they have a systemic problem.

The art in monetary policy is for the Fed to be on top of potential problems that can disrupt the economy and the financial markets and, wherever possible, to attack adversities before they spread. This seems far more useful than concentrating on—and overemphasizing—increases in personal consumption expenditure core prices that occur over a twelve-month period and being pleased with monetary policy if the increase is 1.9 percent and inching lower, or being disturbed if it is 2.1 percent and inching higher.

THE INK IS NOT DRY

While much of the attention in late 2007 was focused on the mortgage-backed market and housing, other dangerous situations were developing, such as financing through asset-backed securities in the commercial paper market (unsecured debt issued by banks and corporations that typically have maturities from one to three months). On August 8, 2007, the amount of commercial paper outstanding peaked at $2,224 billion; by December 12, 2007, it was down to $1,839 billion—a decline of almost $400 billion. What made this situation so dangerous was that it dealt with short-term funding by many companies across a broad spectrum of the economy. If a company cannot fund itself, it is not too far from needing relief—such as borrowing from banks, being bought out, or even bankruptcy. In contrast, the mortgage-backed market has had a meltdown of values on the asset side of the balance sheet. Thus, it does not have the short-term systemic risk inherent in the short-term funding area.

For those who are not aware, this was crisis number two in the commercial paper market. The first was the Penn Central commercial paper crisis that occurred in 1970. The magnitude of the current problem is greater, but the shock when the first one occurred was more dangerous, because regulators and those involved in the financial markets had never encountered a problem of this type. The same thing happened in the housing financing squeeze in the late 1960s, which could have been a greater calamity of a magnitude similar to what transpired in 2007.

In order to understand the severity of the Penn Central problem, it is important to go back and quote from several Federal Reserve documents. As Yogi would say, it was déjà vu all over again, except thirty-seven years later. At the July 21, 1970, FOMC meeting, the following comment was made by Fed officials:

> Pressures in domestic financial markets had abated in recent weeks from the peaks that had been reached in the latter part of June, after a major railroad corporation indicated that it was insolvent and unable to pay off

maturing commercial paper. Uncertainties and strains persisted, however—
particularly in the market for commercial paper, the outstanding volume
of which contracted sharply following the indication of the railroad's
insolvency. It appeared that a large proportion of the funds so freed were
being rechanneled through the banking system; there had been sharp
increases recently both in bank loans to businesses and finance companies
and in the outstanding volume of large-denominated CD's of short maturity,
for which Regulation Q rate ceiling had been suspended effective June 24.
The massive readjustment under way was facilitated by Federal Reserve
assurances to member banks that the discount window was available to
assist them in meeting the needs of businesses unable to replace maturing
commercial paper.

System open market operations since the preceding meeting of the
Committee had been directed mainly at maintaining money market conditions conducive to stability in financial markets generally, amid the churn-
ing occasioned by developments in the commercial paper market. Member
bank borrowings rose sharply during the period—from an average of less
than $900 million in the statement week ending June 24 to nearly $1.7 billion
in the July 15 statement week. The increase was in large part a consequence
of special discount window accommodation of banks lending to firms that
were finding it difficult to roll over maturing commercial paper.

Then, there was this quote from an article in the November 1970 Federal Reserve
Bulletin entitled "Changes in Time and Savings Deposits, April–July 1970":

Interest rates paid at most banks on those time and savings deposits
subject to rate regulation were at or close to the regulatory ceilings at the
end of July 1970. Most of the large banks and many of the smaller ones
had moved their offering rates to the new ceiling during the first few
months following the change in ceiling rates on January 21, 1970. An
appreciable number of the remaining banks moved to the highest permis-
sible rates during the April-July period. For some types of deposits ceiling
were suspended in late June.

The upward movement of rates and the resulting rate structure on July 31
reflect the continued competitive pressure from high yields on market
instruments. The steep decline in short-term interest rates that had characterized the first quarter of 1970 was succeeded by wide swings in rates during
the second quarter. Nevertheless, short-term market rates were generally
above bank offering rates until late June. On June 24 supervisory authorities
suspended the ceiling rates that banks may pay on large-denomination time
deposits with maturities of less than 90 days. This action was designed to
help banks meet any unusual demands for short-term credit resulting from
uncertainties in financial markets, particularly those in the commercial
paper market associated with the financial difficulties of a large railroad.
Following this action, short-term market rates declined further, and banks

again were able to compete effectively for both large-and small-denomination time deposits.

In both 1970 and 2007, there was very rapid and unsustainable growth in the amount of commercial paper outstanding in the years that preceded the meltdown. For example, at the end of 1965, the amount of commercial paper outstanding was a mere $9.3 billion. It then exploded to $13.6 billion at the end of 1966; to $17.1 billion at the end of 1967; to $21.2 billion at the end of 1968, and $32.6 billion at the end of 1969. By the end of May 1970, the amount outstanding had surged to $39.7 billion. After that, there was a major meltdown and by the end of 1970, the amount outstanding was down to $31.8 billion.

With regard to the 2007 situation, the amount of commercial paper outstanding at the end of 2003 was $1,261 billion, and at the end of 2004 it was $1,376 billion. It then moved sharply higher to $1,631 billion at the end of 2005; to $1,981 billion at the end of 2006, and reached $2,224 billion by August 8, 2007. By September 2008, it had slipped to near $1,600 billion.

To understand the magnitude of the problem in 1970, it is necessary to look at the amount of commercial paper outstanding and to compare interest rates on commercial paper versus the interest rates on Treasury bills. The next comparison is to look at similar data in 2007, with some minor modifications: The commercial paper rates used in Table 10-1 for 2007 and 2008 are on asset-backed securities, whereas such data were not available in 1970. In addition, the 1970 rate comparisons are with six-month paper, while the 2007 comparisons are with three-month paper:

Table 10-1
Commercial and Finance Company Paper Outstanding 1970

| Month End | Commercial and Finance Company Paper Outstanding Billions of Dollars | Interest Rates—% | | |
		Commercial Paper 4 to 6 Months	Bills 6 Months	Difference
Jan-1970	34.4	8.78	7.78	1.00
Feb	36.0	8.55	7.23	1.32
Mar	37.2	8.33	6.59	1.74
Apr	38.0	8.06	6.61	1.45
May	39.7	8.23	7.02	1.21
Jun	37.8	8.21	6.86	1.35
Jul	37.0	8.29	6.51	1.78
Aug	36.6	7.90	6.56	1.34
Sep	34.0	7.32	6.47	.85
Oct	34.4	6.85	6.21	.64
Nov	34.0	6.30	5.42	.88
Dec	31.8	5.73	4.89	.84

Table 10-1 *(Continued)*

2007–2008

Month End	Commercial and Finance Company Paper Outstanding Billions of Dollars	Interest Rates—%		
		Commercial Paper 3 Months[*]	Bills 3 Months	Difference
Jan-2007	1,979.0	5.26	4.99	.27
Feb	2,000.9	5.24	5.01	.23
Mar	2,033.7	5.54	4.90	.35
Apr	2,041.0	5.25	4.79	.46
May	2,111.1	5.26	4.60	.66
Jun	2,147.8	5.28	4.68	.60
Jul	2,186.6	5.27	4.82	.45
Aug	1,927.0	6.15	3.91	2.24
Sep	1,872.4	5.24	3.72	1.52
Oct	1,899.0	4.83	3.84	.99
Nov	1,843.6	5.45	3.08	2.37
Dec	1,780.7	4.58	3.29	1.29
Jan-2008	1,860.7	3.07	1.92	1.15
Feb	1,819.2	3.19	1.81	1.38
Mar	1,821.5	2.80	1.36	1.44
Apr	1,758.0	2.99	1.41	1.58
May	1,749.0	2.75	1.85	.90
Jun	1,741.0	3.21	1.87	1.34
July	1,732.7	2.88	1.65	1.23
August	1,777.2	2.84	1.69	1.15
September	1,623.8	4.41	0.90	3.51

[*]Asset backed

One might ask, Why was there such a surge in commercial paper financing during these two periods before the respective debacles occurred? There are some similarities in both instances: Short-term financing was cheaper, especially when there was a considerable upslope to the yield curve; some companies financed long-term expansion with short term funds; others borrowed in the paper market to buy back their shares, and some even used the paper source to help finance takeovers and investments.

When these situations were brewing, and the amount of commercial paper outstanding was growing by leaps and bounds, the Fed should have reined in policy ease. Where were the regulators when we needed them?

THE BERNANKE POLICY STORY IS FAR FROM OVER

The 2006–2008 story with respect to markets coming unglued is still in the process of being written. Yet, at this point we can say that the Fed was late in acting, and when it did act, it did not act forcefully enough. Its actions suggested that it did not have a good feel for what was happening in either the markets or in specific areas of the economy. When the Fed finally started to act in August 2007, rather than cutting the discount rate by only 50 basis points, from 6.25 percent to 5.75 percent, it should have cut it by 125 basis points to 5 percent, and cut the funds-rate target by 25 basis points, also to 5 percent. At that time, the length of repurchase agreements the Fed was willing to do should have been extended out to at least three months, and maybe even six months. Also at this early date, there should have been a coordinated effort on the part of three major central banks—the Federal Reserve, the European Central Bank, and the Bank of England—to announce a coordinated effort to help bring back to life the London Inter-bank market, where borrowing by banks was a problem in terms of both availability and rate.

Funding problems for banks were occurring on both sides of the Atlantic, and the problem in all three cases was not that overnight interest rates, such as the fed funds rate, were too high. If that were the case, when the Fed cut its fed funds target from 5.25 percent beginning in September 2007 to 2 percent in May 2008, there would have been a major rally in the longer part of the U.S. Treasury market. That in fact did not happen. On September 17, 2008, the 10-year Treasury yield was 4.46 percent, and in the middle of May 2008, it was trading somewhat under 4 percent, or a rate decline of only about 50 basis points, and that rate decline was due primarily to a considerable softening of the economy.

If one looks at the details of what the Fed did from August 2007 to April 2008 (which is detailed in the two sidebars), this was another one of those periods of nickel-and-dime policy changes that became famous under Greenspan and carried over to Bernanke. What is strik-ing is that all the changes the Fed made proved to be inadequate and did not

> **FED FUNDS RATE AND DISCOUNT RATE REDUCTIONS**
>
> **August 17, 2007**—The Fed cuts the discount rate from 6.25 percent to 5.75 percent. The funds target is left unchanged at 5.25 percent.
>
> **September 18, 2007**—Both the funds rate and the discount rate are cut 50 basis points—the funds rate to 4.75 percent and the discount rate to 5.25 percent.
>
> **October 31, 2007**—Both the funds rate and the discount rate are cut 25 basis points—the funds rate to 4.5 percent and the discount rate to 5 percent.
>
> **December 11, 2007**—Both the funds rate and the discount rate are cut 25 basis points—the funds rate to 4.25 percent and the discount rate to 4.75 percent.
>
> **January 22, 2008**—Both the funds rate and the discount rate are cut 75 basis points—the funds rate to 3.5 percent and the discount rate to 4 percent.
>
> **January 30, 2008**—Both the funds rate and the discount rate are cut 50 basis points—the funds rate to 3 percent and the discount rate to 3.5 percent.
>
> **March 16, 2008**—The discount rate is cut 25 basis points to 3.25 percent while the funds rate stays unchanged at 3 percent.
>
> **March 18, 2008**—Funds rate and the discount rate are cut 75 basis points.
>
> **April 30, 2008**—Funds rate and the discount rate are cut 25 basis points.
>
> **October 8, 2008**—Both the funds rate and the discount rate are cut 50 basis points.

OTHER FED POLICY OPERATIONS AND PRONOUNCEMENTS—

December 12, 2007—The Fed, the Bank of Canada, the European Central Bank, and the Swiss National Bank announced measures to meet elevated pressures in the short-term financing market. In addition, the Federal Reserve established a Temporary Term Auction Facility (TAF) to auction term funds to depository institutions against a variety of collateral that can be used to secure loans at the discount window.

December 21, 2007—The Federal Reserve indicated that it intends to conduct biweekly TAF auctions for as long a period as necessary to address elevated pressures in the short-term financing area.

March 7, 2008—The Fed announced two initiatives to help meet the heightened liquidity pressures in the term funding markets. One was the amount of outstanding TAF was increased to $100 billion. The Fed also indicated it would continue to hold TAF auctions for at least another six months unless conditions indicated that such auctions were no longer necessary. The second initiative announced that the Fed would start a series of term repurchase agreements that were expected ultimately to total $100 billion. These transactions would occur as 28-day repurchase agreements in which primary dealers can elect to deliver as collateral any of the types of securities, such as Treasury, agency, or agency mortgage-backed securities that are eligible collateral in conventional open market operations.

March 11, 2008—Liquidity pressures in some of the funding markets have increased again. To combat such problems, the Fed, the Bank of Canada, the Bank of England, and the European Central Bank, and the Swiss National Bank announced specific measures. The Fed announced an expansion of its securities lending program. Under a new Term Securities Lending Facility (TSLF), the Fed will lend up to $200 billion of Treasury securities to primary dealers collateralized for 28 days by a pledge of other securities, including federal agency debt, federal agency residential-mortgage-backed securities (MBS), and non-agency AAA/Aaa-rated private-label residential MBS. The FOMC also authorized increases in its existing temporary reciprocal currency arrangements with the European Central Bank (ECB) and the Swiss National Bank (SNB). These swap lines were extended through September 30, 2008.

March 14, 2008—The Federal Reserve Board voted approval of the arrangement announced by JPMorgan Chase and Bear Stearns. Bear Stearns in essence failed on that weekend despite the fact that it was classified by the Fed as part of an elite group of reporting dealers in U.S. Treasury securities, that there had been growing concerns in the weeks before the failure among market participants that Bear Stearns might have a financing problem, and as a reporting dealer, the Fed got considerable and regular position and financing information from Bear Stearns. Maybe this was one of those cases where the approach of "don't ask, don't tell" was followed.

March 16, 2008—The Fed announced two initiatives to improve market liquidity and promote orderly market functioning. The Board approved the New York Fed creation of a lending facility to improve the ability of primary dealers to provide financing to participants in securitization markets. The facility will start March 17, will be in existence for at least six months, and may need to be extended for six months. The operations can be collateralized by a broad range of investment-grade debt securities. The interest rate will be the same as the primary credit rate or the discount rate. The Fed also decreased the primary credit rate from 3.5 percent to 3.25 percent. This lowers the spread of the primary credit rate over the Fed funds rate to .25 percent.

May 2, 2008—The Fed, the ECB, and the SNB announced an expansion of their own liquidity programs. The fed announced an increase in the amounts auctioned in its biweekly TAF from $50 billion to $75 billion. The Fed also authorized increases in its existing temporary reciprocal currency arrangements. These arrangements were extended through January 30, 2009. Then, there was an expansion of the collateral that can be pledged in the Term SLF auctions. The wider pool of collateral should help improve financing conditions in a broader range of financial markets.

July 13, 2008 – The Federal Reserve Board announced that it granted the New York Fed the authority to lend to Fannie Mae and Freddie Mac if such lending should prove necessary. Any lending would be at the primary credit rate and   collateralized by U.S. government and federal agency securities. The authorization is intended to supplement the Treasury's existing lending authority and to help ensure the ability of Fannie Mae and Freddie Mac to promote the availability of home mortgage credit during a period of stress in financial markets.

July 30, 2008 – The Federal Reserve announced several steps to enhance the effectiveness of its existing facilities, including the introduction of longer-terms to maturity in its Term Auction Facility. In association with this change, the European Central Bank and the Swiss National Bank are adopting the same maturities. Actions taken by the Federal Reserve include the Primary Dealer Credit Facility and Term Securities Lending Facility (TSLF) through January 20, 2009, the introduction of auctions of options on $50 billion of draws on the TSLF, the introduction of 84-day Term Auction Facility (TAF) loans as a complement to 28-day TAF loans, and an increase in the Federal Reserve's swap line with the European Central Bank to $55 billion from $50 billion.

September 7, 2008 – The Federal Reserve Board, the Federal Deposit Insurance Corporation, the Office of the Comptroller of the Currency, and the Office of Thrift Supervision are prepared to work with Fannie Mae and Freddie Mac to develop capital restoration plans pursuant to the capital regulations and the prompt and corrective action provisions of the Federal Deposit Insurance Corporation Improvement Act.

Investments in preferred and common stock with readily determinable fair value should be reported as available-for-sale equity security holdings and that any net unrealized losses on these securities are deducted from regulated capital.

get the job done. While analysts can argue about what should have been done early on, there is little doubt that the Fed did not seem to understand the problems and the depth of the difficulties and had to keep coming back to apply more and more medicine. Weekend announcements and operations give the appearance of inadequate pre-planning."

FEDERAL RESERVE DATA RELEASES NEED TO BE MONITORED MUCH MORE CLOSELY

For many years, the bank reserve figures presented by the Fed were simple and straightforward. That is no longer the case, what with all of these methods of attempting to improve the liquidity of the financial markets. The Fed publishes a release called "H.3: Reserves of Depository Institutions." For analytical purposes, I had to totally redo the organization of the current H.3 release (Table 10-2) to make it understandable:

Table 10-2
Reserves of Depository Institutions (millions of dollars)

Month	Term Auction Credit	Primary Borrowings from Fed	Primary Dealer Credit Facilities	Other Credit Extensions	Secondary and Seasonal Borrowings	Borrowed Reserves	Non-Borrowed Reserves	Total Reserves
Apr 2007		32	—	—	48	80	42,580	42,660
May		14	—	—	90	104	43,010	43,114
Jun		43	—	—	145	188	43,420	43,608
Jul		45	—	—	217	262	41,521	41,783
Aug		701	—	—	274	975	43,895	44,870
Sep		1,345	—	—	221	1,566	41,132	42,698
Oct		126	—	—	128	254	42,283	42,537
Nov		315	—	—	50	365	42,313	42,678
Dec	11,613	3,787	—	—	31	15,431	27,169	42,600
Jan 2008	44,516	1,137	—	—	6	45,659	-3,874	41,785
Feb	60,000	155	—	—	4	60,158	-17,578	42,580
Mar	75,484	1,617	16,168	1,249	6	94,524	-50,490	44,034
Apr	100,000	9,624	25,764	0	21	135,409	-91,938	43,471
May	127,419	14,076	14,238	0	47	155,780	-111,624	44,156
Jun	150,000	14,225	6,908	0	145	171,278	-127,867	43,411
Jul	150,000	15,204	255	0	205	165,674	122,277	43,397
Aug	150,000	17,980	0	0	205	168,078	123,510	44,569

Table 10-3
Ben S. Bernanke, Chairman—Federal Reserve Board of Governors ~February 1, 2006~

2006	Fed Funds	Treas 30-yr	Corporates Aaa	Corporates Baa	30-yr Mtge	S&P 500	Euro	Monetary Base	Free Rsvs	Loans	Inv	Real GDP	Unemp Rate	Total	Core	Budget	Oil	Gold
Jan																		
Feb	4.49	4.54	5.35	6.27	6.25	1280.66	1.1925	795.7b	+1530	5540	2108	+4.8%	4.8	+0.1	+0.2		61.63	565.00
Mar	4.59	4.73	5.53	6.41	6.32	1294.87	1.2139	798.0	+1393	5599	2119		4.7	+0.3	+0.3		62.90	557.09
Apr	4.79	5.06	5.84	6.68	6.51	1310.61	1.2624	800.6	+1664	5637	2171		4.7	+0.6	+0.3		69.69	610.65
May	4.94	5.20	5.95	6.75	6.60	1270.09	1.2833	804.7	+1779	5718	2206	+2.4%	4.6	+0.5	+0.2		70.94	676.51
Jun	4.99	5.15	5.89	6.78	6.68	1270.20	1.2779	804.6	+1774	5742	2189		4.6	+0.2	+0.3		70.96	596.15
Jul	5.24	5.13	5.85	6.76	6.76	1276.66	1.2764	804.1	+1508	5787	2195		4.8	+0.4	+0.2		74.41	633.17
Aug	5.25	5.00	5.68	6.59	6.52	1303.82	1.2793	804.7	+1507	5835	2206	+1.1%	4.7	+0.3	+0.2	FY	73.05	632.59
Sep	5.25	4.85	5.51	6.43	6.40	1335.85	1.2687	805.2	+1696	5869	2191		4.6	-0.5	+0.2	-248.2	63.87	598.19
Oct	5.25	4.85	5.51	6.42	6.36	1377.94	1.2773	806.6	+1656	5986	2206		4.4	-0.4	+0.1		58.88	585.78
Nov	5.25	4.69	5.33	6.20	6.24	1400.63	1.3261	809.7	+1655	6011	2224	+2.1%	4.5	0.0	+0.1		59.37	627.83
Dec	5.24	4.68	5.32	6.22	6.14	1418.30	1.3197	812.4	+1693	6099	2221		4.5	+0.4	+0.1		62.03	629.79
						+13.6%	+11.4%	+3.1%						+2.5	+2.6		+4.4%	+23.5%
						D-D	D-D	D-D		D-D	D-D	4Q-4Q		D-D	D-D		D-D	D-D

Table 10-3
(Continued)

2007	Financial Markets							Monetary Policy					Economic Indicators				Commodities	
	Fed Funds	Treas 30-yr	Corporates Aaa	Baa	30-yr Mtge	S&P 500	Euro	Monetary Base	Free Rsvs	Bank Credit Loans	Inv	Real GDP	Unemp Rate	CPI - % Total	Core	Budget	Prices - $ Oil	Gold
Jan	5.25	4.85	5.40	6.34	6.22	1438.24	1.2998	813.5b	+1319	6174	2233		4.6	+0.2	+0.3		54.57	631.17
Feb	5.26	4.82	5.39	6.28	6.29	1406.82	1.3080	813.4	+1490	6232	2248	+0.6%	4.5	+0.4	+0.2		59.26	664.75
Mar	5.26	4.72	5.30	6.27	6.16	1520.86	1.3246	815.0	+1614	6186	2272		4.4	+0.6	+0.1		60.56	654.90
Apr	5.25	4.87	5.47	6.39	6.18	1482.37	1/3513	817.2	+1493	6237	2284		4.5	+0.4	+0.2		63.97	679.37
May	5.25	4.90	5.47	6.39	6.26	1530.62	1.3518	818.8	+1422	6289	2290	+3.8%	4.5	+0.7	+0.1		63.46	666.86
Jun	5.25	5.20	5.79	6.70	6.66	1503.35	1.3421	820.1	+1659	6320	2309		4.5	+0.2	+0.2		67.48	655.49
Jul	5.26	5.11	5.73	6.65	6.70	1455.27	1.3726	821.5	+1619	6376	2318		4.6	+0.1	+0.2		74.18	665.30
Aug	5.02	4.93	5.79	6.65	6.57	1473.99	1.3626	824.5	+4121	6479	2342	+4.9%	4.6	−0.1	+0.2	FY	72.39	665.41
Sep	4.94	4.79	5.74	6.59	6.38	1526.75	1.3910	821.7	+397	6576	2372		4.7	+0.3	+0.2	−162.8	79.93	712.65
Oct	4.76	4.77	5.66	6.48	6.38	1549.38	1.4233	824.7	+1324	6660	2404		4.8	+0.3	+0.2		86.20	754.60
Nov	4.49	4.52	5.44	6.40	6.21	1481.14	1.4683	825.7	+1361	6715	2468	+0.6%	4.7	+0.8	+0.3		94.62	806.25
Dec	4.24	4.53	5.49	6.65	6.10	1468.36	1.4559	823.4	−2041	6785	2414		5.0	+0.3	+0.2		91.73	803.20

Table 10-3
(Continued)

2008	Financial Markets							Monetary Policy				Economic Indicators					Commodities	
	Fed Funds	Treas 30-yr	Corporates Aaa	Baa	30-yr Mtge	S&P 500	Euro	Monetary Base	Total Reserves*	Bank Credit Loans	Inv	Real GDP	Unemp Rate	CPI - % Total	Core	Budget	Prices - $ Oil	Gold
Jan	3.94	4.33	5.33	6.54	5.76	1378.55	1.4728	821.4b	42.1b	6839b	2438b		4.9%	+0.4	+0.3		92.95	889.60
Feb	2.98	4.52	5.53	6.82	5.92	1330.63	1.4759	822.5	42.8	6881	2458	+1.0%	4.8	0.0	0.0		95.35	922.30
Mar	2.61	4.39	5.51	6.89	5.97	1322.70	1.5520	827.0	44.3	6917	2544		5.1	+0.3	+0.2		105.56	968.43
Apr	2.28	4.44	5.55	6.97	5.92	1385.59	1.5754	824.4	43.5	6889	2514		5.0	+0.2	+0.1		112.57	909.96
May	1.98	4.60	5.57	6.93	6.04	1400.38	1.5554	826.5	44.2	6922	2477	+2.8%	5.5	+0.6	+0.2		125.39	888.66
Jun	2.00	4.69	5.68	7.07	6.32	1280.00	1.5562	832.5	43.4	6902	2478		5.5	+1.1	+0.3		133.93	889.49
Jul	2.01	4.57	5.67	7.16	6.43	1267.38	1.5759	838.2	43.4	6907	2491		5.7	+0.8	+0.3		133.44	939.77
Aug	2.00	4.50	5.64	7.15	6.48	1282.83	1.4955	841.8	44.6	6938	2476		6.1	-0.1	+0.2		116.61	839.03
Sept	1.81	4.27	5.65	7.31	6.02	1164.74	1.4342					+0.9%	6.1			FY-est −400b	104.31	829.93

*Free reserves data not available

187

Notice that from April 2007 to November, 2007, everything was straightforward. Nonborrowed reserves were monitored closely by the trading desk at the New York Fed and had desired growth levels. Nonborrowed reserves were arrived at by simply taking total reserves and subtracting borrowed reserves, which comprised primary, secondary, and seasonal borrowings from the Fed.

However, beginning in December 2007, the Fed's financial-statement world got much more complicated. A series of new and supposedly more helpful financing methods appeared on the scene, and the amounts were so large that the Fed had to make sure that these additions were offset by declines in nonborrowed reserves. Otherwise, there would be an explosion in bank reserves, and with it a possible inflation risk. At present, when monitoring reserve growth, it is total reserves that are much more important than non-borrowed reserves. In this regard, if one looks at total reserves from April 2007 to April 2008, reserve growth had been held in check with basically a moderate and steady increase. In April 2007, total reserves were $42.7 billion, in April 2008, they were $43.5 billion, and in September 2008, they were 45.5 billion.

This was not the only mistake the Fed made in this period, especially in the latter part of 2007. Initially, the Fed should have avoided using government securities as collateral when doing repurchase agreements (RPs), because that added to the squeeze in the Treasury securities market. Early on, Fed operations should have been coordinated with the Treasury, which, in turn, should have added considerably to the amounts offered in its short-term securities auctions. The Fed initially should have placed greater emphasis on asset-backed securities as collateral in its RP operations; it should have done a larger amount of RPs; it should have done longer-term RPs; it should have been more aggressive in inducing the banks to borrow at the discount window; and then it should have pushed the banks to help their good-credit clients who were having funding problems.

SUMMARY

The Fed obviously did not use preventive medicine in any of the previously mentioned operations, and when it did act, it was a day late and again, many dollars short in its operations. While Greenspan's Fed may have set the groundwork for these problems, if in mid 2006, Bernanke's Fed had acted in an aggressive and preventive way, Greenspan's Fed would not get as much of the blame as historians are likely to bestow on him and the institution. It has already proven to be a major misjudgment on Bernanke's part that when he took over at the Fed, he wanted to give the impression that policy was steady as she goes and that his policies would be an extension of Greenspan's. The financial world was changing rapidly, but Fed policy was not.

While it may be true that under normal conditions, the Fed should concentrate on prices, these were not normal conditions. When the viability of major markets is at risk, and short-term financing is inadequate, these should be at the top of the Fed's list of concerns. This approach is not meant to bail out those who, by their excesses and greed in high-risk, longer-term markets, were responsible for the crisis; but rather, to inject enough short-term temporary funds to keep the money markets viable until conditions returned to normal. Generically speaking, the fact that securities are backed by asset classes that have developed an adverse reputation is surely no reason by itself for buyers to shy away from that paper. The entire asset-backed market should not be viewed as a pariah. Providing sufficient funds to keep financing markets functioning until underlying basics take hold will primarily help the innocent and not bail out the guilty.

11

THE NEED FOR PREVENTIVE
REGULATION

On October 19, 2007, the Group of Seven Ministers (G-7) asked the Financial Stability Forum (FSF) to analyze the underlying causes of financial turbulence in the world and to come up with recommendations. The response was that the main problems centered in four areas: liquidity and risk management; accounting and valuation of financial derivatives; the role of methodologies and credit rating agencies in structural finance; and basic supervisory principles of oversight, especially with respect to off-balance-sheet items. These areas were spot-on in terms of importance, but unfortunately the request was tardy, to say the least. It should have been done several years earlier, so that some preventive measure could have been implemented. Talk about locking the barn door after the horse has been stolen. Probably the best that can be said of this request is better late than never.

When it comes to these financial market problems, most media attention has focused on mortgage-backed securities. Yet, as indicated in the G-7 request, this is not the only financial-market difficulty. There have been other securities problems, such as those dealing with asset-backed commercial paper where the amount outstanding plummeted in the second half of 2007. There have been collateralized debt obligations (CDOs) problems. These are securities where pools of debt, some tied to subprime mortgages, have been sliced and diced into pieces and carry different levels of risk and return. There have been problems in the London Interbank Borrowing market (LIBOR), where banks have experienced funding and capital concerns; in structured investment vehicles (SIVs), which have been under-regulated for two decades; and the insurance of securities, such as credit default swaps (CDS) and backing for state and local government obligations.

There also have been problems with respect to the management, accounting, and oversight of government-sponsored agencies, and in particular Fannie Mae and Freddie Mac. Their problems culminated in a government takeover of their managements in September 2008. For many years, these government sponsored organizations had the best of all possible worlds—motivated by profits and protected by implicit government guarantees—a combination that had to create major problems, especially in bad times. Because of these conflicting forces, it was necessary to have in place government oversight that was both high quality and timely. Unfortunately this proved not to be the case. Of course, one can also argue that the political power wielded by these two organizations was a factor that made a bad situation worse. The full story of Fannie Mae and Freddie Mac has yet to be written. The next Congress and administration will have to redefine and retool these organizations, and the outcome is far from clear.

All of the previously mentioned problems did not happen overnight. The causes began as early as the 1980s in the SIV area, and over a period of two decades other factors have come on the scene to make the underlying situation worse. Adding to the problems has been that while the United States may have been the center and distributor of most of the problems, the difficulties and the meltdowns spread to all over the world.

Let us start this analysis with the financial institutions that created off-shore organizations that allowed for off-balance sheet accounting and limited regulation. In essence, many of these organizations were not much more than shells and, in some cases, not much more than a post office box. Unfortunately, both the regulators and the rating agencies did little to improve the financial analysis and to report deficiencies that these organizations created. They generally served no useful economic purpose except to earn more money for their owners by avoiding rules and regulations that they would have encountered in their home countries. It was little wonder that, once the organizations were in place and proved to be profitable, much more aggressive and complicated investment and financial vehicles were created. Regulators around the world just seemed to watch, and the same appeared to be true for the rating agencies.

MORTGAGE-BACKED SECURITIES

The most widely-used and well-known asset-backed securities are those backed by mortgages. A mortgage-backed security (MBS) is a securitized interest in a pool of mortgages. It is a bond, but instead of paying investors fixed coupons and principal, it pays out the cash flows from pools of mortgages. The simplest form of mortgage-backed security is a mortgage pass-through. With this structure, all principal and interest payments (less a servicing fee) from the pool of mortgages are passed on directly to investors each month.

The Government National Mortgage Association (Ginnie Mae) issued the first mortgage pass-through in 1970. Currently involved in this market are other quasi-government organizations—the Federal National Mortgage Association (Fannie Mae) and the Federal Home Loan Mortgage Corporation (Freddie Mac). Fannie Mae was formed by the federal government in 1938, and its purpose was to promote home ownership in the United States. It did so by purchasing mortgages from originators, which freed up the originators' capital so they could originate more mortgages.

Private firms—banks or mortgage originators—also pool mortgages and sell them as pass-through securities without implicit government guarantees. Such private-label MBSs traditionally had some form of credit enhancement to obtain a triple-A credit rating. Starting in the early 2000s, private-label MBSs were increasingly issued with little or no credit enhancement, and they were used on pools of risky subprime mortgages. For the first time, MBSs posed significant credit risk.

Because credit risk made these instruments fundamentally different from earlier mortgage pass-through securities, many market participants avoided calling them MBSs, preferring to label them asset-backed securities. Volume in these risky instruments grew rapidly until 2007, when defaults accelerated and the market values of the instruments plunged. This caused a liquidity crisis that spilled over into other segments of the capital markets and into other asset-backed securities. Needless to say, valuing the going market price became very difficult, if not impossible.

What enhanced the problem for mortgage-backed securities even more was that many banks and other financial institutions packaged the securities and sold them all over the world. They had little interest in holding on to them, which, not surprisingly, meant that an excessive amount of these securities was created. If the regulators had asked the sales people at these primarily U.S. institutions what they sold and to whom they sold them, they would have been shocked by the size of the sales and the number of institutions that bought them, especially abroad. If U.S. investors could not figure out the underlying value of these investments, think how difficult it would be for foreign investors.

Many of these investment vehicles were divided into tranches (packages of securities), and the risk factors differed considerably. Unfortunately, many of those who bought the riskier investments had no idea of the risks involved, and credit-rating agencies did little to help in this regard. These securities were typically issued at rate levels over Treasury securities that were grossly inadequate. In addition, there was another major risk that fell between the cracks, and that was when many institutions decided or needed to liquidate these securities at the same time. This caused the market price of the securities to drop dramatically, and in many cases well below what the securities were worth if there had been no panic selling.

When considering all of these factors, one should not be surprised that the worldwide losses on asset-backed investments and related areas will exceed one trillion dollars. Many large banks already have reported multibillion losses, and more reports of large losses are likely to come. Because of the magnitude of these losses, some banks are concerned about the adequacy of their capital and their ability to pay dividends.

In the next few years, their financial problems will limit them in their willingness to make loans, which is hardly a plus for economic growth. Thus, it is only a matter of time before regulators around the world come up with new reports and regulations. When this type of situation happens, it is not unusual for new laws and rules to be unduly burdensome. Obviously, these problems will not prove to be merely a blip on the radar screen, and rating agencies and companies that guarantee securities will operate in a much different regulatory climate in the years to come.

THE STRUCTURED INVESTMENT VEHICLE (SIV) STORY

Most of the world's attention in the huge financial meltdown of asset-backed securities is in the mortgage-backed area. Yet, there are other asset-backed securities markets that also have been hard hit and which significantly add to the scope of the overall problem. One area worth analyzing is the structured investment vehicle (SIV), because it helps explain the complexity of the problems encountered by many unsuspecting investors.

Many of these SIVs had all the problems that were part of the asset-backed mess—they were often formed offshore, were not on the balance sheets of the parent organizations, the originators wanted to sell off the investments and not hold on to them, the securities often differed substantially in risk, and the risks were not fully understood by rating agencies and regulators, and obviously not by the buyers.

The first SIV was Alpha Finance Corporation. It was launched by Citibank in 1988. Shortly thereafter (in 1989), Beta Finance Corporation came into existence. Alpha and Beta composed the SIV market for six years before the arrival of a third SIV, Sigma Finance Corporation, set up by Gordian Knot in 1995. The next twelve years witnessed another twenty or so vehicles administered by a small community of SIV managers globally.

The SIV concept was developed in London, but it reached fruition in the Cayman Islands. The Cayman Islands was an ideal location because of its emergence as the dominant jurisdiction for offshore capital market transactions during the 1980s. It became the leading offshore center as a result of political and economic stability, an effective judicial system, the absence of any direct taxation or currency exchange controls, the availability of professional and administrative support services, and importantly, a minimum amount of regulation.

The first bond issues using Cayman Island companies occurred in the 1970s. The 1980s brought diversification in capital market products in the Caymans, using securitization and structured finance techniques and employing repackaging and derivatives. Then came the development of the SIV as investment managers attempted to take advantage of market arbitrage (taking advantage of price or yield disparities between securities or between markets). The use of the Cayman Islands' companies in the commercial paper and medium-term note markets was already well established, so the SIV was a logical progression.

As of July 2007, Moody's Investors Service rated 36 SIV and SIV hybrids. They managed assets of approximately $400 billion (which has since diminished significantly), and this makes it easy to understand why investors and government organizations have had more than a passing interest in these problems.

As for the structure of an SIV, it is like a finance company that engages in market arbitrage by purchasing financial assets, such as medium- and long-term fixed-income bonds, and funding itself with cheaper senior debt instruments such as commercial paper and medium term notes. Typically, an SIV will be capitalized with either a mix of equity and subordinated debt or subordinated debt only. Equity investors have the benefit of leverage on their exposure to underlying assets. The economic incentives behind the establishment of SIVs have been the generation of management fees for the financial institution managing the SIV and the generation of significant returns for equity investors.

As time passed, the SIV models have become increasingly complex and sophisticated. Early on, the vehicles were relatively limited in scope and were rather static and inflexible. That changed, however, and managers ultimately acquired a greater range of discretion and operational freedom, while at the same time maintaining the risk-management and risk-mitigation features that are deemed essential to the SIV structure. The models necessary to operate an SIV include a wide range of variables covering a variety of asset and liability characteristics. SIV managers issue capital with a variety of asset and liability characteristics, and with a variety of currencies, increasingly using alternative forms of liquidity and structured credit.

Despite the sophistication of the models and the people who developed them, there are elementary and basic risks that sophistication cannot avoid. The most basic of risks is an inability to add to or roll over funding. This can happen due to nervousness on the part of investors because of concerns over SIVs in general, the type of financing vehicles that are being used, the financial condition of the company, or changes in key personnel. When funding becomes a problem, then pressure exists to sell off assets, many of which are not the most liquid even when there are no financial problems.

Of course, the problems do not have to start with funding. They can occur as securities become tarnished because of the type of security, because of the collateral that is behind the security, because the market for the investments has dried up, or because it is very difficult to determine the price of a security that is not actively trading. Investment problems can ultimately lead to financing problems. No matter how sophisticated the models, and the people that develop them, there is no way that such fundamental risks can be fully protected against. The best that can be hoped for is to have backup financing arrangements, and all that does is to create a stop-gap approach to the problem. It does not get at the fundamental difficulties. Potential risks can become actual risks and then become actual problems in a very short period of time.

What is truly amazing about the structured investment vehicle is how long it has been around (since 1988); how large the amounts became (about $400 billion at the peak); the excessive nature of the risks taken above and beyond the fundamental liquidity, credit, and market risks; and how little was known about these vehicles and their problems until the feathers hit the fan. Any investment vehicle that is set up in a way to limit surveillance is ultimately doomed to have some sort of major financial problems that can spread like wildfire, taking down both the guilty and the innocent.

In many cases, the mathematical sophistication of these investments is so great that many investors and regulators do not fully understand the risks involved. Many of these investments are based on highly sophisticated models where past relationships are used as a guide to future relationships. The problem is that these models can come off the track when past risk/reward relationships no longer apply.

For those technically inclined, there are exogenous and endogenous factors that influence economic activity and investments. Exogenous forces come from outside the economic system, while endogenous forces are from within the system. In a highly complex and ever-changing world, past exogenous forces and relationships often change and with them major changes can take place in financial risks and rewards.

To be even more specific, the problem for many models is that the worst case has yet to occur. Moreover, one of the biggest mistakes in economic analysis and forecasting is the phrase "other things remaining equal." It's too bad that those people who managed Long-Term Capital Management, and those people who managed mortgage-backed investments, CDOs, and SIVs, did not realize that the more complex a model, the greater the chance for something to go wrong.

To be very blunt, one can argue that were it not for creating these investment vehicles off balance sheet and offshore, and with little in the way of regulation, transparency, and understanding the risks involved, these investment vehicles would never have seen the light of day. Or, at a minimum, they would have been more conservatively operated. In this regard, the rating agencies (and those companies that insure securities) should have forcefully and publicly stated the risks and possible rating downgrades. If the Fed is so concerned about adequate transparency, why not hold the institutions it regulates to a higher transparency standard than they have at present?

As for the Federal Reserve, and other central banks, some may argue that they should not be concerned about whether asset-backed investors get burned or lose a great deal of money. However, what they have to be concerned about is the collapse of one market leading to collapses in other markets, especially those that are in their regulatory bailiwick. This is one place where transparency by the central banks, and especially by the Fed, is a very important factor, much more important than what the Fed is thinking about with respect to current economic data.

It is little wonder that the rating agencies are finally becoming more active in communicating to investors exactly how asset-backed investments operate and the risks involved. Frankly, it is about time. Generally, they have been a day late and a dollar short in pointing out problems. Fitch, to its credit, published in September 2007 a report entitled: "The Rating Performance of Structured Investment Vehicles in Times of Diminishing Liquidity for Assets and Liabilities." They made some important points, such as the need to have continuous access to funding via the commercial paper (CP) and medium-term note (MTN) markets. Moreover, the cost of financing is a key factor in profitability. If funding proves to be expensive or hard to come by, it can severely limit the profitability of an SIV, and it can create liquidity squeezes and even losses.

The risk of CP funding disappearing, says the report, can differ between SIVs. Some purchasers of SIV senior debt will invest in vehicles only of a certain size. Some investors will invest only in vehicles with long, established track records. Some will also distinguish between SIV investments depending on their asset mix or whether they have strong bank sponsors. The latter can have the advantage that the SIV can place paper with either its sponsors or its affiliates. SIVs in general have come under hard times. Asset sales have led to losses, because the asset sales prices are lower than the purchase prices.

SIVs, the report continues, "are exposed to the market value of their assets in two ways. Firstly, when market value losses lead to realized losses due to assets being sold to cover maturing liabilities. Secondly, a deterioration in the market value of the portfolio may put pressure on the implied support for the senior ratings of the vehicles. A fall in the portfolio value may also explicitly trigger a market value capital test and force the vehicle into a restricted operating state or enforcement." In enforcement, the vehicle cannot issue further senior notes. An irreversible wind-down of the SIV can then commence as assets are sold to meet maturing liabilities.

Finally, Fitch stated in its September 2007 report that it did not expect any near-term improvement in the CP funding environment or the current illiquidity and repricing of credit risk in the market. This situation, if continued, could lead to lower ratings and, of course, more difficult and costly financing.

RESCUING THE FINANCIAL SYSTEM

In the middle of August 2007, a rescue plan for SIVs was quietly developed. The U.S. Treasury was directly involved in developing the plan. One reason for the plan was that key Treasury officials, who previously had been employed in the private sector of the debt markets, had become concerned about the problems. In the middle of October 2007, information about the plan and the organizations involved leaked out, and this caused the Treasury to make a public announcement. The plan was both inadequate and short-sighted, and the organizations involved in the rescue operations were limited, which suggested resistance to the idea. Not surprisingly, the plan never came to fruition.

What is unusual about these circumstances is that when banks are involved in major financial problems, dealing with this type of situation is typically in the bailiwick of the Federal Reserve. Either the Fed takes the lead in such an operation, or it is part of a joint venture comprising the Fed, the Treasury, and some other regulators. Yet, during the formative stages of this plan, or even after the plan was announced, the Fed stayed primarily in the background. One can surmise that the main reason why the Fed was not actively involved was because it did not believe that those who lost or would lose money in areas such as SIVs should be bailed out. For example, on October 15, 2007, Chairman Bernanke in a speech at the Economic Club of New York, made the following statement:

> As I indicated in earlier remarks, it is not the responsibility of the Federal Reserve—nor would it be appropriate—to protect lenders and investors from the consequences of their financial decisions.

From a public policy point of view, this lack of Federal Reserve-Treasury cooperation was a bad set of circumstances. The Fed should have the primary responsibility in dealing with these financial problems. Yet, the Fed was late in
recognizing the problems, especially when it came to the regulatory side, and it
did not act in a timely or aggressive fashion when it did recognize the problems.
Monetary policy is not just federal funds targeting or discount window borrowing; there is a regulatory side which seems to have fallen between the cracks.

There are times when the regulatory side is more important than adjusting
interest rate policies, but that has not been recognized as such. While Bernanke is
correct in saying that it is not the responsibility of the Fed to protect lenders and
investors from the consequences of their financial decisions, this statement does
not get the Fed off the regulatory hook. The Fed regulators should have used a
combination of regulations, more enlightened reporting procedures by the banks,
and jawboning, to stop the banks and investors from getting in over their heads in
these high-risk, leveraged investments.

Both Greenspan and Bernanke share the blame for concentrating too much on
interest rates with not enough emphasis placed on the regulatory portion of monetary policy. In this regard, what would be wrong if, at the conclusion of an FOMC
meeting, part of the Fed's press release is devoted to the regulatory side of policy
and what the Fed thinks should be done? There should always be one member of
the Federal Reserve Board who is a true expert on regulation in general, and commercial bank regulation in particular.

It is important to note that while the Fed is a bank regulator, it is also a regulator for government securities dealers and the government securities market. Bear
Stearns happened to be one of dealers in government securities, and the Federal
Reserve dealt with them on an ongoing basis and therefore had to be aware of
problems, especially when looking at their financials. This is another regulatory
black eye for the Fed, and this one is primarily on Bernanke's watch. Greenspan
cannot be held accountable for what happened here.

INVESTMENT BANKS FOLLOW DIFFERENT PATHS

In the 1960s, three financial institutions each had a similar goal—to becoming
a leader in investment banking. One succeeded—Goldman Sachs—and is now the
preeminent, world-wide investment banking house. The other two—Bear Stearns
and Lehman Brothers—collapsed in 2008. The paths that the three institutions
followed over the last four decades had much to do with these divergent outcomes.

In the early 1960s, Goldman Sachs was primarily an equity house and had little in the way of a bond business. They were not even a dealer in U.S. Treasury
securities, but they did have a modest investment banking operation, and, Goldman Sachs was a well-run organization. Their movement into other financial
areas was gradual and well thought out. Management succession occurred in a
logical and civilized way, and this continued over the next forty years. Thus, it is

no accident that so many senior government officials have come from Goldman Sachs.

However, with Bear Stearns and Lehman Brothers, the circumstances were different. Both firms were run by hard-charging individuals who had little desire to share power. This meant that over the years, many very good people with considerable managerial talent left, or were forced out. This was power sharing—or rather, the lack thereof—at its worst. While Goldman Sachs employees went on to work for the government, Bear Stearns and Lehman Brothers looked to hire former government employees, and especially those with considerable name recognition.

Both Bear Stearns and Lehman believed that the road to being a successful investment banking house was through the bond market. Subsequently, they discovered that they could make a great deal of money in the bond market, and the more money they made, the more aggressive they became . Needless to say, you can have too much of a good thing and that proved to be the case when both firms became overextended in the asset-backed market in general, and the mortgage-backed market in particular.

These observations are not based on second-hand sources. I worked for Lehman Brothers in the early 1970s and was a consultant to Bear Stearns for two decades beginning in the early 1980s.

THE BEAR STEARNS FINANCIAL DEBACLE

On many a Friday in the early 1980s, a limousine would pull up to my house at the ungodly hour of about 5 a.m. Dennis Coleman would be in the car, and it would take about an hour to get to 55 Water Street in Manhattan, which was Bear Stearns headquarters at that time. Dennis was apparently number three at Bear Stearns, although there were several others who probably would have said the same thing. Dennis was in charge of the debt market area, which was the centerpiece of the firm. He had joined Bear Stearns around 1967, just out of Georgetown University, and had been brought on board by "Ace" Greenberg.

The meetings at 55 Water Street were held in modest and rather small quarters and typically included about a half-dozen trading and financing types. The discussions tended to be very detailed and generally centered around Federal Reserve policy, Treasury debt management, and the budget outlook. When Dennis left the firm, Bill Michaelchek took over the responsibilities for the debt market area, and the Griggs & Santow relationship with Bear Stearns expanded considerably. At that time, they were one of our largest clients.

After the firm moved to 245 Park Avenue, I would address the debt market trading desk every Friday. In addition, they had me come in on occasion to lecture the trading desk on predetermined topics. These were the good old days for Bear Stearns; it was unfortunate that both Coleman and later on Michaelchek were "induced" to leave. Perhaps some of the problems that ultimately did in Bear Stearns would not have happened if they had stayed on in senior management positions. Bill and Dennis were the calming forces in a firm prone to take aggressive positions.

Bear Stearns had its own economics department, and early on in our relationship, there were no political problems, which was very unusual for that firm. This was because so much of our work was technical in nature and narrow in focus, and they did not have similar in-house expertise at that time. However, things changed and new people took over in the economics area. They apparently thought that because Bear Stearns was paying millions for their in-house research operation, why should they pay for outside economists? That was the beginning of the end for Griggs & Santow at Bear Stearns, and by 2003, what had dwindled down to a token relationship came to an end.

I bring this up because our relationship of over two decades gives us some insight into a unique firm staffed by unique individuals. I saw the good and the bad and the highs and the lows. It was a firm that was a debt-market trading house that aspired to be a broadly based investment banking house. They wanted to be a "white shoe" type of operation—an old-line, traditional investment banking house that was very selective in whom they hired, and where, in days gone by, the traditional summer outfit included white shoes and straw hats—but the way the firm was organized and staffed, that goal was difficult to achieve.

Each part of the firm was like a fiefdom, and it was not unusual for the relationships among the various departments to be something less than cordial. Some might even classify it as cutthroat. Each department was driven to make money, even if it may have been detrimental to the interests of other areas of the firm. For example, take the financing operation for government securities and related securities. It was one of the most profitable operations in the firm because in essence they charged a "toll" to trading areas for providing them with financing. Unfortunately, the firm could never overcome its lack of a management style.

To offset, or some might say, cover their problems, they would on occasion hire well-known people and give them fancy titles in order to improve the firm's image, but in many cases it appears that it was primarily for show. In one case in particular, they paid a substantial financial price for a well-known economist who, after a few years on the scene, recommended a trading position in the commodities area. This cost Bear Stearns a lawsuit and a great deal of money. Yet, when all was said and done, Bear Stearns had neither the capital, the blue-chip customers, nor the type of management that would allow it to make the jump from being a very aggressive trading house to becoming a first-class investment banking house.

In the years they were a client, there was little doubt that, one way or another, the firm would ultimately be sold. It was just a question of whether it would be sold at a high-water time or a low-water time. Because of their lack of success in becoming a first-rate investment banking house, they kept getting more and more aggressive and, at least on the surface, more sophisticated in their debt-market products. They became a kingpin in the mortgage market and kept adding more bells and whistles on to their products. Of course, the more bells and whistles that are on a securities product, the greater the risks involved, not only for themselves, but for their customers.

In terms of risk-taking, the Federal Reserve was surely aware of most of what Bear Stearns was doing because of all the regular reports the monetary authority received. Yet, reading apparently is not the same thing as understanding, especially when it came to the risks involved. One can be nasty with respect to the Fed by saying it appears to have believed that it had more important things on its mind than what the dealers were doing in the products that they devised and sold. After all, the Fed had other things on its plate such as closely monitoring the core PCE price performance over the last twelve months, and how this performance might change over the next two or three years. It was also very important to be transparent about the current economic performance and to create forecasts that go out over several years, and it was important to make sure that the wording in a press release after an FOMC meeting conveyed the right tone when it came to policy.

THE LEHMAN BROTHERS FINANCIAL DEBACLE

Lehman Brothers failed in September 2008. Some analysts had hoped that Lehman would avoid the financial guillotine because—supposedly—they were different from Bear Stearns, they were less financially vulnerable, and the regulators had new safety nets in place. But in reality, the two firms were quite similar— one might argue that they were two peas in the same pod.

Their businesses were similar and so were the way they operated them. They gambled heavily on their bond businesses in general, and their mortgage operations in particular. Neither wanted to run "vanilla" operations; they were innovative, but to a fault, especially when greater profits could be made by taking on greater leverage and credit risks. Both had aspirations to became a "white shoe" investment banking firm, and both came up short. It was a bridge too far.

GOVERNMENT SECURITIES DEALERS

To understand the formative years of Bear Stearns, when they were viewed as one of the better and more aggressive dealers in government securities, it is worthwhile to talk a little bit about this industry and why it became virtually impossible for a firm just to concentrate on that one business. Not only was there not enough money to be made in the business, but when debt markets began to expand in terms of products, firms could no longer be a boutique. The following information comes from a book I wrote in 1988 entitled *The Budget Deficit: The Causes, the Costs, the Outlook.*

> At the end of 1960, there were 18 firms classified by the Federal Reserve as reporting dealers in government securities. A decade later the number moved to 24, by 1975 reached 30, and by 1980 had grown to 37. It dipped to 36 by the end of 1985, but by early 1988, had reached 42 firms.

The number of dealers then grew to forty-four in 1988 but by late 2008 had fallen to eighteen. Today, none of the dealers are viewed as just specialists in U.S. Treasury securities. All of the once independent dealers have been bought up, gone out of business, or expanded into other areas. Moreover, being a reporting Treasury securities dealer—which at one time was considered very prestigious—is no longer as important or as profitable. This is despite the fact that the Treasury market is still the centerpiece of debt markets in the United States, and in the upcoming years, very large budget deficits will need to be financed. It is the market that both the Fed and the Treasury operate in, and its rates are used as the base for interest rates in general. It is the market where most interest rate forecasts are made, regarding both the level and the slope of the yield curve. Treasury rates form the base level against which higher risk securities are compared.

Every once in a while, an economist makes a long-term forecast that proves to be close to the mark. In my book written over two decades ago, I made the following comment:

> Maybe the most interesting question with respect to dealers and their profit opportunities is how the new firms, or those under new management, will react when their first major bear market develops. The sharp deteriorations in the bond market in the spring, and again in the fall of 1987, were the first tests. The recent wave of expansion in the dealer community was induced largely by the greatest bull market in the history of U.S. Treasury obligations. Many of these firms are not accustomed to huge unexpected losses of a highly leveraged business in a short period.

"Reporting dealers" in U.S. Treasury securities was a designation that a firm could not automatically adopt. It was bestowed by the Federal Reserve, and there was a considerable testing period before the Fed would classify a firm as a reporting dealer. Once this was done, the Fed would conduct open-market operations through the dealer, who would then have the opportunity to be financed when the Fed did repurchase agreements. Many looked upon reporting dealers as being a cut above the rest when it came to market sophistication, because it required considerable expertise in monetary policy, fiscal policy, and debt management.

Bear Stearns was a well-regarded reporting dealer in government securities. Many admired the firm's smarts, aggressiveness, and creativity, but there were also concerns that they were getting in over their heads in terms of risk. Excessive risks taken on the asset side of the balance sheet can ultimately lead to excessive risk on the liability side, and it is the liability side that can do in a firm. It was Bear Stearns' funding problems that ultimately would have become a counterparty problem (where another organization acts as an ultimate guarantor for loans) that proved to be the death knell for the firm. Apparently, the bank that held much of the counterparty risk for Bear Stearns was the organization that bought them. This situation no doubt had something to do with the purchase.

12

Learning from the Past to Improve the Future

During Alan Greenspan's eighteen-year tenure, the swings in the fed funds rate were excessive and the timing was questionable. Especially notable in this regard was the period from 2000 through 2005. From 4.75 percent in early 1999, the funds rate was increased to 6.5 percent by the middle of 2000, and unfortunately, it stayed there through the end of the year. It then dropped like a stone and reached 1 percent by the middle of 2003; then, beginning in the middle of 2004, it started an upward trek of seventeen consecutive 25 basis point increases—fourteen under Greenspan—that took the rate up to 4.5 percent by the time he left office. One can argue that implicit in the magnitude and timing of these advances and the changes in direction is that the Fed was misreading the economy and the price picture. Fortunately, the underlying economic fundamentals were strong enough, and the downward pressure on prices sufficient enough, that the cost of the Fed's errors in judgment were minimal.

Greenspan could have done a better job by using a broader array of policy tools and targets. The Fed should have paid more attention to bank credit expansion and its components and, depending on the circumstances, more actively used reserve requirement changes, discount window policies, margin requirements on stocks, and a more forceful use of the Fed's regulatory powers. Operating policy with one arm tied behind your back is hardly an optimum approach.

Moreover, even in the one area that the Fed concentrated on—the federal funds rate—it can be argued that there could have been major policy upgrades. Under Greenspan, the Fed moved the funds target inch by inch, and ultimately to rate levels that seemed too high or too low. More aggressive changes in the level of the funds rate, but staying within a middle ground, could have avoided agonizingly slow and ultimately large fed funds rate swings.

MISSTEPS STARTING IN 2000

At the beginning of 2000, the funds rate was at 5.5 percent, and the Fed was in the process of firming. By March the rate had been advanced to 6 percent—a questionable move. The most logical procedure would have been to keep the funds rate at 5.5 percent. Real growth had slowed; the unemployment rate had stabilized at about 4 percent; the stock market appeared to be peaking; the core CPI was running between 2 and 3 percent on an annual basis, and the monetary base was slipping. The economic recovery was in its eighth year, and there were signs that the expansion was long in the tooth.

Yet, the Fed continued to jack up its funds target. Stopping at 5.5 percent was appropriate; continuing on to 6 percent and then 6.5 percent was not. In May 2000, the Fed increased the funds target by 50 basis points, to 6.5 percent. At the time, we stated in *The Griggs & Santow Report* that the May increase made little sense. It was almost as if the Fed advanced the rate because the market had expected it to do so, and had already built an increase into market prices. This was no way to run a railroad, let alone monetary policy.

Yet, up to this point, while the Fed's errors in judgment were disturbing, the impact was relatively small. Then, in the second half of 2000 the Fed compounded its mistake. It was clear that both the economy and the stock market were weakening noticeably. If the Fed had been on top of things, it would have cut its funds target several times in the second half of the year. By the end of 2000, something between 4 and 5 percent would have been an appropriate funds target. In fact, it was still stuck at 6.5 percent.

Thus, the Fed sat on its hands for a half year with a funds rate that was inappropriately high in the first place, and then had been inappropriately raised. By the end of 2000, a moderate policy mistake had become a considerable policy mistake. If the Fed had made the right moves throughout 2000, the stampede to ease that started in early 2001 and continued throughout the year—and beyond—would not have been necessary.

For those who might ask, "Where is the evidence in the second half of 2000 that indicates the Fed should have eased considerably?" consider the following: The 30-year Treasury rate declined from a 6.15 percent average in May 2000 to a 5.49 percent average in December 2000. In this same period, Aaa corporate bond rates had fallen from 7.99 percent to 7.21 percent; Baa corporate bond rates had slipped from 8.90 percent to 8.02 percent, and 30-year fixed-rate mortgages had dropped sharply from 8.52 percent to 7.38 percent. These large rate declines and a downward sloping Treasury yield curve indicated that market participants were expecting a considerable weakening in the economy. This was not the only time that Greenspan did not get the message from the financial markets.

Both the stock market and economic data were sending a similar message. The S&P 500 index had dropped from a 1,517.68 average in August 2000 to 1,320.28 in December. In the third quarter, real GDP moved to the minus side and the recovery in the fourth quarter was modest. Yet, the funds rate, which stood at 6.5 percent in

May 2000, was still 6.5 percent at the end of December. At the start of 2001, it was as if the lights finally went on at the Open Market Committee and the Fed realized what it had done wrong. Then came the mad rush to ease policy. The situation was somewhat reminiscent of the Alec Guinness character in the movie *Bridge on the River Kwai*, who was so obsessive about building the bridge that he lost sight of his main objective, which was to blow it up!

Even if one gives the Fed a pass on its policy shortcomings in 2000, its policy approach in 2001 also left much to be desired. Going into 2001, the proper funds rate was between 4 and 5 percent, and the actual target was 6.5 percent; this was no time to gradually move the funds target downward. Moreover, additional Fed easing would have been necessary in the first half of 2001, even if the funds target had been correct at the beginning of the year. By mid-2001 an appropriate funds target would have been about 3 percent, and that should have been the rate going into the 9/11 catastrophe.

When 9/11 occurred, the prudent move would have been to cut the funds target by 1 percent in order to create a positive shock for the financial community and the public. The rate would have stood at 2 percent, which should have been the bottom for the cycle. Thus, the range in the policy cycle should have been about 5.5 percent on the high side and 2 percent on the low side. As it turned out, the actual range was 6.5 percent on the high side and, eventually, 1 percent on the low side.

The Fed eased many times during 2001—at all eight regularly scheduled meetings and three times between meetings. By the end of 2001 the funds target was down to 1.75 percent. For those who do not remember, in 2001 the easing moves totaled 475 basis points, and took place as follows:

Fed Funds Rate Easing Moves—2001

January 3	Special meeting	50 basis points to 6.00 percent
January 31	Regular meeting	50 basis points to 5.50 percent
March 20	Regular meeting	50 basis points to 5.00 percent
April 18	Special meeting	50 basis points to 4.50 percent
May 15	Regular meeting	50 basis points to 4.00 percent
June 27	Regular meeting	25 basis points to 3.75 percent
August 21	Regular meeting	25 basis points to 3.50 percent
September 17	Special meeting	50 basis points to 3.00 percent
October 2	Regular meeting	50 basis points to 2.50 percent
November 6	Regular meeting	50 basis points to 2.00 percent
December 11	Regular meeting	25 basis points to 1.75 percent

Greenspan and some of his colleagues at the Fed would no doubt argue that this analysis is an example of revisionist history. However, after the funds rate was increased to 6.5 percent and left there until the end of 2000, on more than one occasion it was pointed out in *The Griggs & Santow Report* that this was an excessively high target and needed to be reduced. Moreover, we were not alone in making such recommendations. Then, when the funds target was pushed down to 1 percent, we said the rate should not have been driven that low, that it was kept at that level for too long, and then, the degree of firming was agonizingly slow.

One of the purposes of this book is to be as objective as possible in presenting the monetary policy record. The economic indicators data and the Flavor of the Times section are most useful in pursuing that objective. After all, how can the Fed improve monetary policy if past mistakes go unreported? One thing is for sure—with regard to the cyclical management of monetary policy, Greenspan's worst performance occurred from 2000 to 2005. Look at the facts:

- In 2000, the Fed raised its funds target three times—from 5.5 to 6.5 percent.
- In 2001, the Fed eased policy eleven times, with a funds rate of 1.75 percent by year-end.
- In 2002, the Fed eased policy once to 1.25 percent; and in 2003, it again eased policy only once, to 1 percent.
- In 2004, the funds rate was raised five times—25 basis points at a time—and finished the year at 2.25 percent.
- In 2005, the funds rate was raised at all eight FOMC meetings—25 basis points at each meeting—and finished the year with a target of 4.25 percent.
- In 2006, the target was raised by 25 basis points at each of the first four FOMC meetings (once by Greenspan and three times by Bernanke), and ended the year at 5.25 percent.
- In September 2007, the funds target (under Bernanke) was lowered by 50 basis points to 4.75 percent, in October it was reduced 25 basis points to 4.5 percent, in December it was lowered 25 basis points to 4.25 percent, and in January 2008 it was cut twice by a total of 125 basis points to 3 percent. On March 18, 2008, the funds rate was reduced by 75 basis points to 2.25 percent, and on April 30 it was cut to 2 percent, and on October 8, 2008 it was cut to 1.5 percent.

Thus, in a period of roughly six years, the Fed raised its funds target from 5.5 to 6.5 percent then down to 1 percent, then back up to 5.25 percent, and then down to what may prove to be less than 2 percent. Yet, during this period, there were only relatively moderate changes in economic growth and prices, and the changes that did occur hardly justified such a rollercoaster monetary policy ride. Real GDP growth was soft in 2000 and 2001, but there was no recession. The price performance as measured by the PCE core generally stayed within a 1.5 to 2.5 percent range. There was no breakout on either the low or the high side, which suggests that all these funds-rate gyrations had less of an impact on real growth and inflation than many analysts seem to believe. That proved to be fortunate, because the overall performance of the economy during these six years was, on balance, quite good.

To those in the media, this analysis contains a message: Do not get overly excited about what a 25-basis-point or even a 50-basis-point change in an overnight interest rate means for economic growth and inflation. And do not get overly excited about word changes in the press releases following an FOMC meeting. Of course, the business news stations are under constant pressure to find things to talk about all day long, which leads to an overemphasis on any piece of information that comes down the pike—even if it has little meaning. In contrast, there is often a lot going on below the surface, but this requires some digging for information and time-consuming analysis, and so the grunt work tends to get lost in a fast-paced era of news headlines. The financial media usually has most of the facts, but more often than not, very little understanding of what is important and what these facts mean.

For example, ask any financial reporter where current monetary policy stands and that person will tell you it is such-and-such a funds target. Moreover, it is likely that if the person is steeped in facts (not knowledge), that person can no doubt give you a history of fed funds rate changes, and which chairman was responsible for the changes. Yet, ask about other monetary policy measurements, and they are usually clueless. What is frustrating is that the Fed, by telling us how important the funds target is, adds to this lack of understanding on the part of the media and general public.

It cannot be stated frequently enough that the fed funds target rate is only an overnight rate that is designated by the Fed and not by market forces; it is only one measurement—and not a dominant one—of the ease or tightness of monetary policy; that interest rates out on the yield curve have more of an influence on the economy than an overnight rate; and that bank credit expansion and the availability of funds for those who lend or borrow are more important than an overnight interest rate.

If you think that this is an attempt to downplay the value of a fed funds target rate, and criticize the Fed for overemphasizing it, you are absolutely right. In the years from 2000 into 2008, the funds rate target was all over the place, but that was not the case with respect to monetary policy when viewed in its entirety. Policy may have moved too much, and not always in the right direction, but the swings were much less than what the funds target suggests. This is because there is more to monetary policy than what happens to the fed funds target, and on an even broader basis, monetary policy is only one factor among many that weigh on economic growth and prices.

Both Greenspan and the Fed were very fortunate that their funds-target missteps from 2000 through 2007 were muted by other policy factors and were not as important a causative factor as many analysts made them out to be. Monetary policy was never as tight as the 6.5 percent funds rate indicated, and never as easy as a 1 percent funds rate target suggested. Overly tight and then overly easy—yes, but not as those rates suggest.

When Bernanke took over the helm of the Fed in February 2006, the recommendations he received from many so-called pundits were to indicate he should be tough on inflation, should continue to follow the Greenspan policy approach, should not be wedded to models, should add to policy transparency, should get on the good-side of the media and Congress, and should develop the confidence of market makers. On the surface, these seemed like good suggestions. However, if Bernanke had looked at what was right and what was wrong with the policy that he was inheriting, and with forces that had previously been set in motion, one wonders whether he might have tried to put his own imprint on policy at an early date. What is the safest approach in the short run may not be the best approach in the long run.

Bernanke's biggest mistake at the start of his term was his preoccupation with the topic of inflation—how to measure it, the need to contain it, and then how to contain it. He decided that the PCE core that was in use was the best measurement, that the increase should be in the 1 to 2 percent range, and that the funds target needed to move higher for the Fed to be successful in its price objectives. Interestingly, he seldom talked about either real growth or the unemployment rate as possible targets. In other words, when it came to targeting one aspect of the economy, and even though real growth, the unemployment rate, and price changes were supposedly considered to be near equal in importance, the only one with a specific target was prices. That made one of the equals more than having equal.

In support of this analysis, the first major speech that Bernanke made as chairman of the Federal Reserve was on the occasion of the 75th anniversary of the Woodrow Wilson School of Public and International Affairs at Princeton University. The speech, entitled "The Benefits of Price Stability," was delivered on February 24, 2006, less than one month after he took over at the Fed. In this speech, Bernanke suggested that while the Fed had several policy objectives that were equal, price stability was given the highest priority. The following is a quote from that speech:

> Although price stability is an end of monetary policy, it is also a means by which policy can achieve its other objectives. In the jargon, price stability is both a goal and an intermediate target of policy. . . . When prices are stable, both economic growth and stability are likely to be enhanced, and long-term interest rates are likely to be moderate. Thus, even a policymaker who places relatively less weight on price stability as a goal in its own right should be careful to maintain price stability as a means of advancing other critical objectives.

With Bernanke devoting so much attention to prices, it appears that some very important issues slipped between the cracks. The housing bubble, a creature of some of his predecessor's policies, did not get the attention it deserved. Neither did the lack of Fed regulatory oversight and guidance that could have limited bank lending to questionable borrowers in questionable ways. Then we come to the Fed's forecasts for the economy, which left a great deal to be desired. The Fed was way wide of the mark in February 2006 with its forecast for 2007, and those misestimates continued all the way through into 2008.

What was notable in the misjudgments was the Fed's overoptimism about economic growth in general, and the performance of the housing market in particular. For example, in the press release following the July 31, 2007, FOMC meeting, which was just about the time that the housing market and its financing was coming unglued, the Fed said the following: "recent indicators have suggested somewhat firmer economic growth, and some tentative signs of stability have appeared in the housing market." That does not exactly indicate that the Fed was on top of economic and financial events.

The Fed was also overly optimistic about the price picture and performance in 2007 and into the first part of 2008. The PCE core price increase in 2007 (December 2006 to December 2007) came in at about 2.2 percent which was above the 1 percent to 2 percent target band. Moreover, this was despite the fact that economic forces, both at home and abroad, had helped keep prices contained and that seepage from high food and energy prices did not significantly make their way (at least up to that time) into the core price performance.

One can argue that the less than distinguished forecasting results are in part due to the fact that the Fed pays too much attention to targeting and modeling. It is not just a matter of whether the targets and models chosen are right or wrong, or whether the Fed is inside or outside its target ranges, but rather how successful it is in picking up early in the game whether there are problems ahead and what is the proper reaction. Is economic activity accelerating or decelerating by an unacceptable amount? Are there growing problems with respect to the price outlook? Are there growing problems with respect to markets? If the answers are yes, then the Fed should act in a way that could limit unacceptable changes. In the case of inflation, trying to fine-tune to a price range where you have not figured out the cause-effect relationship, is questionable to say the least. This is no way to run a central bank.

The Fed needs to realize that relationships continually change and models have trouble keeping up with the changes and acting accordingly; when a model predicts adversity, it cannot seem to handle the possibility that the worst case has yet to happen; there are periods when external forces that are difficult to predict will dominate over internal economic forces, and that highly complex international events can change domestic economic relationships in unexpected ways.

A FULL ARSENAL OF POLICY TOOLS

If the Federal Reserve uncorks its arsenal of policy tools and comes up with innovative approaches, there would be less reliance on the fed funds rate as a policy tool. With more reliance placed on other policy tools, the Fed could follow a policy that allows market forces to play a larger role. Moreover, with more emphasis on other policy tools, the Fed could avoid guessing about what is the appropriate funds rate and the amount that it should be changed when necessary. Let market forces play an important role in the funds rate, with the Fed only setting the outside rate parameters. Maybe, just maybe, this approach would downplay the importance that market participants and the media place on token changes in an overnight interest rate that has been overemphasized in terms of importance.

The more the Fed dips into its arsenal and uses a variety of policy tools to change policy, the better its chances of attaining what it considers to be desired targets. This is because the impact of using a combination of policy tools can add to the effectiveness of policy changes and reduce the time it takes to work their way through the banking system and the economy. For example, it would make sense to have an acceptable fed funds rate range (not just a specific target) with market forces determining where funds trade inside the range. This approach, if used in conjunction with adjustments in reserve requirements, discount window policies, open market operations, capital requirements, and selective controls such as margin requirements on stocks, should add to the potency to reach policy objectives. This is a more sensible approach than using one policy tool such as a predetermined single federal funds target rate and thinking in terms of what marginal change in this one rate should be made to change policy.

This is not a minor issue. For example, prior to the September 2007 FOMC meeting, market participants and those in the media focused almost exclusively on whether the Fed would cut its funds target by 25 or 50 basis points from a 5.25 percent level. There was little discussion of other alternatives, or a combination of other alternatives, that could better deal with the new and difficult circumstances. This led to confined thinking that easing a fed funds target by 25 basis points would only be a token move, but a change of 50 basis points would be a substantial move. Needless to say, both moves were inadequate when it came to changing monetary policy. As it turned out, both the funds target and the discount rate target were reduced 50 basis points, and some at the Fed apparently believed that it was now ahead of the curve when it came to easing policy.

Yet, the devil can be in the details when it comes to the specifics of what policy techniques the Fed should use. For example, how much fed funds rate flexibility should be allowed if an ordained target is not used? The Fed seems to believe that it can peg a specific overnight interest rate that will lead to a PCE core price increase of 1 to 2 percent over a twelve-month period. If the price increase is outside the acceptable zone, then the Fed will make marginal changes in its funds target to get the job done. If that does not work, then the Fed will try more nickel-and-dime moves. This approach, whether it is appropriate or not, is truly an art that involves much more guesswork than the Fed would care to admit.

One not-so-small problem with respect to the 1 to 2 percent PCE core price approach is that this has not been the central tendency in the last few decades. The Fed chooses not to discuss this situation, but its actions indicate it understands very well that its acceptable range is too low. If the Fed adhered rigorously to the 1 to 2 percent range, we would have had numerous overshootings of policy changes on the firming side. In the real world, the inner acceptable PCE core price range may well be 1.75 to 2.25 percent, but even this range should be flexible if the Fed is not satisfied with real growth or market conditions. The way the Fed operates and what it says are different, and this is not exactly policy transparency at its best.

Adding another complication to Fed targeting is that the Fed uses a controversial inflation approach; so controversial, in fact, that no other central bank uses the exact same approach. As a matter of fact, other central banks such as the Bank of England have officials who criticized the Fed for excluding food and energy from its price computations. Moreover, not only does the price target range used by the Fed exclude food and energy, which makes the Fed unique in that regard, but the computation does not accurately reflect changes in asset prices in general, and home prices in particular. An illogical approach to imputed-rent measurement tends to lead to questionable results on the cost of housing, and this is important since housing is a major item in the cost of living. Also, changes in home prices can be an important factor in people's thinking as to whether inflation fears are becoming more or less embedded.

Not to be lost in this analysis is that inflation expectations of one narrow group of investors are not the same as inflation expectations of consumers in general. PCE core prices relate to consumers, not to investors. Yet, the Fed places considerable emphasis on interest rate relationships between full-coupon Treasury securities and inflation-adjusted Treasury securities (TIPS) when trying to determine the inflation outlook of consumers.

IDEAS FOR FUTURE POLICIES

It is easier to be critical of what seems obviously wrong and needs to be changed than it is to come up with good, solid, practical recommendations. As a starting point, assuming the Fed continues to use the fed funds rate as its basic policy tool, then at least use a desired range rather than a specific number. This allows market forces to give the Fed some information that it does not currently have by pegging the rate.

For example, instead of announcing, say, a 3 percent funds target after an FOMC meeting, the Fed could announce that the acceptable range is 2.75 to 3.25 percent. If the Fed decides to change this funds range, it could move the 50-basis point differential. It could change the range to 3 to 3.5 percent if it wants to firm slightly, or 3.25 to 3.75 percent if it wants to firm somewhat more aggressively. Correspondingly, if the Fed wants to ease, it could move the range down to 2.5 to 3 percent for a modest easing, and 2.25 to 2.75 percent for a somewhat more aggressive easing. Let the supply/demand factors in the funds market have a chance to give the Fed some information.

Irrespective of the exact approach used, the transmission devices from an overnight interest rate to an acceptable consumer price performance, and to an acceptable real growth rate, and to a desirable unemployment rate are indirect and change over time. This indirect relationship is also true when the Fed is trying to alleviate financial market problems by bringing down its funds target. How much of a reduction is too little, how much of a reduction is too much, and how much is about right? No one really knows, including the Fed. If the Fed did know, it would not have edged its funds target lower; it would have acted more aggressively and forcefully. As events have shown in late 2007 and 2008, there is no magical amount of change in an overnight target rate in order to bring about health to the financial markets and financial institutions. How much more evidence is needed to demonstrate that changes in monetary policy—no matter what techniques are used—are primarily an art and not a science?

13

A BIGGER-PICTURE PERSPECTIVE

Inflation is a major concern for central banks around the world. This is not surprising because, what other government organization has the political courage to combat prices when they get out of hand? The problem for central banks has become more complex in recent years because inflation (or deflation) forces have, to a growing degree, come from outside a country's boundaries, and a central bank has little influence over the impact on prices. This situation calls for additional flexibility when it comes to a central bank targeting prices.

INFLATION

The modern U.S. inflation story began during the Burns era, and when he left office in 1978, prices were out of control. During G. William Miller's period in office (March 1978 to August 1979), he tried to contain inflation by pushing short-term rates higher, but he was not successful. In Paul Volcker's first few years at the helm of the Fed, he was only partially successful, although it was not because of a lack of trying. Inflation psychology had become so embedded that it took extraordinarily high interest rates and tight money to wring it out of the system. Even then, inflation fears did not disappear completely; they are still with us, but to a much smaller degree.

Studying a period of excessive inflation can teach us something about improving monetary policy. Because the Fed uses intermediate techniques and targets to control monetary policy, one area that should be studied is whether one intermediate target—such as fed funds—can contain out-of-control inflation, especially because the cause and effect between an overnight interest rate and a rate of inflation is highly uncertain. Also, monetary policy may be more effective against asset inflation than it is against product and service inflation, because in the former case the relationship is more direct. Yet, this distinction is seldom made. Fed actions against inflation may also be more effective when the inflation problem is demand driven rather than supply driven. All one has to do is look at embedded inflation due primarily to huge long-term wage contracts that were implemented in the 1970s and 1980s, and the extremes the Fed had to go to in order to harness these cost increases in order finally to conquer double-digit embedded inflation.

Inflation can be generated from the cost side (cost-push) or the demand side (demand-pull). Cost-push inflation can come about from rising labor and commodity costs, a lack of satisfactory productivity gains, and from events that occur abroad that cause higher prices. Demand-pull inflation can come about because of unsustainable and excessive demand for goods and services, excessive liquidity in the system that allows people who are fearful of rising prices to chase after goods and services, and a growing fear that higher prices are not temporary and are becoming embedded.

The demand side should also include asset inflation, and in particular, prices on houses and residential land. This is one area where the impact of monetary policy on inflation can be the most evident, as witnessed by the excessive amount of ease, unduly low interest rates, and a lack of regulatory oversight in the 2003–2006 period. Unfortunately, the PCE core price index that the Fed uses to target inflation does not directly include changes in asset values. For example, when the balloon broke on housing prices in 2007, it reduced inflation expectations among consumers, and yet had little influence on monthly changes in the PCE core prices. Thus, Fed successes in combating inflation can be determined not only by how aggressively it is tightening policy, but also by where the inflation pressures came from.

When Paul Volcker took over as chairman of the Federal Reserve, he inherited an embedded inflation problem with price pressures coming from many sources outside the direct control and influence of the central bank. The Fed's anti-inflation weaponry was generally confined to severely limiting the availability of funds and helping to push up interest rates to painfully high levels. On the psychological side, the public had little confidence that the Fed would stay the course in battling inflation. Volcker spent eight years combating this belief and putting out inflationary fires, and there were times when he lacked the full support of government officials and other members of the Fed.

When Alan Greenspan took over the reins at the Fed, he faced an entirely different set of circumstances. Although inflation was still running at an unacceptable rate of about 4 percent, the inflation momentum was moderating, and the heavy lifting with respect to breaking the back of inflation had already been achieved. In other words, Greenspan's job was different from Volcker's. Greenspan's job was to continue the movement towards lower inflation. Thus, he was in a position where he could make some short-run and cyclical policy mistakes and not pay the same price as Volcker if he had made those same mistakes.

Obviously, if one had a choice as to which set of circumstances a chairman would want to inherit, it would be those that faced Greenspan. Yet, because of this difference, it was harder for Greenspan to distinguish himself in the job than Volcker. It is hard for an individual to get full credit for continuing on and extending the success of others.

Then there is the matter of karma. It has been said that successful people create their own good luck, and one can argue that Greenspan helped create his own good fortune, especially when it came to bringing down and holding down inflation. Yet, he was fortunate in that he was in office at a time when a multitude of events occurred around the world that helped limit inflation:

- There was solid growth in the world economy.
- The cold war came to an end.
- The European Community had expanded along with the European Central Bank.
- Major improvements had taken place in the foreign exchange market because of the advent of floating exchange rates that helped limit currency crises.
- There were economic successes as many emerging countries took advantage of low costs and growing productivity, especially when it came to exports.
- There was a willingness on the part of countries to recycle money that came from current account surpluses.
- There was the creation and economic success of NAFTA.
- Multinational corporations came into their own, and large amounts of foreign money were invested in plant operation and equipment in the United States.
- There was a technological revolution especially with respect to computer use, that made both developing and developed countries far more productive, even for the little guy.
- And finally, there were advances and rapid growth in the breadth, depth, and resilience of money and capital markets around the world.

All of these factors made the Fed's job—and Greenspan's—a lot easier.

In fairness to Greenspan and the Fed, while they did not create these positive forces that held down inflation, they did not do anything foolish to offset the benefits. At no time during Greenspan's eighteen years in office did inflation become an out-of-control and embedded problem, and at no time was there a first-rate recession. This is an amazingly long period to have such successes. While Greenspan made quite a few policy mistakes during his tour of duty, most dealt with cyclical problems and how he addressed particular events. The main exception—which has yet to fully play out—is the ultimate price to be paid by the U.S. economy and many individuals because of what happened in the housing and asset-backed securities markets due to excessively easy money and a lack of early and proper regulatory responses.

STAGFLATION

On March 7, 2008, I gave a speech in Boston before the Eastern Economics Association entitled: "How to Determine Whether Stagflation Exists." The following is the written presentation of that speech and indicates that the fears of a stagflation problem facing the U.S. economy are overblown. That is fortunate because a monetary authority has more capability in fighting inflation than it does fighting stagflation. The Fed has tools to limit inflation but stagflation, which adds in a real growth problem, is another matter.

> Every few years, economists and those in the media fret that the U.S. economy is moving into a stagflation period (a combination of stagnant economic growth accompanied by excessive prices increases). Fortunately, those have been wrong for the last several decades as Table 13-1 indicates. Moreover, those arguing that stagflation is in the cards this year are likely to be wrong once again.

One of the problems in determining stagflation is that there are no agreed upon parameters for what constitutes this undesirable situation. That is: How weak does economic growth have to be? How high does inflation have to be? And how long do these circumstances have to last to qualify as a stagflation experience? In the absence of some agreed upon definition of stagflation, analysts must decide for themselves what guidelines "should" be used, and whether or not they make sense.

A reasonable approach in determining whether a period can be characterized as one of stagflation is to first determine the items to be used for the measurement; and second is to determine the length of time before it might be considered a stagflation period. In this regard, I decided to use four different measurements—productivity increases, real GDP growth, the unemployment rate, and changes in the CPI. The performance of the four components (in terms of both level and direction) is then looked at in combination in order to make a judgment as to whether we are in a period of stagflation. Finally, it should be realized that stagflation is not something that lasts a quarter, or even a year, it must continue for at least several years.

The two most obvious measurements of stagflation are a lack of real growth and unacceptably high prices. Yet, it is hard to have good size increases in productivity and at the same time have unacceptably low increases in real growth and unacceptably high prices. It is also hard to have a relatively low and stable unemployment rate and at the same time have a stagflation problem. For these reasons, the performance of productivity and the unemployment rate are included alongside real growth and prices in order to determine whether stagflation exists.

Table 13-1
How to Determine Stagflation - Percentage

	Year	Productivity	Real GDP	Unempl. Rate	CPI
Definite Stagflation					
	1979	−0.3	3.2	5.9	13.3
	1980	−0.2	−0.2	7.2	12.4
	1981	1.4	2.5	7.6	8.9
	1982	−1.1	−1.9	9.7	3.8
No Stagflation					
	1983	4.5	4.5	9.6	3.8
	1984	2.0	7.2	7.5	4.0
	1985	1.6	4.1	7.2	3.8
	1986	3.1	3.5	7.0	1.2
	1987	0.5	2.4	6.2	4.3
	1988	1.7	4.1	5.5	4.4
	1989	0.7	3.5	5.3	4.6
Marginal Stagflation					
	1990	1.9	1.9	5.6	6.3
	1991	1.6	−0.2	6.9	3.0
No Stagflation					
	1992	4.1	3.3	7.5	3.0
	1993	0.4	2.7	6.9	2.8
	1994	1.1	4.0	6.1	2.6
	1995	0.5	2.5	5.6	2.5
	1996	2.7	3.7	5.4	3.4
	1997	1.6	4.5	4.9	1.7
	1998	2.8	4.2	4.5	1.6
	1999	2.9	4.5	4.2	2.7
	2000	2.8	3.7	4.0	3.4
	2001	2.5	0.8	4.7	1.6
	2002	4.1	1.6	5.8	2.5
	2003	3.7	2.5	6.0	2.0
	2004	2.7	3.6	5.5	3.3
	2005	1.9	3.1	5.1	3.4
	2006	1.0	2.9	4.6	2.6
	2007	1.6	2.2	4.6	4.1

With these guidelines in mind, you may be surprised to know that beginning
with 1979, there has been only one clear period of stagflation (1979–1982) and
one marginal stagflation period (1990–1991), although in the latter case, the time
frame seems too short. In the first very definite stagflation period from 1979
through 1982, productivity showed negative numbers, real GDP declined in two

of the four years and the average of the period was barely on the plus side; the unemployment rate jumped from a high number to an even higher number, and, early in the period, the CPI was increasing at a double-digit pace. Indeed, it was not until the fourth year of this period that the price increases slowed to a relatively moderate rate.

Finally, as one looks at the 2007 results, it is evident that three of the four components do not indicate stagflation and the fourth one, the CPI, increased 4.1 percent, with the jump from the previous year's 2.6 percent due primarily to food and energy. As for 2008, if productivity advances about 2 percent, real GDP increases somewhat over 1 percent, the unemployment rate moves up to about 6.5 percent, and the CPI stays about 4 percent (energy and food price increases moderate while other prices increase), 2008 will not qualify for a stagflation designation. Results like those suggested would certainly not make 2008 a great year in economic terms. However, not having a good year is not the same as experiencing stagflation. Too many economists throw around a term such as "stagflation" with excessive impunity.

Just because inflation is currently not embedded and stagflation does not exist does not mean monetary policy tools and techniques should not be at the ready to be used quickly and, if necessary, in combination. If problems are already on the horizon, the Fed should be seriously considering something more than just changing targets on an overnight interest rate. Depending on the circumstances, the use of tools such as required reserves, open market operations, yield curve changes, discount window operations, selective liquidity and reserve adjustment techniques, margin requirements on stocks, and regulatory options should all be on the table. These tools, when used appropriately and often in combination, can be far more effective than trying to arrive at the desired macro results by fine tuning an overnight interest rate which involves one narrow sector of the money market.

The use of a broader range of policy tools is necessary, irrespective of whether the Fed is concentrating on real growth, inflation, or some sort of balance between the two. Based on the circumstances and problems, some tools and policy techniques will be more useful at certain times than others. Yet, irrespective of what tools or targets the Fed chooses to use, its economic forecasts need to improve, and for that to happen, more emphasis has to be placed on practical research. The use of sophisticated models means little if the forecasts prove to be wide of the mark.

FORECASTING AND THE FED'S LIMITED SUCCESSES

When it comes to economic forecasting, the Fed is not providing the American people and those in government with satisfactory results. One thing is certain, the Fed is not transparent with regard to explaining its forecasting mistakes. A feature of the chairman's semiannual presentations before Congress is the Fed's compilation of estimates from its governors and district bank presidents. This is not an official Fed forecast; rather, it is how those who participate in the survey feel about a handful of macro items. Moreover, some of the individuals making the forecasts are not economists, and their forecasts are based primarily on what their research people suggest. There is no single official Fed economic forecast.

Thus, during the chairman's testimony, you seldom hear those in Congress question the forecasts, because how do you criticize the results of a survey? Where is the responsibility? There is no chairman's forecast, and there is no official Federal Reserve forecast. This approach allows the Fed, in good part, to avoid responsibility for errant economic estimates. Moreover, since the Fed can update its survey forecast every six months (recently changed to three-months), good-size mistakes can tend to go unnoticed, as they did in 2007.

Speaking about Fed forecasting, in late 2007 the central bank did take some steps in dealing with forecasting and transparency. Unfortunately, these steps dealt with frequency and length of forecasts, not accuracy. On November 14, 2007, Chairman Bernanke delivered a speech at the Cato Institute's 25th Annual Monetary Conference in Washington, D.C., entitled "Federal Reserve Communications." One comment that I found questionable was as follows: "Central bank transparency increases the effectiveness of monetary policy and enhances economic and financial performance." Such a statement presumes that the quality of the data and forecasts is relatively accurate. Otherwise, it could well be counterproductive. There should be enough evidence presented in this book that the quality of the Fed's forecasts is a mixed bag.

The Fed's emphasis on transparency seems to be on looking ahead rather than explaining the whys and wherefores of past and present policies, and in particular, what went wrong with past forecasts. Economic and financial forecasts are frankly a dime a dozen, irrespective of the source. In all the years I have been in the forecasting business, I would be fortunate if I were right on average about 60 percent of the time. The key to good forecasting is how long it takes me to change my mind when I'm wrong, and then how quickly I would communicate that to my clients. That is the key to good forecasting and good transparency.

Notice in the following statement made by Bernanke in his November 14, 2007, speech, there is no mention of quality and accuracy, nor any discussion of past policy missteps:

> Accompanying the numerical projections will be a discussion—a projections "narrative" if you will—that summarizes participants' views of the major forces shaping the outlook, discusses the sources of risk to that outlook, and describes the dispersion of views among policymakers. By providing a medium-term perspective, the narrative will complement the discussion of shorter-term developments contained in the minutes. We will also provide qualitative information about participants' views on both the uncertainty and the balance of risks surrounding the outlook, together with quantitative historical information on the typical range of projection errors. Of course, the specific material provided and its form of presentation may change over time as we gain experience and receive feedback.

COMMUNICATION AND TRANSPARENCY
DO NOT MEAN ENLIGHTENMENT

Unfortunately, communication and enlightenment are not synonymous. If what is being communicated is not accurate, or is off center from what is of primary importance, its value is questionable. What is far more useful is to study what actually happened in the economy and the financial markets. Was the Fed spot-on with its analysis and its policy reactions, and if it was not, what went wrong, why did the Fed get it wrong, and what could it have done to get it right? In this regard, it is important to study the Fed's economic forecasting record in recent years, and this can be done by the forecasts that the Fed has presented before Congress. The forecasting record is not a distinguished one.

When looking at the following table, which shows Fed forecasts and actual data, realize the following factors:

- The forecast is a range of estimates made by the governors and district bank presidents and therefore is not actually a true Federal Reserve forecast—it is a system survey.
- A survey allows the Fed to present a range of forecasts, not a specific forecast.
- In many cases, the range of so-called central tendency forecasts is excessively wide.

It should be realized that getting economic forecasts close to the mark does not mean that monetary policy will be right on. Correspondingly, the Fed might have bad forecasts, but still could get lucky and have the right policy. If one measures monetary policy strictly by the level of the fed funds rate (which is highly questionable), at the beginning of 2000, the funds rate was 5.5 percent. From that point on, it rose to 6.5 percent, then ultimately down to 1 percent, then back up to 5.25 percent, and now down to 1.5 percent, and could go lower.

When we come to the accuracy of the Fed's forecasts, the numbers speak for themselves. In quiet and calm periods, the Fed record is far from sterling; but in periods when consequential economic changes are occurring, the results are embarrassing. For example, look at the Fed's real growth estimates. The worst estimate by far was made in 2000 for 2001. The Fed estimated real economic growth for 2001 at 3.25 to 3.75 percent. The actual increase in 2001 (not adjusted for benchmark revisions) was 0.1 percent.

In only one of the years shown in the table (and 2007 is not it) was actual real GDP growth inside the wide band of the Fed's forecast. Needless to say, if we had made such economic forecasts, we would have no clients. Instead of concentrating on the details and frequency of transparency, the Fed should concentrate on improving the quality and accuracy of its forecasts.

In February 2006, immediately after being appointed chairman, Bernanke had to make the Fed's semiannual presentation before Congress. In that presentation, the survey of district bank presidents and Fed governors indicated that from the

Table 13-2
Federal Reserve Forecasts and Actual Performance—Percentages

Date of			Real GDP		Prices—PCE Core		Unemployment Rate		
Forecast	For 4Q-4Q	Chairman	Forecast	Actual	Forecast	Actual	Period	Estimate	Actual
7/22/99	'99-'00	Greenspan	2½–3	3.5	-na-	2.4	4Q-00	4¼–4½	4.0
7/20/00	'00-'01	Greenspan	3¼–3¾	0.1	2–2½	1.3	4Q-01	4–4¼	5.6
7/18/01	'01-'02	Greenspan	3–3¼	2.8	1¾–2½	1.9	4Q-02	4¾–5¾	5.9
7/16/02	'02-'03	Greenspan	3½–4	4.3	1½–1¾	1.4	4Q-03	5¼–5½	5.9
7/15/03	'03-'04	Greenspan	3¾–4¾	3.7	1–1½	1.6	4Q-04	5½–6	5.4
7/20/04	'04-'05	Greenspan	3½–4	3.1	1½–2	1.9	4Q-05	5–5¼	5.0
2/16/05	'05-'06	Greenspan	3–3½	3.4	1½–1¾	2.3	4Q-06	5–5¼	4.5
2/16/06	'06-'07	Bernanke	3–3½	2.5	1¾–2	2.0	4Q-07	4¾–5	4.7
2/14/07	'07-'08	Bernanke	2¾–3	1.0	1¾–2	2.2	4Q-08	4½–4¾	5.4

fourth quarter of 2006 to the fourth quarter of 2007, real GDP growth would increase between 3 and 3.5 percent. Then, at the July 2006 presentation, the estimate was lowered; in February 2007 it was lowered again; and in July 2007 it was lowered again. In the first half of 2007, real growth was only 2.2 percent, and in the second half of the year it was 2.8 percent.

What is disturbing is not just that the ultimate numbers were substantially different from what was forecast initially, but that none of the updates got it right. Not only did the Fed get the estimates wrong, but more important, the performance is an indication that the central bank really did not have a feel for what was happening in the economy in general and some key areas—such as housing—in particular. If the Fed is in favor of transparency, a good place to start would be to explain when and why it got things wrong. That by itself will help put pressure on the Fed to improve its economic forecasts.

Getting an economic forecast right is not the primary objective of a central bank—getting monetary policy right is. And it can often take years to figure out whether or not a given policy approach was appropriate. Yet, it is worthwhile to know that when the Fed did get policy right, was it due to good forecasts or despite bad forecasts? Or, when the Fed got policy wrong, was it was due to bad forecasts or despite good forecasts? Of course, the policy outcome may also have had something to do with the tools the Fed used to adjust policy, and whether they were used in the best possible way at the best possible time.

Also, realize that under most circumstances, monetary policy is not as powerful a weapon as many analysts make it out to be. Even if the Fed did all the right things, it may not have the capability to turn a bad economic situation into a good one. Thus, the Fed's performance, along with those of its chairmen, cannot be judged strictly on the basis of numbers. There are a wide variety of contributing factors, many of which are outside the direct control or influence of either the Fed or its chairmen.

14

Concluding Thoughts and
Recommendations

The Fed not only needs to dust off its arsenal of policy tools, but it needs to rethink the entire subject of targeting. For example, hitting targets that may not be the most appropriate from an economic well-being point of view has a hollow ring of success. In this regard, economic well-being in 2007 and 2008 was unsatisfactory despite respectable overall real growth and inflation data. The Fed, in reporting on past performance, should indicate where economic data and economic well-being diverge.

CENTRAL BANK TARGETING

Central banks generally do not delve into the economic well-being issues when it comes to setting targets. Instead, they generally have two primary economic objectives—sustainable real growth and acceptable price increases. They tend to make real world compromises, because achieving both objectives at the same time for an extended period is a Herculean task. Because central banks work in the monetary world and are viewed as the primary guardians against inflation, it is not surprising that most of them claim that their primary emphasis should be on containing prices. Thus, central banks typically have officially stated targets and ceilings for prices (the European Central Bank (ECB) uses a 2 percent maximum and the Bank of England has a 2 percent objective). Notice, neither of these central banks have floors with respect to prices, therefore they are assuming that deflation is not a risk.

In the real world of monetary policy management, the ECB not only has a 2 percent price maximum, but it has a phobia that even if the rate is at or below 2 percent, there could be an inflation risk hiding around the corner. There have been times when the ECB has raised its official rate despite the fact that the annual price increase has been running under 2 percent. The obvious question here is, "What would cause the ECB to lower its rates?" The answer is an actual or impending recession, and if it appears to be severe enough, the ECB would likely ease even if it was not satisfied with the inflation picture. In other words, the most difficult time for applying a policy approach is in a period of stagflation. This can prove to be a considerable practical problem, because the members of the ECB all have different price and real-growth stories, and the contributing factors are dissimilar.

The Bank of England (BoE) has less of an inflation phobia than the ECB and seems to rely more on the inflation numbers over the last twelve months rather than on what might happen down the road. The BoE also seems to be less one-sided when emphasizing the importance of prices over real growth. Also, it should be pointed out that its 2 percent inflation number is a target and not a ceiling, which provides some added flexibility. In addition, the current head of the central bank seems more policy flexible than the head of the ECB.

Now we come to the Federal Reserve, where the situation is quite a bit different from that of the ECB and the BoE. The Fed may place considerable emphasis on maintaining satisfactory prices, but it cannot target inflation to the exclusion of other factors, such as real growth. In other words, price containment is the highest equal among several equals. Moreover, when the Fed talks about acceptable prices, it talks in terms of minimums and maximums and has rough guidelines rather than targets. At one point, there seemed to be a belief at the Fed that a zero to 2 percent increase in the CPI was the proper guideline. That has now evolved into a 1 to 2 percent increase in core prices of personal consumption expenditures.

Yet, notice that although the Fed is generally more concerned about inflation than deflation, there was a time in the recent past (the second half of 2003 and early 2004) when there was a fear of deflation. Central banks hate deflation because, as has been shown in Japan, the central bank cannot take interest rates below zero percent to combat high real interest rate levels. What makes this analysis especially important is that Bernanke has shown fears on both sides of prices within a short period of time.

From this explanation, it should be evident that the U.S. monetary policy approach is quite different from that of the ECB and the BoE. The Fed does not emphasize prices to the degree that the other two central banks do; it has guidelines rather than targets; it uses a core approach to prices, which does not include food and energy; and in recent years it has had concerns over both inflation and deflation. The approach the Fed uses versus the other two central banks makes policy here more of an art than a science. That is, the Fed has more flexibility to act when things are not going right, especially when real growth is moving towards unacceptably low levels.

While policy being an art may be an advantage, it can prove to be a disadvantage if the Fed makes bad judgments. The objectives and the transmission techniques used to achieve the objectives become very important. Unfortunately, there are problems with the current Fed approach. The Fed deals in a narrow world of banking and interest rates, and the only rate it can control (most of the time) is an overnight rate. Yet, controlling an overnight interest rate is miles away from fine-tuning a rate of inflation for consumers. There are many intermediate steps between a "right" fed funds rate and a "right" PCE core increase, and the relationships change over time. Moreover, the PCE core is too narrow an approach for measuring inflation, not only because food and energy are excluded, but so are changes in asset values. Nevertheless, the Fed tends to nudge its funds target one way or the other if the PCE core is out of line with what is desired, even though what is desired may not be the right objective.

Despite these problems, the Fed has chosen as a primary target range a 1 to 2 percent increase in PCE core prices, which appears to have little theoretical or conceptual backing. The Fed also appears to be unwilling to change that target range despite real-world events. Thus, to a considerable degree, the Fed is using a seat-of-the-pants approach in fine-tuning its funds target, in order to attain a price-target range that is also based on a seat-of-the-pants judgment. Nothing wrong with this scenario, as long as you admit it, and continue to look for better seat-of-the-pants judgments.

What we have is a central bank that says its primary responsibility is containing prices. This is despite the fact that the Fed has a better chance of fine-tuning real growth than it does prices, although achieving any real-growth objective by adjusting monetary policy is no piece of cake. Raising or lowering an interest rate target would generally hit the real-growth rate first and in a more direct manner, and then work its way through to inflation by some unknown amount over some unknown time.

The Fed indicates that prices are its most important objective. However, a specific single-target, price-range approach over a business cycle leaves something to be desired. I would argue that not only is this approach inflexible, but also it runs the risk of excessive policy adjustments that in the past have been factors leading to excessive and ill-timed fed funds rate movements.

Depending on economic and financial circumstances, what is wrong with having a price-range objective that has a fixed outer band of 1 to 3 percent for total PCE prices, and a flexible inner band in the range of 1 to 2 percent, or 1.5 to 2.5 percent, or 2 to 3 percent. The inner band would be set once a year, and would part of the Fed chairman's February presentation to Congress. Reasons for the range chosen would be outlined in considerable detail. This would be a far better approach than the current, inflexible 1 percent-to-2 percent range for core PCE prices, a band that is too narrow, too low and out of touch with reality. Further, the current approach does little for the credibility of the Fed in general and Bernanke in particular.

Finally, the Fed has little notion of the transmission process and the time and the accumulation of changes that it takes in order to get desired results. Simply put, the Fed does not know how much it should cut or raise its funds target to change PCE core price numbers; nor does it know if it has even guessed correctly as to how long it would take to achieve its policy objective. Why not try to devote more time and effort to improving the art of monetary policy management and less time devoted to looking for magical models?

In summary, there are ways that the transmission process between a funds target and economic objectives can be improved. One is to use an acceptable band for fed funds—such as 50 basis points—and not a specific rate. This allows the Fed to pick up some valuable information on supply/demand factors in the market. Two is to avoid excessive extremes in funds rates, but to move more aggressively in terms of timing and amounts within a middle ground funds rate level. Third is that the Fed should have a price range *objective* (not *target*) that is broader, more flexible, and more practical than the current one.

Yet, even if these recommendations are adopted in some form, there is no guarantee that monetary policy would be more successful. Policy remains primarily an art and not a science, and having improved techniques and better information does not guarantee success. It just enhances the possibility for success. Also, remember that when it comes to economic growth, inflation, and the performance of the markets, Fed policy is only one factor, and usually not the most important one. In other words, the Fed could be doing the right thing but have an appropriate policy sidetracked by events and policies outside its control.

FED WATCHERS AND THE MEDIA

An important requisite to attaining a better monetary policy is to have so-called Fed watchers and media people get involved in the recommendation process. However, there is little evidence this is currently the case, or is about to happen. Although the communication of information is expanding manyfold, the understanding of what is being reported is not, and understanding what is said and how it is written may even have deteriorated.

As things stand now, the discussion of monetary policy in the media is, purely and simply, show business. There is little attempt to educate the investor or the general public on the subject. The media focus on official statements and speeches and dissect the information presented by the Fed and government agencies in excruciating detail. A word change here, a word change there or a slight turn of a phrase, and it is headline information. Where are the old-time media people such as Ben Weberman, Pete Nagan, and Ed Foldessey when you need them?

If you do not think this is a problem, look at how the media reports on the Fed policy statement released after an FOMC meeting. The press release is typically about four paragraphs and maybe a dozen sentences. This will be the basis for media types (and unfortunately some economists) writing many paragraphs, even pages, explaining what the Fed said in just four paragraphs. The attention given to the release is so overwhelming that a reader or a listener might get the idea that all the Fed has to do is fine tune its verbiage and, *voilà!*, it can appreciably influence real growth, inflation, unemployment, and so forth. Hopefully, this book makes it clear that this is not the case.

The Fed has limited influence on the real growth of the economy because it is the private sector that dominates the economic outcome. The Fed typically has the most influence on real growth when its policy stance is unduly easy or unduly tight for an extended period, or when it is changing policy in a meaningful way. Considerable time lags can be involved.

The Fed has limited influence on inflation because the problem can come from many sources, both domestic and international. It can come from cost-push or demand-pull price pressures, from a weak dollar, excessive budget deficits, excessive bank credit creation, and unduly low interest rates. It can show up in goods, services, and asset values. The Fed can tweak overnight interest rates, and fine-tune the language in its press releases, but neither will have much influence on real growth and inflation. The transmission belt between monetary policy and real growth can be long and complex, and the transmission belt between monetary policy and inflation is even less direct and more complex.

NOT ENOUGH PRACTITIONERS AT THE FEDERAL RESERVES

In the business world, when a team is brought together to manage an organization, their breadth of expertise is important. In order to help improve monetary policy, the expertise among seven governors should cover a broader range than currently is the case. There should be experts in the money and capital markets, in practical research and regulation, senior executives from the business world, experts on the budget and Treasury financing, technical experts from inside the Fed, and domestic and international economists who have strong academic and business backgrounds. Moreover, the staff at the Board and various district banks should look to hire more real-world types from the business and financial world. The reason for having such a wide variety of individuals is that the Fed is less likely to get blindsided by events it did not expect. The 2007 and 2008 meltdown in the housing and subprime mortgage markets and in other asset-backed markets is a good example.

A lack of innovative thinking in terms of staff, research, tools, and targets cannot be laid at the feet of any one chairman. They all came up short in varying degrees. It seems as though each chairman came into power with certain high priority items, and these areas got pushed into the background, overshadowed by efforts to improve what some might consider the mechanics of monetary policy. Thus, many of the previous comments are made with a view to improve the future course of monetary policy, rather than criticizing former Fed chairmen.

In assessing performance, there were major differences with respect to what each chairman inherited, what kind of a job each one did, and whether each left the job with the economy and financial markets in better shape than when he took over. A major goal here is to make sure that the monetary policy record from 1970 on has been presented in as detailed and objective a way as possible. After all, how do you make policy better? The answer is by learning from past mistakes. Government officials should not believe they can walk on water.

The simple truth is that the Fed policy record over the last half century has been inconsistent—good at some times, not so good at other times. One might wonder if the Fed could have avoided many of its policy mistakes if it had taken full advantage of its resources such as research capabilities and policy tools. Realize that the Fed has an inherent advantage over virtually every other governmental or quasi-governmental organization because of its resources; and to a considerable degree, it can march to the beat of its own drummer. Yes, there is oversight of the Fed and its policies, but compared with most official organizations, the oversight does not get down to the nitty-gritty of how the Fed manages its ship.

Despite these general comments about the Fed and its chairmen, if there is one thing that each chairman analyzed in this book should be known for, it is as follows:

- In the case of Arthur Burns, it was allowing inflation to get out of control where his words spoke louder than his deeds.
- G. William Miller was out of his element. He tried to do the right thing with respect to quelling inflation but his policies were a day late and a dollar short.
- Paul Volcker's claim to fame was that he and his policies helped break the back of an inflation psychology that had become deeply embedded. Eight years, however, was not enough time for him to finish the job.
- Alan Greenspan's primary claim to fame—for which he gets too little credit—should be his role in the early 1990s in helping restore financial institutions to health. He was an important factor in deregulating financial institutions, and in doing so, helped rebuild the viability of many institutions that were on the verge of bankruptcy. His legacy with respect to his role in the housing and financial market problems has yet to be fully written, but events and policies of the Bernanke era have not helped.
- Ben Bernanke's performance as chairman is still to be determined. His first three years have been a painful learning process for him and for the country. When the Fed has to keep coming up with new stop-gap measurements—often on weekends—things are not going right for for Bernanke, his colleagues and monetary policy. The same can be said for the Fed's handling of the AIG (American International Group) financial debacle, where the importance of this organization in the house-of-cards derivative insurance market was not fully appreciated until the very last minute. At this point, I would rank Bernanke's performance closer to that of Burns and Miller than to Volcker and Greenspan.

RECOMMENDATIONS

The following is a list of recommendation that the Fed should consider. Some are obviously more important than others. Realize that even if the recommendations are accepted and used, they do not guarantee an improved or more appropriate policy—just a better chance of achieving such objectives. The recommendations are not listed in order of importance, and some are broad in scope, while others are narrow. Yet, when all these items are viewed as a package, they could go a long way towards helping to improve monetary policy:

- There should be a chairman and two vice-chairmen heading the seven-person Board of Governors. Regulation would be the responsibility of one of the vice-chairmen. The President of the United States would appoint the chairman and the two vice-chairmen to terms of four years each. The chairman as well as the vice-chairman for regulation would report twice a year to joint sessions of Congress. The chairman would report on the first day and the vice-chairman for regulation would report on the second day.
- Monetary policy should be treated by Fed officials as more of an art than a science, and the chairman should indicate that is the case.
- Model-building is a useful analytical tool, but realize that models have limitations such as changing relationships, and other things do not necessarily remain equal.
- Transparency as a goal is overrated. It is better to be right and quiet than wrong and talkative.
- The Chairman should be required to present to Congress, on a quarterly basis, an updated official economic forecast (not a survey of governors and district bank presidents). The forecasts would be updated and revised every quarter, and it would be the chairman's responsibility to explain why the expected numbers did not materialize if that was the case, what the Fed might have done differently, and the issues the Fed needs to address and concentrate on, looking ahead. In this forecast, economic well-being should be covered because, for the noneconomists, this is more important than GDP.
- There is only one monetary policy, and that should be presented by the chairman. Those officials with different opinions should have these differences included in the FOMC minutes; they should not be made public through speeches.
- Get rid of Fed-speak, it can be misleading and confusing. Actions speak louder than words.
- The Fed should admit policy misjudgments on a timely basis in order to avoid future mistakes.
- Fed policy should not be appreciably influenced by what market participants hope will happen or what is already built into market prices.
- There should be twelve FOMC meetings a year—eight in person and four through teleconferencing.
- Six to seven weeks between meetings is too long in a fast-paced and ever-changing financial world. The eight in-person meetings should be two days in length, the video meetings one day.

- The statements released to the press after FOMC meetings should be brief. They should be long on facts and short on policy hints.
- FOMC meetings should not be held in the middle of major Treasury refundings.
- Vacancies on the Board of Governors should be filled promptly. The Fed should have an unofficial list of prospective candidates.
- The seven governors as a whole should have a broad range of expertise. They should be chosen from backgrounds such as regulation, the federal budget, financial markets, bank management, international business, foreign exchange, and accounting. Real world experience is important.
- There should be seminars conducted by the Fed for the media. They should be conducted by experts from both the private and public sectors to aid in the interpretation of monetary policy.
- There is a need for better coordination, not merely communication, between the Fed and the Treasury, and between the Fed and other central banks. This is especially important in preventing economic and financial meltdowns and market squeezes.
- Both the quality and quantity of practical district bank research and surveys should be enhanced, taking advantage of their regional expertise.
- Greater emphasis should be placed on regulatory powers, especially when it comes to the prevention of serious problems. Surveys by regulators need to be enhanced and improved, and they should be more timely.
- The Beige Book should include comments from Fed regulators. So should the policy statement released at the end of the FOMC minutes and the press release presented after an FOMC meeting.
- The Fed should pay more attention to bank credit expansion and monetary aggregates when setting policy.
- All policy tools should be viable alternatives, and there are times when several should be used together. There is too much emphasis on fed funds targeting.
- Greater policy use should be made of the discount window, the discount rate, and selective policy tools such as margin requirements on stocks.
- Fed funds should not have a specific target level, but rather a trading range of 50 basis points in order to allow market forces to show through.
- Using the fed funds rate to attain a desired consumer price range is too indirect and overly simplistic. The transmission process is not only uncertain, but it is ever-changing.
- When it comes to the Fed trying to target prices, total PCE makes more sense than using the narrow PCE core approach. A more complete price picture is of greater importance than using an approach where the Fed has somewhat greater (but still very imperfect) influence over price performance simply because important food and energy prices are excluded.
- The fed should use total PCE prices as an inflation guideline. The outer band would 1 to 3 percent; the inner and more flexible bands would be 1 to 2 per-

cent or 1.5 to 2.5 percent, or 2 to 3 percent. The inner band should not be set once a year.

- Annualized quarterly or semi-annual changes in prices are more useful than twelve-month changes, because in the latter, the base number has excessive importance.
- The Fed needs to rethink the techniques it uses for measuring embedded inflation. Yield differences between full-coupon Treasury securities and TIPS (Treasury Inflation-Protected Securities) involve more than just inflation concerns.
- Consumer price fears are more important than investor price concerns, because the Fed uses consumer prices as its guidepost to inflation.
- Fed officials should not try to give the impression they can walk on water, and other government officials should not treat them as if they can.

Appendix 1
GLOSSARY

One problem in writing this kind of book is determining the type of reader to be targeted. Should it be someone looking for a general background with respect to the Federal Reserve and its policies, or should it be someone with some background in how the Federal Reserve and monetary policy operate? Should it be someone involved in the markets who is looking for policy insights, or should it be academics and students? Finally, should it be aimed at the Federal Reserve and other public officials with the hope that the ideas in the book could help future policy decisions?

The approach I took was to write for those well versed in the Federal Reserve and monetary policy, but to present the information and analysis in a way that a neophyte in these areas would understand. One way I tried to make the book useful for the non-expert was to stay away from complicated models and mathematical formulas and to make sure that definitions and explanations were written in an easily understandable manner. Of course, what is easily understandable for an economist may not be so for others. Another way I tried to make the book easier for the nonexpert was to present a glossary of definitions and explanations.

Writing a glossary is more difficult than it appears. Many of the terms are the vernacular used in a particular market, and the terms can have different meanings depending on which market one is talking about. Generally speaking, for those who want to pursue definitions and explanations more thoroughly, I found Martha Stigum's book, *The Money Market*, to be the most useful. It is now in its fourth edition, which was published in 2007.

In addition, Barron's *Dictionary of Finance & Investment Terms*, which was in its sixth edition in 2006, can be useful, although its definitions and explanations can vary somewhat from other sources. The Federal Reserve publication, *U.S. Monetary Policy & Financial Markets*, can also be useful, especially when it comes to explaining rather than just defining.

Accrued interest: Interest due from the issue or last coupon date to the present on an interest-bearing security.

Active: A market where there is a considerable amount of trading.

Adjustable rate debt: Predetermined adjustments of interest rates made at specified intervals.

Agency bank: A type of organization that can be used by foreign banks to enter the U.S. market. It cannot accept deposits or extend loans in its own name; it acts as an agent for its parent bank.

Agent: Acts on the behalf of another.

Amortize: Periodic charges made against interest income on premium bonds in anticipation of the call price or par value at maturity.

Arbitrage: Taking advantage of disparities in price between markets.

Asset-backed securities (ABS): Securities that represent pools of loans of similar types, duration, and interest rates. By selling loans to ABS packagers, the original lender can recover cash quickly and therefore make more loans. Many different types of loans are securitized and sold in the investment markets. Asset-backed security sources are agency securities, mortgages, consumer loans, business loans, trade receivables, and Treasury securities. Virtually any debt obligation with regularly scheduled principal and interest payments can be securitized.

Auctions (U.S. Treasury): The Treasury issues new bills, notes, and bonds through a process whereby investors bid for the securities. Most of the bids are on a competitive basis.

Bank credit: The amount of loans and investments outstanding in the banking system.

Bank line: A line of credit granted by a bank to a customer.

Bankers' acceptance (BA): A draft or bill of exchange accepted by a bank or trust company.

Basis point: One one-hundredth of one percent.

Bear: Someone with a pessimistic market outlook.

Bear market: An extended decline in the price of stocks, bonds, or commodities.

Bearer security: The owner of the security is not registered on the books of the issuer.

Beige book: A booklet bound in a beige color (one time called the tan book), in which each Federal Reserve district collects regional information, and submits it to one of the district banks to summarize. The summary is then submitted to the

Federal Open Market Committee (FOMC) participants in advance of their regular meeting.

Bid-and-asked prices: Bid is the highest price a potential buyer is willing to pay, and asked (also called offered) is the lowest price a seller is willing to receive.

Bond: An interest-bearing or discounted security that requires the issuer to pay to the bondholder a specified amount of money and to repay the principal amount of the loan at maturity.

Bond rating: A method of indicating the chances of default by a bond issuer. The three main rating agencies (all private) are Standard & Poor's, Moody's, and Fitch Ratings. The ratings typically range from AAA (top of the investment grade) to D (bottom of the speculative grade).

Book-entry: A bookkeeping system in which securities are not represented by pieces of paper but are maintained in computerized records.

Book value: The value at which a debt security is shown on the holder's balance sheet.

Bridge financing: Interim financing to take a borrower from a short time period to a longer time period.

Broker: One who charges a commission for bringing buyers and sellers together.

Bull: Someone with an optimistic market outlook.

Bull market: Extended rise in the price of stocks, bonds, or commodities. The opposite of a bear market.

Business cycle: Recurrence of periods of economic expansion and contraction. Usually measured in terms of gross domestic product (GDP) adjusted for prices.

Call money: Interest-bearing bank deposits that can be withdrawn on twenty-four-hour notice.

Callable bond: A bond that the issuer has the right to redeem prior to maturity.

Capital market: Where debt and equity securities are traded. In contrast, the money market is where short-term securities, typically with maturities of less than one year, are traded.

Cash market: Transactions in which ownership is transferred from seller to buyer, and payment is made on delivery. In contrast, the futures market is where contracts are completed at a specified time in the future.

Cash settlement: When the purchased securities are delivered against payment in fed funds on the same day the trade is made.

Central bank: A nation's bank that issues currency, administers monetary policy, holds deposits that are the reserves of commercial banks, and has auditing and supervisory responsibilities. In the United States, the Federal Reserve is the central bank.

Certificate of deposit (CD): A debt instrument issued by a commercial bank that pays interest to the holder. Maturities range from a few weeks to several years. Those that involve large amounts are typically marketable and can be traded.

Clearing House Interbank Payment System (Chips): The New York Clearing House's computerized payment system.

Collateral: Assets that are pledged to a lender until a loan is repaid.

Collateralized mortgage obligation (CMO): A mortgage-backed bond that divides mortgage pools into short, medium, and longer-term portions. Each class of owner is paid a fixed rate of interest at regular intervals. The pools that are split into different time periods are called tranches.

Commercial paper: Short-term debt obligations with maturities from two to 270 days issued by banks, corporations, and other borrowers. Such instruments are typically unsecured and are usually discounted. They can be issued directly to buyers or through brokers. Commercial paper is almost always backed by bank lines of credit.

Competitive bid: Typically applies to bids tendered in a Treasury auction for a specific amount at a specified price or yield.

Constant dollars: A base year is used to ascertain purchasing power. Often used in the presentation of economic data such as "real" in real GDP.

Consumer price index (CPI): Measure of changes in consumer prices as determined monthly by the U.S. Bureau of Labor Statistics. A derivation of the CPI is the personal consumption expenditure (PCE) index. When food and energy prices are excluded from the PCE, the result is called the core PCE, and this is the price index the Federal Reserve has chosen to target.

Conventional mortgage: A residential mortgage loan with a fixed rate and a term that is typically thirty years. It is repayable in fixed monthly payments.

Convertible bond: A bond containing a provision that permits conversion to the issuer's common stock at some fixed exchange ratio.

Cost-of-carry: The cost of borrowing money in order to finance an investment position. A "carry profit" refers to the gain made by an investor where the cost of borrowing is less than the rate of return.

Cost-of-living adjustment (COLA): Wages that are adjusted to offset changes in the cost of living.

Cost-push inflation: Rising costs that lead to rising prices. Raw materials and labor cost increases are forms of cost-push inflation. When manufacturers pay more, they often raise their prices to merchants, and when merchants pay more, they often increase their prices to consumers. Inflation can also come from the demand side.

Country risk: Risks that attach to a security because the borrower's country of residence differs from that of the investor.

Credit risk: Financial and moral risks that an obligation will not be paid and a loss will result.

Dealer: An individual or an organization acting as a principal in a securities transaction. They trade for their own account.

Default: Failure to make timely payment of interest or principal on a debt security.

Deflation: A decline in the prices of goods and services. It is the opposite of inflation.

Deflator: A technique that excludes the price-change factor.

Directive (Federal Reserve): Directions issued by the FOMC to the trading desk at the New York Fed regarding domestic monetary policy changes and leanings in the period.

Discount rate: The interest rate the Federal Reserve charges member banks for collateralized loans.

Discount window: Department at district Federal Reserve banks where members can borrow. Traditionally, borrowing from the Fed is considered a privilege and not a right, although this distinction is no longer clear-cut.

Discount window borrowings: The aggregate dollar amount of borrowings from the Fed by depository institutions.

Disintermediation: Movement of funds from low-yielding accounts at traditional banking firms to higher-yielding investments in the general markets.

Draining reserves: Actions by the Federal Reserve to decrease the money supply by curtailing the funds banks have available to lend or invest. The opposite of adding reserves.

Dutch auction: Lowest price necessary to sell the entire offering becomes the price at which all the securities offered are sold.

Edge Act corporation: Banks establish international banking corporations whereby the operations are restricted to activities that are incidental to the parent company's international business.

Euro bonds: Bonds issued in Europe outside the confines of the capital market of a nation.

Euro CDs: CDs issued by a U.S. bank branch or foreign bank located outside the United States.

Equivalent bond yield: Annual yield on a short-term noninterest-bearing security calculated so as to be comparable to yields quoted on coupon securities.

Eurocurrency accounts: Deposits held in a bank or its branches not located in a country in which the currency is denominated.

Eurodollar: U.S. currency held in banks outside the United States.

Excess reserves: Funds a bank holds over and above its reserve requirement. The funds may be on deposit with the Federal Reserve, or with an approved bank, or it may be in the bank's possession.

Exchange rate: The price at which one currency can be converted to another. Almost all relationships change every day, although there are some that do not float freely.

Federal agency security: Debt instruments issued by an agency or quasi-government agency of the federal government. They are not general obligations of the U.S. government but are generally considered to be "sponsored" by the government.

Federal funds: Noninterest-bearing deposits held by member banks at the Federal Reserve. Banks with more deposits at the Fed than they need can sell them to other banks that need such deposits.

Federal funds rate: The interest rate at which federal funds are traded. Rates charged by banks with excess reserves to other banks that need overnight money to meet reserve requirements. The rate tends to fluctuate, but typically by small amounts, as the Federal Reserve has a publicly known target rate.

Federal Deposit Insurance Corporation (FDIC): A federal institution that insures bank deposits.

Federal Financing Bank (FFB): A federal institution that lends to a wide array of federal credit agencies money that it obtains by borrowing from the U.S. Treasury.

Federal Home Loan Banks (FHLB): An organization that regulates and lends to savings and loan associations.

Federal Open Market Committee (FOMC): The Fed's chief policy-making body. The committee is comprised of seven Federal Reserve governors and five of the twelve district Federal Reserve Bank presidents. The New York bank president is always a voting member while the other eleven district bank presidents are rotated.

Federal Reserve Bank: One of the twelve district banks. The role of district banks is to monitor the banks in their regions in order to ensure they follow Fed regulations and to provide access to funds from the discount window.

Federal Reserve Board: Shorthand for the Board of Governors of the Federal Reserve System. It is the governing board of the Federal Reserve. Its seven members are appointed by the President of the United States and are subject to Senate confirmation. The length of a full term is fourteen years.

Financial futures contracts: Investors and traders use these contracts to hedge positions or speculate on the direction of markets.

Financial intermediary: These are financial institutions such as commercial banks, savings and loan associations, mutual savings banks, credit unions, and other so-called middlemen. They redistribute savings to those that spend or invest the funds.

Fiscal policy: It applies to federal government taxation and spending policies and debt management. Fiscal policy is administered by the executive branch of government and is administered separately from monetary policy. In reality, there is no simple or single unified fiscal policy.

Fixed exchange rate: The rate of exchange between two currencies is fixed. The opposite of floating exchange rates.

Flight to quality: Money moves to what is deemed to be the safest investments in order to achieve protection from an unsettled period.

Floating exchange rate: Currencies that are allowed to strengthen or weaken based on market forces. The opposite of fixed exchange rates.

Floating rate note: Interest-rate adjustments are made periodically, often every six months, and they are typically tied to a money market index or instrument.

Floating supply: An amount of securities believed to be available for immediate purchase that is in the hands of dealers and investors waiting to sell.

Flow of funds: The way that funds are transferred from sources to uses. The Federal Reserve publishes quarterly data on the flow of funds.

Flower bonds: Government bonds that are acceptable at par in payment of federal estate taxes.

Foreign exchange: Instruments that are used to make payments between countries.

Foreign exchange rate: The price at which one currency trades for another.

Foreign exchange risk: The risk that a long or short position in a foreign currency might have to be closed out at a loss.

Forward contract: Purchase or sale of a commodity, security, currency, or other tradable instrument at the current price with delivery and settlement at a specified future date.

Freddie Mac: Shorthand name used by market participants for the Federal Home Loan Mortgage Corporation. They issue mortgage-backed securities that are packaged, guaranteed, and then sold to investors.

Free reserves: Borrowings by banks at the discount window are subtracted from excess reserves in the banking system. It is a measurement of the ease or tightness of the Fed's reserve policy. If borrowings are more than excess reserves, this difference is called net borrowed reserves.

Futures contract: An agreement to buy or sell a specific amount of a commodity or financial instrument at a particular price on a stipulated date.

Futures market: Exchanges where future contracts are traded.

General obligation bonds: State and local government securities secured by the full faith and credit of the issuer as well as by its taxing power.

Ginnie Mae: Abbreviation for the Government National Mortgage Association and the securities guaranteed by that agency.

Ginnie Mae pass-through securities: A security backed by a pool of mortgages and guaranteed by Ginnie Mae. It passes through to the investors the interest and principal payments of homeowners.

Glass-Steagall Act of 1933: Authorized deposit insurance and prohibited commercial banks from owning brokerage firms. Many of the restrictions in the Act no longer exist.

Gold fixing: Daily determination of the price of gold set by specialists and bank officials in London, Paris, and Zurich. The price is fixed at 10:30 a.m. and 3:30 p.m. London time every business day.

Gold standard: A monetary system in which units of currency are convertible into fixed amounts of gold. The United States came off the gold standard in 1971.

Government National Mortgage Association (GNMA): A government-owned corporation that is an agency of the U.S. Department of Housing and Urban Development. It guarantees, with the full faith and credit of the United States, full and timely payment of all monthly principal and interest payments on mortgage-backed pass-through securities of registered holders.

Gross domestic product (GDP): The primary indicator of the value of goods and services produced inside the United States over a specified time period. GDP can be computed both in terms of spending and income. With respect to income, the primary items are personal income and corporate profits. On the spending side, there is consumer spending, government purchases, foreign trade, fixed investments, and business inventories.

Hedging: A strategy used to offset or limit risk.

Hedge fund: A term used in the securities industry to describe an investment firm that heavily relies on hedging strategies to limit position risk.

Humphrey-Hawkins Legislation: Full Employment and Balanced Growth Act of 1978. One of its provisions is that the chairman of the Federal Reserve Board report semi-annually to Congress on the Fed's analysis of the economic outlook, and its targets.

Inflation: A rise in the price of goods and services. It occurs when spending increases relative to the supply of goods and services. The most commonly used measurements of inflation are the GDP deflator, the consumer price index, and the personal consumption expenditures price index. The Federal Reserve considers the latter the most important, and, excluding food and energy, targets the rate of advance over a twelve-month period.

Intermediate term: The period between the short term and the long term. The length of these periods depends on the context in which it is used. In the Treasury securities market, a short-term maturity is one year or less, an intermediate-term maturity is over one year and less than ten years, and a long-term maturity is ten years and more.

Intermediation: Funds being placed in a financial intermediary, such as a bank, which invests the money in such assets as bonds, stocks, mortgages, and so forth. It is the opposite of disintermediation.

International Bank for Reconstruction and Development (The World Bank): An international financial organization that finances mainly commercial and infrastructure projects, primarily for developing nations. World Bank loans are backed by the government in the borrowing countries.

International Monetary Market (IMM): A futures exchange.

Interest rate exposure: Risk of gain or loss to which an institution is exposed due to possible changes in interest rate levels.

International Monetary Fund (IMF): Focuses on lowering international trade barriers and stabilizing currencies. Membership in the Fund is worldwide.

Inverted yield curve: Occurs when short-term interest rates are higher than long-term interest rates—not a typical situation. It can also be called a down-sloping yield curve. Normally, lenders or buyers receive a higher yield when committing their money for a longer period of time; this is defined as a positive or up-sloping yield curve. The expected direction of interest rates and the outlook for economic growth and inflation can influence the slope of the yield curve.

Investment bank: An organization that primarily is an underwriter for stocks and bonds. Until a few years ago, the Glass-Steagall Act kept investment banks separate from commercial banks, but that is no longer the case. Both serve as financial intermediaries, with the commercial banks primarily regulated by the Federal Reserve and the investment banks by the Securities and Exchange Commission (SEC).

Junk bonds: A bond with a credit rating that is below investment grade. Junk bonds are issued by companies that do not have a long track record or have a questionable credit record.

Lender of last resort: A lender or investor that provides financial support for an institution that is in financial difficulty. The Federal Reserve and other government or quasi-government agencies are typically viewed as the primary lenders of last resort.

Line of credit: An arrangement by which a bank agrees to lend to the holder under a promise to lend during a specified period up to the full amount that the bank promised to lend.

Liquid assets: Investments that are easily and quickly convertible into cash or are already in cash. Typically, high-grade assets with a maturity of one year or less are considered liquid assets.

London Interbank Offered Rate (Libor): The rate of interest that creditworthy international banks dealing in Eurodollars charge each other for loans.

Long position: Ownership of an asset on an outright basis. A short position means the security has been borrowed and therefore not owned outright. A long position is held on the expectation that the price will rise; a short position is held on the expectation that the price will decline.

Macroeconomics: Analysis of an economy in a broad sense by using data that measures overall performance. In contrast, the study of individual sectors of an economy is called microeconomics.

Marketability: The speed and ease with which an investment can be bought or sold.

Marketable securities: Assets that can be readily converted into cash are considered marketable securities. The U.S. Treasury issues both marketable and non-marketable securities. A savings bond is an example of the latter.

Market price: Usually refers to the last reported price at which a security traded.

Mark to market: Adjusting the value of a security or a portfolio to reflect current market conditions.

Matched sales: Also called reverse repurchases; it is the opposite of a repurchase operation. For example, in a matched-sales operation, the Federal Reserve drains reserves from the banking system by selling securities it owns on a temporary basis, and agrees to buy them back at no later than a specified date.

Microeconomics: A study of individual sectors of the economy such as industries, companies, and households.

Modeling: Designing a mathematical model that attempts to replicate how the economy or markets operate using mathematical relationships typically involving simultaneous equations.

Momentum: The rate of acceleration dealing with economic, price, or volume movements. Many mathematical models that traders use in taking positions are momentum models.

Monetarist: An economist who believes that the money supply is the dominant factor in the performance of the economy, and if excessive, will bring about inflation.

Monetary base: Consists of currency outside the Federal Reserve—including vault cash—held by depository institutions, and required and excess reserve balances at the Fed. It is one of the monetary aggregates most closely watched by the Fed and by those who consider themselves monetarists. The Board of Governors of the Federal Reserve and the St. Louis Federal Reserve Bank publish separate versions of the monetary base.

Monetary Control Act of 1990: A federal law liberalizing bank regulations, but also extending the regulations to certain classes of financial institutions that had not been previously subject to them.

Monetary policy: Policies that a central bank, such as the Federal Reserve, develops to influence such important items as interest rates, money supply, bank credit expansion, prices, real economic growth, employment, and unemployment. Monetary policy is different from fiscal policy, which is carried out primarily through government spending and taxation and is not a responsibility of the Federal Reserve.

Money market: Composed of investment instruments that typically have maturities of one year or less. These include Treasury bills, CDs, commercial paper, and so forth.

Money supply: Typically, money supply is described rather than defined. There are several variations of what constitutes money supply, but all of them center around a variety of deposit and other short-term funds held by the public, as well as currency in circulation.

Money supply variations: The narrowest form of money supply is M1. It consists of currency in circulation, demand deposits, travelers checks, negotiable order of withdrawal accounts (NOW), automatic transfer service accounts (ATS), credit union share draft accounts, and demand deposit at thrift institutions. M2 consists of M1 plus savings deposits, including money market deposit accounts, small-time deposits that include retail repurchase agreements (RPs) and balances in money market mutual funds. M3 (which is no longer published by the Fed) consists of M2 plus time deposits and large-size term RPs issued by commercial banks and thrift institutions; term Eurodollars held by U.S. residents at foreign branches of U.S. banks; and all balances in institution-only money market mutual funds. Then there is a monetary aggregate measurement called "debt," which encompasses the outstanding debt of the U.S. government, the state and local governments, and the private domestic nonfinancial sectors. It is the broadest measurement of the monetary aggregates.

Mortgage: A debt instrument whereby the borrower gives the lender a lien on the property as security for the repayment of the loan.

Mortgage bank: An organization that originates mortgage loans, sells them to investors, services the monthly payments, keeps related records, and acts as escrow agent to pay taxes and insurance.

Mortgage pool: A group of mortgages that share similar characteristics in terms of class of property, interest rate, and maturity.

Municipal bond: The debt obligation of a state or local government entity, or one of its instrumentalities.

Mutual fund: An organization that brings in money and invests it in stocks, bonds, options, commodities, and money market instruments. A wide variety of investment products are typically offered with a variety of risk and reward considerations.

Narrowing the spread: Closing the difference between the bid and asked prices on a security. The narrower the spread, the more likely a transaction will take place.

Negative carry: The net cost incurred when the cost of owning an investment exceeds the yield on the securities being financed. The opposite of positive carry.

Negotiable order of withdrawal (NOW): Checking accounts on which depository institutions may pay a rate of interest subject to federal rate ceilings.

Net transactions accounts: Funds held in deposit form where the money is used primarily to meet spending rather than investment needs.

Non-competitive bid: In a Treasury auction, it is the bidding for a specified amount of securities at the price equal to the average of the accepted competitive bids.

Nonmember bank: A bank that is not a member of the Federal Reserve System.

Options Clearing Corporation (OCC): The organization that issues all listed options trading on national options exchanges.

Odd lot: Less than a round lot. On the New York Stock Exchange a round lot is 100 shares, but the size of round lots can differ by markets.

Open Market Operations of the Federal Reserve: The New York Fed carries out the guidelines of the FOMC in adding or draining reserves from the banking system. The operations can be outright purchases or sales of securities or temporary purchases and sales.

Opportunity cost: The cost of pursuing one course of action measured in terms of the foregone return offered by the most attractive alternative.

Option: A call option is a contract sold for a price that gives the holder the right to buy from the writer of the option over a specified period, a specified amount, at a specified price. A put option is a contract sold for a price that gives the holder the right to sell to the writer of the contract, over a specified period, a specified amount at a specified price.

Overhang: A supply of securities difficult to sell at current market prices.

Portfolio: Collection of securities held by an investor.

Position: To take long or short positions in a security.

Positive carry: Net gain earned when the cost of carrying securities is less than the yields on the securities being financed.

Prime loan rate: The interest rate that banks charge to their most creditworthy customers. Yet there are some customers that obtain funds at a cost below what is called the prime loan rate.

Principal: The face amount or par value of a debt security.

Private placement: An issue that is offered to a single or a few investors as opposed to being publicly offered.

Producer price index (PPI): A measure of the changes in wholesale prices that is published monthly by the U.S. Bureau of Labor Statistics.

Profit-taking: An action by traders or investors to cash in on gains earned in an investment.

Purchasing power of the dollar: A measure of the amount of goods and services that a dollar can buy in a particular market, typically compared with past periods.

Quantitative analysis: Using measurable facts as distinguished from qualitative considerations.

Ratings: An evaluation given by rating services of the creditworthiness of a security.

Real GDP: Gross domestic product excluding inflation.

Real interest rate: A rate of interest after subtracting the rate of inflation.

Reconstruction Finance Corporation (Refcorp): The governmental organization that bought and sold the assets of distressed savings and loan associations, the primary purpose being to restore the industry's health.

Refunding: Replacing an old debt with a new one. Especially important when it comes to U.S. Treasury financing.

Regional commercial bank: Money center banks operate nationally and internationally while regional banks tend to operate in one or several states.

Regressive tax: A tax in which the tax rate declines as the tax base increases. A progressive tax is one where the rate rises as the tax base increases. A sales tax is regressive, and most income taxes are progressive.

Regulations (Federal Reserve): Congress assigned to the Federal Reserve Board the responsibility for implementing the Federal Reserve Act that established the Federal Reserve System. The Board implements those laws in part through its regulations. As of mid-2008, there were thirteen regulations (A through Z and AA through GG). Five of the more important regulations are as follows:

Regulation A (Federal Reserve): This regulation establishes rules under which a Federal Reserve Bank may extend credit to depository institutions and to others. Applies to U.S. branches and agencies of foreign banks that are subject to reserve requirements under Regulation D.

Regulation Q (Federal Reserve): Ceiling on interest rates that banks and other saving institutions can pay. The Depository Institutions Regulation and Monetary Control Act of 1980 phased out much of Regulation Q by 1985. At present, the regulation is limited to prohibiting interest payments on demand deposits by member banks and other depository institutions.

Regulation T (Federal Reserve): Its principal purpose is to regulate extensions of credit by brokers and dealers. It also covers related transactions, and imposes, among other obligations, initial margin requirements and payment rules on certain securities transactions.

Regulation U (Federal Reserve): Imposes credit restrictions upon persons other than brokers or dealers that extend credit for the purpose of buying or carrying margin stock if the credit is secured directly or indirectly by margin stock. Lenders include banks and others who are required to register with the Board. Lenders may not extend more than the maximum loan value of the collateral securing such credit.

Regulation Z (Federal Reserve): Implements the Federal Truth in Lending Act. The purpose of this regulation is to promote the informed use of consumer credit by requiring disclosures about its terms and cost. The regulation also gives consumers the right to cancel certain credit transactions that involve a lien on a consumer's principal dwelling, regulates certain credit card practices, and provides a means for fair and timely resolution of credit-billing disputes. The regulation does not govern charges for consumer credit, and requires a maximum interest rate to be stated in variable-rate contracts secured by the consumer's dwelling.

Reintermediation: Money moving into accounts at depository institutions from general market investments. The opposite of disintermediation.

Repurchase agreement: An agreement between a buyer and a seller whereby the seller agrees to repurchase the securities at an agreed-upon price and, usually, at a stated time. Widely used in the financial community as well as by the Federal Reserve.

Reserve requirement: Federal Reserve rule mandating the financial assets that member banks must keep in the form of cash and other liquid assets as a percentage of demand deposits and time deposits. The money must be kept in the bank's own vaults or on deposit with its regional Federal Reserve Bank.

Secondary market: Where already outstanding securities are traded. In contrast, a primary market is where new issues are offered and sold.

Securities and Exchange Commission (SEC): An agency created by Congress to protect investors in securities transactions by administering securities legislation.

Selling short: The sale of securities or commodities futures contracts that are not owned by the seller.

Senior debt: Securities where the owner has prior claims on assets in the event of a bankruptcy.

Settlement date: The date on which a trade is cleared by delivery of securities against funds.

Short covering: Purchase of securities by a short seller to replace those securities borrowed at the time of the short sale.

Short sale: The sale of securities not owned by the seller based on the expectation that the price will fall.

Short squeeze: Traders believe the price of an investment will decline, therefore they borrow securities hoping they can buy them later at a lower price. If the price should rise, however, pressure intensifies on the investor to buy the security outright in order to avoid losing money.

Spot market: A market for intermediate delivery as opposed to future delivery.

Spread: Difference between yields on securities of the same quality but different maturities. Can also be the difference in yields on securities of the same maturity but of different quality.

Squeeze: A tight money period where loan money is scarce and interest rates are high. This makes borrowing both difficult and expensive.

Student Loan Marketing Association (Sallie Mae): A publicly traded stock corporation that guarantees student loans trading in the secondary market.

Supply-Side economics: A theory that contends that reductions in tax rates will stimulate the economy to a point where the additional economic growth will raise more total tax revenues and therefore benefit society. In contrast, there is Keynesian economics that is based on the belief that the government should be actively involved in order to stimulate demand.

Support level: A price level at which a security tends to stop falling.

Swap: Selling one issue and buying another.

Swap rate: In the foreign exchange market, the difference between the spot and forward rates at which a currency is traded.

Takedown: Usually refers to purchases by investors in a Treasury auction, but can apply to other financial instruments.

Tax-exempt security: A security whose interest is exempt from taxation by federal, state, and/or local authorities.

Technical conditions of a market: Demand and supply factors affecting prices.

TED spread: The difference in yield between Treasury bill futures and CD futures.

Term fed funds: Most federal funds transactions have a one-day maturity. However, they can be for a longer period than the next business day.

Term loan: Loan extended by a bank for more than the normal ninety-day period.

Term RP: A repurchase agreement that has a maturity longer than the next business day.

Tier I: The most permanent portion of a bank's capital. A measure of a bank's capital adequacy.

Thin market: A market where there is little trading volume because of a lack of supply and demand.

Tight market: A market characterized by active trading and a narrow bid-offer price spread.

Tight money: Economic conditions in which credit is difficult to secure. The opposite is easy money.

Total rate of return: The earnings on an investment that takes into consideration capital appreciation (or depreciation), dividends or interest, and tax adjusted for present value and expressed on an annual percentage basis.

Trading desk: The department at the New York Fed that conducts open market operations in government securities for the Federal Reserve System.

Treasuries: Direct obligation of the U.S. government. Composed of bills, notes, and bonds.

Undervalued: A security selling below its liquidation value or the market value analysts believe it deserves.

U.S. unit: This is a reference in the foreign exchange market to the dollar.

Unloading: Liquidating securities, typically when prices are declining, in order to avoid losses or to protect earlier gains.

Variable-price security: A security that sells at a fluctuating market-determined price.

Variable rate mortgage (VRM): A home mortgage where the interest rate varies with a money market rate.

Visible supply: Typically refers to the state and local government market and the amount of securities scheduled to come to the market within the next thirty days.

When-issued: A security that has yet to be auctioned or issued but is trading in the market. Marketable Treasury securities initially are all traded on a when-issued basis.

Whip-sawed: When, in a volatile market, an investor loses money by being on the wrong side of the market over a period of time.

Window dressing: Trading near the end of an accounting period; an investor makes position adjustments to dress up or improve the appearance of the financial statements.

Write-off: Reducing or eliminating the amount of assets or earnings in order to bring them in line with financial reality.

Yankee bond: A foreign bond issued in the U.S. market, payable in dollars, and registered with the SEC.

Yankee CD: A CD issued in the domestic market by a branch of a foreign bank.

Yield curve: Interest rate levels along a series of maturities is typically based on what is called the term structure of interest rates. Can be shown by plotting the yields on the same debt instruments from the shortest to the longest maturities. If short-term rates are lower than long-term rates, then the yield curve is positive or upward sloping. If short-term rates are higher than long-term rates—which is usually not the case—then the yield curve is negative or downward sloping. If there is little difference in yield between short and long rates, then the yield curve is flat.

Yield to maturity: The rate of return if a debt instrument is held to maturity. The return takes into consideration the purchase price, the redemption value, the time to maturity, the coupon rate, and the time between interest payments.

Appendix 2

A FLAVOR OF THE TIMES: SELECTED MEDIA HEADLINES (1970–2008)

A FLAVOR OF THE TIMES

Writing about history, especially when it is still unfolding, is never an easy task. Notable in this regard has been the period of September/October 2008 when one of the great financial debacles of modern American history took place. The entire U.S. financial landscape changed during that period, and only time will tell whether the changes, and the ultimate results, are for the better. One thing for sure, the Federal Reserve, the Treasury, the administration, and Congress were all unprepared for what transpired, and that was evident by how they responded— or should I say did not respond—to events that spun out of control. The $700-billion bailout package originally proposed by the administration was incomplete, and if done properly, was overstated in both size and cost. The details of the plan were not adequately worked out, and the proposals did not recommend sufficient oversight responsibilities, especially for Congress. Public officials, both at home and abroad, did not seem to fully appreciate that throwing money at problems can do only a limited amount of good if markets seize up, because of credit risk concerns, not trusting the accuracy of financial statements, or a lack of adequate long-term capital. The breathtaking speed in which new problems, and old ones, worsened seemed to overwhelm public officials, and this was evident to financial market participants as events spun out of control.

In this period of roughly two months, the most prominent investment banks were either purchased by commercial banks, became bank holding companies, or went out of business. Looking ahead, an obvious question is, Who will carry on all the investment banking functions, such as providing the capital needed for long-term U.S economic growth? One has to believe the Federal Reserve will adjust its regulations—and the regulatory climate—to make sure that typical investment banking functions continue in a way that benefit investors, issuers, and the public. Whether such changes will succeed is another matter.

This section of the book entitled "A Flavor of the Times," gives the reader a broad and general perspective of what happened during the months and years since 1970. This includes the financial-debacle period mentioned above.

1970

January

U.S. recession begins, ending the longest postwar expansion in the country's history.

U.S. federal oil depletion allowance reduced from 27.5 to 22.0 percent.

Strike by electrical workers' union against GE, which started in late October 1969, is settled.

Personal income tax surcharge reduced to 5.0 percent. Withholding cut.

Inflation reaches 6.1 percent, the highest rate since the Korean War.

Maximum rates payable on time and savings accounts are raised to 4.5 percent.

February

January economic indicators fall by 1.8 percent, the greatest monthly decline since the 1957 recession.

March

Nuclear non-proliferation treaty, ratified by forty-three nations, goes into effect.

First major postal workers' strike in U.S. history.

April

Social Security benefits raised by 15 percent.

On April 2, Teamsters go on strike; walkout ends on June 2.

On April 28, the Dow Jones Industrial Averages (DJIA) falls to 724.33, its lowest point since President Kennedy assassinated.

May

U.S. troops invade Cambodia.

Four students killed when National Guard fires at a crowd of more than six hundred anti-war demonstrators at Kent State University, Ohio.

Stock margin requirement cut from 80 to 65 percent.

June

Senate repeals Gulf of Tonkin resolution.

Bankruptcy petition of Penn-Central Railroad approved, followed by disruptions in credit markets.

July

Personal income tax surcharge removed.

September

United Auto Workers strike GM; 400,000 workers idled. Strike ends November 11.

December

OPEC establishes 55 percent minimum tax rate; demands that posted prices reflect changes in foreign exchange rates.

Bill signed by Nixon calls for 90 percent reduction in auto exhaust pollution by 1975.

Environmental Protection Agency, established by executive order in July, activated.

Thirteen-week extended duration unemployment benefits in effect.

1971

February

Tehran agreement signed, companies accept 55 percent tax rate, posted price increased.

OPEC mandates total embargo against any company that rejected 55 percent tax rate.

Regulation of construction wages on federal projects suspended; suspension revoked in March.

Wage-price curbs ordered on federal construction contracts.

March

Social Security bill signed; benefits raised 10 percent. Contribution base raised to $9,000 effective January 1972.

April

Agreement with oil companies raises posted price from $2.55 to $3.45 per barrel. Provides for 2.5 percent annual price increase plus inflation allowance. Tax rate raised from a range of 50–58 percent to 60 percent of posted prices.

May

World Bank signs its first loan agreement for pollution control. $15 million to Brazil.

Amtrak begins operation. Rail strike.

U.S. program for a supersonic transport ended.
Liquidity ratio for savings and loan associations raised from 6.5 to 7.5 percent.

June

Communications workers strike against Western Union ends.
Northern California construction workers go on strike. It ends in July.

July

Venezuela mandates gradual transfer to government of unexploited concession
    areas by 1974.
Longshoremen strike West Coast ports. Strike lasts until October.
Communications workers strike the telephone system. Strike ends in August.
Railroad workers go on strike. Strike ends in August.
Steel strike averted by accord on contract.

August

Federal bailout of Lockheed Aircraft authorized by Congress via $250 million
    loan guarantee.
Teamsters walk out in Northern California against building contractors.
Phase I of Nixon Economic Control Policy goes into effect with ninety-day
    freeze on prices, wages, rents; government spending reduced; temporary
    10 percent surcharge on imports.
Dollar convertibility to gold suspended. U.S. is freed from gold standard; and
    restricts gold outflow. U.S. informs International Monetary Fund (IMF) it
    will no longer freely buy and sell gold to settle international transactions.
Par values and convertibility of dollar—two features of Bretton Woods
    Agreements—cease to exist.

September

OPEC directs members to negotiate price increases to offset the devaluation of
    the dollar.

October

U.N. seats Communist China and expels Nationalist China.
East and Gulf Coast longshoremen go on strike.

November

Phase II of Nixon Economic Control Policy goes into effect. Price and wage
    freeze replaced by a pay board to set standards for wage increases (set at

5.5 percent). Price commission establishes annual price increase guidelines of 2.5 percent.

Domestic petroleum prices remain at Phase I levels. Phase II lasts until January 1973.

December

President Nixon signs Revenue Act into law; $25 billion tax cut.

Stock margin requirements cut from 65 to 55 percent.

Floating prime rate adopted.

Smithsonian Agreement arrived at after four months of negotiations. Provides for realignment of industrial country currencies and increase in price of gold.

IMF established temporary regime of central rates and wider margins.

Smithsonian Agreement devalues dollar by 8.6 percent.

Official price of gold raised from $35 to $38 per ounce.

The 10 percent import surcharge, begun on August 15, 1971 as part of Phase I, is ended.

1972

January

Ten days of meetings between oil companies and representatives of Abu Dhabi, Iran, Iraq, Kuwait, Qatar, and Saudi Arabia. Agree to raise the posted price of crude by 8.49 percent to offset loss from decline in the dollar.

February

President Nixon makes unprecedented eight-day visit to Communist China. Meets with Chairman Mao Zedong.

Rolls Royce announces bankruptcy.

134 day dock strike—longest to date—ends when West Coast longshoremen return to work.

Kaiser Steel Company employees go on strike.

March

OPEC threatens sanctions against companies not complying with member actions.

May

Japanese and European steel producers promise to limit exports to U.S. voluntarily for two years.

U.S. devalues the dollar to $38.00 per ounce of gold.

June

Iraq nationalizes Iraq Petroleum Company's concession owned by foreign oil companies.

OPEC moves to prevent companies nationalized in Iraq from increasing production elsewhere.

Washington, D.C., police arrest five individuals for burglary at Democratic Party Headquarters located in Watergate apartment complex.

All meat import quotas lifted for rest of the year in an effort to control rising meat prices.

July

20 percent increase in Social Security benefits signed into law. Effective September 1972.

Nixon announces three-year grain sale agreement with Russia. Reached $1 billion on August 9.

August

Last U.S. ground combat forces withdrawn from Vietnam.

October

OPEC approves plan for 25 percent government ownership of all western oil interests.

Water Pollution Control Act passed by Congress over a presidential veto.

Supplementary Security Income system approved by Congress—effective 1974.

Revenue Act authorizes sharing $30.2 billion of tax revenues with state and local governments.

Revenue sharing to take place over five years.

Nixon signs Social Security bill providing an additional $5.3 billion in benefits for elderly.

November

Richard M. Nixon re-elected president of the U.S.

November 14: The DJIA closes above 1,000 for the first time.

Stock margin requirements raised to 65 percent.

1973

January

Vietnam peace agreement signed in Paris on January 27, 1973.

European Economic Community expanded to include Britain, Denmark, and Ireland.

Price and Wage Controls—Phase III—liberalizes wage and price controls; allows for voluntary instead of mandatory price controls. Voluntary controls do not prevent sharp rise in heating oil prices due to weather and shortages.

President Nixon suspends mandatory oil import quota on Number 2 heating oil through April 30.

DJIA closes at a record 1,052.

February

Purchasing Managers Association reports shortages of many materials and components.

Dollar devalued by 10 percent relative to other major currencies.

Official price of gold raised from $38.00 to $42.22 per ounce.

March

Iran and consortium nationalize all assets. In return, companies are assured a twenty-year supply.

Atomic Energy Commission says nuclear power needed to avoid dependence on Middle East oil.

Foreign exchange markets close on March 2 because of massive sale of dollars.

Major central banks suspend dealing in foreign exchange markets.

Mandatory price controls reimposed on most petroleum products through Special Rule No. 1.

Mandatory (Phase II) price controls on twenty-three largest oil companies. Small companies—no controls.

"Generalized floating" for European Community currencies against the dollar begins on March 19. European exchange markets reopen with "joint float."

Joint Economic Committee recommends implementation of stricter wage/ price controls.

President Nixon announces a price freeze on prices of beef, pork, and lamb.

April

President Nixon accepts responsibility for Watergate, but not the blame. Nixon accepts resignations of advisers H. R. Haldeman and John Ehrlichman. Fires counsel John Dean.

U.S. government ends Mandatory Oil Import Program that was established in 1959. Limited crude imports and products east of Rockies to percentage of domestic crude production.

Consumer groups initiate a five-day nationwide meat boycott in an effort to force prices down.

May

U.S. oil import quotas ended.

Fed's Regulation Q ceiling suspended for all large certificates of deposit.

Chicago Board of Trade Options Exchange is formed to deal in stock options.

June

Soybean futures hit $12 per bushel; up from $3.50 a year earlier.

Sixty-day price freeze announced on retail prices, called "Phase 3$^{1}/_{2}$." Freeze supersedes Special Rule No.1 for oil companies.

Minimum wage raised from $1.60 to $2.20 per hour.

Export restrictions placed on soybeans and oilseeds.

German mark revalued by 5.5 percent.

Federal Energy Office established by President Nixon.

July

Interest rate ceiling raised for savings and small-denominated time deposits; suspended for four years for $1,000 minimum accounts.

Maximum rate on bank savings accounts increased from 4.50 to 5.00 percent.

Savings and loan rate raised from 5.00 to 5.25 percent.

Federal Reserve "swap lines" with foreign central banks reactivated and expanded.

Phase IV of Nixon Economic Control Policy begins. All food price restrictions and health-care cost controls to be lifted by September 12, 1973. System of mandatory price controls allows price increases to only match cost increases.

August

U.S. bombing of Cambodia ends, marking official halt to twelve years of combat in Southeast Asia.

Nixon's Cost of Living Council imposes two-tier price ceiling on crude petroleum sales.

Production of old oil to be sold at March 1973 prices, plus 35 cents.

Production of new oil to be sold at uncontrolled prices.

September

OPEC supports price hikes. Designates six Gulf states to negotiate with companies over prices.

Congress establishes new par value for dollar at $42.00 per ounce of gold.

Marginal reserves increased on large certificates of deposit and bank-related commercial paper.

October

Mandatory allocations ordered by U.S. on oil products.

Spiro Agnew resigns as vice president. Pleads no contest to charges of income tax evasion.

In "Saturday Night Massacre," Nixon fires special Watergate prosecutor Archibald Cox. Also fires Deputy Attorney General Ruchelshaus. Attorney General Richardson resigns.

Egypt and Syria attacked Israel. Began Six-Day War. Fourth and biggest Arab-Israeli conflict.

Embargo imposed on oil shipped to the U.S. and other nations that supported Israel.

Ceasefire in Arab-Israeli war. Egypt and Israel sign U.S.-sponsored accord.

Fertilizer industry exempted from price controls.

International trade surplus for third quarter was largest since 1965.

U.S. devaluation of the dollar effective.

New law requires interest ceiling on time deposits of less than $100,000.

November

TWA employees walk out. Strike ends on December 18.

President outlines steps for fuel conservation—daylight savings time extended; 55 mph speed limit imposed; Sunday gas sales banned; standby rationing.

Alaskan pipeline bill signed.

Arab summit adopts open and secret resolution on use of oil weapon.

Nixon signs Emergency Petroleum Allocation Act. Authorizes petroleum price, production, allocation, and marketing controls.

Two-tier gold market formally abandoned.

December

Federal Energy Office announces regulations for oil usage.

Four-day traffic slowdown on U.S. highways. Truckers protest high fuel costs and lower speed limits.

December 13–14, truckers get off the road entirely, going on strike to emphasize their protest.

DJIA closes at 788, the low for the year.

Large layoffs planned by auto firms and airlines.

Decline in economy associated with Arab oil embargo begins.

1974

January

President Nixon signs a bill to reduce speed limit to 55 mph.

Federal Energy Office said the Arab oil embargo is fully effective.

Independent truckers begin eleven-day strike to protest high fuel prices and reduced speed limit.

Federal Reserve reduces margin requirements on stock purchases from 65 to 50 percent.

February

Washington Energy Conference opens; attended by thirteen industrial and oil-producing nations; called by U.S. to resolve international energy problems through cooperation among nations.

Kissinger unveils Nixon administration's seven-point "Project Independence."

President Nixon says no to rationing despite lines at gas stations.

March

Arab oil ministers (except Libya) announce end of the embargo against the U.S.

DJIA closes at 892 on March 13; high for the year.

April

Shortages ranging from abrasives to zinc are reported.

Steel workers agree to pattern-setting three-year pact; 40 percent increase in wages and benefits.

Economic Stabilization Act Phase IV expires, ending general wage and price control authority.

Controls on 165 sectors of the economy lifted.

Committee on Interest and Dividends expired.

Thrift institutions report savings losses as disintermediation returned.

June

Arab oil ministers decide to end most restrictions on exports of oil to the U.S.

IMF establishes "oil facility"—a special fund used to make loans. Lends to nations whose balance of payments is severely affected by high oil prices.

Various electric utilities reported to be deferring expansion projects.

German Bankhaus Herstatt collapses with worldwide repercussions.

July

House Judiciary Committee adopts three articles of impeachment for President Nixon: Obstruction of justice, failure to uphold laws, and refusal to produce subpoenaed material.

Usury ceiling on Illinois home mortgages raised from 8.00 to 9.50 percent until July 1, 1975.

Congressional Budget and Impoundment Control Act of 1974 becomes law.

Labor Department reports more strikes than at any time since World War II.

August

Richard Nixon resigns; Gerald Ford becomes president.

Department of Agriculture says drought will hurt crops.

Treasury sells three-month bills at a record 9.91 percent.

Bell System sells forty-year bonds at a record 10 percent yield.

September

President Ford grants "full, free, and absolute pardon" to ex-President Nixon.

Employees Retirement Income and Security Act signed by President Ford.

Natural gas suppliers announce sharp cutbacks to industrial users.

Purchasing Managers report no rise in new orders in August, first time since January 1971.

FNMA auction of commitments produced a record 10.6 percent yield.

Builders report funds for residential and commercial construction all but dried up.

Federal Reserve eliminates marginal reserve requirements on longer-term certificates of deposit.

October

Business activity begins sharp decline.

President Ford obtains cancellation of large grain sales to USSR. Voluntary export controls placed on grains and soybeans.

President Ford's WIN (Whip Inflation Now) program to fight inflation includes 5 percent tax surcharge.

Comptroller declares Franklin National Bank insolvent; largest bank failure in U.S. history.

November

International Energy Agency formed in Paris within Organization for Economic Cooperation and Development framework.

Coal miners strike begins.

Federal Reserve restructures reserve requirements to encourage longer-term time deposits.

Auto makers announce layoffs and capital outlay reductions, as sales slump.

Freedom of Information Act passed over President Ford's veto.
FDIC insurance coverage raised from $20,000 to $40,000.

December

U.S. Crude Oil Entitlements Program enacted, retroactive to November 1974.
Coal production resumed at some mines.
Oil companies reported to be canceling plans to expand refining capacity.
Congress approves the Trade Reform Act, permitting new international trade negotiations.
DJIA closes at 578 on December 6; low for year and lowest since October 1962.
Fed authorizes banks to issue six-year investment certificates yielding up to 7.50 percent.
Comptroller of the Currency says 150 banks are under scrutiny.
Congress exercises new power over presidential impoundment of funds.
Massive auto industry layoff forced by sharply reduced car sales. 142,000 auto workers lose jobs and another 75,000 are temporarily laid off.
American citizens can buy gold for the first time in forty years.

1975

January

John Mitchell, H. R. Haldeman, and John Ehrichman found guilty of Watergate cover-up.
U.S. Federal oil depletion allowance eliminated for large producers.
First U.S. gold auction. Two million ounces auctioned; less than half bid for.
Oil Chemical Atomic Workers Union goes on strike.
Chrysler offers rebates to new car buyers; other makers follow.
New claims for unemployment compensation reach record level.
President Ford proposed substantial tax reduction to stimulate spending.
Major nations propose a fund to aid participating nations in financial difficulty due to oil prices.
Fidelity Mortgage investors file under Chapter 11; second sizable real estate investment trust to do so.

February

Multilateral trade negotiations to reduce barriers to international trade.
New York City cancels large note issue amidst concern over its financial condition.

March

Saudi Arabia's King Faisal assassinated.
Tax Reduction Act signed into law. Cut individual and corporate income taxes by $22.8 billion.

Federal Reserve submits draft legislation, establishes federal chartering and
control of foreign banks.

April

Saigon surrenders to Viet Cong, ending thirty-year war.
Federal Reserve authorizes member banks—phoned withdrawals/transfers
from savings accounts.
Federal Reserve announces cut from 8 percent to 4 percent in reserve requirements on foreign borrowings.

May

Trading under SEC-ordered negotiated broker fees to begin on New York Stock
Exchange.
For the first time, the Federal Reserve reports to the Senate its monthly growth
targets for coming 12 months.
President Ford requests an additional $1 billion for the rapidly expanding food
stamp program.
Congress adopts first concurrent resolution—specifying targets under
Congressional Budget Act.

June

President Ford signs Securities Reform Act, expanding powers of the SEC.
Suez Canal opened to traffic for the first time since the 1967 war.
Unemployment rate hits 9.2 percent in May, highest since 1941, but employ-
ment rises substantially.
World Bank establishes "Third Window" fund. Lends to those nations too rich
to qualify for "soft" no-interest loans, too distressed for normal rates.
Second U.S. gold auction.

July

Social Security payments boosted 8 percent in cost-of-living adjustment.
U.S. grain companies announce large sales to Russia.
"Dumping" charges filed with U.S. Treasury against foreign auto producers.
Environmental Protection Agency reported electricity rates rose a record
30 percent in 1974.

August

Moratorium placed on future grain sales to Russia.
Group of ten major industrial countries and Switzerland agree—no attempt to
peg price of gold.

Total stock held by IMF and monetary authorities of the G-10 countries would not be increased.

IMF's Interim Committee agreed to dispose of 50-million ounces (or one-third) of the Fund's gold. Twenty-five million ounces to be sold and surplus devoted to a Trust Fund. Funds in trust fund available in loans with concessions to low-income members. Other 25-million ounces to be restituted to members at the official price.

September

President Ford escapes second assassination attempt in seventeen days.

National Airlines employees go on strike.

Federal Reserve permits preauthorized transfers from savings accounts for any bill payments.

IMF announces agreement on steps to eliminate role of gold in international finance.

New Illinois law permits Negotiable Order of Withdrawal accounts at state savings and loan institutions effective January 1, 1976.

October

Retailer W. T. Grant files bankruptcy proceedings under Chapter 11. Bankruptcy petitions reportedly climbed to record 254,484 during fiscal 1975, up 34.4 percent from fiscal 1974.

Federal Reserve cuts reserve requirements on time deposits with maturities of four years or longer. Rate reduced from 3.00 to 1.00 percent.

American City National Bank (Milwaukee) is declared insolvent.

Equal Credit Opportunity regulations become effective.

Venezuela and foreign oil companies agree on nationalization as of January 1, 1976.

November

Federal Reserve allows member banks to offer business firms savings accounts up to $150,000.

President Ford announces support for federal loans to New York City to avoid bankruptcy.

December

Strike against United Airlines. Ends December 17, 1975.

FHLB permits S&Ls to offer variable-rate mortgages on multi-family and commercial properties.

Industrial production index rises in November for the seventh straight month.

Last minute compromise bill extends 1975 tax cuts for six months.

Federal Reserve cuts reserve requirements on time deposits with maturities of 180 days to four years.

President Ford signs the Energy Policy and Conservation Act (EPCA) effective February 1976. Act authorizes the establishment of Strategic Petroleum Reserve (SPR). Act also authorized participation in International Energy Program and oil price regulation.

1976

January

Minimum wage raised from $2.10 to $2.30 per hour. First part $2.00 to $2.10 on Jan 1, 1975.

Maximum income for Social Security taxes raised from $14,100 to $15,300.

State S&Ls in Illinois allowed to offer non-interest-bearing NOW accounts.

Futures trading in Treasury bills begins on the Chicago Mercantile Exchange.

February

EPCA (Energy Policy and Conservation Act) three-tier price regulation begins.

March

Federal Reserve amends Regulation Q to member banks in New England, offers NOW accounts

France withdraws franc from European Community "joint float," following sharp drop in pound.

Pound drops to $1.98, under $2.00 for the first time.

April

Teamsters go on strike.

Rubber workers go on strike.

May

Federal Trade Commission issues revision of the "holder-in-due course" doctrine, relating to consumer credit.

New York state permits S&Ls and mutual savings banks to offer checking accounts.

New York Mercantile Exchange reports heavy defaults on potato futures contracts.

OPEC concerned about protectionist actions by certain countries.

June

IMF auctions gold at $126 per ounce, first auction of a series.

California voters defeat proposition curbing operation of existing nuclear power plants. Also defeat ban on additional construction.

GE agrees to labor pact raising wages 33 percent over three years; assumes
   6 percent annual increase in CPI.

July

Social Security payments raised 6.4 percent in cost-of-living adjustment.
London gold price drops to $105.50 per ounce, a thirty-one month low.
Cannery workers go on strike.
Treasury announces budget deficit was $65.6 billion for fiscal 1976.

August

Illinois law sets usury rate on home mortgages at 2.5 percent above yield on
   long-term federal bonds.

September

Mexican peso drops sharply after government withdraws support.
U.S. stripper well oil prices decontrolled.
UAW strike against Ford Motor Co. begins.
American Bank and Trust Company fails; the fourth largest banking default
   ever in U.S.

October

Supreme Court upholds ruling that electronic terminals established by banks
   are branches.
Bank of England raises its minimum lending rate to a record 15 percent.
Ford begins to reopen plants after thirty-day strike. Per-hour compensation to
   increase 13 percent in first year.
Currency values in EC joint float are realigned.

November

James Earl Carter elected president of the United States.
Russia announces big grain crop.
U.S. Agriculture Department estimates 1976 corn crop at a record 6.06 billion
   bushels.
Australian dollar devalued.

December

Steel companies raise prices of flat-rolled products by 6 percent.
New AAA bond yields at 7.9 percent, lowest in three years.

Federal Reserve reduces reserve requirements on demand deposits.

Federal Reserve issues rules against credit discrimination.

1977

January

President Carter pardons Vietnam draft evaders.

Former President Ford proposes a tax cut, $10 billion for individuals and $2.5 billion for businesses.

February

President Carter addresses the nation on energy problems after signing emergency law to allocate natural gas.

Electronic banking system begins operating in Iowa; nation's first statewide system.

Federal Reserve rules that bank holding companies cannot acquire S&Ls.

March

Regulation B revised to implement 1976 Amendment to Equal Credit Opportunity Act.

Monetary aggregates now an important policy determinant.

April

FHLB Board lifts ban on S&Ls having savings accounts at banks.

United Steelworkers agree to pact raising compensation more than 30 percent over three years.

Federal credit unions given broader lending powers, including authority for thirty-year mortgage loans.

President Carter unveils details of proposed National Energy Plan.

May

Major industrialized nations meet in London to discuss sluggish growth and high unemployment.

June

Oil starts flowing through Alaskan pipeline—completed after four years at a cost of $7.7 billion.

Robert Hall, nation's largest retailer, closes 366 stores after losing nearly $100 million in three years.

July

Social Security payments raised 5.9 percent in cost-of-living adjustment.
Water rationing instituted in Los Angeles due to severe West Coast drought.

August

Iron ore miners go on strike.
Strip-mining law requiring restoration of excavations approved.
Federal Department of Energy established.
Major steel companies announce layoffs and plant shutdowns.
Sweden withdraws from the "snake" (international arrangement for maintaining currency values.)

September

Nuclear-proliferation pact signed by fifteen countries; curbs spread of nuclear weapons.
Trading in ninety-day commercial paper futures begins on Chicago Board of Trade.

October

Federal pay boost (7.05 percent) for civilian employees and the military.
Longshoremen go on strike against selected Atlantic and Gulf ports. Wages and container ships the main issues.
IAM-Lockheed strike begins.
President Carter pledges federal action to curb "dumping" of foreign steel.

November

Law signed raising minimum wage from $2.30 to $2.65 on Jan 1, 1978, and to $3.35 by 1981.
Single-family housing starts reported at 1.6 million for October; highest on record.
Major auto producers announce reduction in output schedules as sales lag.
East and Gulf Coast dockworkers end two-month strike against container ships. Three-year settlement included guarantees of job security and a 30.5 percent pay increase.

December

Soft coal miners strike begins, idling 130,000, mainly in eastern mines. Strike settled March 24, 1978.
Most iron ore miners end strike.

Milwaukee Road railroad filed for bankruptcy under Section 77.

President Carter signs Social Security tax increase. Expected to cost workers and employers $227 billion over ten years.

U.S. dollar hits historic low versus the mark, yen, and other major currencies.

United States posts highest foreign trade deficit in history—$31.1 billion for 1977.

1978

January

Federal minimum wage increased to $2.65 per hour.

Pay base for Social Security raised from $16,500 to $17,700. Social Security tax rate increased from 5.85 to 6.05 percent.

Treasury and Federal Reserve intervene in foreign exchange markets to moderate dollar fluctuations.

Japan agrees to open some of its domestic market to U.S. products.

February

Indiana orders electricity usage cut back. Coal supplies depleted by eastern miners' strike.

ICC orders railroads to allocate freight cars to speed grain shipments.

March

Senate approves Panama Canal neutrality treaty. Canal to be turned over to Panama by 2000.

Coal strike ends after 111 days with a three-year pact boosting compensation 39 percent.

April

Gold's formal role in international monetary system disappears.

United Airlines employees go on strike. It ended May 28, 1978.

First Volkswagen produced in U.S. rolls off line in New Stanton, Pennsylvania.

FHLB Board reduces liquidity requirement for S&Ls from 7.00 to 6.50 percent.

U.S. Treasury announces additional sale of gold to stabilize the dollar.

May

Federal Reserve approves plan to allow automatic transfers from savings to checking accounts.

U.S. gold auctions resumed.

June

Iran and Saudi Arabia block efforts of OPEC price hawks to fix oil prices outside the dollar.

Change in Regulation Q allows banks and S&Ls to tie CD rates to Treasury bill rates.

California voters approve Proposition 13, sharply limiting property tax increases. Nearly 60 percent slashed in property tax revenues.

July

Teamsters union strike affects supermarkets throughout northern California.

August

Federal loan guarantee of $1.65 billion for New York City bonds signed by President Carter.

Retail clerks' union goes on strike in Southern California.

October

President Carter announces voluntary guidelines for wage and price increases—Phase II.

Pay increase for federal workers of 5.5 percent plus usual "step" increases.

National Energy Act of 1978 passed by Congress. Tax cut also passed.

November

Iranian prime minister resigns. Riots and strikes disrupt Iranian economy; oil output reduced.

President Carter announces massive intervention in international currency markets.

Major plan to support the dollar in the international currency markets. Part of the plan involves an increase in the discount rate from 8.50 to 9.50 percent and the issue of U.S. Treasury obligations denominated in foreign currencies and sold abroad. Dow Jones rose 35.34 on day.

Issuance of U.S. Treasury obligations denominated in foreign currencies and issued abroad.

December

Shell Oil Company announces plan to ration gasoline to dealers.

OPEC announces three-stage 14.5 percent boost in crude oil prices for 1979, to be implemented quarterly.

FHLB Board reduces liquidity requirement for S&Ls from 6.50 to 6.00 percent.

Cleveland defaults on $15.5 million in short-term notes. First major U.S. city to default since the 1930s.

First offering of Treasury securities denominated in a foreign currency and issued abroad. Eight issues ultimately sold in the program—six in deutschemarks and two in Swiss francs.

1979

January

Shah of Iran flees Iran for asylum in the U.S. Bakhtiar government established by Shah to preside until unrest subsided.

Minimum wage rose from $2.65 to $2.90 per hour.

Social Security tax rose from 6.05 to 6.13 percent. Taxable income rose from $17,700 to $22,900. Mandatory private retirement age increased to seventy.

First emergency Crude Oil Buy-Sell Program allocations.

February

Revolutionary forces under Khomeini take over Iran on February 1.

Department of Energy predicts serious gasoline shortage.

Airlines reduce flights because of fuel shortages.

Major oil companies curtail fuel allocations.

March

Iran resumes petroleum exports.

Gasoline shortages despite world oil glut.

Nuclear Regulatory Commission orders five large East Coast nuclear power plants closed.

Accident closes nuclear power plant at Three Mile Island near Harrisburg, PA.

Machinists strike United Airlines. Strike lasts until May 26, 1979.

European Monetary System established. Participants in exchange rate arrangements had to swap 20 percent of gold and U.S. dollar reserves.

Swap on rolling quarterly basis with European Monetary Cooperation Fund for ECU. Other members not participating in exchange rate arrangements could swap if they chose.

April

President Carter issues an order to deregulate oil prices beginning June 1, 1979.

Teamsters go on strike.

May

Conservatives win British election. Margaret Thatcher new prime minister.

Long lines at gas stations.

Machinists' strike against United Airlines ends.

Diesel fuel shortages slow truck traffic.

DOE announces $5 per barrel entitlement to importers of heating oil.

June

Carter and Brezhnev signed SALT II agreement.

Independent truck drivers halt traffic, protesting price and availability of diesel fuel.

Phased oil price decontrol begins. Involves twenty-eight month increase of "old" oil price ceiling; slower rate of increase of "new" oil price ceiling.

July

Passbook savings rate ceiling raised to 5.50 percent for S&Ls and 5.25 percent for banks.

Nine-percent cost-of-living adjustment for Social Security and welfare payments.

Chrysler Corporation requests a $1 billion federal loan to prevent bankruptcy.

August

Los Angeles Rapid Transit and BART workers go on strike.

October

All federal workers receive 7.00 percent cost-of-living increase in addition to step increases.

Federal government announces grain sale to USSR; up to 25 million metric tons of wheat and corn.

Financial and stock panic sparked when Federal Reserve announced 1 percent discount rate increase from 11 to 12 percent.

Black Saturday—Federal Reserve acts to slow inflation. Focus is on controlling money supply.

Fed reduces efforts to control interest rates.

Buy-Sell oil program. Averages more than 400,000 B/D, Oct 1979–Mar 1980.

Canada eliminates light crude oil exports to U.S. refiners.

Monetary aggregates became dominant Fed policy determinant.

Great funds rate volatility begins; comes to a halt in October 1982 when monetary aggregate domination ends.

November

President Carter orders cessation of Iranian imports to the U.S.

Iran cancels all contracts with U.S. oil companies.

Big three auto makers announce additional layoffs.

State of Illinois suspends mortgage usury laws.

Final U.S. gold auction. During two phases (1975 and 1978/79) 530 tons were sold.

December

Soviet invasion of Afghanistan stirs worldwide protests.

In London, gold reaches $524 per ounce on December 31, an increase of 132 percent in one year.

1980

January

Federal minimum wage rises from $2.90 to $3.10 per hour.

Social Security wage base increased from $22,900 to $25,900. Tax rate stays at 6.13 percent.

President Carter denounces Russian invasion of Afghanistan. Places embargoes on shipments of agricultural products to Russia.

State of the Union message calls for draft registration and 5 percent boost in real defense spending.

February

Trade agreement between U.S. and People's Republic of China goes into effect.

IMF auctions 444,000 ounces of gold at $712 per ounce, up from record $563 on January 2.

Nuclear Regulatory Commission lifts moratorium on new nuclear plants.

March

President Carter announces new anti-inflation program; activates Credit Control Act of 1969.

Federal Reserve announces 15 percent special deposit on growth of money market funds. Announces special deposit on some types of consumer credit, a voluntary Special Restraint Program to restrict business credit, an increase in marginal reserves on managed liabilities from 8 to 10 percent and a three-point surcharge on frequent borrowings from Federal Reserve by large banks.

Banks urged by Federal Reserve to limit loan growth to between 6 and 9 percent.

Administration suspends trigger-price mechanism intended to curb steel imports.

Spot price of silver drops by $5, to $10.80 per ounce. Peak of $50 was reached in January.

Economic Emergency Loan Program to financially distressed farmers extended and expanded.

Depository Institutions Deregulation and Monetary Control Act approved.

April

Act imposing windfall profits (excise tax) on domestic crude oil output is approved.

U.S. breaks diplomatic relations with Iran and cuts off all trade.

China replaces Taiwan as a member of the IMF.

April-September Buy-Sell Program, oil allocations dropped to average of 120,000 B/D.

May

Federal Reserve removes 3-point surcharge on frequent borrowings by large banks.

Last of forty-five IMF gold auctions; 778 tons were sold in all, average price $240. Lowest price $109; highest price $712.

Unemployment compensation claims reach a new high.

Purchasing Managers survey shows business plummeted in April and May.

Federal Reserve eases credit restraint program.

Aluminum workers win 42 percent wage boost over three years, assuming 11 percent inflation rate.

Leading economic indicator index released May 30 falls 4.8 percent in April. Largest drop on record.

June

Chrysler obtained $500 million loan after government board approved federal guarantee.

Carpenters strike in Northern California ended.

Synfuel Act creates Synthetic Fuel Corporation.

July

Checks to 35.2 million Social Security recipients rose 14.3 percent based on COLA formula.

Labor Department reported white-collar salaries up 9.1 percent for twelve months ending in March.

Motor Carrier Reform Act partially deregulates trucking.

FHLB authorizes S&Ls to issue credit cards; offers unsecured loans.

Indefinite layoffs at Big Four auto makers hit a record 246,000.

Motion picture and television industry employees go on strike.

Federal Reserve announces complete phase-out of credit restraint program.

August

AT&T labor contract provides for a 34.5 percent pay hike over three years; assumes a 9.5 percent increase in the CPI.

U.S. import duty on small trucks increased from 4 to 25 percent.

September

Iran-Iraq war begins over disputed border waterway; Iraq invades Iran. Mutual bombing.

Regulation A revised as required by Monetary Control Act. Gives all depository institutions access to the discount window.

October

Federal employees receive a 9.1 percent general pay boost in addition to annual step increases.

Staggers Rail Act provides for gradual deregulation.

Agriculture Department announces drought; cuts major crop output.

Agriculture Department announces four-year agreement with China. Commits China to substantial purchases of wheat and corn.

Regulatory authorities set 5.25 percent ceiling on NOW accounts, effective December 31.

Federal Reserve cuts bank reserve requirements by $11 billion.

November

Ronald Reagan elected president in Republican sweep.

International Trade Commission turns down request by Ford and UAW to impose quotas on imports of cars and light trucks.

New York legislature eliminates usury ceilings on most loans.

First phase of reserve requirement provisions of Monetary Control Act became effective.

Federal Reserve institutes 2-point surcharge for $500 million for institutions that borrowed frequently.

December

Auto makers extend holiday closings to cut inventories.

Iran demands $24 billion ransom to release hostages.

OPEC's pricing structure collapses.

Labor Department announces November CPI was 12.7 percent above the level of a year earlier.

1981

January

U.S.-Iran agreement frees fifty-two hostages held in Tehran since 1979. Held for 444 days.

Minimum wage increased from $3.10 to $3.35.

Social Security wage base increased from $25,900 to $29,700.

Stock market run begins when Joe Granville advises to sell everything. DJIA falls 23.8 percent.

Social Security tax rate increased from 6.13 to 6.65 percent.

Ronald Reagan inaugurated as the fortieth President.

Deregulation of oil and gas industry announced, effective immediately.

Deregulated price and allocation controls originally scheduled to expire in September.

February

Western coal miners accept 37 percent increase in wages over next three years.

GM and Ford rebate plans announced.

Federal loan guarantee for Chrysler raised to $1.2 billion.

President Reagan reveals program for economic recovery.

Asks for cuts in eighty-three federal programs.

March

President Reagan announces plans to cut taxes and the budget by $130.5 billion.

United Mine Workers strike the coal industry.

After reaching a high of $40 per ounce in January, silver stabilizes at $12 per ounce.

April

Peace talks between Iraq and Iran fail.

May

OPEC fails to agree on uniform price schedule. OPEC officials freeze prices at current level.

Japan agrees to limit car exports to the U.S. from April 1, 1981 to March 1983, after U.S. officials threaten to impose quotas limiting Japanese imports.

Surcharge raised by the Fed from 3 percent to 4 percent.

June

AIDS first identified.

United Mine Workers ratify forty-month contract with coal mining industry. 38 percent increase in compensation. Ends strike that began February 10, 1981.

Dollar reaches highest level in international trading since December 1971.

July

Social Security checks increased by 11.2 percent, due to cost-of-living adjustment.

U.S. dollar hits new high exchange rate against European currencies.

Canadian dollar closes at 80.9 U.S. cents. Lowest rate since 1931.

FHLB board allows federal S&Ls to issue graduated-payment adjustable mortgage loans.

Congress passes Reagan's tax-cut legislation; expected to save taxpayers $750 billion over five years.

August

Professional Air Traffic Controller's Organization begins a nationwide strike.

President Reagan announces the strikers have to return to work by August 5 or face dismissal.

Federal Aviation Administration accepts applications for new air traffic controllers.

President Reagan signs the Economic Recovery Act of 1981.

Both the tax- and budget-cut bills become law.

Windfall profits tax reduced.

September

Federal Reserve cuts surcharge from 4 to 3 percent.

October

Egyptian President Sadat assassinated.

Federal Labor Relations Authority decertified Professional Air Traffic Controllers Organization.

Introduction of All Savers Certificates with tax-exempt yields tied to market rates.

Federal employees received 4.8 percent general pay increase plus regular step increases.

Military pay increased 14.3 percent.

Federal Reserve cuts surcharge from 3 to 2 percent.

November

Federal Reserve eliminates 2.00 percent surcharge. Basic discount rate unaffected.

December

Many durable goods producers announce extension of holiday shutdowns into January 1982.

1982

January

Economic Recovery Tax Act of 1981 mandates a series of tax rate reductions for 1982–1984.
Congress approves this three-year 25-percent reduction in personal and business income taxes.
Social Security wage base raised from $29,000 to $32,400.
Tax rate increased from 6.65 to 6.70 percent.
AT&T agrees to divest itself of twenty-two Bell Telephone operating systems.

March

Reagan administration announces economic sanctions against Libya.
U.S. Gold Commission reports to Congress. Official holdings of 264 million ounces should not be cut to zero; minority favors no change.

April

Japan renews its ceiling of 1.68 million auto exports to U.S.
Unemployment rate in U.S. hits 9 percent in March; ties post–WWII high of May 1975.
U.S. consumer price index falls 0.3 percent in March; first decline in seventeen years.

May

U.S. unemployment rate reached 9.4 percent—a post–WWII record.

June

Iran demands $150 billion in war reparations; pledges war until Iraq's Hussein stands trial.
April sales of new one-family homes at lowest level since series started in 1963.

Raw steel plant operating rate 42.5 percent; lowest rate since 1938; continues decline for remainder of the year.

U.S. Commerce Department determines imported foreign steel received government subsidies.

French franc devalued by 6 percent and Italian lira by 3 percent.

July

10 percent personal income tax rate becomes effective.

Social Security benefits increased by 7.4 percent.

August

Mexico announces serious problems servicing its foreign debt. Marks the onset of the Latin American debt crisis. In following months, the IMF supports major adjustment programs in Mexico and other nations.

Unemployment rate reaches 9.8 percent in July; highest level since 9.9 percent rate in 1941.

Bull market begins on Wall Street. Inflation rate falls to 6.1 percent.

Stock market trading soars to a record 132,690,000 shares.

September

Tax Equity and Fiscal Responsibility Act raises taxes by cutting loopholes. Eliminates about one-third of 1981 corporate tax cuts. Raises taxes by $37.5 billion per year.

Highway Revenue Act raises the gasoline tax by another $3.3 billion.

October

Federal employees receive 4 percent general pay increase in addition to annual step increase.

Military pay also increased 4 percent.

In November, Social Security will borrow for the first time.

Monetary aggregates still important but no longer dominant in monetary policy.

November

Voluntary restrictions on steel exports from the European Community to the U.S. put in effect.

Ford announces plans to close California auto assembly operations due to import competition.

Housing market picks up just as general recession came to an end.

December

Introduction of money market deposit accounts by banks and S&Ls.
Unemployment rate hits 10.8 percent, the highest rate since 1940.
Federal fuel tax on gasoline and diesel increased by five cents.

1983

January

Super NOW accounts introduced.
Independent truckers strike begins.
Public Power Supply System of Washington state defaults on $2.25 billion in bonds. Worst government failure in U.S. history.

February

Independent truckers strike ends.
United American Bank of Knoxville, Tennessee, declared insolvent; deposits of $760 million.
Toyota/GM agree to build small car in late 1984. FTC approves the venture on December 22, 1983.

March

Oil glut takes hold. Demand falls as a result of conservation, use of other fuels, and recession.
European Monetary System (EMS) experiences reserve loss problems.
Heavy reserve losses experienced by the weak currencies in the EMS.
Severe restrictions on currency transactions imposed by weak-currency countries.
Fixed foreign exchange rates realigned and austerity programs proposed. Hardly sufficient.

April

U.S. Embassy in Beirut almost totally destroyed by car bomb; sixty-three killed, including seventeen Americans.
Iraq increases missile attacks on Iran.

July

U.S. threatens action to preserve navigation in the Persian Gulf.

August

Communications Workers of America and two other unions strike AT&T. Ends on August 28.

Persistent and substantial strength of the dollar once again becomes an issue of policy importance. Brings about intervention in foreign exchange market by several governments, including U.S.

September

IMF/World Bank meetings focus on solutions to financial difficulties of several nations.

October

Massive car-bomb explosion destroys U.S. Marine headquarters in Beirut.
Interest rate ceiling adjustments implemented.

November

Strike called against Greyhound Lines. Ends December 21.

December

Joint U.S.-Japanese auto venture by GM and Toyota approved by the Federal Trade Commission.
FHA mortgage interest rates start to float. VA rates were still pegged.

1984

January

Breakup of AT&T becomes effective. Company broken up into twenty-four independent units.
U.S. stock market begins a seven-month decline of 15 percent.

February

Contemporaneous reserve accounting, required by Fed, excludes small, deposit-taking institutions.
Iranian and Iraqi armies inflict more than 25,000 fatalities on each other.

March

Reagan ends U.S. role in Beirut by relieving Sixth Fleet from peacekeeping force.
Monetary aggregates' policy importance declines.

April

President Reagan calls for international ban on chemical weapons.

May

President Reagan rules out U.S. military intervention in Iran-Iraq war.

July

Democrats nominate Walter Mondale for president and Geraldine Ferraro for
vice president.

August

Republicans renominate President Reagan and Vice President Bush.

September

Hotel and restaurant strike in San Francisco; starts September 3, ends December 7.
UAW-GM strike; starts September 15, ends October 14.

October

Norway and Britain cut oil prices in response to falling spot market. Nigeria
follows, renewing pressure on OPEC prices.
Chinese Communist party announces economic reforms. Plans to lift government price subsidies. Promises to relax party control over enterprises.

November

Ronald Reagan re-elected president. Wins in a landslide with 59 percent of the
vote.
U.S. and Iraq resume diplomatic relations after President Reagan meets with
Deputy PM Aziz.

1985

January

Federal price controls removed from about half the natural gas produced in
the U.S.

February

Prime Minister Thatcher addresses U.S. Congress. Endorses Reagan's policies.

March

Home State Savings Bank in Cincinnati closed.
Seventy Ohio thrift institutions closed to prevent run on deposits.
Auto manufacturers initiate low-interest loan programs.

April

Controversy in West Germany sharpens over President Reagan's impending
  state visit.

May

U.S. financial firm E.F. Hutton pleads guilty to charges it carried out check-kiting
  scam.
May 17: United Airlines Air Pilots Association goes on strike. Strike ends June 14.
May 20: DJIA closes above 1,300 for the first time.
President Reagan's tax reform plan is unveiled.

June

OPEC output falls to twenty-year low of 13.7 MMB/D.
Israeli army pulls out of Lebanon after 1099 days of occupation.

July

8,200 steelworkers on strike at Wheeling Pittsburgh—industry's first major
  walkout in 26 years.
OPEC loses customers to cheaper North Sea oil. More OPEC price cuts.
Conventional mortgage rates fall to 12.03 percent average—lowest since
  October 1979.

August

GM announces 7.7 percent financing rate program to run through October 2.
Ford and Chrysler announce incentive plans including low interest loans,
  rebates on 1985 autos.

September

Farm Credit System asks for a Federal bailout of its $74 billion loan portfolio.
Plaza Accord called by Secretary of the Treasury Baker. G-5 meets at Plaza
  Hotel in New York.
Purposes of Accord: Adjust trade imbalances and better reflect economic fun-
  damentals.
Wants other currencies to appreciate against the dollar, and head off restrictive
  U.S. legislation.
Helps create panic in foreign exchange market, especially over the weekend in
  Tokyo.

October

Bank of Japan moves interest rates higher to strengthen the yen against the dollar.

November

November 7: DJIA closes above 1,400 for the first time.

President Regan and Soviet Union leader Gorbachev meet for the first time. Agree to step up arms control talks and renew cultural contacts.

Since September G-5 meeting, the Federal Reserve purchased more than $2 billion of foreign currencies.

December

OPEC output hits 18 MMB/D; causes a glut and triggers a price war.

IMF and World Bank leadership expresses broad support for debt initiative proposed by U.S.

Known as the Baker Plan, it calls for comprehensive adjustment measures by debtors; increased and more effective structural lending by multilateral development banks; expanded lending by commercial banks.

President Reagan signs budget deficit bill into law. Raises debt ceiling to $2 trillion.

Gramm-Rudman Amendment raises the debt ceiling passed into law; sets annual deficit targets through 1991.

President Reagan signs farm subsidy bill; creates a five-year plan to bail out Farm Credit System.

Many banks and S&Ls go bankrupt in Texas, Oklahoma, and other oil states; results of pressure from collapsing world oil prices.

1986

January

Spain and Portugal joined European Economic Community.

President Reagan freezes Libyan assets in the U.S.

Ceiling on Super NOW accounts removed.

United Steel workers agree to allow rank-and-file members to vote on labor contracts.

G-5 meets. No plans laid to push interest rates down on a coordinated basis.

February

Gramm-Rudman ruled unconstitutional by a district court; however, could remain in force until ruled upon by Supreme Court.

March

March 3: the DJIA closes above 1,700 for the first time.

March 21: the DJIA closes above 1,800 for the first time.

Yields on 10-year Treasury notes fall to below 8.0 percent for the first time in eight years.

April

Soviet nuclear plant at Chernobyl destroyed by fire; incites world-wide concerns.

Interest ceilings on passbook savings accounts ended.

U.S. dollar reaches a post–WWII low against the yen at 168.60.

Fed Chairman Volcker warns that public and private debt buildup is a threat to the economy.

May

U.S. dollar falls to 159.95 yen.

U.S. proposes 35 percent tariff on Canadian cedar shakes/shingles; leads to trade dispute with Canada.

June

Communications Workers of America strike at AT&T from June 1 through June 26.

State and local government purchases of non-marketable Treasury securities continue to boom.

July

Iran threatens missile attack on any Gulf state that supports Iraq.

Brent prices dipped under $9 per barrel. OPEC production rose to 20 MMB/D.

Supreme Court rules Gramm Rudman Hollings unconstitutional.

President Reagan signs into law economic program calling for spending curbs and higher taxes. Purpose is to reduce projected federal budget deficit by $496 billion over a five-year period.

August

House votes arms appropriations bill; rejects administration's "Star Wars" policy.

United Steelworkers strike for the first time since 1959. 44,000 workers involved.

GM introduces incentive program to lure consumers; unprecedented loan rate of 2.9 percent.

September

On September 4, stock market prices soar; DJIA jumps 38.38 points; closes at record 1919.17.

On September 11, the DJIA plummets a record 86.61—or 4.61 percent—to 1792.89.

October

Congress approves immigration bill barring hiring of illegal aliens, but with amnesty provision.

President Reagan signs tax reform bill: first full scale modification since 1954. Goals: to simplify tax code, broaden tax base, eliminate many tax shelters and other preferences. Top tax rate lowered from 50 to 28 percent and bottom rate raised from 11 to 15 percent. Capital gains face the same tax rate as ordinary income.

Interest on consumer loans such as credit card debt no longer deductible for federal tax purposes.

State and local sales taxes and income taxes no longer deductible for federal tax purposes.

Income averaging eliminated, but personal exemption and standard deductions increased.

Kaiser Foundation Hospital, Permanente Medical Group, and Foundation Health Plan go on strike on October 27.

State and local governments' purchase of non-marketable Treasuries made less attractive.

November

Democrats triumph in elections; gain eight seats to win Senate majority.

Diversion of funds from arms sales to Nicaraguan Contras revealed.

U.S. and Japan reach agreement for increased cooperation. Indicate that current level of dollar/yen was consistent with underlying fundamentals. U.S. apparently committed to stop pushing down the dollar if Japan would stimulate its economy.

Savings bond rate drops from 7.50 to 6.00 percent; only new issues affected.

December

Kaiser group strike ends on December 13.

U.S. international indebtedness reaches $269 billion.

1987

January

OPEC price accord begins to deteriorate.

U.S. November 1986 trade deficit shockingly high at $19.2 billion.

Fannie Mae raises mortgage ceiling to $153,100 from $133,250.

January 8: the DJIA tops the 2,000 mark.

January 19: the DJIA tops the 2,100 mark.

Dollar falls to record low against the yen—150.49 to the dollar.

January 22: the DJIA posts a record 51.60 gain to a new high of 2,145.67.

February

February 5: the DJIA tops the 2,200 mark.

Japanese investors a major factor in all three Treasury auctions in the February refunding.

Brazil suspends interest payments on commercial debt.

Low interest rates and low oil prices combine with weak dollar to boost U.S. corporate profits.

February 22: G-7 nations in the Louvre Accord pledge to take fundamental action; try to develop policies to correct the low price of the U.S. dollar.

Accord wants to encourage expansion, stimulate trade, and produce exchange rate stability.

Central banks intervene unsuccessfully in foreign exchange market in support of the dollar.

OPEC majors stick to a fixed-exchange rate approach, which proves to be a mistake.

March

Fannie Mae announces it will not enter home equity loan market.

On March 20, the DJIA average tops the 2,300 mark.

On March 24, the U.S. dollar falls to a post–WWII low—148.5 yen to the dollar.

On March 29, the U.S. announces trade sanctions against Japan due to dumping charges on computer chips.

Bank of Japan is joined by other major central banks in its effort to stabilize the dollar. Intervention dictated by an understanding at the G-7 meeting in February.

April

April 6: the DJIA tops the 2,400 mark.

May

Modest moves made by Japan and Germany to lower interest rates.

Japan attempts to reduce dollar/yen speculation by Japanese traders.

Uncertainties abound as to what will happen at the upcoming June 8–10 G-7 meeting.

Immigration amnesty program brought into effect.

Farm Credit System formally asks Congress for a $6 billion loan from the Treasury.

June

Penalties enacted for employers of illegal aliens.

Paul Volcker announces he will leave the Federal Reserve; has been chairman since August 1979. Among his problems, individual Board members often

had strong and conflicting views, and showed no reluctance to differ in
public about monetary policy issues.

Upcoming debt ceiling problem. On July 17 ceiling reverted to well below
amount outstanding.

July

President Reagan says Iran-Contra arms policy went astray, and he accepts
responsibility.

On July 17: the DJIA closed over 2,500 for the first time.

August

On August 10, the DJIA closed over 2,600 for the first time.

Alan Greenspan sworn in as chairman of the Federal Reserve Board; attends
first FOMC meeting on August 17.

On August 17, the DJIA closes at a new high of 2,700.

September

Foreign investors have become a very large factor in the long end of the Treasury market.

October

Government bond market deteriorates for the ninth week in a row.

Long bond rates move above 10 percent, and yet the rate of inflation is between
4 and 5 percent and improving.

On October 14, the DJIA falls a record 95 points.

On October 15, the DJIA falls 58 points.

On October 16, the DJIA falls a record 108 points.

On October 19, the DJIA falls a record 508 points for a 22.6 percent one-day
drop and a cumulative four-day decline of 769 points. Computerized program trading and economic factors blamed for the crash. Panic atmosphere
in stock market; Fed's short term objective was to ensure adequate liquidity.

On October 21, the DJIA rallies a record 187 points.

In early trading on October 19, the 30-year Treasury yields 10.375 percent; in
early trading on Friday, October 23, it yields below 9 percent.

No single factor causes "black Monday." Fed firming a factor but not a key
causative force.

Keys: unsustainable stock prices, trade deficit, dollar concerns, comments by
public officials.

Impact on real economy from stock market debacle proves to be surprisingly
short-lived.

November

On November 2, the dollar falls to a forty-year low of 136.95 yen, maintaining a steady, 2.5 year downward trend. Since early March 1985, the dollar has declined more than 50 percent against yen and European currencies; hits postwar lows against yen and mark.

On November 20, Congress arrives at a compromise on Gramm-Rudman; no one completely satisfied; many totally dissatisfied; agreement lacks substance. Plan allows some painful spending decisions to be avoided.

Other G-7 nations want U.S. to deal with its own budget deficit before stimulating their economies.

December

IMF establishes Enhanced Structural Adjustment Facility (ESAF); provides resources to low-income members having strong three-year macro and structural programs.

1988

January

U.S. and Canada reach free trade agreement.

Members of the G-7 lay a bear trap for those who "shorted" the dollar.

On January 4, the trap is sprung with official intervention giving the dollar substantial support.

February

The NYSE announces circumstances under which it would curb the use of its electronic trading system, that is, when DJIA increases or falls more than fifty points in one day.

At its December 15–16 FOMC meeting, the Fed states it would gradually return to normal operating procedures, which were abandoned after October 19 stock market crash in an attempt to stabilize the markets.

March

Texas financial institutions, not just banks, also encountering financial problems, due mainly to weakness in local economies; primarily energy, real estate, agriculture.

Television writers go on strike (from March 7 to August 7).

April

World Bank affiliate—Multilateral Investment Guarantee Agency (MIGA)—is formally established. Intended to supplement national and private agencies, and support foreign direct investment.

In his first eight months as chairman of the Fed, Greenspan has made an unusually large number of policy adjustments. Firming, easing, and then firming policy from August 1987 to April 1988.

June

EEC again seeks limits on China's textile exports.

July

Iran accepts cease fire agreement.
Democrats nominate Michael Dukakis for president, Lloyd Bentsen for vice president.
Dollar strengthens substantially. Shift in Japanese attitudes primarily responsible.
European central banks believe the dollar's improvement is too great. Intervene in market.

August

Republicans nominate George H.W. Bush for president, Dan Quayle for vice president.

September

Technical corrections bill to the Tax Reform Act proposed. Attached to the bill was removal of the ceiling on outstanding Treasury bonds.

November

George H.W. Bush elected President. Republicans sweep forty states.
Economic recovery in its sixth year, yet budget deficit picture shows no improvement.

December

In response to concerns about inflation and rapid economic growth, foreign central banks raise interest rates; the dollar strengthens significantly.

1989

January

Recent economic indicators give no indication of a recession in 1989; causes a number of economists to push their recession forecast from 1989 to 1990.
Comprehensive free trade agreement between the U.S. and Canada signed.

Chairman Greenspan testifies before House Banking Committee. Asserts that the current rate of inflation (between 4 and 5 percent) is unacceptable; does not say what rate is acceptable.

February

Gramm-Rudman budget deficit targets unrealistic. Leads to putting spending programs—such as the rescue of the savings and loan industry—off budget.

March

On March 4, the International Association of Machinists strike Eastern Airlines.
Exxon Valdez runs aground on Bligh Reef in Alaska, spilling eleven-million gallons of oil. Oil prices react to news of the spill and to potential shortages on the West Coast.

April

Increases in the German discount rate and Lombard rate take markets by surprise.
New German finance minister announces he wants to suspend 10 percent withholding tax. Wants to wait until a "European solution" can be found.
Dollar trades near the top end of its acceptable G-7 range.

May

More than one million demonstrate in Beijing. Chaos spreads throughout China. Thousands killed in Tiananmen Square as Chinese leaders take a hard line towards demonstrators.
Mikhail Gorbachev named Soviet president.
IMF strengthens its strategy for dealing with debt problems in developing countries, based in part on proposals by Treasury Secretary Brady, called the "Brady Plan." Countries with strong adjustment programs gain access to IMF resources, to be used for debt or debt-service reduction.
West Germany and Japan experience political turmoil. Japan has Recruit scandal and Germany sees its ruling coalition lose popularity in the polls.
Three areas hurt the U.S. economy—autos, housing, and defense.

July

Chairman Greenspan presents his semi-annual testimony before Congress. Indicates risk of recession has replaced inflation as the Fed's number one concern. Nevertheless, inflation still remains a serious problem.

August

Measures to rescue the savings and loan industry signed into law by President Bush.

October

On October 4, the International Association of Machinists strike Boeing.
Minimum wage increased from $3.35 per hour to $3.80.
Dollar stronger than G-7 desires. Results in a coordinated intervention with dollars being sold.
October 13: U.S. stock market plummets, due to concerns about junk bonds and leveraged balance sheets; this causes a rush to quality which pushes Treasury yields sharply lower. Much of the lost ground is regained in the following week.

November

Deng Xiaoping resigns from China's leadership.
After twenty-eight years, East Germany opens Berlin Wall and its borders.
U.S. economy continues to show strength in some areas but weakness in others.
Strike by International Association of Machinists against Boeing ends on November 20.
Federal Reserve eases policy despite large monthly increases in core CPI.

December

Bundesbank intervenes in foreign exchange market; sells dollars. Amounts not very large.

1990

January

Campeau Corp. files for Chapter 11 bankruptcy protection.
Biggest World Bank loan—$1.26 billion—approved for Mexico to support debt reduction.
Japan aggressively supports its currency in the foreign exchange market, with limited success.
Rates on 10-year Japanese government bonds exceed 1 percent, but market rallies late in month.

February

Soviet Communists relinquish exclusive power over government.
Greenspan states that some leading economic indicators suggest a 10 to 20 percent chance of recession.

Refcorp working capital needs over the next year expected to decline.

Drexel Burnham Lambert Inc. files for Chapter 11 bankruptcy protection.

March

Recent elections in East Germany accelerate the process of German reunification. Timetable for monetary unification actively discussed. East German central bank would surrender sovereignty over monetary policy to Bundesbank.

Japan's 1-percent increase in discount rate seen by some as too little too late.

Controversy in UK on imposition of community tax to replace real estate tax as revenue source.

Amalgamated Transit Union strikes Greyhound Lines, Inc.

April

Many U.S. banks more concerned with capital ratios than growth turn down credit risks that previously were acceptable.

Quarterly plant and equipment survey published by the government is surprisingly strong. Real increase in plant and equipment spending expected to be 7.6 percent in 1990.

Employment cost index disturbing; data suggest upward pressure on core inflation.

Federal minimum wage raised from $3.35 to $3.80 per hour.

June

U.S.-Soviet summit reaches armaments accord.

10-year Japanese government bond rates move up substantially, from 6.96 to 7.34 percent, in a period of eleven days.

July

Western Alliance ends cold war and proposes joint action with Soviet Union and Eastern Europe.

Greenspan comments that the Fed was considering easing monetary policy, in response to banks imposing tougher lending standards; indicates that the balance of risk had changed.

Funds to be sequestered in mid-October if fiscal 1991 deficit estimate is above Gramm-Rudman target. In previous year, 74 percent of non-defense spending and 35 percent of defense spending was exempt.

August

Iraq invades Kuwait. President Bush orders troops to Saudi Arabia.

OPEC nears informal agreement. Raises output to cover 4 MMB/D shortage due to invasion. Cash market trading experiences abrupt decline.

In late August, dollar reaches record lows against several major currencies.

September

Oil markets surge on aggressive U.S. statements toward Iraq.
Reports that U.S. refinery problems will lead to a 200,000 B/D loss in capacity.
Aggressive remarks by Saddam Hussein send crude prices to new highs.
Crude prices outpace increases in product prices; there is talk of cutting refinery runs.
Saddam Hussein states a willingness to strike first; intends to damage oil fields in the region.

October

East and West Germany reunited.
U.S. employment cost index increases 5.2 percent over the last twelve months.

November

Republicans receive a setback in midterm elections.
Gorbachev assumes emergency powers.
Margaret Thatcher resigns as British Prime Minister. Succeeded by John Major.
IMF approves temporary expansion of fund facilities, to support countries affected by Middle East crisis resulting from Iraq's occupation of Kuwait.
Soviet Union reluctant to endorse the use of force against Iraq.
Gramm-Rudman law extended to 1995 rather than expiring in 1993.
New procedures place caps on domestic discretionary spending. Puts entitlement and revenue legislation on a pay-as-you-go basis.
New deficit-reduction targets set, reflecting an upward revision in the estimated deficit. To enforce discretionary spending caps, budget package has a sequestration process. President Bush signs bill to reduce the budget deficit $500 billion over five years.
Index of leading indicators declines for the fourth month in a row.

December

President Bush reiterates his "no concessions" stance against Iraq.
Federal gasoline tax increased five cents a gallon.
Weakness in real estate spreading. What was primarily a New England and Mid-Atlantic problem spreads to other regions.
Federal Reserve cuts bank reserve requirements by $11 billion.

1991

January

Congress approves using force in Iraq.
On January 16, the U.S. begins military action against Iraq called Desert Storm.

President Bush directs a drawdown of SPR. U.S. Energy Secretary Watkins orders 33.75 MMB draw down. Oil prices drop $9 to $10 per barrel in one day. Had risen $3 to $5 per barrel in first half of January.

Kuwaiti oil facilities destroyed by Iraq. Iraqi missile attacks launched against Saudi Arabia.

DOE selects thirteen firms to purchase 17.3 MMB of SPR crude.

February

Warsaw Pact dissolves military alliance.

Surplus of unsold oil held by oil producers reached 80–90 MMB.

First SPR oil delivered to commercial buyers.

On February 27, President Bush orders a cease fire in the war against Iraq.

On February 28, the war ends. U.N. troops moved into Kuwait City.

Carter Hawley Hale files for bankruptcy protection.

April

European Bank for Reconstruction and Development (EBRD) opens for business. Helps former centrally planned states of Eastern Europe, former Soviet Union, and Yugoslavia.

Federal minimum wage raised from $3.80 to $4.25 per hour.

On April 17, the DJIA average closes above 3,000 for the first time.

July

Warsaw Pact dissolved.

Boris Yeltsin inaugurated as first freely elected president of the Russian Republic.

Bush-Gorbachev summit negotiates strategic arms reduction treaty.

August

China accepts nuclear nonproliferation treaty.

Lithuania, Estonia, and Latvia win independence. President Bush recognizes them.

Unsuccessful coup attempted against Soviet President Gorbachev. Minimal effect on oil market.

October

Soviet Union suspends petroleum product exports as its fuel shortage grows.

November

Last of Kuwait oil well fires extinguished by control teams.

U.S. Senate filibuster causes withdrawal of Alaskan National Wildlife Refuge pro-leasing bill.

December

Soviet Union breaks up after President Gorbachev's resignation. Precipitated by Ukrainian vote for independence. Leads to formation of Commonwealth of Independent States (CIS).

GM announced plans to close twenty-one plants and cut 74,000 jobs by the end of 1995.

President Bush signs bill appropriating $25 billion to cover losses in the failure of S&Ls.

1992

January

Yugoslav Federation breaks up.
R.H. Macy files for Chapter 11 bankruptcy protection.
Trans World Airlines files for bankruptcy protection.

February

Bush and Yeltsin proclaim formal end to Cold War.
U.S. lifts trade sanctions against China.
Treaty on European Union signed at Maastricht, includes agreement for qualified countries to proceed to Economic and Monetary Union (EMU). Default date of January 1999.

Provision made for mutation of national central banks into European System of Central Banks.

Headed by European Central Bank (ECB). Able to call an initial amount of investment.

Initial country investment Ecu 50 bln (Euro 50 bln) of gold and foreign reserve assets.

Reserve management of ESCB banks subject to guidelines issued by ECB council.

March

CIS announces that 1991 crude exports dropped by 52 percent.

April

IMF approves membership for countries of the former Soviet Union.

June

Russian Federation joins the IMF, the World Bank, and the IDA.
Last western hostages freed in Lebanon.

July

Democrats nominate Bill Clinton for president and Al Gore for vice president.

August

IMF approves first stand-by arrangement of approximately $1.04 billion for Russia.

North American trade compact announced.

Republicans renominate George H.W. Bush and Dan Quayle.

GM closes Van Nuys plant which employed 2,600; plant was Southern California's last remaining auto factory.

September

U.N. expels Serbian-dominated Yugoslavia.

October

Senate ratifies second Strategic Arms Limitation Treaty.

OPEC production reaches highest level in more than a decade at 25 MMB/D.

November

Bill Clinton elected president; Al Gore vice president.

Democrats keep control of Congress.

Russian Parliament approved START Treaty.

U.S. forces leave the Philippines. Ends nearly a century of American military presence.

Czechoslovak Parliament approves separation into two nations.

December

U.S., Mexico, and Canada signed NAFTA (North American Free Trade Agreement).

1993

January

Inter-American Development Bank affiliate, the Multilateral Investment Fund (MIF), established.

Purpose is to promote investment reforms and encourage private sector development.

February

President Clinton announces economic plan which cuts defense spending by $188 billion from 1994 through 1998.
Bomb blast at New York's World Trade Center.

March

Department of Defense announces plans to close thirty-one major military bases; seven in California.

May

British Commons approves European unity pact.

July

Iraq accepted U.N. weapons monitoring.
Oil prices plunge.

August

Israeli-Palestinian accord reached.
President Clinton signs his economic program bill; calls for spending curbs and higher taxes, and attempts to reduce projected federal budget deficit by $496 billion over a five-year period.

September

President Clinton announces $3.5 million in humanitarian assistance to Vietnam. Allows American corporations to bid on IMF/World Bank contracts for Vietnam.

October

Yeltsin's forces crush revolt in Russian parliament.
China breaks nuclear test moratorium.

November

Europe's Maastricht Treaty takes effect, creating European Union.
Jean Chretien sworn in as Canada's twentieth prime minister.
North American Free Trade Agreement (NAFTA) is passed.
OPEC overproduction, surging North Sea output, and weak demand lower oil prices.

December

Japan and U.S. agree on a plan to open Japan's markets to imports.

1994

January

Serb's heavy weapons pound Sarajevo.

February

President Clinton ends trade embargo on Vietnam.

March

Four convicted in the 1993 World Trade Center bombing.
March 21 through April 4: Stock market sell-off reduces DJIA 9.7 percent from
  its January peak.

April

Treasury 30-year bond yields 7.42 percent; up from 5.79 percent in October 1993.

August

Irish Republican Army declares cease-fire in Northern Ireland.

October

U.S. sends forces to the Persian Gulf.
Ulster Protestants declare cease-fire.
Israel and Jordan sign peace treaty.

November

President Clinton orders Bosnian arms embargo ended.
Former President Reagan reveals he has Alzheimer's disease.
Republicans win control of both the House and the Senate.

December

Russians attack secessionist Republic of Chechnya.
Rumors surface that Orange County, California main fund faces $1.5 billion in
  losses due to higher interest rates. County files for bankruptcy under
  Chapter 9 provisions. Caused by leverage strategy.

Congress approves the General Agreement on Tariffs and Trade (GATT).

President Clinton approves tariff-cutting provisions of the Uruguay Round of GATT. Cuts tariffs globally by roughly 40 percent and extends intellectual property rights. Tightens rules on investment and trade in services.

1995

January

Mexico attempts to secure U.S. Congressional approval for $40 billion of loan guarantees.

Mexico pledges $7 billion per year in profits from state-owned Pemex oil-revenue.

Clinton invokes emergency powers; extends $20 billion loan to Mexico; currency swaps announced. Props up Mexican peso. Plan utilizes existing authority and involves international agencies. Peso has been devalued by more than 40 percent against the U.S. dollar since early December 1994.

U.S. trade deficit soars 68 percent to $12.2 billion.

February

Britain and Ireland unveil "Framework Document" for political settlement in Northern Ireland.

British merchant bank Barings PLC collapses. Trader in Singapore office lost more than $1 billion on Japanese securities.

On February 24, DJIA closes above 4,000 for the first time.

March

China and U.S. reach agreement further opening Chinese markets to U.S. agriculture products.

Discussions on allowing U.S. telecommunications and insurance services into China.

Border controls between seven EU countries disappear as Schengen agreement came into force.

U.S. trade deficit soars by 68 percent to monthly record of $12.2 billion in January.

Senate rejects balanced-budget amendment.

April

U.N. Council votes to ease some sanctions against Iraq.

Dollar hits post–WWII low against the yen and the deutschemark.

Car bomb devastates federal building in Oklahoma City, killing at least 167 people.

President Clinton announces cutoff of all trade by U.S. companies with Iran.

May

Start of major flare-up in Bosnian war. NATO launches air strikes near Pale.
Serbs retaliate by shelling U.N. safe areas; 68 killed in Tuzla.
NASA intends to cut 28,860 jobs, consolidate space-shuttle activities under
   single contractor.

June

Exxon signs a $15.2 billion deal to develop oil and gas fields near Russia's
   Sakhalin Island.

July

Venezuela approves first investment law allowing foreign participation in oil
   exploration and production.
President Clinton signs bill cutting $16.3 billion from spending.
Fed initiates announcement of funds rate target and specific rates in press
   release following FOMC meeting.

August

Iran unable to sell 200,000 barrels per day of crude since unilateral embargo by
   U.S.

September

France explodes nuclear device in Pacific; wide-spread protests follow.
Israel and PLO sign agreement in Washington. Extends Palestinian rule to most
   of West Bank.

October

Warring parties agree on cease-fire in Bosnia.
Quebec narrowly rejects independence from Canada.
Boeing Company union machinists go on strike.

November

Israeli Prime Minister Rabin assassinated as he leaves Tel Aviv peace rally.
Slack world oil demand, rising non-OPEC production, and weak prices.
President Clinton approves legislation lifting twenty-two year ban on oil
   exports from Alaska's North Slope. Legislation also waives royalty payments
   on deep water oil and gas leases in Gulf of Mexico.
U.S. budget impasse causes partial federal government shutdown. Furlough of
   nonessential federal employees begins on November 1; ends on November 19.
On November 20, DJIA tops 5,000.

December

Combatants sign Bosnia peace treaty.
President Clinton authorizes vanguard of U.S. troops to move into Bosnia.
Strikers at Caterpillar reject proposed six-year contract.
However, UAW union calls an end to seventeen-month walkout.
DJIA closes at 5,117.12 on, Friday, December 29; up 33.5 percent for year.

1996

January

France announces end to nuclear tests.
U.S. budget crisis in fourth month.
President Clinton approves resumption of many government operations.
Senate ratifies major arms-reduction treaty.
AT&T to eliminate at least 40,000 jobs over three years as part of a plan to split
    into three companies.

February

President Clinton signs a landmark telecommunications bill into law.

March

Britain alarmed by deadly "mad cow" disease.
IMF approves approximately $10.1 billion for Russia.
On March 6, UAW strike at GM brake-parts plant in Dayton; strike ends on
    March 22.

April

President Clinton signs line-item veto bill.
President Clinton approves sale of $227 million of crude from Strategic Petro-
    leum Reserve.
Gas prices at five-year high.

May

Chechnya peace treaty signed.
White House announces its decision to allow U.S. companies to purchase Iraqi
    oil exports.

June

China agrees to world ban on atomic testing.
Leaders in Balkans sign arms limitation accord.

Venezuela approves eight multi-billion dollar profit-sharing deals. Allows foreign oil companies to explore for and produce oil in Venezuela.

July

Boris Yeltsin reelected in Russia.

August

President Clinton signs bill to raise minimum wage.
Congress passes welfare reform bill; approved by Clinton.
Republicans nominate Bob Dole for president and Jack Kemp for vice president.
Democrats renominate Bill Clinton and Al Gore.
Sanctions imposed on non-U.S. companies investing over $40 million per year in Iran and Libya energy sectors. EU states its opposition to U.S. law; threatens retaliation.

September

IMF endorses a joint initiative for heavily indebted poor countries. Called the "HIPC Initiative."
Allows poorest nations to negotiate writing down debts in exchange for economic reforms.
President Clinton states that the UN oil-for-food sale should be postponed indefinitely.

October

Federal minimum wage raised from $4.25 to $4.75 per hour.
DJIA tops 6,000.

November

Clinton-Gore ticket wins national election. Republicans retain control of Congress.

December

Kofi Annan named U.N. Secretary General.
Many high-technology trade nations agree to abolish tariffs on computers and software-related goods.

1997

January

Mexico announces it will repay U.S. loan three years ahead of schedule.
IMF New Arrangements to Borrow (NAB). Twenty-five members agree to lend to IMF under certain circumstances, extra assistance when needed.

President Clinton starts his second term.

U.S. Treasury issues first inflation indexed notes in the amount of $7 billion with a ten-year maturity.

February

U.K. and France agree to freeze Nazis' gold.

Japan announces plans to cut import tariffs on crude oil and most petroleum products.

Qatar inaugurates the world's largest liquefied natural gas exporting facility.

U.S. foreign trade deficit hits an eight-year high.

On February 13, the DJIA tops the 7,000 mark.

March

Reinstatement of 10 percent federal tax on airline tickets.

April

U.S. Senate approves chemical-weapons treaty by a vote of 74 to 26.

U.S. unemployment rate falls to a twenty-four-year low.

Boeing wins an order from Russia's Aeroflot; first big push into a major untapped market.

First-quarter GDP grows at a robust 5.6 percent; biggest rise in consumer spending in ten years.

May

Russia's President Yeltsin signs Chechnya peace treaty.

Shortages push coffee prices to a twenty-year high.

June

EU bolsters currency merger.

Japan and U.S. announce new defense cooperation pact.

Thai finance minister resigns; Thai stock market drops to its lowest point in eight years. Thai central bank suspends operations of sixteen insolvent finance companies.

Hong Kong's Hang Seng index gains 647.87 points; largest point increase in a single day.

July

China regains sovereignty over Hong Kong after 155 years of British colonial rule.

Thailand government stops supporting its currency. Facing up to the cumulative effect of prolonged imprudent policies. Sparks a financial crisis that spread to other Asian countries. Effects of crisis eventually felt in Hong Kong, Korea, and around the world. Thailand allows baht to float. Leads to immediate depreciation of about 16 percent against the dollar. Asks IMF for assistance.

Malaysia's central bank intervenes heavily to defend its currency. Malaysian Prime Minister Mohamad attacks so-called rogue speculators.

Philippines central bank intervenes heavily to defend its currency. IMF offers the Philippines $1.1 billion to help support its currency.

White House and GOP agree on measures to balance the budget.

Congress passes the biggest tax reduction in sixteen years, including reductions in capital gains.

On July 16, the DJIA tops 8,000.

August

Thailand agrees to IMF rescue plan in return for a line of credit to bolster the economy. Thai central bank suspends operations of forty-eight finance companies. IMF approves a $17.2 billion standby credit for Thailand.

Bank Indonesia floats the rupiah, and the currency plunges.

President Clinton exercises new line-item veto power.

On Aug 4, the Teamsters Union goes on strike against United Parcel; strike ends on Aug 18.

September

Malaysia announces reversal of short-selling ban, postponement of major public works projects.

Chinese President Jiang Zemin called for sale of tens of thousands of state-controlled companies.

Indonesia says it will postpone projects worth almost $14 billion to help reduce its budget deficit.

October

On Oct 8, Indonesia requests help from the IMF.

On Oct 17, Taiwan stops supporting its currency, which immediately falls by 3.3 percent.

Oct 20–23, Hong Kong's stock index falls 23.3 percent.

Decline in value of Asian currencies shakes up world markets.

Oct 27—DJIA falls 554.26 points (7.18 percent), largest single-day decline. The next day, it rebounds by 337.17 points.

November

Yamaichi, Japan's fourth largest securities firm, shuts down. Largest post–WWII corporate failure. Discloses more than $2 billion of losses on unreported trading.

Japanese stock brokerage firm, Sanyo Securities, files for bankruptcy.

Senior finance ministers and central bank officials from fourteen Asia-Pacific nations meet in Manila. Agree on measures to counteract the currency crisis in East Asia.

South Korea asked for assistance from the IMF.

First time in four years OPEC agrees to an increase in its production ceiling.

GOP victorious in off-year elections.

December

EU plans to admit six nations.

Finance officials from fourteen Asia-Pacific nations met in Kuala Lumpur to discuss bailout fund, which would supplement IMF aid to Asian economies.

IMF agreed to $57 billion bailout package for South Korea. Stand-by arrangement was $21 billion. Largest financial commitment in IMF history.

South Korea unveils plan to stabilize financial markets.

Indonesian rupiah and Korean won lose more than half their value against the dollar in 1997.

In wake of financial crisis in Asia, the IMF establishes the Supplemental Reserve Facility (SRF); purpose is to help members cope with sudden and disruptive loss of market confidence.

SRF was activated to support the Stand-By Arrangement for Korea. Approximately $3.5 billion was made available to Korea under the SRF.

Delegates from 150 industrial countries reach agreement in Kyoto to control greenhouse gases.

U.S. would have to reduce greenhouse emissions by 7 percent below 1990 levels.

Europe would have to make cuts of 8 percent, and Japan 9 percent. Developing countries would be exempt.

1998

January

Indonesian President Suharto presents budget; ignores structural adjustment conditions required by IMF.

Suharto announces new IMF package; halts fifteen infrastructure projects. Indonesia guaranteed commercial bank obligations; debt payments frozen.

Japan indicates problem bank loans reported on September 30, 1997, total $577 billion, triple the previous estimate.

South Korea's creditors meet in New York; agree to restructure bank debt.

Thailand removes most foreign exchange controls imposed in May 1997.
President Clinton accused in White House sex scandal.
Bond prices surge; thirty-year Treasury bond to record low yield of 5.73 percent.
Comparable government bond yields reach their lowest levels since the 1960s.

February

Vietnam cuts the value of its currency by about 5 percent as part of gradual
   devaluation.
Japan announces fourth set of policy reforms since October 1997.
President Clinton outlines first balanced budget in thirty years.
On February 2, Standard & Poor stock index passes the 1,000 milestone for the
   first time.

March

IMF threatens to freeze $40 billion bailout package if Jakarta does not comply
   with IMF plan.
Japan's cabinet approves cash infusion of $10.95 billion to bail out seventeen
   banks.
Indonesia drops plans to implement currency board system.
NASD and AMEX boards agree to join the two securities markets.

April

Landmark peace settlement, the Good Friday Accord, reached in Northern Ireland.
Uganda is the first IMF member to receive debt relief.
Japanese Prime Minister Hashimoto announces income tax cut to boost con-
   sumer spending.
RHB Bank of Malaysia takes over failed Sime Bank.
U.S. trade deficit biggest in a decade.
DJIA tops the 9,000 mark.

May

Riots, arson, and looting, mainly targeting ethnic Chinese, break out in Jakarta.
   Banks and offices closed, Indonesian financial market inactive. Trading
   resumes after three days.
Europeans agree on a single currency.
Eleven countries confirm their participation in EMU: Austria, Belgium,
   Finland, France, Germany, Ireland, Italy, Luxembourg, Netherlands, Portugal,
   and Spain. To start January 1999.
Daimler Benz and Chrysler Corporation agree to merge.
Congress approves $216 billion surface-transportation bill.

June

Currencies and stock markets continue to fall throughout the Pacific Rim.

G-7 deputy finance ministers meet in Paris to discuss weak yen and Russia's troubled economy.

Yen falls to eight-year low of 144.75 to the dollar.

Heavy stock selling in South Korea pushes market to eleven-year low.

U.S. spends some $2 billion to support the yen, boosting it from 142 to 137 to the dollar.

The World Bank lends $300 million to Malaysia to help maintain social programs.

Deputy finance ministers from G-7 and Asian countries meet in Tokyo to discuss Asian crisis.

People's Bank of China closes Hainan Development Bank. First bank failure since PRC was founded

Japan announces plans for banking reform, including a "bridge bank."

World Bank and other international donors establish Development Recovery Program; purpose to help Indonesians hardest hit by currency crisis.

Indonesia signs revised IMF agreement, resulting in release of IMF funds.

Oil prices fall to their lowest levels in more than a decade.

Japan officially declares itself in a recession.

UAW strikes against GM. Strike lasts from June 5 to July 28.

July

IMF activates the General Arrangements to Borrow for the first time in twenty years.

Finances an $8.3 billion augmentation of the Extended Fund Facility Arrangement for Russia.

IMF agrees to provide Russia with an overall assistance package worth $14 billion.

ECB decides that 15 percent of its initial reserves of 39.5 billion euros will consist of gold. Will be transferred to the ECB on first day of 1999. Agrees that before year-end, it would adopt an ECB guideline.

ECB approval needed for all operations in foreign reserve assets left with national central banks.

Gold operations also require ECB approval.

Congress voted to overhaul the Internal Revenue Service.

On July 16, the NASDAQ composite index edges over 2,000 for the first time.

August

Indonesia partially defaults on sovereign debt repayments; meets interest but not principal.

Singapore stocks fall to lowest level in nearly ten years.

Hong Kong Monetary Authority intervenes in stock market. Buys $15.2 billion of shares in bid to punish speculators.

Unemployment in Hong Kong reached fifteen-year high at 4.8 percent.

Crisis in the Russian financial system leads world markets into turmoil.

Three-month moratorium on debt payments and over 50 percent devaluation of the ruble crush stock market.

On August 31, the DJIA falls 512.61 points. Wipes out year's gain.

NASDAQ composite falls 140.43, its worst point drop ever.

September

Malaysia announces measures to restrict convertibility of its currency.

Malaysia pegs exchange rate of ringgit at 3.8 to the dollar.

Stock Exchange of Singapore announces closure of trading in Malaysian shares.

Russia devalues currency and restricts international transactions, including debt repayments.

Financial firms lose more than $8 billion so far in the fallout from Russia's financial collapse.

Congress approves an $80 billion tax cut.

On September 30, DJIA falls 237.90 points.

October

At annual IMF/World Bank meetings, governors endorse concept of new financial architecture.

Main tenets—increased transparency and consolidation of banking supervision, along with cautious progress to liberalize capital movements and partnership with the private sector.

Japan announces $30 billion aid package for four Asian economies hit by the currency crisis.

Malaysian government bails out infrastructure conglomerate Renong group with $1.2 billion.

U.S. budget surplus the largest in three decades.

On October 15, the DJIA rose more than 330 points. Leads to rallies in European, Asian, and Latin American stock markets.

November

Brazil reaches pact with leading countries on $42 billion rescue package, aimed at preventing the financial crisis from spreading throughout South America.

Democrats unexpectedly gain five House seats in national election.

Republicans still in control of the House and Senate.

December

IMF activates New Arrangements to Borrow for the first time. Helps to finance an $18.1 billion stand-by arrangement for Brazil.

Japanese government takes control of insolvent Nippon Credit Bank.

Swaps of 20 percent of gold and U.S. dollar reserves deposited with European Monetary Institute unwound.

House panel drafts impeachment charges against Clinton; votes along party lines. Approves four articles of impeachment.

Clinton orders air strikes against Iraq.

House impeaches President Clinton along party lines on two charges—perjury and obstruction of justice.

U.S. lifts economic sanctions imposed on India and Pakistan in May in response to nuclear tests.

1999

January

New reserve currency—the euro—introduced. Creates a single market in Europe. Currency of reference for the eleven countries that participate in the European Monetary Union.

The ECB, which manages euro-area monetary policy, grants observer status in the IMF.

Quota contributions of IMF members are increased. Total quotas raised to 212,000 million in special drawing rights, or about $297 billion.

Transfer of 39.6 billion euros of gold and foreign exchange reserves to the ECB; 15 percent of this is gold.

Brazil devalues its currency, sending U.S. stocks into a freefall.

U.S. agrees to ease restrictions on Cuba.

February

Senate acquits President Clinton of impeachment charges.

March

Poland and Hungary join NATO.

NATO launches air strikes on Serbia to end attacks against ethnic Albanians in Kosovo.

Japanese government grants public funds to fifteen banks to help cover bad loans.

Japan agrees to lend to Indonesia and Thailand to help their recoveries.

Indonesia closes thirty-eight insolvent commercial banks and takes over seven others.

Japan presents budget in an effort to pull the country out of recession.

ADB approves $3.06 billion Asian Currency Crisis Support Facility to assist nations hit hard by crisis.

Thai cabinet announces economic stimulus package backed by Japan and the World Bank.

Bombing of Kosovo begins.

On March 29, DJIA closes over 10,000 for the first time.

April

IMF expands Supplemental Reserve Facility to provide Contingent Credit Lines for those members that have strong economic policies, but might be affected by financial contagion.

ECB cuts its key discount rate for the first time—from 3.00 to 2.50 percent.

DOE announces it will take oil deliveries under its plan to add 28 million barrels to strategic reserves: Phase 1—about 43,000 barrels per day purchased for three months; about 50 percent acquired to be imported. Phase 2—about 100,000 barrels per day purchased of royalty oil over a six-month period.

May

Japanese parliament passes bills to strengthen its security ties with the U.S.

DJIA tops 11,000 mark.

U.S. companies after-tax profits rise 4.3 percent in first quarter. Largest quarterly gain in four years.

June

Serbs sign agreement to pull troops out of Kosovo after eleven weeks of NATO air attacks.

Indonesia holds first free election in forty-four years.

August

Yeltsin replaces Prime Minister Stepashin with Vladimir Putin; fourth shake-up in seventeen months.

September

IMF adopts a one-time exceptional operation—off-market sales of up to 14 million ounces of gold. Part of a package to allow the IMF to finance its share of the enhanced HIPC (Heavily Indebted Poor Countries) Initiative.

Uranium processing plant in Japan leaks radiation. Worst nuclear accident since Chernobyl.

Central Bank Gold Agreement announced by fifteen European central banks.
European Monetary Union members, Sweden, Switzerland, and the U.K. make
    declaration that gold will remain the important element of global monetary
    reserves. Collectively they will cap their gold sales at about 400 tons per year
    over the next five years. Will not expand their gold leasings and use of gold
    futures and options.

October

Russia sends ground troops into Chechnya as conflict with Islamic militants
    intensifies.
Senate rejects 1996 nuclear test-ban treaty; international leaders upset by U.S.
    stand.

November

U.S. and China reach landmark trade agreement.
On November 2, NASDAQ closes above 3,000 for the first time.

December

President Yeltsin makes a surprise announcement—his immediate resignation.
    Vladimir Putin becomes acting president. Presidential elections to be held
    within ninety days.
Northern Ireland's government begins self-rule for the first time in twenty-five
    years.
From December 14, 1999, through April 5, 2000, IMF conducts seven off-mar-
    ket gold transactions with Brazil and Mexico; 12,944 million ounces sold
    and accepted back. Settlement of those members' obligations to the IMF.
    IMF retains book value of the gold (about $47 per ounce) and invests
    remainder. Proceeds help the IMF's contribution to HIPC debt relief and
    support for poorest countries.
Euro falls to parity with U.S. dollar for the first time.
Panama Canal Zone reverts to Panamanian sovereignty.
On December 29, NASDAQ closes above 4,000 for the first time.
Concerns about possible Y2K disruptions accelerate. Fears mount regarding
    the possible inability of some computers and control systems to recognize
    the year 2000.

2000

January

Y2K comes and goes with no significant problems.
On January 14, the DJIA hits a record high of 11,722.98.

February

U.S. jobless rate at 4 percent—lowest in three decades.

FERC (Federal Energy Regulatory Commission) issues changes extending the deregulation of the interstate natural gas pipeline system.

Wary investors cause stocks to plunge; the beginning of the end of the internet stock boom.

March

Putin elected president of Russia on first ballot; wins 53 percent of popular vote.

Japan's parliament enacts budget aimed at reviving economy.

ASEAN (Association of Southeast Asian Nations) finance ministers scrap idea of an Asian Monetary Fund. Decide to create regional financing arrangement, including Japan, China, and South Korea. Purpose was to help protect regional currencies.

Boeing engineers and technical workers returned to work after a forty-day strike; one of the biggest white-collar walkouts in U.S. history.

On March 10, NASDAQ hit record high of 5,048.62.

On March 16, the DJIA rose 499.19 points, biggest point gain on record.

April

President Clinton signs bill allowing older people to work and not lose Social Security benefits.

One of worst weeks on Wall Street—DJIA down 5.5 percent; NASDAQ down nearly 10 percent.

Employment cost index jumps 1.4 percent in first quarter; sharpest increase in eleven years.

May

Israeli troops withdraw from Lebanese security zone after twenty-two years of occupation.

Indonesia signs letter of intent with IMF. Promises to continue economic reforms in return for IMF loans.

Beijing reaches trade agreement with EU. Paves way for China's entry into WTO.

United States grants China permanent most-favored-nation trading status.

U.S. April unemployment rate falls below 4 percent.

June

Britain restores parliamentary powers to Northern Ireland after Sinn Fein agrees to disarm.

U.S. and Mexico sign treaty resolving issue of economic rights in the Gulf of Mexico. Area involved was called "doughnut hole." U.S. receives rights to 38 percent of the area.

German government announces agreement with utilities to complete phase-out of nuclear power.

July

Vicente Fox Quesada elected president of Mexico.

Republicans choose candidates; George W. Bush for president; Dick Cheney for vice president.

Mori reelected prime minister by Japanese parliament.

Vietnam and U.S. sign trade agreement. Clears the way for normalized trade relations.

Venezuelan President Chavez wins reelection with 60 percent of the popular vote.

August

Democrats select candidates: Al Gore for president, Joseph Lieberman for vice president.

Bank of Japan raises interest rates for the first time in ten years.

U.S. oil inventories at lowest level since 1976.

Crude prices contribute significantly to costlier gasoline and heating oil.

DOE awards contracts to create a two-million-barrel reserve of heating oil.

September

Danish voters reject joining the EU's common currency. First popular test of EU's economic and political integration.

High fuel prices spark protests in Europe.

Truck drivers in Britain begin blockade of oil refineries to protest high fuel prices.

President Clinton releases 30 million barrels of oil reserves to offset rising fuel costs.

European, American, and Japanese central banks act to bolster the euro.

China granted permanent normal trade relations status with the U.S.

Six-year Whitewater investigation of the Clintons ends without indictments.

October

U.N. approves Iraqi request to be paid in euros instead of dollars for oil exported under Oil for Food Program.

On October 12, the DJIA falls 379 points (3.6 percent).

On October 18, the DJIA closes below 10,000 for the first time since March 2000.

Social Security and Supplemental Security income payments to be increased 3.5 percent in 2001.

Clinton administration announces a record $237 billion surplus—the third surplus in a row—for fiscal year 2000.

November

U.S. presidential election closest in decades. George W. Bush ultimately declared the winner. His slim lead in Florida leads to automatic recount in that state.

Republicans file suit to block manual recount of Florida ballots sought by Democrats. Florida Supreme Court rules that hand count of presidential ballots may continue.

Republicans file federal suit to block manual recount in Florida. Florida secretary of state Katherine Harris certifies Bush as winner in Florida by 537 votes.

Global warming talks collapse at Hague conference.

Mad cow disease alarms Europe.

Conference of Parties of Kyoto Protocol ends without agreement on cuts in greenhouse gases.

December

U.S. Supreme Court orders halt to manual recount of presidential votes in Florida. Supreme Court seals Bush victory in five-to-four vote, by ruling that there can be no further recounting.

Ukraine permanently shuts down last reactor at its Chernobyl nuclear power plant.

Natural gas prices in U.S. surge above $10 per BTU for the first time ever, in response to cold weather and stock draw-downs.

DJIA and NASDAQ record losing years for the first time since 1990.

2001

January

Bill Clinton issues controversial pardons, including one for Marc Rich (billionaire fugitive).

January 3: Federal Reserve cuts both discount rate and funds rate by 50 basis points. Reductions made at non-scheduled meeting. Discount rate reduced from 6.00 to 5.50 percent; federal funds target cut from 6.50 to 6.00 percent; prime loan rate reduced from 9.50 to 9.00 percent.

Also on January 3, NASDAQ surges a record 14.17 percent.

On January 31: Federal Reserve cuts both the discount rate and funds rate by another 50 basis points.

February

Bank of Japan cuts official discount rate 15 basis points; first cut in five years.

March

British livestock epidemic, hoof-and-mouth disease, reaches crisis levels.
President Bush abandons global-warming treaty (Kyoto Protocol); angers European leaders.
In order to boost the economy, Bank of Japan cuts its official overnight rate to zero.
U.S. Energy Department establishes Northeast Home Heating Oil Reserve— two-million-barrel reserve.
World's largest oil rig located off Brazil suffers three explosions; sinks on March 20.

April

Pacific Gas & Electric files for Chapter 11 bankruptcy.

May

President Bush's energy policy—reduce regulation to encourage more oil, gas, and nuclear output.
Tax incentives are needed to boost coal output, other tax incentives to promote conservation, encourage alternative fuels and increase energy assistance to low-income households. Need to make electricity grid more interconnected, both at home and with Mexico and Canada.

June

Senate balance of power shifts as Senator Jeffries of Vermont changes party affiliation from Republican to Independent, gives Democrats 50-49-1 majority.
Federal tax reduction signed into law. Cuts taxes by $1.35 billion over eleven years.
Syrian forces evacuate Beirut area after decades of occupation.
Exxon Mobil and Qatar sign a letter of intent for a natural gas-to-liquids project. Would be largest in the world with production capacity of 80,000 to 90,000 barrels per day.

July

One hundred and seventy-eight nations (excluding U.S.) reach agreement on climate accord. Kyoto Protocol of 1997 rescued though diluted.

August

U.S. budget surplus dwindles. Some blame slowing economy and the Bush tax cut.

South Korea repays last installment of IMF loan granted at the height of Asia crisis.

Japan's unemployment rate reaches historic high of 5 percent.

Indonesia and IMF sign letter of intent allowing resumption of $5 billion loan program.

President Bush signs the Iran and Libya Sanctions Act, which allows the president to waive sanctions against foreign firms if doing so is in national interest.

September

On September 11, terrorists crash planes into New York's World Trade Center and the Pentagon in Washington, D.C. Largest terrorist attack in history; Trade Center is destroyed; Pentagon is heavily damaged. Another plane taken over by terrorists crashes eighty miles outside Pittsburgh. More than 3,000 die in the attacks. Within days, Islamic militant Osama bin Laden and al-Qaeda network are identified as attackers. Aviation halted and all major trading markets are closed for remainder of the week.

On September 13 relative calm returns to world oil markets; gasoline prices return to normal levels. On September 17 major trading markets in the U.S., including NYSE and NYMEX, reopen. DJIA records biggest point drop in history, falling 684.41. At unscheduled meeting, Federal Reserve cuts its discount rate from 3.00 to 2.50 percent; federal funds rate reduced from 3.50 to 3.00 percent.

On September 24, crude oil and petroleum products futures fall to their lowest levels in two years. It is feared that a recession would reduce energy demand. Over last six trading sessions, crude oil and gasoline futures fall more than 26 percent.

October

Responding to the September 11 attacks, U.S. and Britain bomb al-Qaeda in Afghanistan.

Irish Republican Army announces it has started to dismantle its weapons arsenal. Dramatic leap forward in Northern Ireland peace process.

Japan's parliament approves legislation allowing military to provide logistical support overseas.

President Bush signs legislation allowing resumption of economic and military aid to Pakistan.

November

President Bush orders the Strategic Petroleum Reserve be filled to capacity over next few years.

The NBER states that the U.S. entered a recession as of March 2001.

December

Taliban regime in Afghanistan collapses after two months. Hamid Karzai
  sworn in as new interim Afghan leader.

Enron files for bankruptcy protection.

Stock markets decline for a second straight year—the first time since 1974.

2002

January

ASEAN Free Trade Area officially comes into force.

Euro becomes legal tender in twelve European countries.

Energy Department opens bidding process for oil companies to deliver 22 million
  barrels to SPR.

President in State of the Union address identifies Iraq, Iran, and North Korea
  as part of "the axis of evil."

March

U.S. and Afghan troops launch Operation Anaconda. Attack remaining
  al-Qaeda and Taliban fighters in Afghanistan.

Citibank opens its doors to Chinese customers, first for a foreign bank.

April

Paris Club group of creditor nations agrees to reschedule some Indonesian
  debt.

General strike begins in Venezuela; shuts down many stores and factories and
  nearly halts oil production, refining, and export terminal operations.

SEC launches a formal investigation of Wall Street analysts' conflicts of
  interest.

May

U.S. and Russia reach landmark arms agreement to cut both countries' nuclear
  arsenal.

Presidents Bush and Putin agree to major new energy partnership. Entails
  more investment from U.S., mainly in Russia's oil and gas sector. Leaders
  agree to joint efforts to improve ports, pipelines, and refineries.

June

United States abandons thirty-one year old Antiballistic Missile treaty.

U.N. announces China was on the brink of HIV/AIDS catastrophe.

July

Foreign direct-investment flows to developed countries decline by 56 percent in 2001. United States has the largest falloff to its lowest level since 1997.

Dollar sinks against the euro for the first time in more than two years.

WorldCom files for bankruptcy protection. Largest claim in U.S. history.

The DJIA sinks to its lowest level in nearly four years.

Both the NASDAQ and S&P 500 hit their lowest levels since the first half of 1997.

President Bush signs the Public Company Accounting Reform and Investor Protection Act.

Energy Department announces it intends to increase the rate at which the SPR is filled.

Venture capital investments hit four-year low.

August

IMF signs an emergency loan to Brazil.

Mexico is the only major non-OPEC exporter cooperating with OPEC.

September

Tyco executives Dennis Kozlowski and Mark Swartz indicted in stock-fraud scheme.

Japanese stocks closed at lowest level since 1983.

Cargo operations halted at twenty-nine West Coast ports when terminal operators lock out unionized workers.

EU releases a plan for coordination of member countries' crude oil reserves.

October

China will soon allow international financial institutions to issue yuan bonds for foreign trading.

China's first gold exchange opens for trade in Shanghai.

On October 10 and 11, U.S. Congress gives President Bush the authority to use force, if necessary, against Iraq. Purpose is to induce Hussein to abandon biological, chemical, and nuclear programs.

November

Republicans retake Senate in midterm elections, gain additional House seats.

China's Jiang Zemin officially retires as general secretary. Hu Jintao named his successor.

EPA relaxes Clean Air Act.

Bush signs legislation creating cabinet-level Department of Homeland Security.

November 15: The U.S. SPR reaches 592 million barrels; largest amount since initiated in 1977.

December

North Korea switches all foreign currency holdings from the U.S. dollar to the euro.

Business and labor groups in Venezuela go on strike. Strike continues through December, with adverse affects on several Caribbean refineries. Crude production was over 3 million barrels before strike; sinks to less than 500,000 barrels well into December.

United Airlines files for bankruptcy protection.

2003

January

Fourteen U.S. firms launch Chicago Climate Exchange. Companies unable to meet emissions goals would be able to buy credits.

White House announces budget deficit to top $200 billion in 2003.

Discount rate system changed.

On January 9, 2003, Regulation A is amended; results in new method of establishing discount rate.

March

Tokyo's stock market falls to the lowest level since March 1983.

China names Hu Jintao president. Completes leadership transition started at 16th Congress.

NYMEX puts into effect expanded price limits on its energy contracts.

On March 19, Operation Iraqi Freedom begins. Commences with bombing raid and missile attack.

April

President Bush declares conclusion of major combat operations in Iraq.

European Union expanded by ten nations.

Brazil announces the largest-ever natural gas discovery in Brazil. Raises Brazil's natural gas reserves by about 30 percent.

May

The U.N. approves the immediate end of thirteen years of economic sanctions on Iraq.

Bush signs ten-year, $350 billion tax-cut package; third largest in U.S. history.

June

Three Gorges Reservoir in China, world's largest water-control project, begins electricity production.

July

U.S. Treasury begins mailing $400 per child tax rebate checks.

National Bureau of Economic Research states that U.S. recession ended in November 2001.

September

China participates as dialogue partner with G-7 finance ministers and central bank governors.

U.S. Federal Regulation and Oversight of Energy-Electricity (FERC) approves plan for the new Cameron liquefied natural gas import terminal in Louisiana; first such project in U.S. in over twenty years.

U.N. lifts eleven-year sanction against Libya. Development of sizeable oil resources had been limited.

Chicago Climate Exchange announces its first auction of emission allowances.

November

President Bush signs $87.5 billion emergency package for post-war Iraq reconstruction. Supplements of $79 billion approved in April.

U.S. Congress abandons plans to pass an energy bill before the end of the legislative session.

December

President Bush signs $27.3 billion energy and water bill, which includes funding for nuclear waste facility.

President Bush ends steel tariffs.

December 12: The DJIA closes above 10,000 for first time since May 24, 2002.

Saddam Hussein captured by American troops.

U.S. confirms first case of mad cow disease.

2004

January

Interior Secretary approves plan to open parts of Alaska's North Slope to oil exploration/drilling.

February

On February 11, the DJIA closes at highest level in more than 2.5 years.

March

Senator John Kerry secures Democratic nomination for president; wins nine out of ten primaries and caucuses.

NATO formally admits seven new countries: Bulgaria, Estonia, Latvia, Lithuania, Romania, Slovakia, and Slovenia.

China faces first complaint at WTO. Filed by the U.S. over semiconductors.

Second Central Bank Gold Agreement announced. CBGA renewed for another five years, starting on September 27, 2004. Annual limit of sales 500 tons.

April

On April 30, international oil prices hit a 3.5 year high.

June

U.S. hands over power to Iraqi interim government. Ayad Allawi becomes prime minister.

U.S. announces plans to withdraw 12,500 of 37,000 troops stationed in South Korea by 2006.

U.S. current account deficit (in absolute terms) sets a new record for the first quarter of 2004.

Senate passes $447 billion defense bill.

Fed raises its funds target by 25 basis points. First increase in over four years. Start of 25-basis point advances at seventeen consecutive FOMC meetings.

July

Democrats nominate John Kerry for president and John Edwards for vice president.

August

Republicans renominate Bush and Cheney.

Venezuelan president Chavez survives recall referendum.

September

President Bush eases trade restrictions on Libya.

Congress extends tax cuts due to expire at the end of 2005.

Japanese Cabinet approves privatization of postal service; will split Japan Post into four companies in 2007.

October

China participates in meeting with G-7 countries in Washington.

Japan wins seat as nonpermanent member of the U.N. Security Council.

Russian lower and upper houses and cabinet ratify Kyoto Protocol climate treaty. Returns legislation to executive branch for approval. Russian ratification necessary for treaty to take effect.

November

George W. Bush reelected president of the U.S.

U.S. Senate probe finds Iraq illegally earned $21.3 billion; circumvented U.N. sanctions from 1991 through 2003. Amount is double that mentioned in the October 2004 Darfur report.

December

Russian government gives its long-awaited final approval for major oil pipeline to Pacific port. Would allow exports to Japan and western United States.

2005

January

Worldwide aid pours in to help eleven Asian countries devastated by tsunami.

February

In State of the Union address, President Bush announces his plan to reform Social Security; plan receives lukewarm reception.

Eight years after it was first negotiated, Kyoto Protocol on climate change goes into effect. U.S. did not join; says it will pursue other voluntary reduction programs.

May

Tony Blair becomes first Labour Party prime minister to win three successive terms; however, his party loses a large number of seats in the elections.

June

European Union abandons plans to ratify the proposed European Constitution by 2006. Both France and the Netherlands vote against it.

Oil prices above $60 per barrel for the first time since the launch of the contract in 1983.

July

China removes yuan peg to the dollar; revalues currency by 2.1 percent.

Malaysia unpegs currency from dollar; adopts managed float.

Teamsters and Service Employees unions announce their withdrawal from the AFL-CIO. Considered organized labor's worst crisis since 1935 when CIO split from the AFL.

United Food and Commercial Workers also withdrew from AFL-CIO.

August

Bush signs Central American Free Trade Agreement (CAFTA). Will remove trade barriers between U.S. and six other countries: Costa Rica, Dominican Republic, El Salvador, Guatemala, Honduras, and Nicaragua.

China reveals a plan to help set the price of the yuan. Market prices of several currencies such as the U.S. dollar, the euro, the yen, and the won are used in the computation.

Hurricane Katrina strikes U.S. Gulf of Mexico region near New Orleans; 95 percent of oil and 88 percent of natural gas production in federal waters shut down during height of storm. At least fourteen oil refineries also affected.

U.S. government announces it will lend out crude from the SPR.

September

President Bush directs DOE to release as much as 30 million barrels of crude from SPR.

DOE had already released 13.2 million barrels under short-term exchange agreements.

First emergency-induced release from the SPR since the 1990–1991 Gulf War.

Hurricane Rita makes landfall along the U.S. Gulf Coast. Damages, along with those resulting from Katrina, represent over one-quarter of total U.S. refinery capacity. Significant effects of Hurricane Rita linger into 2006.

October

Bankruptcy Abuse Prevention and Consumer Protection Act of 2005 goes into effect.

November

Gold tops $500 an ounce for the first time in eighteen years on Asian markets.

2006

January

China's auto market surpasses Japan's in 2005, becoming the second largest after the United States.

Alan Greenspan retires as Federal Reserve Board chairman. Replaced by Ben S. Bernanke.

February

President Bush signs law renewing the Patriot Act.
House releases a report on the response to Hurricane Katrina. Assigns blame to all levels of government.

May

President Bush announces plans to normalize relations with Libya.

June

China's central bank orders limit on lending by commercial banks.

July

Japan lifts ban on U.S. beef imports.
U.S., ASEAN sign trade liberalization pact.
Banks worldwide agree to cut off business with North Korea.
Israel sends thousands of troops into Lebanon. Battles run from July 13 to August 15.

September

South Korea terminated three-year ban on U.S. beef imports.

October

U.N. adopts sanctions on North Korea. Bars sale of materials that could be used to produce weapons. Authorities of other countries can inspect cargo entering and leaving North Korea.
The DJIA closes above 12,000 for the first time.

November

Democrats gain control of both houses of Congress in the midterm elections.
WTO approves Vietnam's application for membership.

December

U.N. bans Iranian imports and exports of materials and technology to enrich uranium. Freezes assets of individuals and firms that were active in nuclear and ballistic missile programs.

2007

January

Romania and Bulgaria enter the European Union, which now totals twenty-seven nations and 490 million people.

President Bush announces change in strategy in Iraq. Additional 20,000 would be deployed to Baghdad. Wants Iraq to take control of its forces and commit to a number of benchmarks, which includes increasing troop presence, oil revenue, and jobs. Proposal meets with bipartisan criticism.

Congressional Budget Office forecasts the federal deficit will drop to about $200 billion in 2007.

February

British Prime Minister Tony Blair announces plans to withdraw troops from Iraq.

U.S. stock market plummets; DJIA falls 416 points. The 3.3 percent drop was due to a plunge of nearly 9 percent in Chinese stock market.

March

French president Jacques Chirac announces his retirement after more than forty years in politics.

Northern Ireland's leaders reach historic agreement. New administration to take control in May.

In policy shift, U.S. says it will impose duties on Chinese goods.

U.S. Treasury Secretary Paulson calls for the end of currency controls in China.

June

EU agrees on guidelines for a new treaty to replace its current constitution.

July

The DJIA closes above 14,000 for the first time in history.

The DJIA falls more than 300 points. Concerns about weakness in U.S. housing markets.

Upper House elections in Japan: Ruling coalition of LDP and New Komeito Party lose seats.

August

President Bush signs a bill to implement recommendations of the 9/11 Commission.

On August 9, the DJIA falls by nearly 400 points, due to credit worries.

Canadian and European stocks fall. ECB, Federal Reserve, and Bank of Canada
  inject money.
On August 10, U.S. stocks finish slightly lower. Federal Reserve injects $38 billion.
Asian share markets fall sharply following trends in Europe and North America.
Bank of Japan and Reserve Bank of Australia inject liquidity to try to restore
  confidence.
Markets shaken by the subprime mortgage market problems in the U.S.
On August 16, subprime mortgage financial crisis intensifies. Share prices continue to fall in Asian markets. South Korea, Indonesia, and the Philippines
  hardest hit.
The Financial Times Stock Exchange index (FTSE) falls in the morning session
  on the London Stock Exchange. Other European markets fall as well.
The DJIA recovers in late trading on the New York Stock Exchange. Had lost
  340 points.
On August 17, stock prices in U.S. and Europe rally after the Federal Reserve
  eases policy; done to restore confidence in the banking sector after the subprime mortgage financial crisis.

September

Labor Department says payrolls shrank in August; the first decline in four years.
Oil prices reach $80 a barrel.
U.S. dollar slips to parity with the Canadian dollar; falls to record lows against
  the euro.
United Auto Workers walk off the job at GM plants in the first nationwide
  strike during auto contract negotiations since 1976. Tentative pact ends
  walkout two days later.

October

Dow-Jones industrial average rises 191 points, surpassing mid-July closing
  record of 14,000.
United Auto Workers tentatively agree on a contract with Chrysler.
U.S. budget deficit falls to $162 billion in fiscal year 2007; the smallest deficit in
  five years.
Gold trades above $800 an ounce for the first time since 1980.

November

One week after workers ratified new contract, Chrysler announces 12,000 job
  cuts.
The Federal Reserve injects $41 billion in temporary reserves into the U.S.
  money markets.
United Auto Workers agree on a tentative contract with Ford Motor Company.

Citigroup Inc. CEO Charles Prince resigns as company loses billions in debt crisis.

Members of the Writers Guild of America go on strike.

Citigroup, Bank of America, and JPMorgan Chase agree to a $75 billion superfund to restore confidence to the credit markets.

DJIA closes below 13,000 for the first time since August.

U.S. House of Representatives passes the Mortgage Reform and Anti-Predatory Lending Act of 2007.

Oil prices reach $99.29 a barrel.

Government data shows U.S. home prices in the third quarter showed a decline for the first time in 13 years.

December

President Bush announces a plan to voluntarily and temporarily freeze the rates of a limited number of debtors holding adjustable-rate mortgages.

Federal Reserve injects $40 billion into the money market and coordinates such efforts with central banks from Canada, U.K., Switzerland, and the EU.

Federal Reserve approves measures to give mortgage holders more protection to prevent the current housing crisis from worsening.

Financing with adjustable-rate and multiple mortgages dropped sharply. Foreclosure activity is at record levels.

Banks, mortgage lenders, real estate investment trusts, and hedge funds continue to suffer significant losses as a result of mortgage payment defaults and mortgage asset devaluation.

2008

January

Bank of America agrees to buy troubled Countrywide Financial, a major mortgage market player.

Fitch Ratings, Ltd., an international rating agency assigns a negative rating watch to California.

President Bush proposes an economic stimulus package. Announcement due primarily to crisis in housing market and advancing oil prices. House passes stimulus package on January 29.

Global stock markets plunge. Fear that U.S. is heading for a recession.

The Fed cuts its funds target from 4.25 percent to 3.50 percent.

Eight days later, the Fed cuts its funds target to 3.00 percent from 3.50 percent.

February

The Senate passes the economic stimulus package on February 7. On February 13, President Bush signs the legislation, which totals $168 billion, of which $152 billion will take effect in 2008.

In January the economy lost jobs for the first time in 52 months.

President Bush proposes a Federal budget of $3.1 billion for fiscal 2008-09 and forecasts a budget deficit of $410 billion.

Crude oil moves above $100 a barrel.

The Fed lowers its economic growth forecast and estimates a rising unemployment rate for the rest of the year.

Wheat prices increase due to drought and high demand from abroad. Lowest U.S. supply in thirty years.

Northern Rock Bank, which is in major financial difficulty, is nationalized by British government.

March

Federal Reserve presents a $200-billion loan program that allows the biggest banks to borrow Treasury securities and use mortgage-backed securities as collateral.

White House announces a plan to help ease credit crisis.

Federal Reserve approves a $30 billion loan to JPMorgan Chase so it can take over Bear Stearns.

Stock markets around the world decline sharply after announcement.

JPMorgan Chase agrees to purchase Bear Stearns for $2 per share. Ultimately raised to $10 per share.

Gold peaks at $1,011 an ounce at mid-month; backs off to $934 per ounce by month's end—highest prices since January 1980.

Crude oil prices exceed $110 per barrel. Gas prices rise to another record high.

Dollar temporarily deteriorates to below 100 yen to the dollar. Lowest dollar level since November 1995.

The Fed expands the number of programs to increase financial market liquidity. It also cuts its funds rate target from 3.00 percent to 2.25 percent.

Final fourth-quarter real GDP report shows an advance of only 0.6 percent.

April

The Senate passes housing relief bill. Aim is to help homeowners that are near foreclosure.

Retail chains have large increase in bankruptcies.

World Bank asks for action to tackle increasing goods price problems; announces a group of emergency measures.

The Fed reduces it funds rate target from 2.25 percent to 2 percent.

First-quarter real GDP reported to have increased 0.6 percent. Ultimately revised upward to 1.0 percent.

Brazil sovereign credit rating is raised. It is the first time it receives an investment grade rating.

May

The Fed auctions $24 billion in Treasury securities to help reduce the subpar mortgage crisis.

The Fed reports that banks are tightening lending standards in areas such as home mortgages, other types of consumer loans, and business loans.

Crude oil prices reach and then exceed $120 per barrel.

The House of Representatives passes legislation to allow the government to insure up to $300 billion in mortgages to help individuals avoid foreclosure.

Price of crude oil rises above $130 and then above $135 per barrel.

The S&P/Case-Shiller Home Price Indices for the twelve months ending in March, shows a decline of 14.1 percent.

World Bank announces a $1.2 billion program to help alleviate a global food crisis.

June

Barack Obama wins the Democratic party nomination for president. Will face John McCain in the national election in November.

House of Representatives votes to extend unemployment benefits.

Price of crude oil price jumps by a single-day record of almost $11 per barrel to $138.54.

At the June 24-25 FOMC meeting, the Fed leaves its funds rate target unchanged at 2.00 percent. The first FOMC meeting since September 2007 where the rate was not cut.

Concerns grow about the financial condition of regional banks.

The Conference Board Consumer Confidence Index falls to a sixteen-year low.

Unemployment rate jumps to 5.5 percent from 5.0 percent in April. Biggest one-month increase in twenty-two years.

July

On July 3, oil prices reach an all-time high of $145.29 per barrel.

European Central Bank raises official rate by 25 basis points to 4.25 percent in an effort to fight inflation.

Treasury Department proposes a rescue plan to Congress for Freddie Mac and Fannie Mae. Federal Reserve says it is willing to lend to both organizations.

FHA Housing Stabilization and Homeownership Act is passed by Congress and signed by the President. Helps housing in general and Freddie Mac and Fannie Mae in particular.

Office of Thrift Supervision closes the IndyMac Bank, the largest savings and loan in the Los Angeles area, after determining it is unlikely to Meet depositor demands.

Federal Reserve tightens mortgage regulations to eliminate practices that led to the subprime mortgage crisis.

GM announces a plan to suspend it dividend, sell off assets and reduce salary costs by 20 percent.

August

U.S. unemployment rate rises to 5.7 percent in July and 6.1 percent in August. The last time it was 6.1 percent was September 2003.

Initial unemployment claims rise to their highest level since March 2002.

The Federal Reserve held policy steady and suggested it continues to balance the risks of rising prices and slower growth.

Freddie Mac reported an $821 million loss and warned of further losses.

AIG reported a $5.4 billion loss, as the troubled housing market continued to create problems for the insurer.

The European Central Bank and the Bank of England kept their key interest rates steady.

Five credit unions reported paper losses on mortgage-related securities that are large enough to wipe out their net worth.

Quarterly GDP in the eurozone contracted for the first time since the early 1990s.

The Conference Board's leading economic indicators index had its biggest drop so far this year.

The Federal Deposit Insurance Company said the agency might have top borrow from the Treasury because of bank failures.

Hedge funds are having their worst year since 1990.

September

U.S. government takes control of Fannie Mae and Freddie Mac. Places them in a conservatorship. The Federal Housing Finance Agency will manage the companies on a temporary basis.

Washington Mutual, the largest savings and loan bank in the country, ousts its CEO as a result of losses stemming from the subprime mortgage crisis.

OPEC announces it will cut oil production by 500,000 barrels a day.

Lehman Brothers announces a third-quarter loss of $4.9 billion. Several days later it files for bankruptcy.

Price of oil falls below $100 per barrel.

Bank of America buys Merrill Lynch.

Federal Reserve announces initiatives to increase emergency lending to combat financial crisis.

AIG seeks an emergency loan from the Federal Reserve. Initially the loan is turned down, but then the Fed provides an $85.6 billion bridge loan.

Barclays buys Lehman Brothers core capital markets businesses for $1.75 billion.

Federal Reserve and five other central banks announce coordinated measures to address elevated pressures in the U.S. dollar short-term funding markets.

FOMC authorizes $180 billion expansion of Temporary reciprocal currency arrangements.

SEC imposes emergency ban on short-selling.

Federal insurance considered for money market mutual funds after several are closed.

Goldman Sachs and Morgan Stanley become bank holding companies.

Bush administration proposes $700 billion financial bailout plan to Congress.

Federal Reserve willing to extend non-recourse loans to U.S. depository institutions and bank holding companies to finance purchases of asset-backed commercial paper from money market mutual funds.

Federal Reserve plans to purchase federal agency discount notes from primary dealers.

Federal Reserve eases rules limiting the ability of buyout firms and private investors to take big positions in banks.

SEC revises recently issued rules on short-selling.

New York regulators require some sellers of credit-default swaps to become insurance companies.

October

Bank bailouts spread globally; world economic growth moves substantially lower.

Federal Reserve takes more steps to bail out markets and investors. Floods U.S. banking system with reserves and pushes down Federal funds rate.

Dow Jones falls below 10,000 for the first time since 2004.

U.S. Treasury yields plummet despite likelihood of huge budget deficits and treasury financing.

Trading is suspended on Russia's leading Stock Exchange.

Stock markets around the world drop sharply.

Growing number of nations explicitly announce they will guarantee bank deposits.

Budget deficits for many U.S. states are likely to grow by leaps and bounds.

Federal Reserve cuts funds rate to 1.5 percent.

INDEX

About the Author

LEONARD J. SANTOW is Managing Director of Griggs & Santow Inc., an economic and financial consulting firm in New York City. His clients include government agencies, central banks, investment and commercial banks, corporations, pension funds, insurance companies, government securities dealers, and money managers. He is the author of *The Budget Deficit: The Causes, the Costs, and the Outlook; Helping the Fed Work Smarter*, and coauthor of *Social Security and the Middle-Class Squeeze* (Praeger, 2005). Santow holds a Ph.D. in Finance from the University of Illinois.